MAYA
NARRATIVE ARTS

MAYA
NARRATIVE ARTS

Karen Bassie-Sweet and
Nicholas A. Hopkins

UNIVERSITY PRESS OF COLORADO
Louisville

© 2018 by University Press of Colorado

Published by University Press of Colorado
245 Century Circle, Suite 202
Louisville, Colorado 80027

All rights reserved

 The University Press of Colorado is a proud member of the Association of University Presses.

The University Press of Colorado is a cooperative publishing enterprise supported, in part, by Adams State University, Colorado State University, Fort Lewis College, Metropolitan State University of Denver, Regis University, University of Colorado, University of Northern Colorado, Utah State University, and Western State Colorado University.

ISBN: 978-1-60732-821-6 (cloth)
ISBN: 978-1-60732-741-7 (pbk)
ISBN: 978-1-60732-742-4 (ebook)
DOI: https://doi.org/10.5876/9781607327424

Library of Congress Cataloging-in-Publication Data

Names: Bassie-Sweet, Karen, 1952– author. | Hopkins, Nicholas A., author.

Title: Maya narrative arts / Karen Bassie-Sweet and Nicholas A. Hopkins.

Description: Boulder : University Press of Colorado, 2017. | Includes bibliographical references and index.

Identifiers: LCCN 2017048381| ISBN 9781607327417 (pbk.) | ISBN 9781607327424 (ebook) | ISBN 9781607328216 (cloth)

Subjects: LCSH: Mayas—Antiquities. | Mexico—Antiquities. | Palenque (Chiapas, Mexico)—Antiquities. | Narrative art—Mexico. | Monuments—Mexico—Palenque (Chiapas) | Inscriptions, Mayan.

Classification: LCC F1435 .B37 2017 | DDC 972.81—dc23

LC record available at https://lccn.loc.gov/2017048381

Cover photograph of Vessel K793 courtesy of Justin Kerr

Contents

LIST OF FIGURES	xi
ACKNOWLEDGMENTS	xv
INTRODUCTION	3
Paradigms in the Study of Maya Hieroglyphs, Past and Present	5
Toward a New Paradigm	9
Contrast and Complementarity in Language	10
Contrast and Complementarity in Mythology	14
Contrast and Complementarity between Text and Image	18
The Composition of a Classic-Period Monument	19
The Organization of This Book	23
CHAPTER 1	
The Creator Grandparents and the Place of Duality	27
The Nomenclature and Manifestations of Maya Deities	28
The Multiple Manifestations of Deities and Humans	29
The Chahk Deities	30
The Triad of Thunderbolt Gods	30
The Thunderbolt Deity GI	32
The Thunderbolt Deity GIII	34
The Thunderbolt Deity GII	35
K'awiil	37
The Meteor Deity Tlaloc	37

Avian Avatars	38
The Creator Grandparents and Complementary Opposition	38
The Waters of the Place of Duality	40
The Waterlily Bird-Serpent and the Waters of the Place of Duality	45
Water Shrines	48
The Sky	50
The Quadrilateral World of the Creator Deities	51
House Metaphors	53
The Hearthstones	54
Heat	55
The Place of Duality in the Sky	56
The Sun and the Place of Duality	59
The Sun God	59
The K'inich and K'inich Ajaw Titles	61
The Number Four God	62
Flower Motifs and the Place of Duality	63
Sky and Earth Gods as a Class of Deities	66
Summary	67

CHAPTER 2

The Family of the Creator Grandparents and Complementary Opposition — 68

The Second Generation of Creator Deities	68
The Third Generation of Creator Deities	73
The Wisdom and Knowledge of the Creator Deities	75
The Complementary Opposition of the Deities	77
The Moon and Complementary Opposition	82
Impersonations of One Moon and Lady Moon	86
Summary	87

CHAPTER 3

The Calendar and the Narrative Time Frame — 89

The Divination and Solar Calendars	90
The Long Count	92
The Glyph G Series	94

The Lunar Series	94
Patron Gods of the K'atun Period	95
The Mythological Period Ending Event of 4 Ajaw 8 Kumk'u	98
Periods of 900 Days	99
The Narrative Time Frame	100
Variation	101
Summary	107

CHAPTER 4
The Literary Nature of Mayan Texts, Ancient and Modern	109
Categories of Speech	111
Poetry in a Modern Maya Text	114
Narrative Structure of Modern Texts	115
The Sarcophagus Lid Text of the Palenque Temple of the Inscriptions	118
The Palenque Palace Tablet of House A-D	125
Distance Number Treatment	133
Topical Divisions of the Text	134
Distance Number Introductory Glyphs	135
Elaboration and Relative Weight	137
Summary	138

CHAPTER 5
Text and Image	142
Semantic Markers in Maya Art	142
Text and Image Interchange in Headdress Motifs	146
Text and Image Interchange in Place Names	148
Text and Image Placement: Framing and Bracketing	151
Visual Focus	159
Verbal Couplets	161
Visual Couplets	163
The Poetic Structure of Co-Essences Vessels	166
Other Forms of Visual Couplets	169
Chiasmus Structure	169

Text and Image Couplets	171
Sequential Couplets on the Palenque Temple XIX Platform	176
The Couplet Structure of the Palenque Temple XXI Bench	178
Reversed Texts as Chiasmus Structure	183
Summary	190

CHAPTER 6

The Palenque Tablet of the 96 Glyphs — 193

The Historical Background of the Protagonist	193
The Setting of the Monument	194
The Tablet of the 96 Glyphs Narrative	195
The Protagonist	200
Literary Devices: Focus	200
Literary Devices: Fronting and Promotion	201
Visual Variations	202
Summary	203

CHAPTER 7

The Narrative of the Palenque Temple of the Inscriptions Sarcophagus — 206

The Setting	206
The Tomb	208
The Sarcophagus Lid Scene	209
The Sarcophagus Lid Text	213
Two Alternative Analyses	215
The Sarcophagus Box	216
The Secondary Lords of the Sarcophagus Lid	220
The Death and Afterlife of K'inich Janaab Pakal I	221
Summary	225

CHAPTER 8

The Palenque Cross Group Narrative — 228

The Setting	228
Peripheral Cross Group Texts	230
The Alfardas	232
The Sanctuary Jambs	235

The Sanctuary Piers	236
The Sanctuary Tablets	238
The Tablet of the Cross	238
The Main Text of the Tablet of the Cross	242
The Main Texts of the Temples of the Sun and Foliated Cross	244
The Reading Order of the Three Cross Group Tablets	247
The Place Names in the Cross Group Narrative	249
The Location of the Tablet of the Cross Scene	250
The Location of the Tablet of the Sun Scene	255
The Location of the Tablet of the Foliated Cross Scene	259
GII and the Jester God	263
Summary	264

CHAPTER 9
Conclusions   269

REFERENCES   275

INDEX   301

Figures

0.1.	Yaxchilán Stela 12	15
0.2.	Genealogy chart of primary deities	17
1.1.	Dumbarton Oaks Tablet	31
1.2.	The deity GI	33
1.3.	The deity GII	35
1.4.	The deity GII	36
1.5.	Water symbols	41
1.6.	Vessel K771	42
1.7.	Vessel K4681	43
1.8.	Vessel K1892	44
1.9.	The Waterlily Bird-Serpent	46
1.10.	Palenque Temple XIV Tablet	50
1.11.	Copán Bench 10K-2	53
1.12.	Yaxchilán Stela 1	58
1.13.	Yaxchilán Structure 44, Step III	63
2.1.	Glyph C of the Lunar Series	84
2.2.	Copán Bench 8N-11	85
3.1.	Yaxchilán Lintel 1	101
3.2.	Yaxchilán Lintel 2	102
3.3.	Yaxchilán Lintel 3	103
4.1.	Palenque Palace Tablet, scene	125
4.2.	Palenque Palace Tablet, main text	126
5.1.	*Ch'ab-ak'ab* couplet	145
5.2.	Piedras Negras Stela 7 and Stela 8 obsidian spears	146

5.3.	La Pasadita Lintel 2	147
5.4.	Place name from Tres Islas Stela 1 and Stela 2	150
5.5.	Copán Margarita Panel	151
5.6.	Palenque Tablet of the Cross, scene	155
5.7.	Yaxchilán Lintel 5	160
5.8.	Vessel K5466	162
5.9.	Vessel K2695	163
5.10.	Vessel K1387	164
5.11.	Dieseldorff vessel	164
5.12.	Chamá Bat vessel	165
5.13.	Vessel K5354	166
5.14.	Vessel K1183	166
5.15.	Vessels K793	167
5.16.	Vessel K791	167
5.17.	Altar de Sacrificios vase	168
5.18.	Quiriguá Stela I	171
5.19.	Dresden Codex Wayeb pages	172
5.20.	Yaxchilán Lintel 8	174
5.21.	Yaxchilán Stela 35	175
5.22.	Palenque Temple XIX platform	177
5.23.	Palenque Tablet of the Slaves	178
5.24.	Palenque Temple XXI Bench	179
5.25.	Laxtunich wall panel	186
5.26.	Site R, Panel 3	187
5.27.	Yaxchilán Lintel 25	188
6.1.	Palenque Tablet of the 96 Glyphs	196
7.1.	Palenque Temple of Inscriptions, sarcophagus lid	210
7.2.	Dos Pilas Burial 30 vessel	212
7.3.	Palenque sarcophagus lid, text	214
7.4.	Palenque sarcophagus box, east side	217

7.5.	Palenque sarcophagus box, north side	217
7.6.	Palenque sarcophagus box, west side	218
7.7.	Palenque sarcophagus box, south side	218
7.8.	Vessel K6547	222
8.1.	Palenque Temple of the Cross, alfarda inscription	233
8.2.	Palenque Temple of the Sun, alfarda inscription	234
8.3.	Palenque Temple of the Foliated Cross, alfarda inscription	235
8.4.	Palenque Temple of the Foliated Cross, jamb	236
8.5.	Palenque Tablet of the Cross, main text	239
8.6.	Palenque Tablet of the Sun	241
8.7.	Palenque Tablet of the Foliated Cross	242
8.8.	Vessel K2849	252
8.9.	Palenque Temple XVII Panel	256
8.10.	Chichén Itzá cenote pectoral	265

ONLINE SOURCES FOR SUPPLEMENTARY ILLUSTRATIONS

Corpus of Maya Hieroglyphic Inscriptions (CMHI), Harvard University
https://www.peabody.harvard.edu/cmhi/

Mesoweb, Palenque Resources, Monuments and Inscriptions (photographs and drawings)
http://www.mesoweb.com/palenque/monuments/monuments.html

Justin Kerr's Maya Vase Data Base (rollout photographs of Maya vessels; search by "K number")
http://research.mayavase.com/kerrmaya.html

Schele Drawing Collection, Ancient Americas at LACMA (Los Angeles County Museum of Art)
http://ancientamericas.org/collection/search

Acknowledgments

In an age in which the hoarding of data is commonplace, we celebrate the free and open access to images provided by David Schele, Inga Calvin, Justin Kerr, and Karl Herbert Mayer. We would like to express our sincere appreciation to David Schele for allowing us to reproduce drawings by the late Linda Schele in our volume. Thanks are also due to Inga Calvin who provided us with permission to reproduce her fine rollout image of the Altar de Sacrificios vessel. We are indebted to Elin Danien for supplying us with images of Mary Louise Baker's paintings of Chamá vessels and to the University of Pennsylvania Museum of Archaeology and Anthropology for permission to reproduce them. We are especially grateful to Justin Kerr for supplying us with many pottery images from his peerless database of Maya vessels and for allowing us to reproduce his wonderful photographs. We also have benefited greatly from the documentation of Maya art by Karl Herbert Mayer. Just like Justin, Karl generously shares his work and insights.

Since our early studies of Classic-period narrative structure and the relationship between text and image, a number of researchers have explored these topics and significantly advanced the understanding of the field. We have benefited greatly from discussions with Michael Carrasco, Allen Christenson, Kerry Hull, Timothy Knowlton, and Alfonso Lacadena, and we have learned a great deal from their fine publications.

We would also like to thank Jessica d'Arbonne, Daniel Pratt, and Darrin Pratt of the University Press of Colorado for their support and editorship.

MAYA
NARRATIVE ARTS

Introduction

This book treats domains of Classic Maya language, art, and culture that at first glance might seem to be unrelated. One is narrative structure in text, dealing with the way stories (including history) are presented to the reader and the manipulations of language that constitute the text genres and rhetorical devices that are recorded on Classic period monuments. This domain is partly linguistic and partly hieroglyphic, entailing how language is used to achieve the purposes of the writers (*pragmatics*) as well as the written forms the texts may take (*epigraphy*). The second domain involves the structure of art forms and conventions, and how these principles relate to the narrative structure of the text. The third domain is cognitive and mythological, the belief systems that form the context in which stories were written and illustrated, including the ways in which history is portrayed in monumental text and image. This domain is partly iconographic and partly ethnographic, and entails the ways in which personal and social relations were conceived as well as the ways in which such relationships were represented in Classic Maya art.

Our approach to these matters draws on many different kinds of sources. We take into account the archaeological record, including site layout and building construction, since these form the background against which monuments are displayed, and inform us about chronological alterations to the context. We follow epigraphic advancements to the degree possible, although

DOI: 10.5876/9781607327424.c000

we maintain an independent perspective. A combination of archaeology and epigraphy provides us with a sketch of Maya history. We are informed by the increasingly comprehensive linguistic studies of individual Mayan languages and the Mayan language family in general. We make use of ethnohistorical records where they are available, and rely on modern ethnographic studies for insight into Maya culture. It is our contention that these varied domains are not unrelated, and we believe that our understanding of Classic Maya culture and society must be based on an integration of all accessible data, and that while models drawn on single domains may be useful, they are useful as suggestions and not as conclusions.

In modern Maya studies the narrative structures of language and art have been largely ignored in favor of extracting the historical data from the inscriptions (as concisely summarized by Martin and Grube 2000). But to extract the history from the monuments requires neither an appreciation of how the story is told nor a sophisticated view of Classic Maya society and culture. One need not have an intimate acquaintance with Mayan languages to read that a particular ruler was born on a certain date, took the throne on another, and died on a third. Indeed, the foundational studies of Tatiana Proskouriakoff (1960, 1963, 1964), in which she established the historical nature of the inscriptions and the hieroglyphic verbs that refer to these life stages, made no explicit use of Mayan linguistics.

It is one of the paradoxes of modern Maya studies that one can extract the data from an inscription without knowing any Mayan language at all, including Epigraphic Maya, as the language of the inscriptions is now called. Likewise, there is no need to understand the details of costuming and ceremony to record that a ruler engaged in ceremonial activity. History is not necessarily concerned with this level of detail. What is important to the historian is that the ruler performed these acts and then went out and took his rival prisoner, extending his domain. On the other hand, there was some reason why the carvers of Classic monuments chose to dress their protagonists in certain ways and show them engaged in particular activities. It had meaning to the contemporary population, and if we are to fully understand Maya art, iconography, and epigraphy, we must develop at least hypotheses about these matters, many of which have to do with Classic conceptions of the pantheon and its manifestations.

Our principal focus here is the relation between narrative text and narrative art. We find that underlying many areas of Classic Maya belief and action is a philosophical complex of structural oppositions that define the surface units of expression, and that not only are the units of text and image defined by dimensions of contrast and complementarity, but the two domains are played against each other on Classic monuments in yet another manifestation of the principles of structural opposition. Our approach is empirical and inductive; we do not attempt to impose these binary oppositions on the data as a justification for our theories. Rather, we believe that we are exposing them in the data to build our theories. We readily admit that we are in the initial stages of this process, but we hope that the exposition that follows will encourage others to take up the task.

PARADIGMS IN THE STUDY OF MAYA HIEROGLYPHS, PAST AND PRESENT

The study of Classic Maya texts and their accompanying images as illustrated literature constitutes a new chapter in Maya epigraphy. Pioneer studies were produced as early as the 1980s, but the field has yet to achieve prominence, and Classic inscriptions continue to be valued mainly for the historical data they provide. However, as our understanding of the Classic language has improved and we can read many inscriptions essentially verbatim, our ability to analyze the texts as literature has also greatly improved. The written language is referred to as Epigraphic Maya, and is understood to be a variety of the Cholan branch of Western Mayan. Work on modern narratives in the Western Mayan languages, especially Ch'ol, has contributed to our understanding of Classic literature. The historical texts are not simply lists of events; they are narratives of history that conform to established (and discoverable) norms of the narrative arts.

We seek to exemplify the utility of treating texts as literature—that is, identifying the literary structures that characterize Classic narratives and discussing the effects of the use of such structures. Rhetorical devices emphasize some events, suppress others, and suggest parallels between sets of events that give these events new meanings. We illustrate here the productivity of such analyses by comparing the results of current conventional analyses with innovative ones. In addition to the narrative structures of the texts themselves, we also discuss the placement of texts with respect to the accompanying images, a line of study that also dates to the 1980s.

Our approach is empirical and inductive, constructing our models from observed data. This is distinct from the deductive approach that derives models from theory and then attempts to exemplify them by selecting appropriate data. Nonetheless, after the fact, we do find theoretical support for our approach, which we discuss in terms of the relevant theories, namely the model of scientific revolutions put forth by Thomas Kuhn (1962), especially the concept of *paradigms*, and the theory of *semiotics*, the study of signs, as laid out by its founder, Charles Morris (1946).

The concepts of "paradigm" and "paradigm shift" were popularized in a very influential book by historian of science Thomas Kuhn, *The Structure of Scientific Revolutions*, published by the University of Chicago Press in 1962. Kuhn noted that when a science textbook discusses the history of the science, it generally presents the process as a steady march forward, each step leading inexorably to the next, a simple matter of accumulation of knowledge. But as Kuhn points out, that is not the way things happen. The road forward in any science is a tortured path with lots of side roads leading nowhere, ultimately abandoned in favor of stepping back and beginning a new path. Rather than a straight line leading to enlightenment, the history of a science looks a lot more like a dead tree. But the historians ignore the unsuccessful side roads and straighten out the path, noting only the discoveries that ultimately led to the present state of knowledge.

In fact, said Kuhn, science did not march steadily forward, it staggered along with significant interruptions, when the lines of thought shifted from one model to another and things began to take a new direction. The advance of science is not a steady accumulation of knowledge, but a sociological phenomenon that involves "the society of scientists, and the culture of science." To describe this phenomenon, Kuhn coined the term *paradigm*, a term that has moved from the history of science to the world of business. By this, Kuhn meant what is usually referred to as a "school" of science or research, like wave optics or molecular physics, or structural linguistics and transformational grammar. Progress comes about when there is a *paradigm shift*, the abandonment of one paradigm in favor of a more powerful one.

A paradigm is characterized by the following: there is a central idea or concept that explains a wide field of phenomena, a concept that accounts for most of the observations that have been made. That central idea defines research questions, and it promotes some questions as being interesting and others as being devoid of interest. Since new lines of research are opened up, the new paradigm attracts adherents. Little by little the new paradigm comes to dominate employment, publications, research grants, and so on. Those who do not adopt the new paradigm are displaced to refuge areas, away from the center of the profession. Inevitably, as the major problems are solved, the research questions posed by the paradigm become narrower and narrower. The paradigm turns inward and ignores the world outside its bounds. Finally, the observations that the paradigm is not concerned with accumulate to form a critical mass, and someone rises to the occasion and comes up with a new central idea that not only explains the old data, but also accounts for the data that are being ignored. A new paradigm is born, and the process continues.

As discussed below, Maya epigraphy has passed through two dominant paradigms in its march toward its current state. These are best understood by examining them in terms of semiotics, since they illustrate two of the parts of the semiotic framework proposed by Charles Morris.

Morris (1946) divided the field of semiotics, the study of signs and sign systems, into three parts. The first he called *syntax*, the study of signs apart from their meanings. (Note that this is not the sense in which linguists use the term *syntax*, the order of elements and their combinations.) Morris's syntax involves questions such as how many signs there are in a system, how they are distinguished from one another, and what variants they have. Leonard Bloomfield, an early modern American linguist and a founder of structural linguistics (Bloomfield 1933), would agree that the study of signs need not make reference to meaning.

These were the concerns of the first paradigm of Maya epigraphy, encompassing the work done in the nineteenth and early twentieth centuries, from the initial discoveries of Constantine Rafinesque, Charles Étienne Brasseur de Bourboug, Cyrus Thomas, Leon de Rosny, Charles Bowditch, and Ernst Förstemann to the epoch-marking summary of results and catalog of hieroglyphs of Eric Thompson's *Maya Hieroglyphic Writing: An Introduction* (1950) and *A Catalog of Maya Hieroglyphs* (1962).

Note that the *Catalog* is concerned with grouping hieroglyphic variants into numbered sets (the numbers now referred to as *Thompson numbers*, or *T-numbers*); the question of the meanings of these sets was left for future research based on the concordance provided for each set. However, in this period scholars did work out the mathematics and calendrics of the inscriptions and related topics like astronomy. The basic nature of the writing system was discovered, the chronology worked out, major sites were identified, and the relationship to the Mayan languages established. The text between the dates was largely undeciphered, although the reading of some individual glyphs had been proposed. Thompson famously remarked that there was no history to be found in the inscriptions.

The second part of Morris's semiotics is called *semantics*, the study of what the signs and their combinations mean (more or less corresponding to linguistic usage). In Maya epigraphy, this is called *decipherment* and was the focus of the second paradigm, from Thompson to the present. The first paradigm came to an end with Tatiana Proskouriakoff's publication of what is sometimes called "the historical hypothesis." In a tour de force article, Proskouriakoff (1960) demonstrated convincingly that the inscriptions did, in fact, relate history, and that they did so in sentences with regular syntax (in the linguistic sense). Her initial work on the inscriptions of Piedras Negras (1960) was followed by her work on Yaxchilán (1963, 1964) and David Kelley's derivative study of the inscriptions of Quiriguá (1962). The paradigm shift was not immediate, but had to wait until enough scholars had adopted the new "historical" paradigm to have enough weight to change the direction of work.

Contributing to the paradigm shift, Heinrich Berlin, a frequent correspondent of Proskouriakoff's, tied history to specific sites through Emblem Glyphs, signs that related to specific sites (Berlin 1963). Yuri Knorosov (whose work was translated to English by Proskouriakoff and Sophie Coe) showed how the Maya were writing syllabically, a major key to decipherment (Knorosov 1958, 1967, 1982), and Kelley laid out the procedures of the "structural method" of decipherment in a much-neglected manual, *Deciphering the Maya Script*, published in 1976 but written much earlier.

With the shift to the new paradigm, research questions moved away from calendric and astronomical interests. Now, work focused on identifying the events associated with dates and identifying the actors named, in order to reconstruct history as it had been recorded by the Maya, and then interpret this history in light of external data from archaeology, linguistics, ethnohistory, and so on. Apart from the effort to reveal the history, the study of the writing system itself was advanced, partly by increased knowledge of the hieroglyphic corpus, and partly by increased knowledge of Mayan languages. As a result, scholars could now proclaim with some confidence that they knew what specific words were being written and how they were pronounced. It became possible to propose oral readings of Classic texts and imagine that the Classic Maya would have understood the language of our readings.

A summary of the results of the historical paradigm can be found in Simon Martin and Nikolai Grube's *Chronicle of the Maya Kings and Queens* (2000), which discusses what is known about the rulers of specific Maya sites and the events over which they ruled. On the other hand, the debate about the nature of the language being written continues. While there is little disagreement over the contents of the inscriptions, the history being related, and the events recorded, linguists continue to quibble over points of grammar and the precise pronunciation of words. Issues in the linguistics of the inscriptions are discussed in Søren Wichmann's *The Linguistics of Maya Writing* (2004a; Hopkins

2006b). These two works are for the historical paradigm what Thompson's *Introduction* and *Catalog* were for the first paradigm.

At this point Maya writing can be said to be "deciphered" in the sense that we can "read" most of the texts and we have advanced ideas about the grammar and vocabulary of the language being written. As Kuhn would predict, now that the major research questions have been answered, research has turned inward, and is dedicated to smaller and smaller issues.

TOWARD A NEW PARADIGM

The third part of Morris's semiotics is called *pragmatics*, the study of how a sign system is used—that is, how the sign system is manipulated to achieve social ends. There has been some attention devoted to the placement of monuments (e.g., Proskouriakoff's discussion of the arrangement of historical monuments at Piedras Negras in series, each devoted to the career of a single ruler), and some discussion of biases in the relation of site histories—although Marcus's dire accusation of constant falsehood seems to be without basis (Marcus 1993; see Hopkins 1994). However, there has been little attention to the discourse nature of the texts themselves.

The central concept of this new paradigm is that, while they largely relate history, the Classic Maya inscriptions do so in a traditional narrative style, and they use specific rhetorical devices to manipulate the text. Research questions thus revolve around the nature of the narrative style and the rhetorical devices. And since we are aware that the placement of texts and monuments with respect to images and surrounding architecture is also a meaningful art, questions of the relation of text to image and context are also relevant. How did the Maya artists choose between alternatives to do things like identify more- and less-important protagonists and events, and call the reader's attention to some but not all events? How did they amplify the meanings conveyed by relating the text to the accompanying images?

We know the Maya were largely concerned with recording and promulgating the history of their societies from the viewpoint of the elite. As in every history, this involved the selection of facts to be recorded and the manner in which they were to be presented. To understand this process, we have to go beyond the decipherment of the sentences and the compilation of the presented facts. That is, we have to go beyond the grammar of the sentences and the list of events we can read. We need to know how the language is being used and how the events are being presented to the public. This entails the literary analysis of the texts and the art historical analysis of the monumental contexts of the inscriptions. The next paradigm should be concentrated on discourse analysis of the texts and the relation between the texts and their accompanying monuments, including individual images, iconographic programs, the architecture of buildings, and site layout (an expanded form of text and image studies). This shift has begun. At the 2008 American Anthropology Association annual meeting, Kerry Hull and Michael Carrasco organized a session on verbal art in honor of Kathryn Josserand. With additional contributions, they published the papers of this session in a 2012 volume titled *Parallel Worlds: Genre, Discourse, and Poetics in Contemporary, Colonial, and Classic Maya Literature*. The chapters of this collection demonstrate the impressive retention of literary forms and rhetorical devices over some 2,000 years. The topic of the 2012 Maya Meetings hosted by the Mesoamerican Center of the University of Texas at Austin was ancient Maya texts as literature. The themes addressed were genres and subcultures of writing, rhetorical structures, and analysis of text and message in the context of physical and architectural presentation. If these literary forms are so central to Maya culture that they have survived centuries of turbulence, from the Classic period to the Spanish conquest and modern forces of assimilation, we ignore them at our own peril. If we truly wish to understand Classic inscriptions, we have to begin to see them as literary creations, and treat them as such.

CONTRAST AND COMPLEMENTARITY IN LANGUAGE

In his pionerring study of Nahuatl texts, Ángel María Garibay (1953) identified various types of parallelisms and other rhetorical devices such as couplets, triplets, and metonyms that are also found in Mayan and other Mesoamerican literature. Miguel León-Portilla (1969) initiated the study of Maya poetics when he organized examples of various colonial period texts into verse form. He was followed by Edmonson (1971, 1982, 1986), who arranged the entire text of the Popol Vuh (a sixteenth-century K'iche' manuscript) and two colonial period Yucatec books into parallel lines and demonstrated their couplet structure. Such poetic forms are still found in the oral stories, chants, and prayers recorded by numerous ethnographers across the Maya region (Fought 1972, 1985; Gossen 1974a, 1974b; Laughlin 1977; Edmonson and Bricker 1985; Hofling 1991; Hopkins and Josserand 1990, to name but a few).

Couplets are parallel words, phrases, or lines that differ minimally. They are ubiquitous in Maya formal speech and prayer, and prayers consist almost entirely of coupleted lines, as in this opening to a Tzeltal curing chant (Pitarch 2013:91, our translation):

A	God Jesus Christ, father,
A	God Jesus Christ, my lord,
B	I have come with a sincere mind,
B	I have come with an open heart,
C	to place in order now,
C	to place in a line now,
D	two sacred bouquets of flowers, father,
D	two sacred bouquets of lilies, my lord.

Couplets (AA, BB, etc.) are the most common rhetorical device in Mesoamerican literature. Edmonson stated that "the Popol Vuh is in poetry, and cannot be accurately understood in prose. It is entirely composed in parallelistic (i.e., semantic) couplets" (Edmonson 1971:xi). Tedlock (1983:220–229) importantly noted that the Popol Vuh also includes triplets as well as single phrases that begin or end various groupings of couplets and triplets. He compared these examples to the well-known couplet and triplet forms found in Nahuatl texts.

Another important rhetorical feature of the Popol Vuh first recognized by Christenson (1988, 2003a, 2003b, 2012) is chiasmus structure (inverted parallelism). In this literary device, two clauses (half couplets) or couplets (AA and BB) are contrasted by inversion—that is, by inserting one inside the other such that AABB becomes the chiasmus form ABBA. Christenson noted that chiasmus structure occurs on a small scale in the paired titles of the creator grandparents. For instance, when the creator grandparents Xpiyacoc (male) and Xmucane (female) act together, they are named using paired titles such as Framer and Shaper, White Great Peccary and White Great Coati, Possum and Coyote, where Xpiyacoc is the first member of the pair (Framer, White Great Peccary, Possum) and Xmucane the second (Shaper, Great White Coati, Coyote). However, in the paired titles that refer to their status as parents and elderly office holders (Alom and K'ajolom, I'yom and Mamom), Xmucane (Alom, K'ajolom) is always named first. This reflects the K'iche' metonym for ancestor (mother-father) in which mother always precedes father. When paired titles from the former kind are combined with the latter kind, they form a chiasmic structure of ABBA such as this example (Christenson 2003a:29):

A	Our Grandmother
B	Our Grandfather
B	Xpiyacoc
A	Xmucane

Another passage also gives their names in chiasmic form:

A	Twice She Who Has Borne Children	(Xmucane)
B	Twice He Who Has Begotten Sons	(Xpiyacoc)
B	Great Peccary	(Xpiyacoc)
A	Great Coati	(Xmucane)

A more elaborate chiasmus structure is seen in this example (Christeson 2003b:30):

A	They said therefore the One Grandmother	(Xmucane)
B	One Grandfather to them	(Xpiyacoc)
B	This the grandfather	(Xpiyacoc)
	This master of *tz'ite*	
	Xpiyacoc his name	
A	This therefore the grandmother	(Xmucane)
	Mistress of Days	
	Mistress of Shaping at its foot	
	Xmucane her name	

Christenson also discussed grander scales of chiasmus structures where entire sections of the Popol Vuh were presented in this form. In addition, he identified such structures in a variety of other K'ichean documents and demonstrated its widespread usage.

The use of couplets and parallelisms is not just to enhance the poetic elegance of a text. It has real power. In his study of Tzeltal shamanic curing chants, Pedro Pitarch notes that "the use of *difrasismos*—semantic parallels—is not just a mnemonic resource, but also a means of increasing the efficacy of the text through sustained persistence" (Pitarch 2013:24, our translation).

Another common rhetorical device found in Mesoamerican literature is a *metonym* in which two typical members of a class are juxtaposed to stand for the whole domain. While we prefer this term, such compounds are also referred to as *diphrastic kenning* and (Spanish) *difrasismos* (Garibay 1953; Norman 1980; Hull 1993, Knowlton 2002). Metonyms are common in the Popol Vuh and other colonial period texts as well modern tales and prayers. This form is also found in hieroglyphic texts, demonstrating its great antiquity (Riese 1984; Edmonson 1985; Hull 1993, 2002, 2003, 2012; Hopkins 1996; Knowlton 2002, 2010, 2012; Stuart 2003a). Other rhetorical devices that have been identified in hieroglyphic texts are parallelism, chiasmus, anaphora, metaphor, hyperbole, synonymy, ellipsis, and hyperbaton (Lounsbury 1980:107–115;

Fought 1985; Hopkins and Josserand 1987; Josserand 1991, 1995, 1997; Josserand and Hopkins 1991; Hull 2002, 2003; Carrasco 2005, 2012; Lacadena 2009, 2010).

In our present volume, we focus on the importance of couplets as not only a literary but also a visual device employed by the Classic Maya in their illustrations of various events. Many of these couplets represent complementary opposition, and we argue that this principle was the underlying organizational principle of Maya worldview.

On the language side, contrast and complementarity are present in linguistic structures ranging from word composition to text structure. A common technique for coining metonyms is to juxtapose two members of a lower order to form the name of a higher order. A well-known example is the term for "ancestors," composed of the juxtaposing of "father(s)" and "mother(s)"—for example, Ch'ol *tyaty-na'-äl-ob* (*tyaty* "father," *ña'* "mother," a generalizing suffix *–äl*, and a plural suffix *-ob'*)—that is, a class of persons that includes fathers and mothers. In the Tzotzil and Tzeltal areas, the ancestors are called the *totilme'iletik* ("fathers-mothers") and *me'tiktatik* ("mothers-fathers"), respectively (as noted earlier, the K'iche' term is "mother-father"). The term for "ancestors" is paralleled by the term for "descendants," juxtaposing "child of woman" and "child of man," Ch'ol *'al-p'eñel-ob'* (Aulie and Aulie 1998:5). An early attestation of such terms was Metzger and Williams's (1963) elicitation of a Tzeltal term for "animals," *chan-balam*, combining "snake" and "jaguar" to represent the class that includes both reptiles and mammals. Some examples in the Popol Vuh are the terms for the world (sky-earth), the earth (mountain-valley), water (lake-sea), and warfare (arrow-shield) (Tedlock 1987:148; Christenson 2003b).

In Classic Maya inscriptions, *tok'-pakal* "flint-shield" juxtaposes weapons of offense and defense to signal weaponry in general, and by extension, warfare (Genet 1934; Houston 1983; Hull 1993, 2003, 2012; Stuart 1995; Hopkins 1996). Another example of such opposition is seen in the *tz'ak* "whole, complete" glyph (Hull 1993, 2002, 2003, 2012; Hopkins 1996; Knowlton 2002, 2012; Stuart 2003a). The standard form of this sign is often replaced with a complementary pair of signs such as day-night, sun-moon, star-moon, cloud-water, wind-water, unripe-ripe. Hopkins (1996) has noted that many of the *tz'ak* pairs have not only a complementary opposition relationship, but a sequential one. For example, *k'in* "day" is followed by *ak'ab* "night" and unripe corn turns into ripe corn. This principle of opposing two members of the same order to imply something of a greater order is basic to the phenomena that we present below.

Beyond lexical composition, the principal element of Maya formal speech is the couplet, a pair of lines that contrast in at least one part, the contrasting parts functioning like the juxtaposed elements in the compound nouns cited above. A

Ch'ol prayer published by Vázquez (2001) includes the couplet *kpasel tyi yeb'al 'awok, tyi yeb'al 'ak'äb'* "I come beneath your feet, beneath your hands," where the play between "feet" and "hands" implies "in your presence." A similar construction was reported in Tzotzil formal speech by Cancian (1965:223), preceded by another couplet (in English translation): "has your earth arrived, has your mud arrived, here beneath the foot, here beneath the hand, of Señor Esquipulas?" The play between earth and mud is a deferential reference to the petitioner.

Couplets can also be used to imply parallelism between two events. An early epigraphic example is found in the text of the Leiden Plaque, a jade celt dating from the fourth century AD (Schele and Miller 1986:129, plate 33; 320, fig. A.3; Lounsbury 1989:208; Josserand 1991:16–17; Josserand and Hopkins 1991:38; 2011:21). The recorded event is the "seating" (enthronement) of a king, and this is played against the "seating" (eve of) a particular month: "it was the seating of Yaxk'in, the seating of the king." The implication is that the succession of rulers is as natural and inevitable as the succession of time periods. Yaxchilán Stela 12 (figure 0.1) reports the death of a ruler in the left two columns of the inscription, and contrasts this point for point in the right two columns with the succession of his son:

> [*Left*] 6 Ix 12 Yax. Died the *Ch'ajom*, five-*k'atun* Lord Shield Jaguar, Captor of Ah Ajual. Ten years and six days later, it came to be
>
> [*Right*] 11 Ajaw 8 Tsek. Was seated as lord Tekuy, Noble, Captor of Aj Uk, Bird Jaguar, Lord of Yaxchilán, *Bakab*.

The play between two elements of speech can be extended to whole sections of text. For instance, the Palenque Cross Group panels contrast a block of text concerning mythology on the left side of a scene with a block of text on the right that deals with history (see the Cross Group monuments discussed in chapter 8). The implication is not only that the historical actors are following the model established by their ancestral deities, but that there is a greater scheme that both deities and humans are participating in.

These structural oppositions can be extended further. Beyond complementary wall panels, architecture and city planning may also participate in the design of a ceremonial complex, with buildings played against buildings and building complexes played against each other.

CONTRAST AND COMPLEMENTARITY IN MYTHOLOGY

The Classic Maya pantheon is an excellent example of the kinds of structures created by binary oppositions. The structure is complex, as befits a pantheon.

FIGURE O.I. *Yaxchilán Stela 12, after Ian Graham.*

However, an examination of the repertory of major deities shows that they are defined by a series of features that include some of those established by Kroeber (1909) for the definition of kin types in different ethnographic settings: sex, relative age, generation, and lineality (figure o.2). Omaha-type patrilineal Maya kinship systems (Hopkins 1969, 1988, 1991) are relevant here, since the major Classic (and colonial) deities, from the creator grandparents to the Hero Twin grandchildren, are related by cross-cousin marriage, uniting the descendants of a celestial and an Underworld lineage (another important binary opposition).

The paternal and maternal creator grandfathers, Xpiyacoc/Itzamnaaj and Gathered Blood/God L (their colonial and Classic names) head contrasting lineages joined by marriage (of Xpiyacoc to Xmucane/Ix Chel, sister of Gathered Blood) (Bassie-Sweet 2008). Both lineages give rise to a contrasting generation of children, again joined by (cross-cousin) marriage. The triad formed by the children (One Hunahpu and Seven Hunahpu), their parents (Xpiyacoc and Xmucane), and the mother's brother (Gathered Blood) constitutes what Claude Lévi-Strauss (1949) called the "elementary structure of kinship," since it contains the oppositions of generation (parents, children), sex (brother, sister), and direct relations (ancestors and descendants) versus collaterals (uncle, aunt).

The Maya pantheon adds relative age (elder brother, younger brother), as well as the proliferation of the senior line through polygamous marriages that generate four potential patrilines headed by the brothers One Chouen and One Batz and their cousins Hunahpu and Xbalanque. With only a few deities, all of the critical oppositions of Maya kinship are present (Romney 1967:222–228; Hopkins 1988): direct versus collateral relatives, male versus female, generation versus generation, and elder versus younger siblings.

There are many more deities in the popular Maya pantheon, including most prominently the Earth and Sky gods. Earth Lords abound, from the generalized figures of the rain/storm/earth lord known as (native) Chahk or (introduced) Tlaloc, to specific local mountain and cave gods related to a particular polity. The Sun and Moon dominate the celestial lords, and in the mythology are related by kinship to Venus as well. As is characteristic of Mesoamerican deities, many members of the Maya pantheon are bivalent, manifesting as male in some instances and female in others, for instance, or as young and old.

The distant ancestors of humans also take their place in the pantheon. Ancestors are frequently depicted floating in the air above living descendants or conjured by blood sacrifice. The relevance of the pantheon to Maya history lies in the fact that historical figures are often portrayed in the guise of deities: they are shown in scenes that are framed by celestial and terrestrial deities, they perform acts that are reminiscent of those performed by the ancestors and deities, and they take titles that relate them to their gods and ancestors. The meaning of the scenes in monumental art cannot be fully appreciated

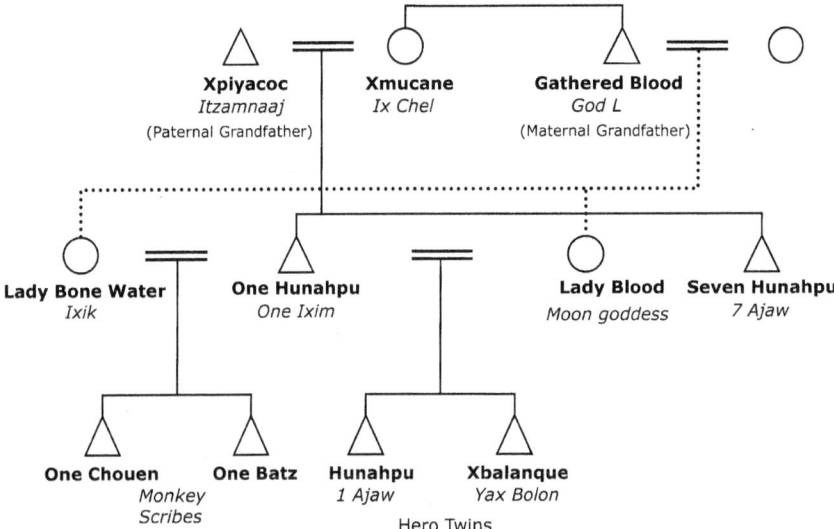

FIGURE 0.2. *Genealogy chart of primary deities*

without an understanding of these subtle clues manifested in the iconographic designs of the artists.

Sets of binary oppositions form many of the cognitive systems of the Maya. The four directions (actually, the four quadrants)—east, north, west, and south—exemplify these structures (Bassie-Sweet 1996; Josserand and Hopkins 2011). The major axis is east–west, and Mayan languages typically refer to these with reference to the sun's path through the sky: for example, Classic Maya "east" and "west," *lak'in* and *chik'in*, from **elab' k'in* "the sun's exit" and **ochib' k'in* "the sun's entrance" (because the sun comes out of the Underworld in the east and reenters it in the west). North and south are default categories, the quadrants between the eastern and western quadrants defined by the rising and setting ranges of the sun along the horizons. In fact, it is difficult to find native terms for "north" and "south" in Maya vocabularies. However, the north and south axis represents variation in the annual path of the sun. Thus the binary opposition east–west defines one axis, and north–south forms another, resulting in a four-way contrast.

Colors are also associated with the directions: red (east), white (north), black (west), and yellow (south). In addition, there are animal associations, as seen in the Dresden Codex: east (mammals, especially deer), north (birds), west (reptiles), and south (fish), and these correspond to the four major categories of animals in Maya taxonomies: mammals, birds, reptiles/amphibians, and fish

INTRODUCTION   17

(Hopkins 1980). Note that there are again two contrasting binary axes: the terrestrial (mammals and reptiles/amphibians) versus the non-terrestrial (birds and fish). The four classes are effectively defined by their modes of locomotion: walkers, crawlers, fliers, and swimmers.

Maya plant taxonomies typically feature another four-way contrast defined by two opposing axes (Hopkins 2006a, 2009; Breedlove and Hopkins 1970–1971). A hypothetical reconstruction of the life-form taxa features the opposing categories of trees, herbs, vines, and grasses. Again, there is a major axis, trees versus herbs, whose taxa include the majority of plant names. Contrasting with this axis is another, vines versus grasses, and there are typically only a few members of each. Parallel to the animal classes, the minor axis features plants with unusual climbing and spreading habits. A hypothetical reconstruction is necessary to show the underlying nature of the classes, because the reported systems vary in how plants are treated: some contrast domesticated versus wild plants (with the four categories replicated within each), some replace grasses with maize and wheat (relegating the other grasses to the herb category), and so on. As Cecil Brown (1977) has noted, only the "tree" term can be reconstructed to proto-Mayan. The ethnobotanical system may have evolved during the Classic period as the Maya sciences developed, the system then being imposed on languages that had independently labeled the other life forms. This may be an example of the extension of an ideological principle (that binary oppositions combine to form four-way contrasts) on disparate preexisting local ethnobotanical taxonomies.

When a modern Highland Guatemalan prayermaker lays out his or her altar, the colored candle arrays represent these categories: red candles to the east, white candles to the north, black candles to the west, and yellow candles to the south. Having thus defined the terrestrial universe and represented its animals and plants, a fifth color is placed in the center of the circular array: the combined fields of blue and green (*yax*). This stands for humans (vs. animals), the center (vs. the directions), and by putting both blue (sky) and green (earth) candles together in the center of the terrestrial universe, the celebrant defines an opposing axis, up–down. That is, the universe is formed by a series of binary oppositions.

CONTRAST AND COMPLEMENTARITY BETWEEN TEXT AND IMAGE

Classic Maya images often depicted members of the elite acting in their official roles, often dressed in the guise of mythological figures, wearing symbolically significant apparel and handling significant objects. They may be framed by sets of deities and ancestors. Apart from these symbolic aspects, they are also carrying out actions and interactions that represent historical events. The combined images tell a story of their own. Another, complementary story is told in the texts that surround and impinge upon the images. The play between these two domains is an art in itself.

There are several levels on which texts and images interact. First, there are physical interactions. Caption texts, which may be either short text segments that simply identify actors in the images or lengthy statements, are placed within the scene. Conversely, elements of the images may impinge on the texts in significant ways, as when the feathers of the bloodletter being held by the ruler on Quiriguá Stela J curl around the corner of the monument to touch the glyphs reporting his accession, in the text. On Yaxchilán Stela 11, Bird Jaguar's headdress extends into the text above to touch his name, and the toes of Shield Jaguar III, at the base of the image, touch the latter's name in the inscription. Less-intrusive text may be manipulated simply to locate ruler's names close to their faces, verbal glyphs close to the corresponding action in the images, and so on.

Text segments may frame the images of the actors being referred to, as on Palenque's Tablet of the Cross, where the image of the young Kan Bahlam on the left panel is framed by an L-shaped caption text that states his pre-accession name and parentage, and the figure of the older Kan Bahlam on the right-hand panel is framed by a text that records his accession and later events (Bassie-Sweet 1987, 1991). The lintels of Yaxchilán offer numerous examples of such text placement.

On the other hand, there are interactions between text and image that are not physical. The image on a monument does not necessarily represent the events related in the text. Rather, the two can be in complementary opposition, evoking a third element of meaning.

THE COMPOSITION OF A CLASSIC-PERIOD MONUMENT

Looking first at the texts, we can postulate three stages in the production of the inscriptions of a Classic monument. First, a text must have been composed that met the standards of the literary norms of the society. As we discuss below, the texts are carefully crafted narratives.

Second, a choice of hieroglyphic representations had to be made. There was not just one way a given sentence could be written in Classic script. Words could be written logographically, phonetically, or in a combination of both, and both offered the artist an incredible degree of freedom, since there was not just one way in which any logograph or phonetic glyph could be rendered. For the same meaning, the choice of hieroglyphic variants might include an abstract geometric representation, a *head variant* (the glyph personified as the head of a human or animal), or a *full-figure variant*, the personified glyph shown full figure, possibly interacting with other such variants representing other words (see Montgomery 2002:41–52 for examples). The representation of human and animal forms also gave the artist the opportunity to draw on the iconography of mythology to introduce subtle meanings having nothing to do with the literal reading of the text.

The inscription on the back of Copán Stela D, for instance, is entirely composed of full-figure glyphs, and a simple statement of the date of the dedication of the monument is converted into sixteen panels of interactive pairs of figures, with the numbers carrying or wrestling with the time periods, or the ruler's name sitting with his Emblem Glyph, for example. Elsewhere, a simple pronoun prefix for third person, transcribing the syllable *'u*, could be represented by at least nine variants (each with idiosyncratic treatment), ranging from abstract geometric forms to personified head variants (Montgomery 2002:143). This almost infinite flexibility was necessary to carry out the third and final stage of inscriptional composition.

Finally, the hieroglyphic inscription had to be placed in a meaningful way on the monument. The text should frame its referents, placing important words near their corresponding images, and making sure that prominent sections of text occupied prominent locations. Peak events, for instance, are almost always in or near the "hot corner," the upper right-hand corner of a text. To accomplish these locational constraints, sentences, phrases, even words, could be expanded or contracted to move segments of the text into the desired positions. An Emblem Glyph, for instance, composed of three elements ("holy," "lord," and a polity name) could be compacted into a single *glyph block*, one of the squares by which glyphs are arranged into a grid of rows and columns. In fact, this was the norm, with a central glyph representing the polity and with the other two elements attached as affixes. For compositional purposes, however, the phrase could be broken out into three glyph blocks, as on Piedras Negras Lintel (Wall Panel) 2, where three successive glyph blocks read *k'uh* (or *ch'uh)* "holy (God C)," *Yochib* (Piedras Negras), *ajaw* ("lord"). Manipulating these choices made it possible for the artists to move text elements up, down, right, and left to place significant elements in the most meaningful locations with respect to the images.

On a larger scale, related texts could be divided between separate monuments in the same context, as in the mythological versus historical sections in the Palenque Cross Group panels. Furthermore, the texts of the three structures of the Cross Group were intended to be read as a unit, three chapters of the same story (see chapter 8). An interesting example is found in Structure 22 of Yaxchilán (Tate 1992:200–202). Five lintels were set over the doorways of the building. Four of the lintels (Lintels 18, 19, 20, and 22) were ancient, inscribed in Early Classic script. The fifth lintel (Lintel 21) is in a later style, but bears an Initial Series date of 9.0.19.2.4 2 Kan 2 Yax, an Early Classic date (October 16, AD 454) (see chapter 3 for a discussion of Initial Series dates). The event is the dedication of a named building by a ruler whose name phrases indicate he is a member of the Skull clan. The text then moves forward with a Distance Number (15.1.16.5, just under 300 years) that brings events into the Late Classic: 9.16.1.0.9 7 Muluc 17 Tzek (March 12, AD 752). The new event is the dedication of a building with the same name by Bird Jaguar. Thus Bird Jaguar has had four ancient lintels reset in a new (or reconstructed) building to honor an ancient ruler who just happens to be of the same clan as Bird Jaguar's wife, Lady Great Skull.

Another example of the integration of several lintel texts into a single program comes from Yaxchilán's Structure 12 (Tate 1992:168–170), another building with a set of ancient lintels as well as newer ones. The building had seven doorways along its front wall, and at least one doorway on a side wall. The reading order of the lintels apparently began with the central doorway's Lintel 36 and proceeded leftwards through Lintels 48, 47, and 34, all ancient lintels difficult to decipher but featuring beautiful calligraphy. Reading resumed with Lintel 60, on the surviving side wall, and then turned the corner to the front wall again to the other more recent Lintels 49, 37, and 35, the latter adjacent to the central lintel, Lintel 36. The historical content of these last four lintels concerned the seating of rulers, numbered from one to ten in order of their accessions, with notes on either visitors witnessing the accessions or captives of the rulers (epigraphers differ in their interpretations of a critical verb). In any case, on the first lintel, Lintel 60, the first four accessions are noted. On Lintel 49, the next three accessions are recorded. On Lintel 37, the following two accessions are noted, and on the final lintel, Lintel 35, only one accession is mentioned, no doubt that of the ruler who commissioned this monumental display. The decreasing number of accessions leaves room for more and more details, so the tenth ruler is given four times the amount of text as the founding rulers of the site.

Classic Maya artists faced a world of options that included much more than the content of the inscriptions. There were decisions to be made about which hieroglyphs to use to represent the language of the text and how to distribute the text across a monument in the most strategic fashion with respect to the accompanying images, and even the option of dividing the text into discrete units and placing them on adjacent monuments. A similar set of alternatives must have faced the artists in the composition of the images: what scenes to represent, what personages to portray, and what actions to show, as well as what costumes to dress participants in, what stances to place them in, and what paraphernalia to include. The production of a Classic monument, then, was concerned with manipulating language (drawing on literary traditions) and images (drawing on history and mythology). Both were concerned with creating integrated works of art that met the demands of the rulers and conveyed messages to the general public.

An excellent example of the complexity of monument creation is Structure 33 of Yaxchilán (Tate 1992:213–225). The structure itself sits high above the river terrace where the majority of the site's buildings lie, with a broad staircase leading up from the terrace plaza to the Structure 33 platform (Graham and von Euw 1977:7–8). At the foot of the structure is a set of hieroglyphic stairs depicting the ruler Bird Jaguar as a ballplayer, and his image was also displayed above the doorways. As with many of the site's buildings, there are three doorways, each with a carved lintel, in this case Lintels 1–3. Again, these feature Bird Jaguar, in ceremonial dress and holding ritual objects, with his wife (Lintel 1), his son (Lintel 2), and a named subordinate lord (a *sahal*, Lintel 3) (figures 3.1–3.3).[1]

Texts are placed to frame their subjects and note their ceremonial activities (Bassie-Sweet 1991:55–60). The principal actor is Bird Jaguar, the subject of the performance verbs, and lengthy title phrases accompany his names. Secondary actors are identified in short caption texts, with limited titles, including the note that the wife, Lady Great Skull, was the mother of Shield Jaguar IV (also known as Chel Te'). The events depicted on Lintel 1 occurred on Bird Jaguar's inauguration date, 9.16.1.0.0 11 Ajaw 8 Tzek (May 3, AD 752); Lintel 2 depicts activities on the five-*tun* anniversary 9.16.6.0.0 4 Ajaw 3 Sootz' (April 7, 757), when the child Chel Te' was five years old, and Lintel 3 bears an earlier date, the four-*tun* anniversary on 9.16.5.0.0 8 Ajaw 8 Sootz' (April 12, 756).

A similar set of lintels adorned Structure 54, on the river terrace plaza. Lintel 57 depicts Chel Te' with Lady Great Skull; the only text is the caption that identifies her as "the mother of Chel Te'." Lintel 54, with the date 9.16.5.0.0 8 Ajaw 8 Sootz', shows Bird Jaguar in ceremonial activity with Lady Great Skull, and the undated Lintel 58 depicts the unnamed Bird Jaguar facing an axe-bearing warrior identified as "the uncle [*yichan* "mother's brother"] of Chel Te',

Shield Jaguar." Sets of three, four, and more lintels characterize the inscriptions of Yaxchilán and contrast in rhetorical style with the longer wall panel texts of Palenque, for instance, or the stelae of other sites.

Within the confines of lintel sets and wall panels alike, there were almost infinite opportunities to index mythology while reporting history by making certain choices of hieroglyphic variants. Likewise there were numerous ways in which text could be manipulated to create literary structures that emphasized some events and downplayed others. All these elements could be played against the accompanying images. A full appreciation of the art of the Classic Maya requires not only knowledge of the Epigraphic Maya language, the workings of the script and Maya iconography, but also Classic Maya history and its protagonists as well as the mythological background against which the recorded events are played out. Such references to mythology add layers of meaning to the monuments that cannot be appreciated without detailed knowledge of that mythology. For that reason, although our principal goal is to discuss the narrative arts of the Classic Maya—both linguistic and visual—we devote considerable space below to Classic Maya mythology. In all aspects of our research we make use of all available sources, including not only Classic materials but colonial documents and modern ethnography. We justify the use of the latter sources by pointing out the demonstrated continuity in Mayan narrative arts (Hull and Carrasco 2012).

THE ORGANIZATION OF THIS BOOK

This introductory essay has laid out the principal concerns of the authors and illustrated some of the application of their models to Classic Maya monuments. What follows is a much more detailed discussion, beginning with background material (chapters 1–5), and proceeding to the analysis of individual monuments from the Classic period site of Palenque in Chiapas, Mexico (chapters 6–8).

In the first chapter, "The Creator Grandparents and the Place of Duality," basic concepts of Maya cosmology are introduced along with notes on the iconography with which these mythological elements are portrayed on Classic monuments. While linguistic affairs are hardly mentioned in this and the following chapter, the complex of conceptual principles fundamental to the mythology also foreshadows the rhetorical principles discussed later.

The second chapter, "The Family of the Creator Grandparents and Complementary Opposition," extends the mythological genealogy to succeeding generations, again illustrating the principles of opposition and complementarity that are basic to Maya art and literature. Many of the personages introduced here figure later in the art of Classic monuments.

The third chapter, "The Calendar and the Narrative Time Frame," introduces the reader to the chronological framework of Classic Maya inscriptions, an essential part of the narrative text. Almost every sentence in the Classic corpus contains elements of chronology, since the primary purpose of most inscriptions was to record history (or, from the point of view of the contemporary reader, recent and current events).

The fourth chapter, "The Literary Nature of Mayan Texts, Ancient and Modern," lays out the basic structures of Maya rhetoric, from word structure and poetic forms to the devices of long narrative texts. Examples of discourse from modern Maya sources are shown to be related to the discourse style of the Classic Maya, and the analysis of several Classic texts illustrates the application of our model.

The fifth chapter, "Text and Image," does for Classic visual arts what chapter 4 did for language. The basic structures of the interplay between text and image are outlined and illustrated by ample references to the monumental repertory.

The sixth chapter, "The Palenque Tablet of the 96 Glyphs," analyzes a text that is unillustrated, but whose internal iconography—as well as its carefully constructed narrative—gives credit to the creativity of the Classic Maya artist. This text was the first to be subjected to a modern attempt to read a Classic text in a semblance of its original language, but we decline to include here a still imperfect version of that reading, knowing that if we were to be magically transported to the Palenque court and asked to perform the text, the listeners would probably react in dismay and exclaim, "Holy Itzamnaaj! Where did these people go to school?"

The seventh chapter, "The Narrative of the Palenque Temple of the Inscriptions Sarcophagus," continues the detailed discussion of one of the best-known Classic Maya monuments. The discovery of the tomb of the ruler Pakal opened the modern era of Maya archaeology, and the enclosed sarcophagus is one of the most famous artifacts in the Classic Maya world. Nevertheless, the nature of its inscriptions was not fully understood until the model of narrative text was applied.

The eighth chapter, "The Palenque Cross Group Narrative," deals with another famous set of buildings from Palenque, three temples that contain a plethora of inscriptions, all integrated into a single narrative. Combined, the texts constitute one of the longest and most complex narrative texts of the Classic Maya world.

Finally, a brief chapter of "Conclusions" returns to our principal concern, the holistic interpretation of Classic Maya monuments.

In the chapters that follow this Introduction, the discussion alternates between the analysis of specific Classic Maya monuments, especially those of Palenque, and the mythology, iconography, chronology, and discourse traditions that underlie our analyses. We believe that the former cannot be adequately understood without a good foundation in the latter. The conventional approach to a Classic monument is to work out its chronology, decipher the text, and identify the personages and objects depicted in the accompanying images. This information about dated events and royal careers is then added to the corpus of Maya history.

How much deeper our understanding can be if we dissect the structures and rhetorical strategies of the inscriptions, take note of the iconography and visual layout of the images, and relate the imagery to the mythology that much of it represents! Not only is our understanding deeper, it is also closer to that of the creators and contemporary viewers of these narrative arts, who would have been sensitive to all these features. Readers are thus advised that they will be subjected to a seemingly endless array of deities and deity impersonators, mythological beings and associated folklore, costume elements, ritual activities, and esoteric calendrics, as well as literary texts in an unfamiliar language that responds to alien norms of discourse. (Nobody said this would be easy!)

However, a degree of familiarity with the cultural background against which these works of art were composed and executed is necessary if we are to comprehend the messages their creators intended to convey. While the nature and history of the gods, the titles and functions of ceremonial office, the vagaries of the calendric cycles, the norms of formal discourse, and the details of costuming are all new to the modern observer, they were not new to the Classic Maya, but were taken for granted. A contemporary audience could be expected to be sensitive to the details of an inscription and the related images, as well as the interaction between the two. It is our task to unravel the tangle of clues with which we are presented, and to do so requires more than one guide book to the relevant domains.

It is in that spirit that we discuss a wide range of factors both verbal and visual. It is our contention that the only way to fully understand Classic Maya monuments is to see them as holistic creations that incorporate diverse concerns. These creative works of public art and literature were intended to impress the viewer/reader, not just to record history. They certainly do the latter. It is hard to think of Maya events as "prehistory," given the extensive written record they left behind. But while they were concerned with reporting and recording that history, they did it in the most creative way possible, by incorporating it into truly impressive works of art and literature. To begin to appreciate just how meaningful those works were, we offer the following introduction to the narrative arts of the Classic Maya.

NOTE

1. The redrawn illustrations in this book are for illustrative purposes only. The reader is directed to Harvard University's Corpus of Maya Hieroglyphic Inscriptions website for photographs and documentation-quality drawings.

1

The Creator Grandparents and the Place of Duality

There are abundant depictions of deities in Maya art and references to them in hieroglyphic texts. It is our contention that a family of creator deities is at the heart of this diverse pantheon, and that kinship and complementary opposition are the key organizing principles among these deities (Bassie-Sweet 2008). The most comprehensive source regarding the family of creator deities family is contained in the Popol Vuh, an extraordinary piece of literature that was written by members of the Postclassic K'iche' aristocracy after the Spanish conquest (Christenson 2003a, 2003b). The Popol Vuh contains an ancient core myth about the creation of the world and humans by a group of primordial deities. The meager artwork left behind by the K'iche' does not even hint at this rich mythology; however, episodes from the Popol Vuh story have long been used to explain some of the mythology illustrated in lowland Classic-period art. The Popol Vuh relates the deeds of three generations of deities: the creator grandparents called Xpiyacoc and Xmucane; their sons, One Hunahpu and Seven Hunahpu; and One Hunahpu's sons, named One Chouen, One Batz, Hunahpu, and Xbalanque (Christenson 2003a). Classic-period lowland parallels for all of these gods have been identified (Coe 1973, 1977, 1989; Taube 1985, 1992a; Bassie-Sweet 1996, 2008; Zender 2004a) (figure 0.2).

The Maya often categorize, organize, and structure their world using complementary opposition such as

DOI: 10.5876/9781607327424.c001

male/female, right/left, and senior/junior (see Bassie-Sweet 2008:3–4 for an overview). This concept was a fundamental principle in the ancient Maya worldview, and it was reflected in all aspects of life. In this and the following chapter we review the manifestations and complementary nature of the major Popol Vuh deities and their Classic-period parallels, and explore how this family of primary deities functioned as role models for humans. The physical environments in which these deities operated is also discussed. This will provide a framework for understanding the events and ceremonies illustrated in Maya art. We begin with an overview of terms related to deities.

THE NOMENCLATURE AND MANIFESTATIONS OF MAYA DEITIES

Paul Schellhas (1904) categorized the various deities in the three Postclassic codices from northern Yucatán and gave them alphabetic designations. Many of these Postclassic deities or close variations of them also occur in Classic-period art. In some cases, the name glyph of a deity has not been deciphered so the Schellhas designation is retained.

In Maya epigraphy, the head of God C (T1016) with its prefix (T35–40) is taken to represent the word *k'uh*, meaning "god" (Barrera Vásquez 1980:416). A common occurrence of this compound is in Emblem Glyphs, where the head is positioned behind the place glyph, leaving only the prefix visible. There are no phonetic complements or substitutions to insure the reading, which might in some cases take its Cholan form *ch'u(h)* as well (Montgomery 2002:243–245). In either case, the term is derived from proto-Mayan **k'uuh* (Kaufman 2003:458–460) and is well distributed throughout the Mayan family.

The meanings associated with the reflexes of **k'uuh* vary somewhat. About equal numbers of languages in Kaufman's cognate list report the primary meaning of the term to be "god," "sun," "day," and "thunder/lightning" (*trueno, rayo*). However, the meaning "god" prevails in Yucatecan and Cholan languages—the languages most closely associated with Classic culture—and the latter meaning occurs only in the Cuchumatanes, where "sun" and "day" are alternate meanings. The proto-Mayan term **q'iinh* (Kaufman 2003:461–463), giving Epigraphic Maya *k'in*, has the meaning "day, sun" in almost all Mayan languages, but the languages of the Cuchumatanes have shifted the meaning to "fiesta" (and *k'uh* means "day," as in Chuj *hoye k'uh*, Five Days, the period corresponding to the ancient Wayeb).

In Ch'ol (Hopkins et al. 2011:50), the root *ch'uj* "holy" is an adjective, as in *ch'uj-tye'* "cedar" or "holy wood" (from which sacred figures are carved), and *ch'uj-lel* "soul." It commonly occurs with the addition of a suffix, *ch'uj-ul*, as in *ch'ujul tyaty* "holy father" or "God." The suffixed form may reduce to *ch'ul*, or this may be an independent development: in Bachajón Tzeltal (Slocum and Gerdel 1980:136–137) the three forms *chuh ~ ch'uj ~ ch'ul* occur with the same meanings. In early modern Ch'ol sources (Starr 1902:96; Becerra 1935:273) the form *ch'ul* was attested as "holy," as in *ch'ul tyaty* "saint, Sun" (literally, "holy father").

In Maya of Yucatán (Barrera Vásquez 1980:416–423), the meanings "day" and "sun" are assigned to *k'in*, and *k'u* and its derivatives are associated with divinity: *k'u* "God," *k'u na* "temple," *k'uil* "divinity," as well as *k'ul* "adoration, to adore, sacred thing." Kaufman (2003:459) takes the latter to derive from the suffixed form **k'uh-ul*, attested in Epigraphic Maya and common throughout the Greater Lowlands (Yucatecan, Cholan, Tzeltalan, and neighboring languages), with the meaning "divine (thing)."

THE MULTIPLE MANIFESTATIONS OF DEITIES AND HUMANS

Some of the major Maya deities such as the creator grandfather Itzamnaaj, his wife Ix Chel, and the Chahk thunderbolt deities have quadripartite forms that are related to the four quadrants of the world and their associated colors (east-red, north-white, west-black, and yellow-south). In addition, Maya deities have multiple manifestations that relate to their various functions and duties. These manifestations could have the form of flora, fauna, geological formations, or natural phenomena like lightning, whirlwinds, and meteors. As an example, the deities designated as God D and God N were different manifestations of Itzamnaaj.[1] Generally speaking, God N is identified with earthly locations and his diagnostic trait is a net bag headdress while the celestial God D is a conflation of God N and his avian manifestation. Itzamnaaj also had turtle, conch, opossum, and peccary manifestations. The first two forms are obviously associated with water and the latter are identified with fire in Mesoamerican thought. As will be discussed later, Itzamnaaj was the source of the fire and heat that engendered life.

The Maya believe that humans have co-essences that can take the form of fantastic animals or phenomena like thunderbolts, whirlwinds, and meteors. Houston and Stuart (1989) and Grube and Nahm (1994) independently deciphered a glyph (*way*) that represents this concept. Given that the deities were role models for human behavior, the notion that humans have supernatural manifestations is clearly linked to the concept that deities had many forms of manifestation.

THE CHAHK DEITIES

In the Popol Vuh, the family of creator deities interacts with a triad of thunderbolt gods who reside in the sky called Thunderbolt Huracan, Youngest Thunderbolt, and Sudden Thunderbolt. The Chahks (God B in the Schellhas system) are thunderbolt gods. They are often portrayed as zoomorphic creatures wearing a *Spondylus*-shell earring, and such portraits are used to represent the word *chahk* "thunderbolt." *Pars pro toto* representations are common in Maya art, and the Chahk's shell earring is used as an abbreviated reference for the word *chahk* "thunderbolt" in hieroglyphic writing. There is a common Maya belief that lightning bolts are the axes of the thunderbolt gods, and that they can also take the form of snakes (both strike with fast, deadly results). A clear example is found on the Dumbarton Oaks Tablet originally from the Palenque region (figure 1.1). In this scene, the young K'inich K'an Joy Chitam II is shown dancing in the costume of a Chahk deity while swinging a lightning axe. The handle of the axe has the form of a serpent. There are many different kinds of Chahk deities with names that include references to age, color, rain, clouds, fire, and the sky (Grube 2000; Lacadena 2004; García Barros 2008).

THE TRIAD OF THUNDERBOLT GODS

Berlin (1963) identified three gods in the Classic-period texts of Palenque, and he gave them the nicknames GI, GII, and GIII because their nominal glyphs were not deciphered at the time. When these gods are named together as a triad the order is always given as GI, GII, and GIII, but according to the Palenque Cross Group narrative, the birth order of these three brothers was GI, GIII, and GII. All three of these gods have thunderbolt characteristics, and there is evidence that that they are parallel to the three thunderbolt deities (Huracan, Youngest Thunderbolt, and Sudden Thunderbolt) who play a central role in the creation story found in the Popol Vuh (Bassie-Sweet 2008:102–124). When named together, Youngest Thunderbolt is always in the second position, like GII. Maya hearths are composed of three large stones that contain the fire and support the cooking vessels. There is evidence that the three hearthstones were thought to be manifestations of the three thunderbolt deities GI, GII, and GIII (Bassie-Sweet 2008:63, 121–122).

The Palenque Cross Group is composed of a plaza with a small platform at its center and a temple-pyramid on its north, west, and east sides (Temple of the Cross, Temple of the Sun, and Temple of the Foliated Cross). The inscriptions of these temple-pyramids indicate that each building was dedicated to

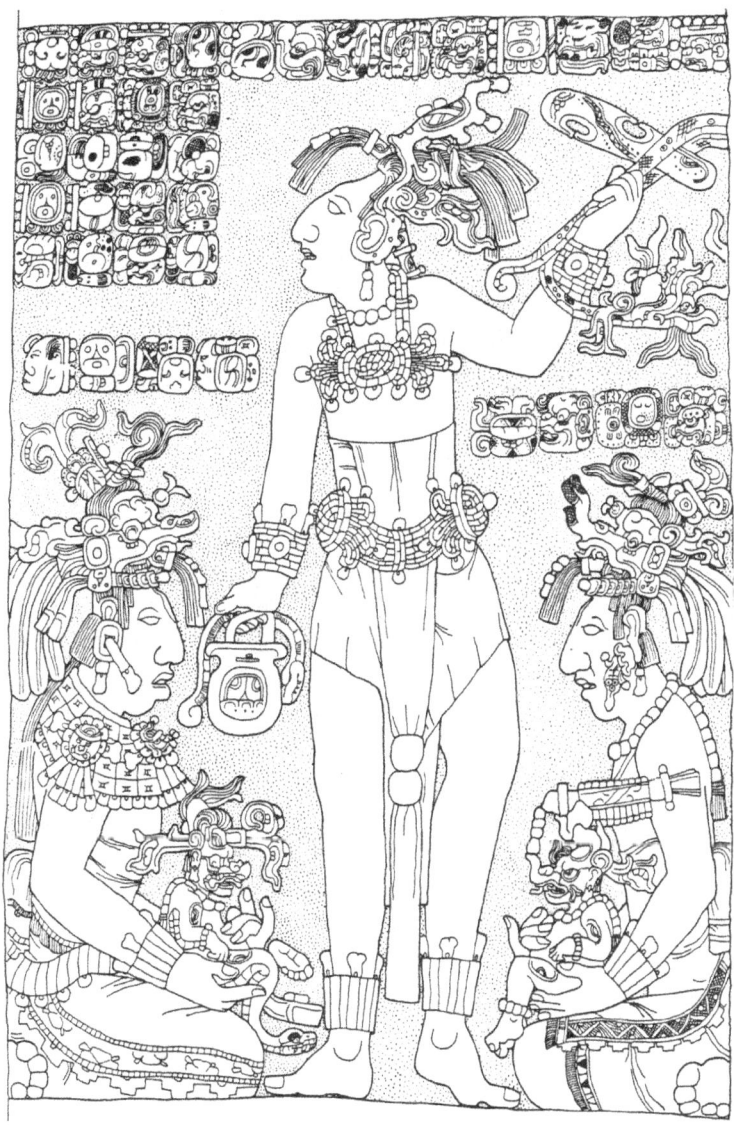

FIGURE 1.1. *Dumbarton Oaks Tablet, drawing by Linda Schele, courtesy David Schele.*

one member of the thunderbolt triad (GI-TC, GIII-TS, and GII-TFC). Each temple-pyramid has a wall panel on the back wall of its inner sanctuary, and these three panels form a continuous narrative beginning with the north panel

(Tablet of the Cross), continuing on the west panel (Tablet of the Sun), and ending on the east panel (Tablet of the Foliated Cross). This reading order follows the birth order of these three deities (see chapter 8 for further discussion). Each panel and temple is nicknamed after the central icon of its respective sanctuary panel. The Tablet of the Cross is so named because its central icon is a cross-shaped tree. The central icon of the Tablet of the Foliated Cross also has a cross-shape, but it is a stylized corn plant with twin ears of corn. The icon on the Tablet of the Sun includes a shield emblazed with the face of GIII, who has facial characteristics similar to the sun god.

THE THUNDERBOLT DEITY GI

The deity GI is an anthropomorphic god with a Roman nose who wears a Chahk earring, and his name is most often represented by a portrait glyph of him wearing the Chahk earring (figure 1.2). An expanded version of his full name phrase on the Palenque Creation Tablet demonstrates that his name includes the word *chahk* (Bassie-Sweet 2008:111). The first glyph is a portrait of GI wearing a headdress in the form of a fish-eating water bird. Such birds are intimately associated with him, and it is likely that this is an avian manifestation of GI. This portrait of GI does not wear the Chahk earring, but the second glyph in this nominal phrase is a portrait of Chahk. Although the portrait glyph of GI has yet to be deciphered, this example demonstrates that his name ended in the word *Chahk*, and consequently it must be concluded that GI was a thunderbolt god. Many of the storms that descend on the Maya region come from the north, and given GI's association with north, it has been argued that he was a Chahk specifically associated with northern storms (Bassie-Sweet 2008:109–113). Furthermore, GI's eye is frequently depicted as a swirl similar to swirls used to depict turbulent water, a highly appropriate eye for a storm god.

Numerous examples of GI illustrate him wearing a headdress in the form of the so-called Quadripartite Badge motif, and the narrative on the Temple of the Inscriptions panels specifically states that the Quadripartite Badge was the headdress of GI. The main element of the Quadripartite Badge motif is a bowl marked with a *k'in* sign that typically contains three objects: a *Spondylus* shell, an upright stingray spine, and an element infixed with a crossed band (Robertson 1974). The bowl is often illustrated as a skeletal zoomorphic creature. The *k'in* bowl itself is found in contexts that indicate it was used for burning offerings including incense, blood, and hearts (Stuart 1998:389–390; 2005a:168; Stuart and Stuart 2008:175; Taube 1998, 2009). The stingray spine in the *k'in* bowl was an instrument used by Maya as a perforator during

FIGURE 1.2. *The deity GI.*

bloodletting rites (Joralemon 1974). Hellmuth (1987) noted that Early Classic depictions of the Quadripartite Badge illustrate the tooth of a shark in place of the typical Late Classic stingray spine. Many portraits of GI have a shark's tooth for an incisor. The implication is that these marine bloodletters were thought to be a manifestation of GI. The *Spondylus* shell pictured in the *k'in* bowl is also identified with blood offerings and thunderbolt gods. Such shells have been found in burials and caches, and they were often used as receptacles for blood offerings. As noted above, a *Spondylus* shell serves as the *pars pro toto* for the word *chahk* "thunderbolt."

The Quadripartite Badge motif is occasionally held by rulers as a scepter, such as on the Tablet of the Cross, the Temple of the Cross jambs, and House D, Pier C. In these two former examples, liquid pours from the mouth of the zoomorphic creature. Although such liquid is often interpreted to represent blood, the Quadripartite Badge motif is also found on the rear end of a celestial crocodile that represents the Milky Way (House E doorway) (Freidel et al. 1993:87; Milbrath 1999:275–282; Stuart 2003b:15). In the Dresden Codex, the liquid that pours from the Milky Way Crocodile is depicted as blue water.[2] As a god of storms, GI was intimately connected to this pathway across the sky that the Maya associated with rain (Bassie-Sweet 2008:36–38). Rulers are illustrated wearing GI's Quadripartite Badge headdress. Copán Stela H is a portrait of a Copán ruler wearing a face mask in the form of GI while wearing the Quadripartite Badge motif as a headdress. He has clearly taken on the guise of this god.

THE THUNDERBOLT DEITY GIII

GIII has the same Roman nose as his older brother GI, but he has jaguar traits, *ak'bal* "night, darkness" signs on his cheeks, and a twisted cord over his nose (figure 1.3). Such cords were used to drill fire and two of GIII's titles refer to him as the vassal of fire (*Yajawk'ahk'*) and a *k'inich* "sunlike" torch (Taube 2000; Zender 2004b). He was also identified with meteors, which the Maya identified as a type of thunderbolt (Taube 2000; Bassie 2008:117–121). GIII's undeciphered nominal glyphs are prefixed with the modifier *k'inich* "sunlike," and he is named with the *k'inich ajaw* "sunlike lord" title in the Temple of the Inscriptions center tablet (E4). GIII has been given the misleading nickname "the jaguar god of the Underworld," and it has been speculated that he represented the night sun in its journey through the Underworld (Thompson 1950:134; Coe 1973). There is, however, no evidence that the Maya believed the sun was transformed into a jaguar at night.

Several authors have asserted that GI and GIII were different aspects of the sun god (Stuart 2015a; Houston and Taube 2000; Taube and Houston 2015). While they follow the Thompson identification of GIII as the "night" sun, they have identified GI as the aquatic form of the sun as it rises from the Caribbean Sea at dawn. They presumably make this identification because GI (like GIII) shares the same Roman-nosed face as the sun god and because they identify GI's brazier headdress as the pyre used in mythological times to transform a god into the sun. In an example of circular reasoning, they assert that the swirl eyes of GI and GIII indicate night while the square eye of the sun god indicates day, based solely on their identification of GIII as the night sun. There is no evidence that the shape of supernatural pupils indicates day or night. Taube and Houston (2015:214) proposed that the GIII portrait on a

FIGURE 1.3. *The deity GIII.*

stairway of Copán East Court may have been paired with a portrait of the sun god on the opposite side of the court, and thus would have represented the complementary opposition of the night sun and the day sun. There is little evidence that such a pairing actually even existed. In fact, the Copán Structure 8N-11 bench, where there is a clear contrasting of day and night, does not employ a portrait of GIII to represent night (see following chapter for a discussion of this bench). Furthermore, the rising sun on this bench is a standard form of the sun god, not GI. Another Copán bench from Structure 10K-4 also illustrates the rising sun, not as GI but as the standard sun god (Baudez 1994:234).

Bassie-Sweet is of the opinion that GIII's name is prefaced with modifier *k'inich* and that he is named as *k'inich ajaw* in reference to his role as a fire deity. This is similar to Itzamnaaj, who is also named as a *k'inich ajaw* (see below for further discussion of the sun god and the *k'inich ajaw* title). Furthermore, the *k'in* signs that on very rare occasions replace the *ak'bal* signs on GIII's cheeks may simply be a reference to his *k'inich* "sunlike" title, and not an indication that he was the sun. This would be a case of conflation, a common convention in Maya text and image. GIII is closely associated with war imagery, and with the war deity Tlaloc.

A Palenque Group B incensario stand portrays a full-figure rendition of GIII wearing a headdress that represents his office of *Yajawk'ahk'* (López Bravo 2000, 2004; Zender 2004b). The central feature of the headdress is a portrait of Tlaloc. To be a *Yajawk'ahk'* is to take on the role of Tlaloc. Many illustrations of Maya warriors show them carrying a shield emblazoned with the face of GIII. The juxtaposing of Tlaloc and GIII is seen on Aguateca Stela 2 where the king wears the mask of Tlaloc and is draped in Tlaloc clothing while holding the GIII shield. The central icon on the Tablet of the Sun is such a shield.

THE THUNDERBOLT DEITY GII

In contrast to the anthropomorphic GI and GIII, GII is a zoomorphic Chahk (figure 1.4). The name of this youngest-born thunderbolt deity has

FIGURE 1.4. *The deity GII.*

been read as *Unen K'awiil* "Baby *K'awiil*" and he is parallel to the thunderbolt deity named simply as *K'awiil* in the codices (God K in the Schellhas system) (Stuart 1987; Martin 2002). For brevity, we will continue to refer to Unen K'awiil as GII. GII is depicted as the personification of a thunderbolt axe in many illustrations. His body represents the handle, while his head has the axe blade protruding from it. The axe head is often shown emitting smoke or flames, and lightning is a natural source of fire. One of his legs is often shown as a snake. It is stated in various texts that GII was a red dwarf, and he carries the *ch'ok* "youth" title (Houston 1992). Red is associated with the east in Maya worldview, and his temple is situated on the east side of the Cross Group plaza. It is likely that GII was the thunderbolt god who broke open the mythological mountain containing corn (Bassie-Sweet 2008:262–263).

Maya kings are frequently shown holding a GII scepter, and this deity has long been associated with rulership. However, there are numerous examples of young lords and secondary lords with GII scepters as well, which suggests that this emphasis on GII was not identified with sovereignty per se, but on the ability to control the power of the thunderbolt. The Maya believe that humans have supernatural co-essences who share their soul and destiny. The co-essences of spiritually strong individuals are thought to have the form of thunderbolts and meteors (Bassie-Sweet et al. 2015). Many lords incorporate the names *Chahk* and *K'awiil* in their name phrases (Martin and Grube 2000).

K'AWIIL

The name *K'awiil* appears in association with other deities as well. Landa noted that during the New Year ceremonies for years that began on a K'an day, the Maya made offerings to Itzamnaaj K'awiil (Tozzer 1941:143). This aspect of Itzamnaaj is also mentioned in the Chilam Balam of Chumayel and by Andrés Avendaño y Loyola in his account of the Postclassic Petén Itzá Maya (Roys 1933:153, 168; Avendaño y Loyola 1987). Maya rulers frequently incorporate the names of deities in their nominal phrases, and rulers from Dos Pilas and Naranjo were called *Itzamnaaj K'awiil* (Martin and Grube 2008). It has been suggested by some researchers that these names are simply conflations of two deities (Houston and Stuart 1996:295), but there are scenes on a number of pottery vessels that suggest otherwise. In these scenes, Itzamnaaj in his God N form emerges from the mouth of K'awiil's serpent leg (see K5164). The name *Itzamnaaj K'awiil* appears to be a direct reference to this aspect of Itzamnaaj. The rainy season in the Maya region is a time of intense thunder storms, and God N has long been identified with thunder (Taube 1992a:92–99; Bassie-Sweet 2008:146). Given Itzamnaaj's identification with fire, it is reasonable to conclude that he was also thought to be not only the thunder of the lightning bolt, but the source of its fire.

THE METEOR DEITY TLALOC

Teotihuacán cultural presence in the Maya region during the Early Classic period has long been recognized in the form of talud-tablero-style architecture, iconography, ceramic vessels, and Central Mexican obsidian, although the nature of the relationship between Teotihuacán and various Maya centers continues to be debated. It is well established that certain elements of the war imagery found in the Maya lowlands are also found at Teotihuacán and originated from this site (Pasztory 1974; Coggins 1975; Hellmuth 1975; Carrasco 1982; Berlo 1983; Stone 1989; Taube 1992b, 2000; Proskouriakoff 1993; Stuart 2000, 2004a, 2005b; Braswell 2003). Classic Maya rulers and their wives often dressed in the costume of a Teotihuacán war deity who has been identified as the precursor of the Aztec thunderbolt deity named *Tlaloc*. It is unknown what name was used by the Teotihuacanos for this deity so we will continue to refer to him as *Tlaloc* for lack of a better alternative. At Teotihuacán, the Tlaloc god has attributes that indicate he was associated with lightning, and he has been referred to as a storm god by some scholars. The Maya categorized meteors as a type of lightning, and the Maya specifically associated the Teotihuacán Tlaloc with meteors, obsidian, and fire (Bassie-Sweet and Hopkins 2015:128–144). Tlaloc was incorporated into Maya worldview as a patron god of war. Like other Mesoamerican deities, Tlaloc had a number of avatars, including serpent (18 Ub'aah Chan), jaguar, Black Witch Moth, and owl manifestations. There is significant evidence that the lords and ladies who held the office of *Kaloomte'* (literally, "splitter of trees") were high priests and priestesses for Tlaloc.

AVIAN AVATARS

Birds play an important role in Maya cosmology, and avian manifestations of various deities have been identified. The role of birds as messengers for the gods is well known (see Houston, Stuart, and Taube 2006:229–252 for overview). Various avian deities have wings that are a conflation of a bird wing with a serpent head. The serpent head personifies the bone of the wing. Bardawil (1976) suggested that all supernatural birds with serpent-wings and hooked beaks were variations of the same avian creature, and he grouped all these birds under the nickname Principal Bird Deity. Although Bardawil noted that his Principal Bird Deity could have the head of Itzamnaaj, the deity GIII, or an owl, he wrongly concluded that these were celestial and Underworld manifestations of the same deity. Over the years, more examples of deities with serpent-wings have emerged, including the avian form of One Ixim (K1387, K1388), the vulture deity (K5356), the Sibikte' deity, hummingbirds, and numerous water birds (Berjonneau et al. 1985:figs. 329, 335, 340; Zender 2005), which further nullifies Bardawil's conclusion. Lumping together all avian supernaturals as manifestation of one deity is simply wrong, and in our opinion the term *Principal Bird Deity* should be permanently retired.

THE CREATOR GRANDPARENTS AND COMPLEMENTARY OPPOSITION

In the Maya worldview, humans are thought to be both male and female with the right side being male and the left side being female (Bassie-Sweet 2002, 2008). However, it is believed that an adult has to be married to be complete. Husbands and wives work in unison in their tasks just as the right side of the body works with the left. An expression of this complementary nature is found in agricultural production where a farmer may plant and harvest corn, but he must have a wife to transform it into food. Their complementary nature is also seen in the rituals that must be performed together to ensure agricultural abundance. In some traditional communities, a male cannot attain the position of ritual specialist or leader without being married. The wife shares her husband's titles and position, and has complementary roles to perform. The ritual specialist can also have a junior male assistant who is viewed as a symbolic wife. The Popol Vuh account of the creator couple Xpiyacoc and Xmucane indicates that they were the first priests, diviners, healers, and artists. Their many paired titles and offices such as *Tz'aqol* ("Framer") and *B'itol* ("Shaper") and *Mamon* (glossed as "Patriarch," but literally meaning "Grandfather"), and *I'yom* ("Midwife") reflect their complementary nature, and indicate that they were the embodiment of complementary opposition (Christenson 2003a:60–61).

Before the creation of the earth, the creator grandparents lived in a pooled body of water. The Popol Vuh describes this water:

> This is the account of when all is still silent and placid. All is silent and calm. Hushed and empty is the womb of the sky. These, then, are the first words, the first speech. There is not yet one person, one animal, bird, fish, crab, tree, rock, hollow, canyon, meadow, or forest. All alone the sky exists. The face of the earth has not yet appeared. Alone lies the expanse of the sea, along with the womb of all the sky. There is not yet anything gathered together. All is at rest. Nothing stirs. All is languid, at rest in the sky. There is not yet anything standing erect. Only the expanse of the water, only the tranquil sea lies alone. There is not yet anything that might exist. All lies placid and silent in the darkness, in the night. All alone are the Framer and the Shaper, Sovereign and Quetzal Serpent, They Who Have Borne Children and They Who Have Begotten Sons. Luminous they are in the water, wrapped in quetzal feathers and cotinga feathers. Thus they are called Quetzal Serpent. In their essence, they are great sages, great possessors of knowledge. (Christenson 2003a:67–69)

Above this Place of Duality was a dark sky that was inhabited by the trio of thunderbolt gods known collectively as Heart of Sky (Thunderbolt Huracan, Youngest Thunderbolt and Sudden Thunderbolt). Below was a place called Xibalba that was populated by a host of death deities, and ruled by a pair of gods called One Death and Seven Death. In concert with the three Heart of Sky thunderbolt gods, Xpiyacoc and Xmucane (Heart of Earth) made the earth rise up from the waters of the Place of Duality, and they then set about to create humans who would honor them. The Framer and Shaper titles of Xpiyacoc and Xmucane refer to their role in ordering and shaping the earth and the first human beings.

The description of the creation event makes it clear that all the water in the world originated from the Place of Duality:

> First the earth was created, the mountains and the valleys. The waterways were divided, their branches coursing among the mountains. Thus the waters were divided, revealing the great mountains. For thus was the creation of the earth, created then by Heart of Sky and Heart of Earth, as they are called. They were the first to conceive it. The sky was set apart. The earth also was set apart within the waters. Thus was conceived the successful completion of the work when they thought and when they pondered. (Christenson 2003a:73)

Itzamnaaj and his wife Ix Chel were lowland parallels for Xpiyacoc and Xmucane. The attributes of these deities suggest that Itzamnaaj was originally a god of the sky while his wife Ix Chel had death attributes associated with Xibalba (Bassie-Sweet 2008:236). The contrasts between these two deities led Bassie-Sweet to propose that the Place of Duality was likely first formed when Itzamnaaj-Xpiyacoc of the sky married Ix Chel-Xmucane of Xibalba. In the context of complementary opposition, the creator grandfather, and by extension males, were generally associated with senior, up, hot, day, and life while the creator grandmother and females were identified with junior, down, cold, night, and death.

THE WATERS OF THE PLACE OF DUALITY

Although many researchers follow the proposal that mythological water locations in Maya art represent the Underworld (Hellmuth 1987), the Popol Vuh narrative emphasizes the generative power of the creator grandparents and by extension, the waters of the Place of Duality within which they lived before the creation of the earth. The following is a brief overview of water signs and motifs that appear in Maya art, and how they relate to the Place of Duality (see Bassie-Sweet 2008:84–101 for a more detailed description).

Celestial and terrestrial waters are often depicted as a layered band or bands containing lines of dots or bubbles of various sizes (Hellmuth 1987) (figure 1.5). The edges of water bands or streams of liquid can be defined by a beaded edge. Horizontal water bands representing rain are sometimes juxtaposed with the *muyal* "cloud" signs (Houston and Stuart 1990). The S-shaped cloud sign also has a beaded edge that refers to the water that it contains. In the case of

FIGURE 1.5. *Water symbols, after Justin Kerr.*

terrestrial water, the water band can include waterlilies, seashells, and aquatic animals. There are also two elements that resemble the phonetic T23 *na* sign and T188 *le* sign, although their meaning in the water band context is unclear.

Water bands can also include stacked rectangles or ovals of diminishing size that have been nicknamed "water stacks" (figures 1.5, 1.6). It has been suggested that they refer to waves, spray, foam, evaporation, rain, or the spiral tip of a conch shell. In the Postclassic codices, three inverted water stacks represent the word *ha'al* "rain" (Lacadena 2004:89). Some examples of water bands are edged by water scrolls, or they have diagonal or wavy lines that suggest turbulent motion like river rapids, whirlpools, waterfalls, and waves or rain during intense storms. The water scrolls are reminiscent of the Popol Vuh description of the earth rising from the waters of the Place of Duality. Christenson (2003a:71) noted that one of the verbs used to describe this event (*pupuje'ik*) is used in other contexts to describe clouds rising up from mountains. The image is one of billowing, turbulent clouds much like the water scrolls or the S shape of the cloud sign.

In nature, waterlilies only occur in relatively still bodies of fresh water. In Maya hieroglyphic writing, a stylized waterlily blossom is used to represent the word *ha'* "water" (Fox and Justeson 1983:55; Stuart and Houston 1994:19). In Classic-period writing, it is also used to form the word *ha'al* "rain" (Lacadena 2004:89). *Nahb* "pool" refers to pooled bodies of water such as ponds, lakes, backwaters, deep rivers, lagoons, and the sea (Kaufman 2003:429, 430, 554–556). The word *nahb* is represented by a skull with the water-band cartouche infixed

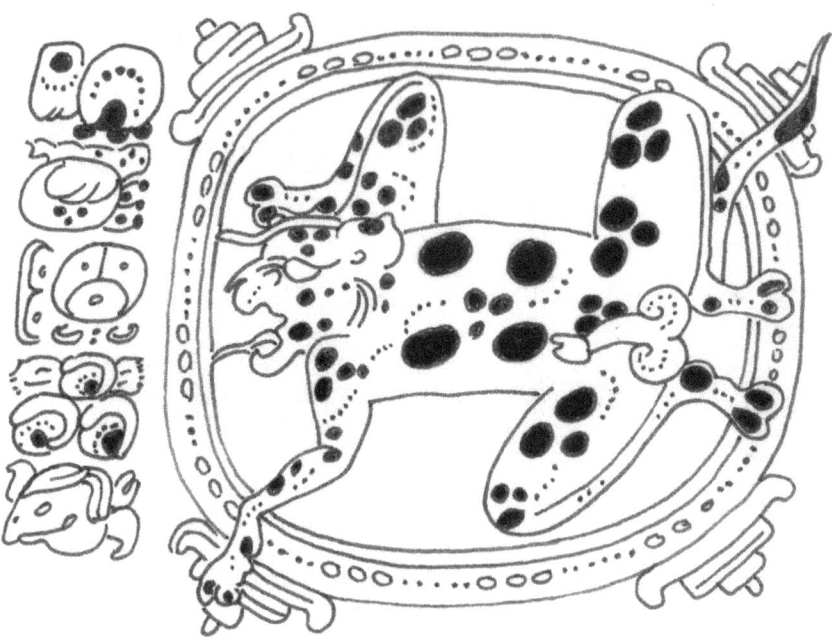

Figure 1.6. *Vessel K771, after Justin Kerr.*

in its forehead and the waterlily plant growing from its skull cap (Hellmuth 1987:figs. 368–382; Stuart and Houston 1994:19). The *nahb* sign frequently appears at the base of a scene to indicate that the location is a pooled body of water (see chapter 2 for a further discussion of the *nahb* skull). It is well demonstrated that the full form of a sign or motif can be reduced to just one element (Stuart 1987). The *nahb* sign can be abridged to just the waterlily pad and water-band cartouche or just the waterlily pad. The clearest examples of these forms of the word *nahb* are seen in the numerous variations used to spell the name phrase of the Palenque ruler K'inich Ahkal Mo' Nahb III (Stuart 2005a:150–151).

A circular band of water is also used in many images to denote a pooled body of water (Hellmuth 1987:figs. 45, 57). For example, the perimeters of vessels and their lids are often decorated with a water band to indicate such a pool. The use of a band to form a water pool is found in a scene on K771 (figure 1.6). Each corner of this water pool is marked with water stacks. A roaring, well-endowed male jaguar sprawls across the pool. Grube and Nahm (1994:690) noted that the adjacent caption text names this being as a *way* "co-essence" of a lord of Seibal. The personal name of the jaguar (Nahb Hix) is composed

FIGURE 1.7. *Vessel K4681, after Justin Kerr.*

of a waterlily blossom ("water"), a cartouche representing the water band ("pool"), and the word *hix*, which is a known term for a jaguar. The illustration of the "water pool jaguar" is a full-figure depiction of his glyphic name. In other examples of this jaguar, the water pool is represented by a circular band of brown wash (K791). The use of brown wash to represent water in pottery scenes is well known (Robicsek and Hales 1981:80, 94).

The earth is often represented by a turtle, one of the animal manifestations of the creator grandfather Itzamnaaj-Xpiyacoc (Taube 1988, Bassie-Sweet 2008:130–140). Such an earth turtle is illustrated on K4681 and K1892 (figures 1.7, 1.8). The head of the turtle wears the net headdress of Itzamnaaj (God N). One Ajaw and Yax Bolon, who are the Classic period parallels of the Hero Twins Hunahpu and Xbalanque, are pictured on either side of the turtle (Coe 1989). These two gods, who represent the sun and full moon, respectively, are illustrated on opposite sides of the turtle earth just as sun and full moon occur in opposition to each other in nature (Bassie-Sweet 2008:222) (see below for a discussion of these deities). The base of the K4681 scene is defined by a water band with diagonal lines. On K1892, the earth turtle floats in a brown wash representing water that scrolls up and around the turtle. At the base of the earth turtle is a water scroll and water stack that take on the form a stylized conch shell. The conch is flanked by a waterlily blossom and pad. Given that

FIGURE 1.8. *Vessel K1892, photograph courtesy Justin Kerr.*

the motif is placed directly under the earth turtle, it seems logical to conclude that it refers to the pooled waters of the Place of Duality from which the earth turtle rose. The positioning of place name motifs at the base of a scene is a common convention in Maya art (Houston and Stuart 1994).

It is curious that waterlilies and seashells are juxtaposed in various representations of water given that waterlilies grow only in fresh water while conch shells are from the salty sea. Many researchers have noted this anomaly, but have not provided an explanation other than to say that the Maya did not distinguish freshwater and marine environments in their art (Filamore and Houston 2010; Houston and Taube 2011; Stone and Zender 2011). There is, however, a reason for such a seemingly unnatural combination of elements when viewed as a metonym. In the Popol Vuh, mountain and valley are paired to describe the earth; sky and earth are paired to describe the world; and Heart of Sky (the three thunderbolt gods) and Heart of Earth (the creator grandparents) are paired to describe all the creator deities (Christenson 2003b:16, 19, 20). In this same manner, *cho* "lake" and *palo* "sea" are paired as a reference to all water (Tedlock 1987:148; Christenson 2003b:16, 157). These two terms are a contrast between the largest body of fresh water and the largest body of salt water. We suggest that the combination of waterlilies and seashells seen in Maya art is a visual metonym that refers to all water, both fresh and salt. Given that the Popol Vuh narrative indicates that all the water in the world originated from the Place of Duality, the juxtaposing of waterlilies and seashells is ultimately a reference to the waters of this primordial place. The creator grandfather Itzamnaaj is intimately associated with such water. In addition to his turtle form, Itzamnaaj in his God N form was also portrayed as a conch (Taube 1992:96). On Vessel K3324, Itzamnaaj's conch shell has a waterlily blossom attached to it.

THE WATERLILY BIRD-SERPENT AND THE WATERS OF THE PLACE OF DUALITY

There is a zoomorphic creature that frequently occurs as an occupant of water, and that is directly associated with the waters of the Place of Duality (fig. 1.9). It has been nicknamed the Waterlily Monster, Lily Pad Headdress Monster, or Waterlily Serpent (Schele and Miller 1986:46; Hellmuth 1987; Stuart 2005a). It is composed of a bird head with the body of a serpent. In some examples, such as on K1162, the body is decorated with feathers. The beast wears a waterlily pad tied to its forehead with a waterlily blossom. We prefer the more descriptive name Waterlily Bird-Serpent. The Waterlily Bird-Serpent also appears as the god of the number thirteen and as the full form of the *tun* glyph (the period of 360 days).

A fish or hummingbird often nibbles at the blossom of the Waterlily Bird-Serpent headdress. The headdress can also contain a zoomorphic animal nicknamed the shell-wing dragon or oyster-shell dragon because it has *Spondylus*-shell wings (Schele 1979; Hellmuth 1987). It has been suggested that the dragon is the personification of a *Spondylus* (spiny oyster) shell (Houston and Taube 2011). In several examples of the Waterlily Bird-Serpent, its undulating body is decorated with layered water and shells or marked with large circles representing mirrors (a pooled body of water is like a mirror). The conflation of water symbols with the serpent's body indicates that the body represents water.

Maya kings, lords, and ladies emulated many different kinds of deities. As an example, the young lord K'an Joy Chitam II of Palenque is illustrated

FIGURE 1.9. *The Waterlily Bird-Serpent, after Nicholas Hellmuth.*

dressed as a Chahk thunderbolt deity on the Dumbarton Oaks Tablet while the young lord Bird Jaguar wears a similar costume on Yaxchilán Stela 11 (figure 1.1). Houston and Stuart noted that:

> Classic Maya lords episodically adopted the names and costuming of particular gods and performed rituals appropriate to those deities, such as fire-drilling.

The similarities to better documented practices in central Mexico (Hvidtfeldt 1958, Klein 1986) are sufficiently striking to suggest that Maya impersonations were not simply mummery and costumed drama. Rather, rulers and certain non-regnal figures shared in some manner the divinity of those gods. The costuming offered not so much a theatrical illusion as a tangible, physical representation of a deity. (Houston and Stuart 1996:299)

A number of scenes illustrate Maya elite dressed as the Waterlily Bird-Serpent and the associated caption texts give three names for this being (Houston and Stuart 1996:299; Stuart, Houston, and Robertson 1999:55, 56; Stuart 2007a; Ishihara et al. 2006). Its nominal phrase begins with the color *yax* "blue-green" and a sign that can be phonetically read as *chit* although the meaning of the word is unclear. The next glyph is the head of the Waterlily Bird-Serpent prefixed with the number one. In some rare examples, the portrait glyph includes phonetic complements that suggest a reading of *witz'*, which means "water spray," "water splash," or "waterfall" in several Maya languages (Stuart 2007a). The final name has been read as *noh kan* "great serpent" by Stuart although the prefix is the T4 sign *nah*.

It has been proposed that the Waterlily Bird-Serpent is a zoomorphic representation of standing bodies of water such as the ocean, lakes, swamps, and agricultural canals (Schele and Miller 1986:46; Miller and Taube 1993:184; Ishihara et al. 2006); that it represents the coursing water of rivers and streams (Stuart 2007a); that it is related to the Underworld, chthonic sources of water (Hellmuth 1987:145, 157; Taube cited in Filamore and Houston 2011:45) or that it represents the sea (Stone and Zender 2011:56). On K1892, an anthropomorphic form of the Waterlily Bird-Serpent emerges from the rear of the turtle shell, suggesting it is intimately identified with the waters of the Place of Duality. The juxtaposing of waterlily and seashell imagery found with the Waterlily Bird-Serpent also suggests such an association.

There is a feathered water serpent in the Popol Vuh who appears to be directly parallel to the Waterlily Bird-Serpent. As noted above, the creator grandparents were manifested in the waters of the Place of Duality as Sovereign and Quetzal Serpent (Qucumatz). They were wrapped in blue cotinga feathers and green quetzal feathers that were metaphors for luminous, shimmering water. The pairing of the blue cotinga feathers and the green quetzal feathers spans the spectrum of the color *yax*. In addition to their joint title Heart of Earth, the creator grandparents were also called *U K'u'x Cho* "heart of the lake" and *U K'u'x Palo* "heart of the sea" (Christenson 2003a:61). It is highly likely that the Waterlily Bird-Serpent is parallel to Quetzal Serpent, and as one of the water manifestations of the creator grandparents the Waterlily Bird-Serpent represents the essence of all water (Bassie-Sweet 1996:83; 2002; 2008:90–92).[3] Both the Waterlily Bird-Serpent and Quetzal Serpent are composite beings that embody the complementary opposition of a bird (a sky animal) and a snake (a land animal).

Rivers are called roads of water (Kaufman 2003:430–431). Given the use of lowland rivers as transportation avenues, this is not unexpected. In hieroglyphic texts, the death of a deity or person is described as entering a road or entering water (Stuart 1998). These verbs likely refer to the washing of a deceased deity or a person in a river or pool of water as part of the burial and apotheosis preparation. As an example, there are a number of scenes in which the deity One Ixim is washed and dressed by the Hero Twins and a bevy of goddesses as part of the preparation for his apotheosis as the morning star (Bassie-Sweet 2008:289–294). These deities stand in waist-high water and the adjacent caption text states that One Ixim entered the water or that he entered the road (K1004, K1202). Mythological locations of water are common in Maya art as are place names prefixed with a number (Houston and Stuart 1996; Tokovinine 2008). The place of One Ixim adornment is called the *Seven Water Place* (Stuart and Houston 1994:73). An interesting example of this place name employs the Waterlily Bird-Serpent to represent the word *ha'* "water" (figure 1.9, bottom). In this context, its serpent body has been replaced with a water band encircling a waterlily. Rather than just being a fancy way of writing the word *ha'*, the use of the Waterlily Bird-Serpent in this place name suggests that the artist was deliberately emphasizing the connection between the Seven Water Place and the waters of the Place of Duality. Water played an important role in healing and regenerative acts (Bassie-Sweet 2008:293). This should not be surprising, given that the earth was thought to have been created from the waters of the Place of Duality, and, of course, the rain that falls at the beginning of the rainy season is essential for the annual regeneration of the world.

WATER SHRINES

The stability of Maya society depended in large part on the successful production of the corn crop. The timely arrival of the rains at the end of the dry season was always a major concern as was year-long access to potable water. Too much water was just as destructive as too little. In addition, storms with heavy rainfall frequently inundated the Maya region. Water was ultimately owned by the creator deities. To access and regulate this resource, humans had to properly petition and honor these deities. The Popol Vuh emphasizes that the duty of humans was to honor the creator deities. It is well established that the Maya replicated mythic locations in their communities for the purpose of making offerings to the deities associated with these places, and many historical events illustrated in Maya art occurred at water sites that replicate mythic water locations.

In hieroglyphic inscriptions, a large number of place names include the word *ha'* "water" or *nahb* "pool of water" (Houston and Stuart 1996; Tokovinine 2008). The images associated with some of these place names indicate that these watery locations were located inside caves or mountains. For example, the exterior of K1609 is painted with water bands that are decorated with seashells and waterlily pads (figure 1.5). Schele and Miller (1993:304) identified this water with the primordial sea. The interior of this shallow bowl illustrates a Chahk standing in water which is enclosed by the jaws of a centipede-snake. Such mouths are used to denote cenotes and cave openings as well as tombs (Grube and Nahm 1994; Bassie-Sweet 1996:89–91; Boot 1999; Carrasco and Hull 2002; Taube 2003a). The caption text names the location of the scene in couplet form. The first couplet refers to the location as a place of emergence (a concept that will be discussed below). The second couplet begins with two place names, the first of which is composed of the color black and the jaws of the centipede-snake. The second place name is *ik' nahb* "black pool," and this same sign appears in the water in the scene. The Seven Water Place of One Ixim's adornment is juxtaposed with cave imagery in several scenes. On K7268, One Ajaw stands in a mountain cave adjacent to the adornment scene while the adornment is framed by a centipede-snake on K1004.

Some of the Maya terms used to describe the discharge point of a river ("foot of water"), the edge of a river ("edge or lip of water"), and the headwaters ("head of water") compare these places to body parts (Kaufman 2003:554–555). In the same fashion, the lakeshore is called "mouth of water" (Hofling 1997:855). There are numerous cases where the term *ti'* "edge, lip, mouth" is used to qualify place names in hieroglyphic texts (Tokovinine 2008). The main text on the Palenque Temple XIV Tablet describes an event that happened in the very distant past while the scene illustrates the young lord Kan Bahlam performing a ritual dance with his mother at this location or more likely at a replication of this location (figure 1.10). The place is illustrated as a band of water that is marked with three place names. The first and third place names have not been deciphered with any certainty, but the second one reads *ti' k'ak' nahb* "the mouth of the fiery pool." Although the term is not commonly used, *k'ak' nahb* "fiery pool" refers to the sea, a pool in a river, or a deep river in several Maya languages (Houston and Stuart 1994:69; Kaufman 2003:429), and

FIGURE 1.10. *Palenque Temple XIV Tablet, drawing by Linda Schele, courtesy David Schele.*

in eighteenth-century Ch'ol it meant "sea" (Hopkins et al. 2011:102). It has been suggested that the fiery nature of this place name refers to the sun rising and setting into the sea (Bassie-Sweet 1996:77; Houston and Taube 2011) or the reflection of the sun atop the surface of the sea (Ishihara et al. 2006). It should be noted, however, that the glyph and motifs used to refer to the rising sun illustrate the sun emerging from either an earth or cave sign, not water. It may be that the term refers to the waters of the cave from which the sun was thought to rise (the concept of solar heat will be discussed below).

THE SKY

Locations are often indicated in Maya art by the use of bands that are marked with hieroglyphic signs. For example, the earth can be represented by the 526 *kab* "earth" sign or by a band marked with this sign. In a similar manner, the word *chan* "sky" is represented by the T561 sign or by a band marked with this sign. The head variant for the T561 "sky" sign is usually an owl, but there is an example at Yaxchilán where *chan* is represented by a *muwan* "hawk" (Martin 2004). One wonders if the use of the diurnal hawk was to emphasize a day sky in this particular context.

The word *chan* also means "serpent," and the T764 sign, which is the portrait of a serpent, freely substitutes with the T561 sky sign. Houston (1984) sees this as a purely homophonous substitution, but the body of a serpent is often used to represent a pathway across the sky. Both celestial and terrestrial serpents are closely identified with pathways of water in Maya imagery and in the ethnographic record (Bassie-Sweet 1996:81–89; 2002; 2008:90–92). Such a celestial example is found on the Madrid Codex (page 30a) where Ix Chel and a Chahk stand on a sky serpent while they dispense rain from their water jars. Furthermore, the T561 "sky" sign is similar in form to a stylized wing (Stone and Zender 2011:149). Such wings are found on a number of different supernatural birds where they are a conflation of a bird wing and a serpent's head (Bardawil 1975).

The words for "sky" and the number "four" are homophones (or near homophones) in most Mayan languages, and the T561 sign is also replaced with the number four in some contexts (Houston 1984). Again, this substitution may not be based solely on homophony. As will be discussed more fully below, the sky and the surface of the earth were divided into quadrants. While the rise and set points of the solstice sun mark the corners of these quadrants, there are also certain times of the year when the nocturnal sky is divided into quadrants by the ecliptic and the arch of the Milky Way (Bassie 2008:267). In many examples of the T561 "sky" sign, the central element is a pair of crossed bands, and in some examples of sky signs, the T561 sign is reduced to just this crossed-bands element. As noted by Hopkins and Josserand (1994), these crossed bands are replicated in modern Yucatec ceremonies by the construction of a celestial dome over the ritual *mesa* (table). The dome is created by bending two flexible branches into arches that span opposite corners of the table, and cross each other at the zenith position above the table. The crossed bands of the T561 sign are often marked with an element that resembles the semantic sign T87 *te'* "wood."

THE QUADRILATERAL WORLD OF THE CREATOR DEITIES

In Maya worldview, the surface of the earth was thought to occupy a quadrilateral space (see Bassie-Sweet 1996:21–29, 195–199; 2008:58–78 for an overview). The solstice sun rises and sets at the corners of this space, and the sun hovers above its center at noon on the two annual zenith passages. Four roads radiated out from the center of the quadrilateral world to the four directions. These world roads represented the daily path of the sun (east–west) and annual path of the sun (north–south). Consequently, the eastern quadrant of the world was associated with the rising sun while the west was associated with the setting sun. In a similar manner, the north was associated with the time period when the sun was north of zenith (late April to mid-August) while the south was associated with the time period when the sun was south of the zenith (mid-August to late April). Each quadrant was identified with a particular color: red-east, black-west, white-north, and yellow-south. These colors were directly related to the environment and the sun. Red was identified with the rising sun and black with the setting sun. One of the signs used by the Maya to indicate that the time to burn their fields and plant their corn was when the sun moved past the zenith position into the northern sky. At that time, the sky would be filled with white smoke and all of the milpas were covered in white ash (Bassie-Sweet 2008:61). When the sun moved back into the southern sky, the fields would turn yellow as the corn ripened. The east quadrant and west quadrant of the world are opposites, as are the north and south quadrants. Given the association of the north with the beginning of the planting season and the south with the ripening of the crop, north and south are comparable to the *tz'ak* pair unripe/ripe (see chapter 2 for a further discussion of the complementary opposition of the directions).

Yellow was also identified with the center of the earth (Taube 1998). The middle of the turtle earth is often defined with the *k'an* "yellow" sign, and Itzamnaaj's conch shell is also marked with this glyph. The *k'an* sign is a cross that represents the center of the world with its four world roads. A radial pyramid platform with its four staircases also replicates the center of the world and the four world roads, and such a platform marks the center of the Palenque Cross Group.

Much like earth bands and water bands, there is also a band marked with sky-related signs that indicates celestial locations (Carlson 1982, 1988; Carlson and Landis 1985). Although the precise meaning of many of the sky band signs has not been ascertained, they include T561 sky signs, *k'in* "sun, day" signs, moon signs, star signs, and *ak'ab* "night, darkness" signs.

Sky bands are used in some contexts to represents the path of the sun across the sky, the ecliptic, the Milky Way, or the horizon. The glyph that represents the rising sun is usually represented by the *k'in* "sun" sign between a T561 "sky" sign and T526 "earth" sign. A variation of this motif is found on each corner

FIGURE 1.11. *Copán Bench 10K-2, after Barbara Fash.*

leg of Copán Bench 10K–2 where it represents the dawning sun on the solstices (figure 1.11). In these examples, the T561 "sky" sign is replaced by a sky band that represents the path of the sun across the sky, and the *k'in* sign is represented by the sun god in a reclining position on a T526 "earth" sign. As noted by Martin (2002), such a pose is associated with birth or emergence in Mesoamerican art, and it is a highly appropriate position for the rising sun.

HOUSE METAPHORS

The quadrilateral world was often metaphorically referred to as a house or milpa, and the Popol Vuh describes the quadrilateral ordering of the surface of the earth by the creator deities as though they were staking out a house or measuring a cornfield (Tedlock 1996:220; Christenson 2003a:65). The Popol Vuh narrative indicates that after the creation of the world the creator deities had a house located at the center of the world, and it is apparent that house metaphors are a reference to their center house (Bassie-Sweet 1996:21–31; 2008:64–65). When the Maya constructed a quadrilateral space, whether it was a house, a corn field, or a ritual space, they were replicating the household of the creator grandparents, that is, a Place of Duality. This means that even at the simplest level of a farmer's house, they were replicating the house of the creator deities, the Place of Duality, and the ideal state. In fact, the Popol Vuh describes the household of the creator deities as though it were a simple farmer's house. In the worldview of the Maya, people could safely live within these idealized spaces if they made the proper petitions to the creator deities.

In house metaphors, the corner posts are identified with the corners of the quadrilateral world while the roof is associated with the sky. The intimate relationship of the creator grandparents with these structures is seen in various cosmograms where Itzamnaaj in his God N form often appears at the corners.

These God N variants wear waterlily headdresses and have *tun* "stone" signs marking their bodies. On a La Corona altar that illustrates a temple decorated with the Waterlily Bird Serpent, these Itzamnaaj–God N deities appear on the corner posts with their upraised hands supporting the roof (Martin 2008:fig. 1).

THE HEARTHSTONES

The center of a Maya household is marked by a fireplace that is composed of three large stones. Three-stone hearths are a defining cultural trait for Mesoamerica in general (Kirchhoff 1943). The stones are used to contain the fire, to create the air draft to fuel the fire, and to support the cooking vessels. Corn processing requires that the seed be slowly simmered all night in a pot of water and lime. Maya household fires are, thus, places of constant heat where corn seeds are transformed into food. In the Popol Vuh episode concerning the creation of humans, the creator deities obtained corn seed from a cliff cave on Paxil Mountain (a mountain located in northwestern Guatemala; see Bassie-Sweet 2008 for an overview). To access the corn, the creator deities had to break open the mountain using a bolt of lightning. The narrative indicates that the creator grandmother Xmucane ground this lightning-infused seed into dough and mixed it with water to fashion the flesh and blood of the first humans. One assumes Xmucane prepared this corn dough on her three-hearthstone fireplace at the center of the world just as women prepare their corn meal every day beside their household fires.

In various hieroglyphic narratives, there are references to the mythological three-hearthstone fireplace of the creator deities (Freidel and MacLeod 2000). There is evidence that the three hearthstones of this fireplace were thought to be manifestations of the three thunderbolt deities GI, GII, and GIII and that these deities were parallel to the three Heart of Sky thunderbolt gods of the Popol Vuh (Bassie-Sweet 2008:63, 121–122). Each of the three buildings of the Palenque Cross Group was a shrine dedicated to one member of the thunderbolt triad. The three buildings represented the three hearthstones (Hansen 1992; Freidel et al. 1993; Taube 2002), and they mark this ceremonial space as well as Palenque as a whole as a replication of the Place of Duality. The climax of the Cross Group narrative was the 9.13.0.0.0 Period Ending ceremony (see chapter 8). A number of Maya monuments indicate that the three hearthstones were renewed during Period Ending ceremonies. This hearth renewal was, in effect, a renewal of the house of the creator deities.

HEAT

There is a strong association of heat with the center of the quadrilateral milpa as well. The April zenith passage of the sun is one of the markers that indicates that the dry season is about to end and the all-important rains will begin. The Maya traditionally sow their primary corn crop during the full-moon phase nearest the April zenith passage because corn planted at full moon is thought to grow better (Bassie-Sweet 2008:32–39). Richard Wilson (1995:94–103) documented the ritual planting practices of the Q'eqchi'. He observed that when a farmer first plants his milpa, he waits for the morning star to rise in the east and then he departs to his field. At the center of the field, he plants a corn mound and burns offerings to the deities. Corn seed is considered to be dead and must be heated just as sick people must be ritually heated to regain their lost souls. Much of the planting ceremony involves heating both the corn seed and the planters through the use of ritually heated foods, drinks, incense, candles, cigarettes, and blood. Another important source of heat is the prayers addressed to the deities (Gossen 1974a).

Formal language—that is, sacred language—is thought to be hot:

> The principal element that gives a discourse its formality, its "heat" or holiness, is the use of the couplet, a pair of lines that differs minimally. These occur in conversation when one speaker repeats another, but the density of couplets increases through heated speech, including court language, and reaches its maximum in sacred speech, prayer, where virtually the entire discourse is coupleted. (Hopkins 2012a)

As noted by Wilson (1985), it is thought that the sun provides the final heat to germinate the planted seed. The noon passage of the sun on the zenith not only demarcates the center of the world and the sky, but it provides the heat that germinates the corn beneath it. The use of the *k'an* "yellow" sign to demarcate the center is a multivocal reference to both the fire of the center hearth and the zenith passage of the sun.

The importance of heat in Maya world view was well summarized by Evon Vogt in his description of Tzotzil Maya beliefs:

> The symbolic state of "hotness" as opposed to "coldness" is one of the most seminal Zinacanteco concepts of opposition. Although ultimately this heat is derived from or partakes of the sun, it is measured not by degrees, but by conventional modes of Zinacanteco thought. Heat is a general quality of existence. It provides a language for describing the differences in power in the universe, whether this be the political power of an Indian leader, the ritual power of

an expert shaman or competent cargoholder, the supernatural strength of the *ch'ulel* [soul] of a respected older man (and his associated animal), the curing power of a hot ritual plant, or the highly intoxicating potential of hot cane liquor.

Heat is a dynamic state, for people and things become hotter as power and age increase. An infant is born cold; its heat gradually increases as it grows up and its *ch'ulel* becomes stronger. Each year adds heat; each stage in the cycle (marriage, acquiring more political influence) adds strength; the hotness reaches a peak just before death, when the heat is again reduced to nothing. In the annual cycle of a cargoholder's ritual duties, the man becomes hotter and hotter, reaching maximum heat in the change of office ceremony at the end of his years in cargo. (Vogt 1976:206–207)

Wichmann (2004b:81) suggested that a maximally hot person would be an aged ruler, but the concept can also be applied to the deities. The god with the most heat would be the creator grandfather Itzamnaaj, who was identified with the Place of Duality and the fire of the hearth that symbolizes the center of this life-generating place. As is discussed below, there was a Mesoamerican concept that even the sun obtained its heat from the primordial fire of the creator grandparents.

THE PLACE OF DUALITY IN THE SKY

The God D form of Itzamnaaj is a conflation of God N and his avian manifestation (see Bassie-Sweet 2008:235–236 for an overview). The Itzamnaaj bird frequently holds a double-headed serpent in his beak. This mythological bird was based on the snake-eating laughing falcon or *guaco* (*Herpetotheres cachinnans*). The laughing falcon's "ha-ha-ha" song mimics the word *ha'* "water" (Alonso Méndez, personal communication), and throughout Mesoamerica, the call of the laughing falcon is thought to announce the coming of the rains. Itzamnaaj was considered to be the first priest and rainmaker, and his rain-making role is reflected in the nature of his avian manifestation.

As discussed above, Itzamnaaj in this God N form is identified with mountains, and some scenes show God N deities holding up a sky band or acting as the corner posts of a structure. While God N is associated with terrestrial locations, Itzamnaaj in his God D form is frequently shown sitting on a throne decorated with sky bands (K1183). His court is populated by a host of officials who wear the same headdresses worn by human court officials, which indicates that the court of Itzamnaaj was a role model for that of Maya rulers (Boot 2008). The role of Itzamnaaj as the supreme deity is exemplified in the

Palenque Temple XIX narrative where it is said that Itzamnaaj oversaw the mythological accession of the deity GI into ajawship, and the accession into ajawship of the ruler K'inich Ahkal Mo' Nahb III that replicated GI's accession (Stuart 2005a, 2005c).

Many of the Itzamnaaj–God D court scenes are delimited by sky bands, suggesting that his court was identified with a celestial realm. In one Late Classic pottery scene, Itzamnaaj is pictured sitting within a room of his palace (Boot 2008). The Itzamnaaj bird sits behind Itzamnaaj, and he perches on a glyphic place name that reads the "Six-?-Sky Place" (the middle element of this place name is undeciphered; Stuart 2006). Three court officials sit beneath Itzamnaaj and the Itzamanaaj bird on a sky band that forms the base of the palace stairs. The sky band consists of three pairs of flint and *k'in* signs. The sun is often illustrated in Maya art in a flint cartouche (Taube 2003a). The flint and *k'in* sky band of Itzamnaaj's court appears to be another form of this sun reference (see below). The couplet form of the flint and *k'in* signs is consistent with formal, sacred language. In Mesoamerica, the sky was conceived as a layered environment and it is possible that the name *Six-?-Sky Place* refers to the sixth layer of the sky.

The three officials are named by adjacent caption texts as a dog deity (*k'in yas ok*), a possum deity (*k'in yas uch*), and the Vulture God (*tan us*) (Boot 2008:6). The first two incorporate *k'in* sun glyphs in their names. Sitting in opposition to Itzamnaaj are the thunderbolt deity GI, the sun god K'inich Ajaw, and a Chahk deity whose specific name has not been deciphered. These gods are situated on another sky band consisting of two pairs of "flint" and *k'in* signs. Beneath them and in opposition with the three court officials are four more deities. These four are not named with caption texts, but the main text refers to them as the Chan Te Chuwen (the four artisans). These Chan Te Chuwen artisan deities are seen in many other contexts as members of Itzamnaaj's court.

On the Boot vase, the Chan Te Chuwen deities are presented in pairs that form a visual couplet. The first deity in each pair has anthropomorphic features with hair tied into a knot and held by a band of rectangular material. Each sits with arms crossed over his chest and left hand resting on his upper right arm. Each of the second deities has simian features and wears a pendant necklace and cloth headdress. Their right arms are extended while their left hands are held in a palm-up pose touching their pendants. While these deities are most frequently characterized as scribes and they certainly do perform that function in some scenes (Coe and Kerr 1998), such a categorization is probably too narrow a description of their duties. The simian deities have been identified

FIGURE 1.12. *Yaxchilán Stela 1, after Ian Graham.*

as being parallel to the twin grandsons of Xpiyacoc, who were changed into monkeys by their half-brothers and designated as the patron gods for artisans (Coe 1977). The Popol Vuh describes the monkey twins in couplet form as flautists and singers, writers and sculptors, jade workers and precious metalsmiths (Christenson 2003a:113). It is possible the hand gesture of the Chan Te Chuwen simian deities juxtaposed with the pendant is a subtle reference to their role as the makers of jewelry. It is also possible that these two pairs of deities represent the manifestations of the monkey twins before they were transformed and then afterwards.

When the zenith-passage sun is positioned directly overhead, it visually demarcates not only the center of the earth, but the center of the diurnal sky. Given that the center of the earth represents the household of the creator grandparents, it would be expected that Itzamnaaj's celestial court would be located directly overhead at the celestial center. In other words, Itzamnaaj ultimately ruled both the earth and sky. The Primary Standard Sequence found around the upper rim of the Boot vessel is divided into three parts by *k'an* signs. As noted above, *k'an* signs were used to demarcate the center of the world. Each *k'an* sign is flanked by a flower blossom. The association of Itzamnaaj's court with flowers is discussed below.

Many scenes illustrate the ancestors of rulers as inhabitants of the Place of Duality in the sky. On several Yaxchilán stelae, such as Stela 1, the ruler is illustrated performing a Period Ending event. Above the head of the ruler is an elaborate sky band. A patron god of Yaxchilán is pictured above the sky band and two flint cartouches flank him (figure 1.12). The parents of the ruler sit within the flint cartouches. They form a pair of complementary opposites. Although many of the Yaxchilán stelae are in fragments or badly eroded, the top portions of Stela 3, Stela 4, Stela 6, Stela 8, Stela 10, and Stela 11 all have this cartouche and sky-band motif (Tate 1992:59–63). On Stela 4, the father's sun cartouche is contrasted with a moon cartouche, in which the mother sits. The *tz'ak* glyph also contrasts a sun sign with a moon sign, echoing this complementary opposition (see the following chapter for further discussion of the complementary opposition of the sun and moon).

THE SUN AND THE PLACE OF DUALITY

The T544 sign that represents the word *k'in* "sun, day" is a red flower with four petals (Thompson 1932:122; 1939:138; 1950:142). The association of red with the sun and in particular the rising sun of the east is appropriate. *K'in* signs can also appear in the center of cartouches that are depicted as an eccentric flint or carved shell with centipede-snake heads or floral elements projecting out from the corners. Stone and Zender (2011:153) noted that the four petals of the *k'in* sign invoke the four world directions, and they stated "the four-petaled flower stood for the bright heavens of the diurnal sun, conceived as a flower- and bird-filled paradise." Following earlier interpretations by Taube and Stuart, they interpret the solar centipede-snake heads and floral motifs as representing sun beams. As noted above, the surface of the earth was thought to contain a quadrilateral space. The solstice sun rose and set at the corners of this space, and the sun hovered above its center at noon on the two annual zenith passages (Bassie-Sweet 1996:21–29, 195–199; 2008:58–78). In Maya mythology, it is believed that the sun rises from a cave, and the mouth of a centipede-snake is often used to represent this cave. In the context of the *k'in* cartouche, each centipede-snake corner represents not only a ray of sunlight but also the cave from which the sun was thought to rise and set on the solstices. In short, the *k'in* cartouche is a solar-celestial cosmogram with the center of the flower representing the position of the sun on zenith passage, and by extension, the celestial Place of Duality.

THE SUN GOD

There are a number of different Classic-period deities who have anthropomorphic form with Roman noses and large circular eyes. One of these gods has T544 *k'in* signs on his face or body. In some portraits of this sun god, he has a stepped-fret motif emerging from his nose that has been interpreted to be "solar heat as the sun god's breath" (Stuart 2005a:23). The sun god is found in Classic-period contexts where he is used to represent the word *k'in* and where he clearly represents the sun itself. As an example, the calendrical *k'in* cartouche often shows the sun god instead of the T544 *k'in* sign at its center (Thompson 1950:fig. 27). Another example is the sun god on Copán Bench 10K-2 that was discussed earlier (figure 1.12).

As noted above, the sun god is depicted at the celestial court of Itzamnaaj (Boot 2008). The caption text adjacent to the sun god gives his full nominal phrase: Uhuk Chapat Tz'ikin ("Seventh Centipede Bird"), K'inich Ajaw ("Sunlike Lord"), and Bolon Yokte' K'uh (Houston and Stuart 1996; Boot 2008; Wichmann 2004b). The latter title appears in a variety of contexts where it seems to refer to a class of deities rather than an individual god (Stuart 2006). On vessel K1398, the sun god wears a headdress composed of the white paper headband of the deity One Ajaw and a centipede-like creature that is likely the Uhuk Chapat "seventh centipede" of his title. As noted above, the sun god emerges from the jaws of a centipede-snake at dawn.

**Tz'ikin* is the proto-Mayan word for "bird" (Kaufmann 2003:618). The proto-Cholan term for eagle is **t'iw* (Kaufman and Norman 1984:133). In the Maya *tzolk'in* calendar, the fifteenth day name is represented by a bird wearing a plain headband. Although this day name is called *Men* in the Yucatec list of Landa, it is *Tz'ikin* in the calendars of the Eastern Mayan languages and in the Tzeltal-Tzotil calendar (Thompson 1950). A number of researchers have identified the Tz'ikin-Men bird as an eagle and have even translated *tz'ikin* as eagle based solely on the fact that the fifteenth day name in the Aztec and Mixtec 260-day calendar is *Cuauhtli* "eagle" (Zender 2004b:232; Martin 2005; Taube, Saturno, Stuart, and Hurst 2010; Houston and Martin 2012). In the Central Mexican mythology of the Terminal Classic and Postclassic periods, the golden eagle played a dominant role, but such birds do not reside in the Maya region. During these time periods, Central Mexican eagle imagery and other status markers were adopted at various Maya sites such as Chichén Itzá and in the Guatemalan highlands. In particular, the eagle-jaguar warrior cult played a prominent role in rulership validation. However, there is no linguistic or epigraphic evidence that the Classic Maya identified the sun with golden eagles or any of the eagle species that do reside in their zone. It is, therefore, advisable to translate the word *tz'ikin* as "bird."

As noted above, *k'in* means both "sun" and "day." In the Long Count calendar (see chapter 3 for an explanation of this calendar), the day position is usually represented by the T544 *k'in* sign, but its personified form is often a portrait of the sun god. His portrait is also employed in the logograph for the month Yaxk'in. This compound glyph is most often composed of a *yax* "blue-green" sign and a T544 *k'in* sign. In some rare forms of *Yaxk'in*, the *k'in* sign is replaced with the head of the sun god (Thompson 1950:fig. 17).

THE K'INICH AND K'INICH AJAW TITLES

In his description of the sixteenth-century New Year ceremonies, Bishop Diego de Landa noted that in the years that began with the day name *Muluc*, the Maya made a statue of a god called K'inich Ajaw, and placed it in the house of a community leader, where it would receive offerings from the populace (see chapter 4). The Dresden Codex New Year scene that is parallel to Landa's description of K'inich Ajaw shows the sun god (God G) sitting in a house where he is receiving offerings. God G is the Postclassic version of the Classic-period sun god, and he is portrayed with the same Roman nose and with *k'in* signs on his body. His name phrase in the accompanying caption texts is composed of two signs that read *k'inich* and *ajaw* "lord." While *k'in* is the word for "sun" or "day," *k'inich* is an adjective with the connotation of being sunlike or hot (Wichmann 2004b). However, the name *k'inich ajaw* ("sunlike lord") was not restricted to the sun god but was also used by other deities, which suggests that it functioned as a title as well.

Bishop Diego de Landa refers to Itzamnaaj many times in his account of the northern Postclassic Yucatec Maya. In his description of the New Year ceremonies, Landa noted that the Maya made offerings to K'inich Ajaw Itzamnaaj to avert calamities during a year that began with the day Ix (Tozzer 1941:147). In the month Woh, the priests also made offerings to K'inich Ajaw Itzamnaaj, and Landa states that the Maya considered him to be the first priest (Tozzer 1941:153). While solar heat is an important element in the Maya worldview, there is a concept in Mesoamerica that the sun god obtained his heat from a sacrificial fire, as in the case of the Central Mexican deity Nanauatzin, who jumped into such a fire in order to transform into the sun (Taube 1998; Sahagun 1950:vol.7:4–5). It is highly like that the creator grandfather Itzamnaaj was not only the ultimate owner of that fire, but that fire was thought to be a manifestation of his generative powers (Bassie-Sweet 2008:65–67). Hence, he carries the *k'inich ajaw* title in reference to his role as a fire deity.

The drilling of new fire to inaugurate reigns or time periods was also common in Mesoamerica. The titles *k'inich* and *k'inich ajaw* appear in Classic-period inscriptions. After taking the throne, Maya rulers frequently incorporated the adjective *k'inich* in their nominal phrases, such as the Caracol ruler K'ak' Ujol K'inich ("Fire is the Head of the Sunlike Being") or the Palenque ruler K'inich Kan Bahlam ("Sunlike Serpent Jaguar") (Wichmann 2004b). The Copán ruler named K'inich Yax K'uk' Mo' is also named as *k'inich ajaw* on Copán Stela 19. The identification of a Maya ruler with the heat of the sun is discussed more fully in the following chapter.

A full-figure rendering of the name of K'inich Yax K'uk' Mo' found on the façade of the Copán Margarita structure demonstrates the innovative and creative ways in which Maya artists could depict words using images (figure 5.5). This façade shows a quetzal bird (*k'uk'*) intertwined with a macaw (*mo'*). *Yax* signs decorate the heads of both birds. The word *k'inich* is represented by sun gods emerging from the mouths of the birds. Another example of the K'inich Yax K'uk' Mo' name is found in a headdress worn by the left figure on the Copán Motmot Marker (Fash 1991:fig. 31). Headdresses often contain glyphs that spell out the name of the person wearing the headdress or the name of a god or ancestor that the wearer is impersonating. The left headdress is composed of a bird with the head of a quetzal and the beak of a macaw. It is clearly a conflation of the name *K'uk' Mo'*. On top of the bird's head is the head of the sun god representing the word *k'inich*. Another example of the sun god representing the word *k'inich* may be found on Pier D of Palenque House A. The stucco panels on the House A piers illustrate standing lords holding a GII staff. Each lord is flanked by a seated male and female. The caption texts that would identify these figures are destroyed. On Pier D, the headdress worn by the standing lord includes a sky band that terminates in the head of the sun god (Robertson 1985:fig. 70). It is likely that the Pier D sun god headdress element simply represents the word *k'inich*.

THE NUMBER FOUR GOD

Each of the numbers from one to thirteen can be represented by a specific god. The number four (*chan*) is the sun god (Thompson 1950:fig. 24). Head variants and full-figure glyphs are often used in scenes to represent place names (Stuart and Houston 1994). An example of the use of the sun god to represent the number four in a place name is found on the hieroglyphic staircase of Yaxchilán Structure 44. The text on Step IV refers to a location called the Four Crocodile Place (Plank 2004:58). It is written using four dots (the standard form for the number four) and the head of the Milky Way Crocodile. On Step III, the narrative refers to the capture of the lord Aj Nik by Shield Jaguar III, and the image shows this lord as a kneeling, submissive captive. Beneath Aj Nik at the base of the scene is the place name where his submission occurred. It is the full-figure rendition of the Four Crocodile Place (figure 1.13). It is composed of the sun god in a cartouche that is superimposed over the body of the Milky Way Crocodile. Although Taube (2003:411) characterizes this motif as the sun god being in the belly of the crocodile, the placement of one glyph in front of another is common in Maya hieroglyphic writing.

FIGURE 1.13. *Yaxchilán Structure 44, Step III, after Ian Graham.*

This style of writing where one glyph is superimposed in front of another is called *infixing* by epigraphers (see chapter 5 for a further discussion of infixing and this Four Crocodile Place name).

FLOWER MOTIFS AND THE PLACE OF DUALITY

Flowers appear in numerous contexts in Maya art. The background of many scenes includes floral motifs. As noted, images of fish and hummingbirds feasting on waterlily blossoms and other flowers are often seen in headdresses worn by Maya elite. In fact, flowers and feathers are ubiquitous in headdresses. Some examples of deity headdresses with flowers are Itzamnaaj's avian headdress, which is composed of a flower with an *ak'ab* sign infixed in its center, and the wind god's headdress, which includes a red flower. One Ixim's jade jewelry as well as the jade jewelry worn by Maya elite frequently takes the form of flowers. The naked goddesses who are pictured assisting in the washing and dressing of One Ixim in his jade jewelry also wear blossoms in their hair (K1202, K7268). On K7268, a hummingbird sucks at the goddess's blossom. On K5166, the flower of the moon goddess's headdress also includes a tiny hummingbird. A floral headdress pictured on K5421 also shows a hummingbird sipping at the blossom. The flowers in this headdress are shown both frontally and from the side.

A hummingbird sipping at a flower is a well-known sexual metaphor. There is a widespread myth in highland Guatemala regarding the courtship of a beautiful goddess by a young hunter (Bassie-Sweet 2008:182). At first the young hunter tried to impress the girl with his hunting abilities. When this tactic failed, he borrowed the feathers of a hummingbird and transformed into this bird. While the young girl sat weaving beside a tobacco plant on her patio, the hummingbird hunter flew to the tobacco flower and sucked its nectar (this motif is common in the weaving of Alta Verapaz). The goddess was so taken with the beauty of the hummingbird that she had her father shoot the bird so she could copy its form in her weaving. She placed the stunned bird in her bosom. During the night, the young hunter transformed into his human form and seduced her. The hummingbird and flower motif represents the complementary pairing of male and female.

While waterlily blossoms have been recognized in the hieroglyphic text, the identification of other flower species is more elusive. The T646 logograph which represents the generic term *nik* "flower" is a stylized blossom with four petals. Each petal is marked with *chak* "red" signs. These red petals are often decorated with scrolls representing the fragrance of the flower (Houston and Taube 2000). The wind god who appears as the god of the number three and the patron of the month Mac wears this red *nik* flower on his forehead or attached to his headband. On a Tikal Burial 196 vessel (K8008), a hummingbird god has a red *nik* flower impaled on his beak. Whether the T646 represents a specific plant species is not known, but red is the primary color that attracts hummingbirds. T646 is clearly not a tobacco flower, which is tubular and white.

Robertson (1985:figs. 29, 42, 43, 49, 59) documented over 140 floral motifs painted on the front façade of Palenque House E. These motifs appear to refer to specific kinds of flowers. For example, the T646 *nik* flower appears 64 times, but several of these cartouches have a different central element, such as a *k'an* "yellow" sign or an eye sign. Most of the House E floral motifs are hanging blossoms combined with other signs such as deer, birds, and even a Tlaloc god. The use of additional signs to qualify the type of flower is also found in a mythological scene illustrated on an Early Classic vessel. In this scene, a hummingbird with a *nik* flower on his bill perches on an anthropomorphic tree. Adjacent to the tree is the place name 6 Wind Sky Cave. The tree is marked with three *nik* flowers, but these flowers are trimmed with bone elements and the center has a U-shaped motif. Clearly these signs are labeling the tree flowers in a specific way that distinguishes them from the hummingbird's flower. A similar situation occurs on Dresden Codex page 12c where a *te'* "tree" sign is attached to the four-petaled T646 *nik* glyph to form the word *nikte'*, a term referring to the *Plumeria* tree, which has a five-petaled flower (Roys 1931:269). The phrase "five *nikte'* place" appears as part of the place names on the water band of Palenque Temple 14 (Stuart 2005a:180). A set of inscribed bones from Tikal Burial 116 include references to a "five *nik* place."

Other flower glyphs also appear as place names. Although undeciphered, the Five T538 place and Five T627 place glyphs appear in a number of creation narratives, and seem to refer to flowers (Tokovinine 2008:89, 144, 284). One flower that has been phonetically deciphered is the T624 *janaab* sign. Despite its clear phonetic decipherment, the word *janaab* has not been recorded in any Mayan language, so the species that it references is unknown. The *janaab* sign is found in place names and the nominal phrases of elite males and females such as K'inich Janaab Pakal I of Palenque and his grandson U Pakal K'inich Janaab Pakal I. The place name Five Janaab Witz ("Five Janaab Mountain") designates the burial locations of rulers from Piedras Negras and from Cancuén. On Yaxchilán Stela 3, the right male figure in the upper cartouche is named by a caption text. Although eroded, the text refers to "he of 5 Janaab Witz."

Although House E was dedicated in AD 654 when K'inich Janab Pakal was 51 years old and had already been on the throne for 39 years, it is believed that this building was his throne room and was used as such by four subsequent rulers (Stuart and Stuart 2008:157). Given that Itzamnaaj's court was the role model for humans, House E was likely a replication of Itzamnaaj's palace. Carrasco (2015) demonstrated that House E and its architectural decoration replicate the mythological location where the deity GI was installed into *ajaw*-ship under the authority of Itzamnaaj, as described in the Temple XIX platform narrative. The House E floral motifs are arranged in six rows across the façade. One wonders if these six layers of flowers might be a reference to the Six-?-Sky Place of Itzamnaaj's court. It has been argued that the Maya used flowers to represent the souls of deceased ancestors (Taube 2004). If so, the House E façade may be a reference to the celestial Place of Duality as the repository of ancestral souls.

Hill (1992) examined the poetic and metaphorical use of flowers in Uto-Aztecan languages, and how flowers are used to describe a mythological place associated with the path of the sun and the afterlife. Expanding on this research, Taube (2004, 2008, 2010) explored the concept of a flowery mythological world in ancient Maya art and hieroglyphic writing. He noted that flowers appear on a variety of mountain symbols. He lumped all of these flower-decorated mountains together, nicknamed them Flower Mountain and argued that they all represent a celestial flower paradise associated with the path of the sun. He asserted that "Flower Mountain appears widely in ancient Maya art, and is both the dwelling place of ancestors and the means by which they and celestial gods ascend into the sky" (Taube 2004:81). Although there is ample evidence that the Mesoamerican Place of Duality was a garden-like environment filled with flowers and fruit, the notion that all of these mountains refer to the same place is unlikely. In his catalogue of Classic-period place names, Tokovinine (2008) noted a number of locations that referred to mythological places as well as historical locations that replicated these places. While some of these locations are named using glyphs that represent various flowers, the contexts of these locations does not support the interpretation that these were all specifically identified with a solar paradise.

SKY AND EARTH GODS AS A CLASS OF DEITIES

A number of Classic-period inscriptions contain a listing of deities. Two parallel examples are found on vessels K2796 and K7750, where the caption texts give a series of names that likely refer to categories of deities rather than individual gods (Stuart 2011a:224). Two of these names (*chanal k'uh* "celestial gods" and *kabnal k'uh* "earthly gods") form a couplet, and are found paired in other contexts as well (Boot 2008; Stuart 2011a; Stuart, Houston, and Robertson 1999). On Tikal Stela 31, the narrative begins on the half-Period Ending date of 9.0.10.0.0. The verb of the first sentence (*tahn lamaj* "it half diminishes") is followed by a list of deities: *jun pik chanal k'uh-kabnal k'uh*, the two Paddler Gods, a wind god, a bird deity, possibly the sun god, the Water Bird Serpent god, and Bolon Tz'akab Ajaw. These deities or classes of deities were apparently important gods during the *k'atun* period that began on 9.0.0.0.0. Outside of the Long Count context, the term *pik* refers to units of 8,000 in the vigesimal counting system of the Maya (Stuart 2012a). The phrase *jun* "one" *pik* would, thus, literally refer to 8,000 gods of the sky and earth. The number nine is used in some contexts to refer to "many" rather than a specific number. It has been proposed that the phrase *jun pik* functions in a similar manner, and carries the value of innumerable rather than specifically 8,000.[4] This pairing of sky and earth is highly reminiscent of the Popol Vuh metonym of sky and earth that is used to describe the world. It is possible that the juxtaposing of sky god and earth god in this couplet is a contrast between the various manifestations of the creator deities such as the sky form and earth form of Itzamnaaj.

SUMMARY

This chapter has given an overview of the creator grandparents, the thunderbolt gods, and the sun god. The complementary nature of the creator grandparents as well as the aquatic, earthly, and celestial environments within which they were thought to reside have also been reviewed. As role models for humans and for human behavior, the creator grandparents represented the epitome of the ideal being. Their complementary nature created a balanced world and ideal state. The following chapter focuses on the children and grandchildren of this couple and explores their relationships.

NOTES

1. Although the name of God N was initially deciphered as Pawahtun (Coe 1973:15), Stuart has demonstrated that the reading is incorrect, and thus, this identification must be set aside (see Bassie-Sweet 2008:130–145 for an overview).

2. This crocodile is known by a number of nicknames such as the Cosmic Monster, Starry Deer Alligator, and Starry Deer Crocodile.

3. There are numbered mythological place names painted on the northeast and southwest corners of Rio Azul Tomb 12 that use a water-band motif as the main sign. The northeast place name is the Six Nahb "Water Pool" while the southwest location is the number six and a simple band of turbulent water with a phonetic wa complement. Two different readings have been proposed for this latter sign: Six Palaw "sea" (Lopes 2004) and Six Tikaw "warm, hot water" (Stuart cited in Filamore and Houston 2011:75). If the Six Palaw decipherment is correct, Six Nahb and Six Palaw would contrast each other in the same manner as lake and sea.

4. The *jun pik chanal k'uh-kabnal k'uh* phrase is also found in a later passage of the Stela 31 narrative that refers to the 8.18.10.0.0 half-period ending event (E25–E26). A third reference (G8) related to the 8.19.10.0.0 half-period ending is abbreviated to just the term *jun pik k'uh* (8,000 gods). The couplet *chanal k'uh-kabnal k'uh* is also found in the caption text of a vessel published by Boot (2008). In this instance, *chanal k'uh* is preceded by the term *jun pik* while *kabnal k'uh* is preceded by a phrase composed of the *huun* "headband" sign and a T541 "sky" sign.

2

The Family of the Creator Grandparents and Complementary Opposition

The Popol Vuh indicates that many deities inhabited the surface of the earth in addition to the creator grandparents. The story does not explain the origins of these supernatural characters, but much of the narrative revolves around their subjugation and that of the Underworld deities by the children and grandchildren of Xpiyacoc and Xmucane. These conflicts established the hierarchy of deities and provided role models for appropriate human behavior. Many of the Popol Vuh episodes are cautionary tales focusing on the importance of properly honoring the creator deities. As noted in the previous chapter, Classic period parallels for all the primary Popol Vuh deities have been identified. The following is a brief overview of the family of the creator grandparents, their complementary opposition, and their role as models for human behavior.

THE SECOND GENERATION OF CREATOR DEITIES

The second generation of creator deities was Xpiyacoc and Xmucane's two sons, named One Hunahpu and Seven Hunahpu. Their Classic period parallels were called One Ixim and Seven Ajaw (see figure 0.2, where the dotted lines indicate inferred relationships). The eldest son, One Hunahpu, took a wife called Lady Bone Water (Xbaquiyalo) while Seven Hunahpu remained a bachelor and a junior partner to his brother. The origin of Lady Bone Water is not discussed in the Popol Vuh, but there is circumstantial evidence to indicate that she was the daughter of an Underworld god called Gathered Blood and that she died giving birth to One Hunahpu's sons, called One Chouen and One Batz (Bassie-Sweet 2008:178–193). Lady Bone Water was identified with corn. After her death, One Hunahpu impregnated Lady Blood, another daughter of Gathered Blood, who then gave birth to Hunahpu and Xbalanque, the Hero Twins. Lady Blood was a waxing moon goddess.

The Popol Vuh authors explicitly state that their narrative is only part of the story of One Hunahpu ("but we shall tell only the half of it, the smallest part of the tale of their father" Christenson 2003a:12), and it is clear as the narrative progresses that many episodes are abbreviated or left out entirely. For example, nothing is said about the courtship and union of One Hunahpu and Lady Bone Water. There are, however, numerous highland Guatemalan myths that refer to the marriage of a corn goddess called Basket Grass to a young deity called Thorn Broom who has all the attributes of One Ixim–One Hunahpu. Given the widespread distribution of these courtship myths across the Guatemalan highlands and the parallels of its main characters with Popol Vuh deities, Bassie-Sweet has argued that these tales reflect the core story concerning One Hunahpu's first marriage (Bassie-Sweet 2008:181–186).

In these stories, Thorn Broom falls in love with the beautiful daughter of the mountain god Xucaneb. He avoids the traditional marriage negotiations and bride payment by seducing Basket Grass and eloping with her. Xucaneb sends a thunderbolt deity after the couple to kill them for their inappropriate behavior. The thunderbolt deity catches up with them at the edge of a lake (or the sea in some versions). While the couple tries to flee across the water in a canoe, the thunderbolt deity throws his bolts at them. Thorn Broom dives deep into the water with the aid of a turtle and survives, but his wife is unable to do so and is killed by the lightning. When Thorn Broom surfaces, he finds that her blood has spread across the water (or her blood and flesh). He gathers the blood into thirteen jars with the help of aquatic animals and leaves the jars with an old woman who lives beside the lake. After making amends with his father-in-law, he returns to the lake and opens the jars. He finds that the blood of the first twelve jars has been magically transformed into various kinds of venomous animals and these beings escape into the world. The Maya often characterize diseases as harmful animals, and Basket Grass's venomous forms were likely thought to be the source of the first diseases (Braakhuis 2005).

When he opens the final jar of remains, Thorn Broom finds Basket Grass restored to life, and they then continue their life together until she becomes pregnant. Thorn Broom leaves his pregnant wife in a cliff cave and travels on his own to inform her father of the impending birth. She dies in childbirth, and her remains are left in the cave where they transform into corn seed. God then directs a thunderbolt deity to break open the cave with his bolt, and the corn, which is referred to as "the body of our mother," pours out and forever provides sustenance for humans. Thus, Basket Grass is the origin of both killing diseases and life-sustaining sustenance.

The Popol Vuh narrative indicates that at the same time that the creator deities were battling with the deities on the surface of the earth and in the Underworld, they were attempting to create humans. Their stated purpose was to create beings that would honor them. Their first attempts were not successful and had to be destroyed, but finally they found special corn seeds buried within Paxil Mountain. As discussed in the previous chapter, the creator grandmother used this corn seed to create the first humans. These humans multiplied and created different tribes that spread across the surface of the earth and established their own territories. After receiving their patron deities, they then climbed their sacred mountains and waited for the first appearance of the morning star and the dawning of the sun. Although the Popol Vuh does not state the origin of the Paxil corn seed, there is evidence that Basket Grass was parallel to Lady Bone Water, and that the Paxil corn was the remains of this goddess (Bassie-Sweet 2008:178–193). Bassie-Sweet has also identified a Classic period goddess (Ixik) who was the prototype for these goddesses (see below for an overview of this goddess).

Houston and Martin (2012) have discussed the convention in Maya hieroglyphic writing of using a mythic prototype to represent a general class. As an example, the Milky Way Crocodile is used in some contexts to represent the word *ahin* "crocodile." The waterlily skull that appears in Classic period depictions of pooled water and that was used to represent the word *nahb* ("pooled body of water") may be another example of this practice. In the various versions of Basket Grass's death in the lake, her blood spreads across the surface of the water much like waterlily pads. An assortment of aquatic animals either eat her blood (in some cases her flesh) or assist Thorn Broom in collecting her blood. What is curious about these myths is that there is no mention of Basket Grass's head, skull, or bones. The implication is that her skeletal remains were left behind in the water. This raises the possibility that the waterlily skull was that of Basket Grass's Classic period parallel, Ixik. Surely any Maya who knew the story of this fundamental goddess would recognize whose skull was in the water. In the same regard, one of the glyphs used to represent the word *ch'een* "cave" is a profile view of a cave opening that contains a jawbone. The quintessential cave is the Paxil cave where corn was discovered. Bassie-Sweet has suggested that the jawbone in this sign represents Ixik–Lady Bone Water's skeletal remains (Bassie-Sweet 2001).

The Popol Vuh narrative explains that after the death of Lady Bone Water, her sons One Batz and One Chouen were raised by their father, One Hunahpu, and their uncle, Seven Hunahpu, who trained them to be great sages, diviners, musicians, singers, writers, artists, and artisans of jade and precious metals. They also taught them to be skillful ballplayers. One Hunahpu owned a ball court on the road to the Xibalban Underworld. The ball playing of the four gods at the border of the Underworld territory enraged the death lords, and One Death and Seven Death challenged the four gods to come down to the Xibalba Underworld and play ball against them. Leaving One Batz and One Chouen behind to maintain the family household, One Hunahpu and Seven Hunahpu journeyed through a cave passageway to the very heart of Xibalba. After failing the various tests of the death lords, the two brothers were sacrificed. One Hunahpu's severed head was subsequently placed in an Underworld tree. Suddenly the tree sprouted gourds, and it became impossible to tell the difference between the fruit and One Hunahpu's skull. Fearing the power of the miraculous tree, the Underworld lords commanded that no one harvest the fruit or even go near the tree.

The Xibalban lord Gathered Blood told his daughter Lady Blood about the tree, and despite the restriction, she was so fascinated by the story that she couldn't resist visiting it. One Hunahpu's gourd skull then spit in her hand and impregnated her. After six months when her pregnancy had become noticeable, Lady Blood had to flee the Underworld and journeyed to the household of the creator deities on the surface of the earth. Lady Blood was a moon goddess. The first six months of her pregnancy represented the lunar half year that is used to predict eclipses. Her journey across the surface of the earth from the Underworld to the creator deities' household represented the cycle of the waxing moon (Tedlock 1985:39; Bassie-Sweet 1991:191; 2008:203–208).

After proving to Xmucane that she was indeed her daughter-in-law and that she was carrying her grandsons, Lady Blood was accepted into the household. She gave birth to twin boys named Hunahpu and Xbalanque who had extraordinary abilities and who were exemplary beings. With great skill and wisdom, they subordinated the other deities who were living on the surface of the earth, including their older half-brothers, and then the twins journeyed to the Underworld to challenge the lords of death. After many contests and deceptions, they defeated One Death and Seven Death and subjugated the Xibalbans. The Hero Twins then adorned their father

One Hunahpu and promised him that he would be the first to be honored by humans.

The next chronological event in the timeline of the Popol Vuh story was the primordial rising of the morning star, which was witnessed by the humans waiting on their sacred mountains. In nature, the first appearance of the morning star occurs on the eastern horizon close to the rising point of the sun. In Mesoamerican thought, the morning star is thought to herald the arrival of the sun and prepare its path across the sky. The Popol Vuh narrative describes the morning star as glittering in the sky and as "the Great Star that gives its light at the birth of the sun" and "the green star" (Christenson 2003a:207, 217, 228). The humans rejoiced at this sight and immediately burnt their copal offerings in censers that they waved towards the rising sun. Hunahpu then rose into the sky as the sun, followed by his brother Xbalanque as the full moon. Given that the sun rises at dawn and the full moon rises at sunset, the rising of these two deities demarcated the first day of a new era.

Despite the fact that the Popol Vuh does not directly state that One Hunahpu became the morning star, it can be inferred from the narrative that his adornment transformed him into this celestial light (Bassie-Sweet 2008:287–300). In fact, the Dresden Codex Venus tables indicate that the first mythological appearance of the morning star occurred on the date 1 Ajaw, and One Hunahpu's name is the K'iche' equivalent of this calendar date. This first celestial rising of One Hunahpu (morning star) and the subsequent rising of Hunahpu (sun) occurred on the first day of zenith passage at the beginning of the rainy season and initiated the corn-planting cycle (Bassie-Sweet 2008:284–301).

The cultural hero Thorn Broom has attributes that indicate he was directly identified with the morning star and with jade (Bassie-Sweet 2008:299–300). Across Mesoamerica, the morning star is thought to sweep the path for the rising sun, and Thorn Broom's name refers to this action. The Motagua fault zone is the only known source of the green jade coveted by the Classic Maya. In highland mythology, each deity is identified with a specific mountain. Cerro Raxon ("Green Mountain") is thought to be the manifestation of Thorn Broom. This mountain is the highest peak on the mountain ridges of the Motagua fault zone, and jade sources skirt its slopes. One Ixim (One Hunahpu's Classic period parallel) was also identified with jade.

A number of pottery scenes illustrate the resurrection of One Ixim, in which he is washed in a river and adorned by his sons and a bevy of naked goddesses (K626, K1004, K1202, and K6979). On K1202, One Ixim and the goddesses are pictured within the water, and the caption text gives the location as the

Seven Water Place. In another portrayal of this myth (K7268), One Ixim and the goddesses are seen standing beside the water while his sons stand within and beside a mountain cave adjacent to the water. In these scenes, One Ixim is dressed in a green jade costume by the Hero Twins and the goddesses. There is evidence that One Ixim didn't just dress in jade but that jade was thought to be one of his manifestations. This is similar to the identification of the deity Tlaloc with obsidian and the deity Chahk with flint (Bassie-Sweet 2011, 2012, in press, in review).

One Hunahpu carries the full *tzolk'in* day name 1 Hunahpu as his personal name. His son is simply called Hunahpu. One Hunahpu's Classic period parallel was not named using a *tzolk'in* date; rather, he was called One Ixim (literally, "one corn"). It is Hunahpu's Classic period parallel who was named using the *tzolk'in* date of 1 Ajaw. On the surface this may look like a discrepancy or change, but there is a simple reason why both the father (morning star) and the son (sun) could have the same *tzolk'in* date for a name. In Mesoamerica, there are abundant references to both deities and humans being named for the *tzolk'in* date on which they were born or for the *tzolk'in* date on which they were transformed into another state. While the day in the 365-day tropical year *haab* calendar changed at dawn, the day in the 260-day *tzolk'in* calendar changed at sunset (Mathews 2001; Stuart 2004b). This means that the first rising of the morning star and sun occurred on the same *tzolk'in* date, and both father and son could legitimately carry the 1 Ajaw *tzolk'in* date as a personal name.

The *tzolk'in* date on which a person was born was thought to be an omen of their fate. Each of the thirteen numbers and twenty day names in this 260-day cycle was represented by a different deity. Modern ethnographic evidence indicates that both the number deity and the day-name deity influenced the events of the particular *tzolk'in* date. The day lord for Ajaw was the deity One Ajaw. It is surely no coincidence that the deity for the number one was One Ixim. Hence both father and son ruled on this primary date.[1]

THE THIRD GENERATION OF CREATOR DEITIES

The primary deities in the third generation of creator deities were Xpiyacoc and Xmucane's twin grandsons Hunahpu and Xbalanque. The Popol Vuh stresses the fact that the Hero Twins were the true and proper replacements for their father, and by extension, for their paternal grandfather. The victory of the Hero Twins over the Underworld deities (the homeland of their mother) placed the paternal line of the creator deities in the senior position in the hierarchy and the maternal line in the subordinate position. The Maya employed a patrilineal descent system for kingship that was based on these deities.

As noted, Hunahpu's Classic lowland parallel was the deity One Ajaw. The word *ajaw* and the day name *Ajaw* are often represented by a portrait of One Ajaw, who wears a cloth or paper headdress. Across Mesoamerica, cloth and paper were created from the bark of wild fig trees (*Ficus* sp.). The word *huun* refers to the tree, bark cloth, and bark paper, and in addition describes the headdresses and books created from bark paper.² One Ajaw's headdress is named in hieroglyphic texts as the *sak huun* "white paper." It was composed of a flexible headband of white bark paper that was tied (*k'ahlaj* "fastened, enclosed, bound, or tied") onto the head with a large knot in the back (Schele et al. 1990:4–5; Schele 1992:22–24; Grube cited in Schele 1992:39–40; Stuart 1996:155). Some examples of the *sak huun* headdress show black markings on the forehead and ends (for example see the Palenque Temple 19 platform and K1183).³

While all young lords were called *ajaw* and clearly emulated One Ajaw, the accession statements for Maya kings indicate that the crown of kingship was the *sak huun* of One Ajaw. When humans donned the costume and headdress of a deity, they became the embodiment of that deity (Houston and Stuart 1996). If we apply this basic fact to the accession of a Maya king, it must be concluded that a young lord became specifically identified with One Ajaw when he took the throne. This identification with the deity One Ajaw is most apparent in variations of the Ajaw day signs where the deity One Ajaw is occasionally replaced with a portrait of the ruling king wearing One Ajaw's headdress (Martin and Grube 2008:108).

The title *bah ch'ok* "first youth" is a designation for the heir apparent (Schele 1990). The narrative on the Palenque Tablet of the Foliated Cross names the six-year-old K'inich Kan Bahlam as the *bah ch'ok* during the reign of his father, K'inich Janaab Pakal I. Although the Palenque Temple XVIII stucco panel is in a fragmentary state, enough remains to demonstrate that it represents the ruler K'inich Janaab Pakal I flanked by his three sons K'inich Kan Bahlam, K'inich K'an Joy Chitam II, and Tiwol Chan Mat (Ringle 1996; Stuart and Stuart 2008:163). Each son is named as a *ch'ok* "youth."

The Popol Vuh narrative indicates that the final destiny of Hunahpu was to become the sun. The identification of a Classic period lord with the sun on the day of his accession is reflected in the *k'inich* "sunlike" title of the sun god that lords frequently acquired on this day (Colas 2003; Wichmann 2004b). The Maya believe that corn seed is cold and dead, and that it requires ritual heating during the night before planting or it will not germinate (Bassie-Sweet 2008:44–45). The first seeds are planted at dawn, and the rising sun completes the ritual heating. When the new king took on the role of One Ajaw on the day of his accession, he became identified with the solar heat that germinated the corn seed. It was a fundamental expression of power.

It should be pointed out that the most prevalent rituals illustrated in Classic period monumental art are Period Ending ceremonies based on units of *tuns* (360 days each). A *k'atun* was a period of 20 *tuns* (7,200 days). Simply because of the mathematics of the calendar, it took 13 *k'atun* cycles before the same *tzolk'in* date would begin another *k'atun*. Landa (Tozzer 1941) indicated that each of the thirteen different *k'atun* periods had its own patron deity who was worshipped during that time. Regardless of what patron deities were being honored during a particular Period Ending, the god One Ajaw always played a central role in Period Ending events because all Period Ending events occurred on Ajaw days of the *tzolk'in*.

THE WISDOM AND KNOWLEDGE OF THE CREATOR DEITIES

The Popol Vuh emphasizes the spiritual power, knowledge, and divination skills of the creator grandparents, their two sons (One Hunahpu and Seven Hunahpu), and their four grandsons (One Batz, One Chouen, Hunahpu, and Xbalanque). One of the episodes explains how the Hero Twins Hunahpu and Xbalanque usurped their older brothers, transformed them into monkeys, designated them as the patron gods for secondary lords who were artisans, and made themselves the proper inheritors of their father's and grandfather's supreme wisdom and skills (Christenson 2003a:145–147). The Popol Vuh narrative also explains that the first four K'iche' lineage heads were given knowledge and prognostication abilities by the creator deities, but in lesser degree than the gods (Christenson 2003a:196–201). The importance of the wisdom and knowledge of the first K'iche' leaders is stressed, and they are referred to as great sages (Christenson 2003a:110). What separated these K'iche' lords from the previous creation of men made from wood was their knowledge and their ability to worship the creator deities.

The word *huun* "fig tree, paper, book, headband" can be logographically represented by a book, a tied paper headband, or an avian figure with a hooked beak and often wearing a paper headband (Grube, cited in Schele 1992:39–40). In iconographic contexts, the avian *huun* god often has three leafy head elements that resemble the hat of a medieval court jester, hence, the nickname the "jester god" (Schele 1974:49). Three distinct forms of zoomorphic creatures have been lumped together under the moniker "jester god": the avian *huun* god, an anthropomorphic figure, and a piscine form (Stuart 2012). It has been determined that the avian *huun* god is the personification of a fig tree (Houston, Martin, and Stuart cited in Stuart 2012). As noted by Stuart, this is best demonstrated by the avian *huun* god illustrated on the walls of Rio Azul Tomb 19, where its foliage includes the T87 *te'* "tree" sign.[4] The conclusion of these researchers is that the avian *huun* god's appearance on books and headbands indicates that these materials were made of paper, and that the avian *huun* god was not, in itself, a symbol of rulership. While that is clearly the case, we suggest that there is a far deeper meaning to the jester god that is directly related to the knowledge and prognostication skills of the creator deities. It is our contention that the *huun* jester god and the paper used to record the esoteric knowledge of the deities were used in Maya art as a symbol for that knowledge. Such metaphorical symbolism is prevalent in Maya art and hieroglyphic writing.

It has been proposed that during the Classic period all young heirs to the throne and secondary lords first underwent training in the art of divination as part of their preparation for office (Bassie-Sweet 1997). An analogy was made with the training of indigenous leaders in the K'iche' region. The first level attained in the hierarchy of the K'iche' community leadership requires that the apprentice learn the structure and function of the *tzolk'in* calendar, divination techniques, times, and locations where offerings are to be made, the proper prayers used to evoke the gods, and how to prepare the incense offerings. These apprentice leaders are, in effect, novice priests. Zender (2004:153–226) expanded on this proposal and identified specific Classic-period offices that involved priestly duties, such as *ajk'uhuun*, *ti'sakhuun*, and *yajawk'ahk'*. Paper was a primary component of their headdresses as well as the headdresses worn by the secondary deities who inhabited Itzamnaaj's court.

To possess paper and by extension books, was to possess knowledge. These lords and their books were the repositories of ancient knowledge. In his discussion of the Paris Codex *k'atun* pages, Love (1994:32) noted that "the never-ending series of *katuns* was the grand framework within which Maya life proceeded. The priest consulting these pages held in his hands the sacred guidebook giving him power to consult the past and predict the future, and make ultimate sense of life itself." We concur with this cogent observation, and suggest that it is equally applicable to the Classic period ruler and his entourage of secondary lords.

The headdress of One Ajaw is distinguished from other *huun* headdresses by the adjective *sak* "white." While it is quite possible that *sak* simply refers to the white color of the headband, colors also carry additional connotations. In many Mayan languages, the root *sak* is used in words to describe brightness, light, and the dawn (Laughlin 1988:295; Kaufman 2003:222–223, Hopkins, Josserand, and Cruz Guzmán 2010:198). In the Popol Vuh, the creation of humans is repeatedly described metaphorically as their sowing and dawning (Christenson 2003a:60, 71, 78, 80, 82, 110, 206, 207, 227). The climax of the sowing and dawning of the first K'iche' lords occurred with the first rising of the morning star (One Hunahpu) and sun (Hunahpu), when the lords acknowledged the creator deities and made their offerings of incense and blood sacrifice (Christenson 2003a:227). It is quite possible then that the *sak huun* headdress alludes to this concept.

THE COMPLEMENTARY OPPOSITION OF THE DEITIES

Complementary opposition is one of the primary organizing principles in Maya worldview. The complementary opposition that characterizes the creator grandparents is also found between all of the major deities. Such is the case between the paternal and maternal grandfather of the Hero Twins. The lowland parallel of the maternal grandfather, Gathered Blood, was a deity nicknamed God L (Bassie-Sweet 2008:226–238), who was the patron god for long-distance traders, in particular obsidian merchants (Bassie-Sweet 2013a; in press). His diagnostic trait is a headdress composed of an owl and owl feathers that metaphorically represent obsidian blades. The avian manifestations of the paternal grandfather Itzamnaaj and maternal grandfather God L contrast with each other. Itzamnaaj's bird form was based on the laughing falcon, a diurnal raptor whose call is thought to announce the life-giving rains at the beginning of the planting season (Bassie-Sweet 2008:235–236). In opposition, the call of the nocturnal owl manifestation of God L is thought to announce death. The struggle between the creator deities and the lords of the Underworld was not a battle between good and evil, but rather it was an expression of the complementary opposition of life and death that reflects the cyclical renewal of the world.

The *tz'ak* "whole, complete" glyph was discussed in the previous chapter. There are many examples of the pairing of *k'in* "day" and *ak'ab* "night" that occur outside of the *tz'ak* context. A number of illustrations of the Itzamnaaj bird display *k'in* and *ak'ab* signs on its wings (Taube et al. 2010:31–33). Another example occurs in the name phrase of a pair of aged thunderbolt deities who have been nicknamed the Paddler Gods because they are pictured paddling a river canoe (Freidel, Schele, and Parker 1993:90; Mathews 2001). The diagnostic trait of the first Paddler is a stingray spine through his nose while the second is a jaguar deity with a fire cord over his nose. Their name phrases are often represented by their portraits, but in some examples their portraits are replaced with two canoe paddles that are infixed with *k'in* and *ak'ab* signs. The paddles indicate their close association with canoe travel. Although some researchers have suggested that the *k'in* signs in these contexts label the Itzamnaaj bird and the Paddler Gods as solar deities (Taube et al. 2010:33; Stone and Zender 2011:145), it is far more likely that the pairing refers to the concept that these deities express the ideal state of complementary opposition. There is evidence that the Paddler Gods are parallel to the Popol Vuh river deities called Xulu ("Descended") and Paqam ("Ascended"), whose names are also complementary opposites (Bassie-Sweet 2008:281–282).

The Hero Twins were complementary opposites. Twins are naturally associated with a senior/junior pairing, given that they are born sequentially, and one twin is always stronger and healthier. Hunahpu was the senior member of the Hero Twins in his role as the hot sun of the day in contrast to his brother Xbalanque, who was the cold full moon of the night. There is a male/female aspect to the Hero Twins' relationship that is reflected in Xbalanque's name, which always begins with the *x* female/diminutive/collective marker, while Hunahpu's name includes the male/individual marker *ah*. There is also a visual opposition between the sun and the full moon. As the sun rises in the east, the full moon sets in the west and vice versa. Xbalanque's Classic period parallel is a deity nicknamed Yax Bolon. As noted in the previous chapter, the scene on K1892 illustrates the surface of the earth as a turtle shell with One Ajaw on one edge of the world and his brother Yax Bolon on the opposite side, just as sun and full moon appear in nature (figure 1.8). The Hero Twin Yax Bolon is distinguished from his brother by jaguar markings on his body. The jaguar is the quintessential nocturnal mammal.

Twin ears of corn were thought to be manifestations of the Hero Twins. On rare occasions, a corn plant will develop unusual or multiple ears of corn (Bassie-Sweet 2008:21–22). The Maya interpret such growth as omens. Positive omens are two ears of corn growing inside one husk, two ears of corn in separate husks but growing from one node, and one large ear of corn in its own husk with several smaller ears growing around its base. Two ears of corn in one husk or growing from the same node are often called twins. The central icon on the Tablet of the Foliated Cross illustrates a corn plant with two ears of corn attached to the same node, and both ears are shown as handsome young males, just like the Hero Twins (see chapter 8 for further discussion of this panel). Note that real maize plants have alternate leaves, not two opposing leaves from the same node, so this is a deliberate anomaly. Twin corn ears are placed with stored ears of corn to protect the female spirit of corn. It is believed that the twin corn ears will actually make the stored corn multiply. In the Popol Vuh, Hunahpu and Xbalanque planted two ears of unripe corn in their house before they descended into the Underworld (Christenson 2003a:160). In nature, unripe corn cannot germinate. However, the planting of the corn ears by the Hero Twins inside their house immediately evokes the guardian ears of corn used to protect the spirit of corn and increase its yield. The Hero Twins told their grandmother that this corn was an omen of their fate. If they died, the corn would also die. Initially when the Hero Twins perished during one of their Underworld challenges, the corn ears died, but then they sprouted again when the Hero Twins were revived. The obvious conclusion to draw from this episode is that twin ears of corn were thought to be manifestations of the Hero Twins (Bassie-Sweet 2008:222). This identification explains why the waxing moon, their mother Lady Blood, is thought to make the corn grow better. The waxing moon makes the corn increase because she carries the magical twin ears of corn in her womb (Bassie-Sweet 2008:205). The Maya plant and harvest at full moon. During the planting and harvesting of corn, the Hero Twins in their roles as sun and full moon stand in opposition to one another at sunrise and sunset to ensure the protection of the planted corn seed and the field ready for harvest. They, in effect, transform the corn field into a Place of Duality, the ideal state.

Kaufman and Norman (1984:150) have reconstructed three proto-Ch'olan corn terms: *ajän*, "roasting corn" (unripe corn), *nal* "ear of corn," and *ixim* "grain corn." The term *ixim* is often used to refer to corn in general. Stuart (2005a:181–182) has argued that the portrait glyph of One Ixim represents the word *ixim*. One Ixim's head has corn foliage and jade features, but it also has the form of a gourd, just as did his Popol Vuh manifestation One Hunahpu. Taube (1985) nicknamed him the Tonsured Maize God. A second corn deity, named the Foliated Maize God by Taube, appears as the god of the number eight. In other contexts, this corn god includes a phonetic *na* sign, and some epigraphers have concluded that it represents the word *ajan*, the proto-Cholan word for "unripe corn" (Boot 2009; Stone and Zender 2011:22, Zender 2014).[5] This is the early stage of corn when the kernels are filled with milky white liquid. *Ajan* is considered a delicacy, and a small number of such ears are harvested from the milpa and eaten at this stage. *Ajan* corn can be cooked by either steaming or roasting, hence the term "roasting ear" is often used to describe the *ajan* stage in North America. The central icon on the Tablet of the Foliated Cross is a stylized corn plant with twin ears of corn. As noted above, twin ears of corn were thought to be manifestations of the Hero Twins, and the ears of corn on the Tablet of the Foliated Cross have the form of handsome young men like the Hero Twins. Given that corn was so vitally important to the survival of the Maya, it is not surprising that the imagery and metaphors associated with it would be complex.

The creator grandmother Xmucane and the wives of One Hunahpu were the complementary opposites of their husbands, and they had many duties and functions that reflected their roles as married females within a family or community (Bassie-Sweet 2008). One Hunahpu's first wife, Lady Bone Water, was a young goddess who like Marilyn Monroe died an early death and thus remained an image of eternal youthfulness. As noted above, the lowland goddess Ixik was likely the prototype for Lady Bone Water. In hieroglyphic texts, the words *ix* and *ixik* "lady, woman" are represented by the portrait of a beautiful young female with a lock of hair at her forehead and ear. When this female portrait is rendered with paint, the hair lock is shown as a circle of black. On sculpture, it is often shown with cross-hatching, which is a sculptural convention used to indicate the color black (Bassie-Sweet 1991:141). One Ixim's nominal glyph is composed of the number one (represented by a dot) and a portrait of him that has been interpreted to represent the word *ixim* (Stuart 2005a:181–182). One Ixim's portrait glyph has frequently been mistaken for the *ix-ixik* glyph because they are so similar, but as noted by Stuart, One Ixim is distinguished by the jade jewelry in his hair, a curl of corn foliage, or his tonsured hairstyle.

As demonstrated by the illustrations of goddesses in the codices, the *ix-ixik* glyph is not a generic portrait of a female but the portrait of a specific goddess (Bassie-Sweet 2008:163–165, 201–202). The young goddesses in these books can be divided into categories according to their name glyphs. The codex version of the *ix-ixik* portrait glyph is used as the personal name of one of these goddesses. The Postclassic Ixik is portrayed with a lock of hair on her forehead. In Classic period inscriptions, the titles and personal names of elite women are preceded by the *ix-ixik* portrait, as are the names and titles of a number of goddesses. This is another example where a mythic prototype (the goddess Ixik) was used to represent a general class (a title for elite women and goddesses). It can be directly compared to the use of the deity One Ajaw as the mythic prototype for the general class of *ajaw* (a title for elite males).

Across the Maya region, corn seed is identified as being female. It is also characterized as bone. Bassie-Sweet presented evidence that Ixik and Lady Bone Water were parallel goddesses that were specifically identified with the corn ear and its seeds (Bassie-Sweet 2008:163–169, 234–235). The black hair of Ixik represented the darkened silk of the ear after fertilization. As noted above, One Ixim (the Classic period parallel of One Hunahpu) was a corn god

(Taube 1985). Many of the major Maya deities had quadripartite forms that were identified with the four directions and their associated colors (east-red, north-white, west-black, and south-yellow). The Maya also categorized corn according to these four colors (Bassie-Sweet 2008:19, 61, 93).[6] There are a number of Classic period scenes that indicate the corn god One Ixim had a quadripartite form that was related not only to the four directions and their colors, but also to the four colors of corn (Stuart 2004c; Bassie-Sweet 2008:173). The Popol Vuh mentions four corn goddesses in the section of the story that refers to Lady Blood (Christenson 2003a:136–138). When the pregnant Lady Blood appeared at the household of the creator deities, the grandmother Xmucane doubted that the young moon goddess was carrying her grandchildren. She told Lady Blood if she could gather a bag full of corn ears from the milpa of One Batz and One Chouen, then she would believe her. When Lady Blood arrived at the field, she was dismayed to discover that only one corn plant had produced an ear of corn. In desperation, she petitioned four goddesses to help her, and when she pulled out the silk from the corn ear it magically produced enough corn to fill the bag. The four corn goddesses were named Lady Toh, Lady Canil, Lady Cacao, and Lady Tzi. *Toh*, *Canil*, and *Tzi* refer to days in the 260-day *tzolk'in* calendar, and are parallel to the lowland day names *Muluk*, *Lamat*, and *Ok*, respectively. It is likely that these four corn goddesses were the quadripartite form of the corn goddess Lady Bone Water (Bassie-Sweet 2008:234). Lady Blood, in essence, was pulling out the hair of Lady Bone Water, the deceased first wife of her husband, One Hunahpu.

A corn plant consists of a single stalk topped by a male tassel. As the plant matures, a single female ear develops from a node on the stalk (only rarely does a Maya corn plant produce more than one ear of corn). In the cornfield, the male tassels drop their pollen on the silk of the female ears and fertilize them. A mature corn plant is incomplete without its ear of corn, just as the corn god One Ixim was incomplete without his wife. Like the corn plant, this couple embodied the principle of complementary opposition. Given the paramount importance of corn to Maya civilization, it should not be surprising that their primary deities reflected the basic nature of this plant.

One Ixim frequently wears a jade skirt despite the fact that skirts are mainly the costume of females. The diamond pattern of the jade decoration symbolically represents the surface of the earth covered in corn fields (Bassie-Sweet 2008:165). When a man takes a wife, one of his responsibilities is to supply her with a new set of clothing. Given One Ixim's identification with jade, it seems reasonable to conclude that he gave his new wife this jade skirt. The images of One Ixim wearing the jade skirt are likely related to the concept that a god and his wife can be illustrated as a single deity, as in a depiction of the creator grandfather Itzamnaaj that is found in the Dresden Codex (Bassie-Sweet 2008:fig. 7.1). The caption text identifies this deity as Itzamnaaj and the deity has Itzamnaaj's face, but he has the breast, headdress, and skirt of his wife, Ix Chel. A similar situation is found in Aztec mythology where the creator pair can be viewed as an elderly couple or as a single entity.

As noted above, the Popol Vuh indicates that Lady Blood was the daughter of the Underworld lord Gathered Blood, but it does not discuss the parentage of Lady Bone Water. When a wife prematurely dies, it is a common Maya practice for the husband to then marry a sister-in-law to maintain the established relationship with his wife's family. Given that the actions of the deities established human customs, it is likely that One Hunahpu's first wife, Lady Bone Water, was also a daughter of Gathered Blood (Bassie-Sweet 2008:178–193). The ultimate destiny of Lady Bone Water was to be a corn goddess identified with the surface of the earth while that of Lady Blood was as a moon goddess identified with the celestial realm. Like One Hunahpu and his brother Seven Hunahpu, and Hunahpu and his brother Xbalanque, Lady Bone Water and Lady Blood were probably thought to be complementary opposites, one an earth-related corn goddess and the other a celestial-related moon goddess. As sisters and as prototypical young wives of a primary creator deity, it is possible that Lady Bone Water and Lady Blood were also viewed as different manifestations of one goddess, much like the Aztec goddesses Chalchiuhtlicue (Jade Skirt), Chicomecoatl (Seven Snake), Huixtocihuatl (Salt Woman), Xilonen (Tender Ear of Corn), and Xochiquetzal (Flower Quetzal), who are described either as manifestations of the same deity or as sisters (Sahagún 1959–1963:2:22; Durán 1971:221; *Codex Ríos*).

THE MOON AND COMPLEMENTARY OPPOSITION

Since the beginning of Maya studies, lunar imagery has been recognized and the T683 sign as a reference to the moon demonstrated (Temple 1930). Early studies also identified a goddess juxtaposed with this sign in Classic art and the Postclassic codices. Patron gods of the lunar cycle have only been recently recognized, and One Ixim is one of these patrons. In this context, he too is juxtaposed with the T683 sign. Many images that were previously thought to be the moon goddess are, in fact, One Ixim in his role as a lunar patron deity. The following is a brief review of the moon goddess as well as the lunar patron deities and how they are contrasted with the sun and other celestial patron deities.

The T683 moon sign appears in the *tz'ak* glyph in contrast with the *k'in* sign. As noted in the previous chapter, *k'in* means both "sun" and "day" (Kaufman and Norman 1984:124). While the contrast between *k'in* and *ak'ab* in the *tz'ak* glyph is between "day" and "night," when contrasted with the moon, the *k'in* sign obviously carries the value of "sun." This is a natural complementary combination, given that the moon is the brightest celestial object of the night and the sun is the brightest of the day.

There was a Classic period goddess who was parallel to the waxing moon goddess Lady Blood of the Popol Vuh. This goddess is portrayed in a number of scenes with a T683 moon cartouche extending from her body (K504, K5166). In one instance she wears the diamond-patterned skirt often worn by One Ixim (Robicsek and Hales 1981:fig. 48c). A number of scenes on Maya pottery illustrate the deity God L and the Paddler Gods being subordinated by One Ixim and the Hero Twins (Stuart 1993; Wald and Carrasco 2004; Miller and Martin 2008). The scene on K5166 illustrates an episode from this myth. God L kneels before the moon goddess, who sits on a bench holding a rabbit and the accoutrements of God L. Her moon sign extends from her body. In another example of this goddess, the adjacent caption text names her using the *ixik* "lady" sign and the moon cartouche (Robicsek and Hales 1981:fig. 9). We refer to her as Lady Moon.

Lady Moon appears in the Dresden Codex Venus pages as a patron deity for one of the Venus intervals (Thompson 1972). Patron gods for celestial cycles and time intervals are well known. Numerous sources indicate that various deities were thought to rule the day, the month, the year, the *k'atun*, the lunar phases, and the Venus intervals (see following chapter). A synodic period of Venus is divided into four intervals: morning star, superior conjunction, evening star, and inferior conjunction. Venus makes distinct paths in relation to the background of stars during its morning star and evening star intervals. It takes five synodic cycles of Venus before the same morning star path or evening star path will repeat (Aveni 1990). A table representing the five synodic periods of Venus is found in the Dresden Codex (pages 46–51) (Thompson 1972). The Dresden Venus table notes the patron deity for each interval in the five synodic periods. Some of these twenty Venus patrons are well-known deities, such as One Ajaw, but many are obscure. Lady Moon is named and illustrated as the patron deity of the fourth morning star interval (Dresden Codex page 49). Her moon cartouche extends out from under her arm and she is shown bare-breasted. The text refers to her as Lady Moon Ajaw (B6, page 24).

There is a Classic period sign composed of a portrait glyph and moon sign that has been interpreted to be the name of the moon goddess, but a close

FIGURE 2.1. *Glyph C of the Lunar Series.*

examination of this sign indicates that the portrait represents the deity One Ixim (for an overview of this identification, see Bassie-Sweet 2008:206–207; Zender 2012). This sign appears most frequently in Glyph C of the Lunar Series as one of three different lunar patrons (figure 2.1). The Maya grouped the lunar synodic periods into three sets, each composed of six lunar synodic periods (177–178 days) (Linden 1996). Each of the three lunar semesters had its own patron deity. The first Glyph C lunar patron is composed of One Ixim's portrait and the moon sign; the second Glyph C deity is a portrait of GIII (no reading has been proposed for his name) and a moon sign; and the third is a portrait of God A (a skeletal deity) and the moon sign. In a previous publication, Bassie-Sweet (2008) read these signs as One Moon, Seven Moon, and Ten Moon based on the fact that One Ixim, GIII, and God A are the gods for each of these numbers. She had incorrectly assumed that the One Moon name referred to the moon goddess, but there is clear evidence on K5166 that One Moon of Glyph C refers to One Ixim in his role as a lunar patron (Chinchilla Mazariegos 2011:199–209). In the scene on K5166, four male deities have moon signs extending from their bodies. The first deity is One Ixim and the last deity is God A. Further evidence of male lunar deities is also found on a vessel that illustrates the moon goddess with GIII sitting adjacent to her (Robicsek and Hale 1981:fig. 9). The moon cartouche is attached to his back. There are several examples where a full figure of One Ixim is juxtaposed with the moon sign. Although these examples have been characterized as a merging of One Ixim and the moon goddess (Taube 1992a:64–67), a better explanation is that they are simply full-figure depictions of the name of the lunar patron, One Moon.

In hieroglyphic writing, it was common for the scribe to replace a logographic sign or head variant of a sign with a full-figure depiction. The Copán Structure 8N-11 bench demonstrates this convention and illustrates One Ixim as a lunar patron (figure 2.2). The edge of the bench is decorated with a sky band that contrasts full figure depictions of day and night and moon and star

FIGURE 2.2. *Copán Bench 8N-11, after Barbara Fash.*

(Webster et al. 1998). Sky bands are linear bands containing celestial-related glyphs (Förstemann 1886; Carlson and Landis 1985). To the right of the central motif (a T1017 sign that likely represents a personified flash of lightning), day is represented by the sun god emerging from a solar disk with *k'in* signs on his body. On the left side of the T1017 sign, night is portrayed as a Chahk deity with *ak'ab* "night, darkness" signs on his arm and leg. He is in the reclined pose representing emergence. As noted above, this same complementary pairing of *k'in* "day" and *ak'ab* "night" is found in the *tz'ak* glyph (Stuart 2003a:fig. 1b). The *tz'ak* glyph on the Palenque Tablet of the 96 Glyphs (E7) pairs a star sign and a moon sign. A similar pairing is found on the Copán bench. The right outer cartouche on the bench is composed of a deity with his arm looped through a star sign. The tail of a scorpion extends from the star sign. Another example of this scorpion star motif is found on K4546 where the deity in question is clearly One Ixim. Scorpion deities are extremely rare in Maya art, but the Dresden Venus tables indicate that the patron of the first evening star interval was a deity named Scorpion. The left outer cartouche of the Copán bench is a portrait of One Moon holding a rabbit, an animal that is linked with the moon throughout Mesoamerica. So it would seem that on the Copán bench, the patron deities for Venus and the moon are paired rather than images of Venus and the moon. This pairing of *k'in-ak'ab* and Venus patron-moon patron replicates the environment of the Place of Duality and in doing so creates an idealized location for the owner of the bench to sit.

When Maya hieroglyphs were first being phonetically deciphered, epigraphers searched for parallel occurrences where logographs had phonetic elements that would hint at the correct reading of the sign or where logographs were completely replaced with phonetic signs that provided a precise reading. One of the first examples noted was the logograph of a shield (*pakal*) used in the personal name of a Palenque ruler, which was replaced with phonetic signs that represented the syllables *pa*, *ka*, and *la*. This decipherment method was very productive, but not all substitutions represent a direct equivalence. As an example, the head variants for the *k'in* "day" position in the Long Count are either a portrait of the sun god or a monkey scribe. The monkey scribe was parallel to the firstborn sons of One Hunahpu, who were transformed into monkeys by the Hero Twins (Coe 1977). They were gifted diviners who counted out the day names during their prognostications and were, thus, intimately connected to the *k'in* cycle. The sun god and the monkey scribe, however, do not substitute for each other because they are manifestations of the same deity. We believe that the usage of One Moon is similar. He does not substitute for the moon cartouche because he is the moon, but because he is one of the patron deities for the lunar cycle.

As noted by Stuart (1998), some benches with hieroglyphic texts include a reference to the dedication of the building that houses the bench. We speculate that in addition to creating a Place of Duality, the pairing of the scorpion Venus patron and One Moon on the Structure 8N-11 bench might be a subtle reference to the Venus patron and moon patron who were in power on the date of the building dedication.

IMPERSONATIONS OF ONE MOON AND LADY MOON

There are numerous examples where a lord, his wife, or his mother are pictured wearing the diamond-patterned skirt of jade that is often worn by One Moon–One Ixim and Lady Moon. For example, the Palenque Temple XIV Tablet illustrates the young K'inich Kan Bahlam many years prior to his accession, performing a ritual with his mother Lady Tz'akbu Ajaw, who is dressed in this skirt (Bassie-Sweet 1991) (figure 1.10). The Palace Tablet illustrates a pre-accession event for her second son K'inich K'an Joy Chitam II, and she is again pictured wearing this skirt. On the Oval Palace Tablet, K'inich Janaab Pakal I's mother is also featured wearing the skirt. Another instance is found on Naranjo Stela 24. A brief digression is in order to discuss these contexts and whether these deity impersonations refer to One Moon (One Ixim) or Lady Moon (Lady Blood).

During the late seventh century, Naranjo was engaged in wars with Caracol and Calakmul that may have annihilated or at least greatly reduced the royal line at Naranjo. Piecing together evidence from various inscriptions, researchers have concluded that an unnamed Naranjo lord married Lady Six Sky, the daughter of the Dos Pilas king Bajlaj Chan K'awiil in order to reestablish or legitimize the Naranjo line (Martin and Grube 2008:74). Like some of the other foreign princesses who married into local dynasties, Lady Six Sky was a Tlaloc priestess (Bassie-Sweet 2013). She arrived at Naranjo on August 30, AD 682, and three days later dedicated a building. It is quite possible that the building was a Tlaloc temple and that she brought with her Tlaloc effigies for the shrine. This would be similar to the Tlaloc priest Sihyaj K'ahk', who brought such effigies to Tikal. Five years after Lady Six Sky's arrival, K'ahk'

Tiliw Chan Chaak was born, and five years later this young lord was placed on the throne. Although the inscriptions that might have contained the parentage statements for this king are eroded, his close association with Lady Six Sky has led epigraphers to conclude that he was her son. Lady Six Sky conducted many of the important ceremonies during the early life of K'ahk' Tiliw Chan Chaak, including Period Ending rituals.

The caption text on the front of Naranjo Stela 24 begins with the date 9 Lamat 1 Sootz' (April 19, AD 699), and it states that the image is a portrait of Lady Six Sky in the guise of the *"yax* deity." In the scene, she wears the diamond-pattern skirt although her headdress is regrettably eroded. The main text on the left side of the stela begins with an Initial Series date and describes the arrival at Naranjo of Lady Six Sky (682) and the birth of the future Naranjo king K'ahk' Tiliw Chan Chaak (688). The narrative continues on the right-side text with the 9 Lamat impersonation date and states that Lady Six Sky impersonated the deity One Moon (E4). The E4 glyph clearly has the corn curl of One Ixim's portrait and not the black cross-hatching of the *ixik* glyph. The narrative ends with the Period Ending event performed by Lady Six Sky in 702. It seems reasonable to assume that the One Moon impersonation event of the main text is a restatement of the *yax* deity caption text impersonation. Because the One Moon name was identified as that of the moon goddess, it has been concluded that when women (e.g., Lady Six Sky) donned this skirt they were taking on the guise of the moon goddess (Looper 2001). In light of the evidence that the name *One Moon* refers to One Ixim in his role as a lunar patron, this interpretation of Naranjo Stela 24 must be set aside. We cannot, however, apply this interpretation to all cases of women dressed in the diamond-patterned skirt and assume they are impersonating One Moon because there are several examples where Lady Moon also wears this skirt (Robicsek and Hales 1991:fig. 48c). The advantage of the Naranjo monument is that it clearly states who it is that Lady Six Sky is impersonating.

SUMMARY

This chapter has reviewed the children of the creator grandparents, their Underworld spouses, and their children. Along with the creator grandparents, these second and third generations of creator deities were the embodiment of complementary opposition, and they were the role models for human behavior. The kinship of this family was the basic organizing principle for Maya political structure. Most cultures have mythological narratives that provide justification for state authority and the Maya appear to be no exception.

The various illustrations of Itzamnaaj's court illustrate secondary deities who have direct parallels with human courtiers and officials (Boot 2008). These secondary deities also seem to have complementary natures, such as do the Chan Te Chuwen deities discussed in the previous chapter. Complementary opposition was the ideal state that created a balanced and safe world where the cycles of time unfolded. The next chapter is a basic overview of the calendar systems used by the Maya.

NOTES

1. There are scenes on Classic period pottery that illustrate the predatory Itzamnaaj bird landing in a tree where he is then shot by One Ajaw. In one such scene the event is recorded as occurring on the date 1 Ajaw (Zender 2004b). Stuart (2012) has proposed that the deity One Ajaw acquired the day name 1 Ajaw as his personal name because of this blowgun event. However, there is no evidence that Mesoamerican deities were ever named in such a manner. What is more likely is that 1 Ajaw was thought to be an auspicious day for the hunting of birds given that One Ajaw was the quintessential bird hunter.

2. The words for "paper" and the number "one" become identical in some late Mayan languages, but in the Classic period they were still distinct, from proto-Mayan *hu'nh* "paper (*Ficus*)" and *juun* "one" (Kaufman 2003).

3. It is possible that this dark mark is a reference to the dark spots that adorn One Ajaw's body. As sun and full moon, One Ajaw and Yax Bolon are intimately associated with solar and lunar eclipses, respectively. In Maya belief, eclipses cause dark marks and jaguar spots on fetuses (Bassie-Sweet 2008:204).

4. The hooked beak of the jester god suggests an avian model, although Stuart and Taube's assertion that the jester god is directly equivalent to the Itzamnaaj bird is highly doubtful. The penchant for identifying any hooked-beak avian with the predatory Itzamnaaj bird is prevalent in Maya studies.

5. Stone and Zender (2011) incorrectly translated *ajan* as corn cob. As noted by Kaufman and Norman (1984:150), the proto-Ch'olan word for the cob is *b'äkäl*. In a later article, Zender (2014) correctly defined *ajan* as "fresh ear of corn" (Spanish *elote*).

6. Among the 10 or so terms for distinct types of maize in Chuj (Hopkins 2012b) are *chak chi'in* (a red corn), *k'ik' chitam wa'* (a black corn), *k'an sat* (a yellow corn), and *sak nhal* (a white corn).

3

The Calendar and the Narrative Time Frame

In the Maya calendar, each day had several interrelated designations that referred to its position in the *tzolk'in* (a 260-day cycle), the *haab* (a 365-day cycle), the *k'atun* (a 7,200-day cycle), the nine-day period of the Supplementary Series Glyph G, the Lunar Series, the greater Venus cycle, and the 819-day count. The Maya believed that a different deity or combination of deities ruled each period within these cycles and that these deities influenced the outcome of events when they were in power. The numbers from one to thirteen were also each represented by a specific deity, and these gods also factored into this system. Some deities were patrons in multiple cycles. For example, the sun god appears as the god of the number four and as the patron of the month Yaxk'in (Thompson 1950). GIII was the god of the number seven, the patron of the month Woh, the *tzolk'in* day lord of Kib, and a lunar patron.[1]

The vast majority of Classic period main texts on monumental art begin with a reference to a calendar date that establishes the time frame of the story. A typical initial date includes an introductory glyph that indicates what *haab* patron was in power, a Long Count notation (a count of days lapsed since an ancient starting date), a *tzolk'in* date, a pair of glyphs known as Glyphs G and F (usually assumed to represent Lords of the Night), lunar information, and finally the *haab* date.[2] The narratives found on many public monuments do not relate events in a chronological order. Rather, the story often steps back in time and relates

DOI: 10.5876/9781607327424.c003

earlier events, including mythological ones. The most commonly noted ceremonies documented on monumental works of art are events related to the end of Long Count periods (*k'atun* anniversaries of the starting date). This chapter is an overview of the calendar system, the patron gods, the Period Ending ceremonies, and the narrative time frame.

THE DIVINATION AND SOLAR CALENDARS

The Maya had a divination-based calendar called the *tzolk'in* ("sequence of days") that consisted of 13 numbers and 20 day names (Imix, Ik', Ak'bal, K'an, Chikchan, Kimi, Manik', Lamat, Muluk, Ok, Chuwen, Eb, Ben, Ix, Men, Kib, Kaban, Etz'nab, Kawak, and Ajaw). Each day the number and day name changed. A sequential series of *tzolk'in* dates would be 1 Imix, 2 Ik', 3 Ak'bal, 4 K'an, and so on. It takes 260 days before the same number and day name reoccur. The *tzolk'in* was used to time many events and ritual obligations. It is likely that the cycle initially represented the gestation period of humans.

The almanacs in the codices are organized using the *tzolk'in* calendar, and indicate the timing of ritual obligations on particular *tzolk'in* dates. Barbara Tedlock's overview of modern K'iche' calendar events indicates a similar structure (B. Tedlock 1992). She also noted that offerings were made every 20 days at specific locations whenever a particular day name repeated. One set of Postclassic rituals called the burner period illustrates how the *tzolk'in* was used to time ritual events (Thompson 1950:99–100). In this cycle, the *tzolk'in* was divided into four periods of 65 days with each period associated with a particular direction. Each 65-day period had a series of events timed to coincide with the next appearance of the *tzolk'in* day on which it started. For example, the burner period that began on 3 Chikchan involved an action described as "the taking of the fire." Twenty days later on 10 Chikchan, the action is described as "the fire of the burner flares up." Twenty days later on 4 Chikchan, the action is "the fire spreads." Twenty days later on 11 Chikchan, the action is "the burner extinguishes the fire." Five days later (the end of the 65-day cycle) is the date 3 Ok, and the series begins again with the same sequence of rituals on 3 Ok, 10 Ok, 4 Ok, and 11 Ok. Five days later is the date 3 Men, and the series begins again with the same sequence of identical rituals on 3 Men, 10 Men, 4 Men, and 11 Men. Five days later is the date 3 Ajaw, and the series begins again with the same sequence of rituals on 3 Ajaw, 10 Ajaw, 4 Ajaw, and 11 Ajaw. Five days later is the date 3 Chikchan and the whole cycle starts again.

The 365-day solar calendar, which is referred to as the *haab* ("year"), was composed of 18 periods (Pop, Woh, Sip, Sootz', Tsek, Xul, Yaxk'in, Mol, Ch'en,

Yax, Sak, Keh, Mak, K'ank'in, Muwan, Pax, K'ayab, and Kumk'u) of 20 days each, plus five additional days at the end of the year, together called the *Wayeb*. A sequential series of *haab* days would be 1 Pop, 2 Pop, 3 Pop, and so on. For ease of discussion, the 20-day period (Maya *winal*) will be referred to as a month. Unlike the Gregorian calendar, the Maya did not make adjustments to their *haab* calendar to accommodate the true length of the solar year, thus, their month positions did not stay in synchronization with the seasons.

It takes 18,980 days (73 *tzolk'in* cycles or 52 *haab* cycles) before the same *tzolk'in* date will reoccur on the same *haab* date. This cycle, in which each day has a unique combination of *tzolk'in* and *haab* designations, is nicknamed the Calendar Round. The numerous examples of paired *tzolk'in* and *haab* dates in Classic and Postclassic texts indicate that the synchronization between the *haab* and *tzolk'in* remained the same until after the Spanish conquest. The *tzolk'in* changed at sunset while the *haab* date changed at sunrise (Mathews 2001; Stuart 2004b).

The Maya practiced divinations based on the *tzolk'in* calendar for virtually all of their activities. The importance of the *tzolk'in* as a scheduling device cannot be overstated. Each day number and day name of the *tzolk'in* was thought to be personified by a particular deity and these deities were thought to influence the events that happened on that day. It was believed that the *tzolk'in* date on which a person was born established their destiny. This belief was extended to time periods as well. The *tzolk'in* day that began the *haab* year established the nature of the year. The mathematical relationship between 260 and 365 dictates that the first day of the new year can only begin on one of four *tzolk'in* days. These four *tzolk'in* days were known as the Yearbearers. Each month of a particular year began with the same Yearbearer day name because each month was 20 days long and there were 20 day names in the *tzolk'in* cycle.

In addition to the *tzolk'in* deities, each time period also had a patron god who ruled that period. Each year had a patron god, as did each month and the Wayeb period. In his detailed description of the Wayeb and New Year ceremonies, Landa noted the patron deities for each of the four kinds of *haab* years (Tozzer 1941).

An important aspect of the *haab* is that the twentieth day of the month was never recorded by glyphs representing the word *twenty*. Instead, it was recorded in two different ways (Thompson 1950:fig. 19). In the first case, the month sign was preceded by the phrase *ti' haab*. The word *ti'* means "mouth, lips, edge, margin" (Stuart cited in Zender 2004b:217). Such an example is found on the Palenque sarcophagus lid, where the death date of Lady Yohl

Ik'nal is record as 2 Eb *ti' haab* Keh. Alternatively, the last day of the month could be referred to as the *chum* "seating" of the following month. Thus, Lady Yohl Ik'nal's death date could have been written as 2 Eb *chum* Mak. For convenience sake, researchers often refer to the *chum* of a month as 0 (zero), as in "2 Eb 0 Mak," but it must be emphasized that the Maya never recorded this date using glyphs for zero.

The last day of the month was a transition period when the current patron deity for the month was replaced with the new patron deity for the coming month. The *chum* "seating" verb is also used in the context of the seating of a lord into an office. While there does not seem to be a *tzolk'in* day that was widely favored for the accessions of kings, a surprising number of accessions took place on the seating of a month (Whitmore 2012:516–519). An Early Classic inscription on the Leiden Plaque draws a direct analogy between the seating of the month and the seating of a king, as discussed in the Introduction. Just as the patron god of the month ruled his time period, the king ruled the time period of his reign.

There has been some debate about which *haab* day was thought by the Maya to be the first day of the month. There is ample evidence from the codices, colonial sources, and ethnographic reports that *haab* dates with a coefficient of one were thought to be the first day of the month and that 1 Pop was the first day of the New Year. However, some epigraphers have argued that during the Preclassic and Classic periods, the *ti' haab/chum* date was considered to be the first day of the month and that the seating of Pop was the first day of the New Year (Bricker 1997; Stuart 2004c; Taube et al. 2010). This has significant implications for identifying which of the *tzolk'in* days were the Yearbearers. Bassie-Sweet (2013b) has argued that the offset schedule of the *tzolk'in* and *haab* is the critical factor for determining the Yearbearers, and that the first of the month was always thought to be the *haab* day with the coefficient of one. This means that in the precolumbian period, the four Yearbearers were the *tzolk'in* dates of Ak'bal-Lamat-Ben-Etz'nab.

THE LONG COUNT

Most narratives on Classic period monumental art include a calendar notation that has been nicknamed the Long Count. In essence, the Long Count records the number of days (*k'ins*) since a zero base date, and it places the Calendar Round date in linear time. This base date is often referred to as the "era event," and it occurred on the Calendar Round date of 4 Ajaw 8 Kumk'u. The era event corresponds to the Gregorian date of August 13, 3114

BC, according to the Thompson correlation of 584,285 (the Julian day number corresponding to the Maya date 13.0.0.0.0; Kelley 1976:30–33).

A typical Long Count date is arranged in units of 400 *tuns* (one *bak'tun*), 20 *tuns* (one *k'atun*), 360 days (one *tun*), 20 days (one *winal*), and single days (*k'in*). As an example, the Long Count date for Lady Yohl Ik'nal's death indicates it is 9 *bak'tuns*, 8 *k'atuns*, 11 *tuns*, 6 *winals*, and 12 *k'ins* after the era event: the shorthand notation for this Long Count is 9.8.11.6.12. When a Long Count appears at the beginning of a narrative, it is referred to as the Initial Series date. Such dates begin with a compound nicknamed the Initial Series Introductory Glyph (ISIG). While the ISIG has not been deciphered, it contains an element that refers to the *haab* patron deity who was in power on that particular date (Thompson 1950:fig. 22–23).

Given that the Maya counted in units of 20, one would expect the length of the *tun* to be in units of 400 days (20 × 20) not 360 (18 × 20) if the Maya were merely interested in calculating the number of days. In the beginning of Maya studies, it was postulated that the Maya chose 360 days because it was the closest multiple of twenty to the solar year of 365. Powell (1997) suggested an alternative explanation. He insightfully argued that a period of 360 days in the Long Count would allow for the commensuration of the cycles of the *haab*, the *tzolk'in*, the nine-day Glyph G cycle, and the synodic cycles of Venus, Mars, and Mercury.

A small number of Long Count inscriptions include cycles higher than the *bak'tun*, which indicates that a typical Long Count date is an abbreviated version of a much longer date (Lounsbury 1976). Hence, the era event is not the beginning of time. In Mesoamerica, there was a concept that the world was created, destroyed, and then re-created by the deities a number of times. Some researchers have suggested that the era event represents the last re-creation. Whether this is true remains to be seen. What can be said is that the era event was a Period Ending date and provided the role model for human Period Ending events.

Numerous Classic period inscriptions indicate that the Maya performed elaborate Period Ending events at the end of each *k'atun* as well as the end of the fifth, tenth, thirteenth, and fifteenth *tun* of the *k'atun* cycle. In fact, it is likely they celebrated in some way the end of every *tun* within a *k'atun* cycle, but probably more modestly than the larger cycles.

Because the era event occurred on an Ajaw date, all subsequent *bak'tun*, *k'atun*, and *tun* periods ended on Ajaw dates as well simply because of the mathematics of the calendar (all are even multiples of twenty days). A series of *k'atun*-ending *tzolk'in* dates would be 4 Ajaw, 2 Ajaw, 13 Ajaw, 11 Ajaw, 9

Ajaw, 7 Ajaw, 5 Ajaw, 3 Ajaw, 1 Ajaw, 12 Ajaw, 10 Ajaw, 8 Ajaw, and 6 Ajaw, before beginning with 4 Ajaw again. In other words, it takes 13 *k'atuns* before the same *tzolk'in* date will reappear. This greater *k'atun* cycle of 260 *tuns* was equal to 256.43 tropical years.

The *tzolk'in* day Ajaw is represented by the deity called One Ajaw. When a lord became king, he was dressed in the headdress of One Ajaw and assumed the identity of this deity. As the living embodiment of One Ajaw, the king was intimately identified with Ajaw dates and the events that occurred on these dates.

THE GLYPH G SERIES

A Long Count date is usually followed by the *tzolk'in* date and then a supplementary notation known as Glyph G and Glyph F. Glyph G is, in fact, represented by nine different glyphs (G1, G2, G3, G4, G5, G6, G7, G8, and G9) that changed daily. This nine-day cycle has been equated with the Nine Lords of the Night series found in Aztec culture because of their structural similarity, but what this Maya cycle actually represents is not yet known (Thompson 1950:208). Although Glyph F has been phonetically deciphered as *ti'* "mouth, lips, edge, margin" *hun* "paper," there has also been a long debate about what this phrase means as well (Johnson 2010). The 4 Ajaw 8 Kumk'u era event occurred on a G9 day, thus all *bak'tuns*, *k'atuns*, and *tuns* ended on a Glyph G9 day because 360 is divisible by 9. In a similar manner, all *bak'tuns*, *k'atuns*, and *tuns* began on a G1 day. It is unclear when Glyph G changed because there are no surviving records of night events that include a Glyph G notation for comparison.

THE LUNAR SERIES

Like many cultures, the Maya revered the moon and paid close attention to its cycle. The scheduling of events such as the planting of corn and the cutting of wood was timed according to the phase of the moon (Bassie-Sweet 2008:33–35). Corn was planted at full moon. Solar and lunar eclipses were thought to be omens of great disaster (Thompson 1950:232; Closs 1989; Hull 2000:4). The Maya had many myths regarding the moon, its cycles, and its relationship to other heavenly bodies (Aveni 1980; Milbrath 1999). As noted in the previous chapter, the Popol Vuh indicates that the Postclassic K'iche' identified each phase of the moon with a different deity. The cycle of the waxing moon was seen as the manifestation of Lady Blood during her pregnancy with the Hero Twins while the rising of Xbalanque from the Underworld was equated with the rising full moon (B. Tedlock 1985:39; Bassie-Sweet 1991:191, 2008:203–208). The first six months of Lady Blood's pregnancy represented the lunar half year. After her expulsion from the Underworld, the pregnant Lady Blood journeyed to the household of her husband (the home of the creator deities located at the center of the world). A climactic moment in her story was her arrival at this household and her acceptance by the creator grandmother as the legitimate wife of One Hunahpu. The first appearance of the new crescent moon occurs just after sunset close to the western horizon and near the setting position of the sun. Each subsequent night, the crescent moon appears slightly fuller, and further away from the setting sun. Lady Blood's journey and pregnancy was equated with this nightly progression towards the east (B. Tedlock 1985).

The Classic period Lunar Series gives information including the number of days since the new moon, the number of the lunar half-year, the patron of the lunation, the name of the lunation, and the length of the lunar month (Thompson 1950; Aveni 1980; Linden 1996; Saturno et al. 2012). One of the purposes of grouping lunar periods into half-year cycles is to track eclipses, which are more likely at the end of each half-year period. The Dresden Codex contains an eclipse table, and the destructive flooding of the world illustrated on Dresden page 74 includes eclipse signs. As discussed in the previous chapter, there were three lunar patrons and one of these was One Ixim, the Classic period parallel of Lady Blood's husband. A recently discovered mural at Xultun also shows a lunar table that illustrates the three lunar patrons (Saturno et al. 2012).

The moon was not the only celestial body whose synodic period concerned the Maya. The Dresden Codex also contains a Venus table that refers to five synodic periods of Venus (the Greater Venus Cycle) (Thompson 1972). Each period is divided into four phases (morning star, disappearance, evening star, and disappearance), and the table gives the patron deity for each of these phases. In total, there were 20 Venus patron deities. Although some of these patrons are obscure, many are well-known deities such as One Ajaw and the Moon Goddess. As discussed in the previous chapter, these Venus tables indicate that the first appearance of the morning star was thought to have occurred on the date 1 Ajaw.

PATRON GODS OF THE *K'ATUN* PERIOD

Like the celestial cycles and other calendrical periods, each *k'atun* in the greater 13-*k'atun* cycle had a patron deity who was worshipped during his term in office. The seventeenth-century priest Andrés de Avendaño y Loyola noted that each *k'atun* "had its separate idol and its priest with a separate prophecy of its events" (Avendaño 1987:39). Regrettably he did not individually name these deities. Landa also mentioned the *k'atun* patron gods, but failed to name them as well. He stated that an idol representing the *k'atun* patron god was worshiped intensely in the temple during the first ten *tuns* of his reign and then less so for the remaining ten *tuns* (Tozzer 1941). Although his explanation is somewhat unclear, Landa stated that a second idol representing the patron deity for the following *k'atun* period was placed beside the idol of the reigning patron. The implication appears to be that this future patron deity was placed there to learn his role from the reigning patron deity. This is similar to the junior assistant who shadows the senior ritual specialist, and in doing so learns the correct procedures and duties. It is also similar to the young heirs who learn the duties of the king in preparation for their future role.

Although very badly eroded and incomplete, pages 2–11 of the Paris Codex illustrate *k'atun* ceremonies performed by the deities (Love 1994). Each page is divided into three registers. The middle register illustrates two deities. The most intact example of the right deity is found on page 3, which illustrates a 13 Ajaw *k'atun* Period Ending. The position of his legs suggests that he is in the act of just sitting down or in the act of rising or leaning forward. The deity is situated on a structure decorated with two stacked crocodiles. The upper crocodile has his feet tied to his body by a cord. This is a common method used to safely transport crocodiles that have been captured. War captives are frequently depicted in a similar way. The lower crocodile has a sky band for a body. The Maya envisioned the Milky Way to be a celestial river with a crocodile swimming in it, and the lower crocodile represents this celestial pathway (Bassie-Sweet 2008:37–38). The seated deity faces towards a standing deity. This deity holds a K'awil head in his hands and appears to extend it to the enthroned deity. Whether this head is an idol or a headdress is unclear. A bird representing the omen of the *k'atun* hovers above (Love 1996). On Paris page 4, the omen bird is the Itzamnaaj bird. At the foot of the standing deity is a bowl of tamales. Such food offerings for deities are also found in the Dresden Codex Wayeb ceremonies. If the standing deities in the Paris Codex *k'atun* pages represent the patron gods of the *k'atun*, then these include Itzamnaaj, K'awil, and the Vulture God.

A scaffold throne similar to one in the Paris Codex is found on Classic-period monuments such as Piedras Negras Stela 11 and demonstrates a degree of continuity between the Classic and Postclassic traditions (Hellmuth 1987). This stela, which illustrates the *k'atun* ending 9.15.0.0.0 4 Ajaw 13 Yax, illustrates Piedras Negras Ruler 4 sitting cross-legged on a scaffold throne while holding a bag decorated with the *tzolk'in* date of 4 Ajaw (Bassie-Sweet 1991:50, Stuart and Graham 2003:57). The Itzamnaaj bird with his diagnostic double-headed serpent perches on the sky band above him. Beneath Ruler 4, the scaffold is decorated with two crocodiles. The upper beast is a bound and headless crocodile while the lower one is the Milky Way Crocodile. At the base of the scaffold is a human sacrifice. A heart with a sacrificial knife embedded in it protrudes from the abdominal cavity of the victim. The sacrifice of captives is a well-documented Period Ending act.

Although many Period Ending scenes focus solely on the actions of the king, a number of monuments also illustrate his ritual assistants. On the sides of Piedras Negras Stela 11, three secondary lords are shown flanking the king. The second lord on the left side, who stands below the Period Ending text, is named by the caption text adjacent to him as a *ti'sakhuun*, an oracular priest and spokesman for the ruler (Zender 2004b:324). As discussed in chapter 1, a Late Classic period vessel shows some of the secondary deities who inhabited the celestial court of Itzamnaaj (Boot 2008). These deities wear the same headdresses as the secondary lords who populate the court of human rulers, indicating that Itzamnaaj's court was a model for the ruler's court.

Regrettably, Classic period texts appear to make no direct references to the patron gods of the *k'atuns*. The specific verbs used to describe the events that occurred on various Period Endings most commonly refer to actions involving the stone used to commemorate the *k'atun* (Stuart 1996). These verbs refer to the *k'al tun* "binding of the stone" and its placement, which is characterized as chum "seating" or ts'ap "thrusting into the ground" (Grube 1990; Nahm and Stuart cited in Schele and Mathews 1998:382; Stuart 1996). One assumes these acts were the climax of the festival. *K'atun* stones can take the form of upright stones or altars (Stuart 1996). Some illustrations of Period Ending stones and altars appear to be tied with strips of material, and Stuart has suggested that the binding of the stone involved literally wrapping it in cloth. These wrappings are similar to the manner in which Maya lords were wrapped for burial, such as is illustrated on K6547. In this scene, the deceased lord is shown laid out on stone bier, and his body is wrapped in strips of knotted cloth. The implication appears to be that the stone representing the end of the period is treated like a deceased person.

Unlike the terse statements in the texts, the illustrations of Period Ending events present a rich picture of these proceedings. Rulers are depicted making offerings or holding a variety of objects. These include GII scepters or ceremonial bars that frequently have deities materializing from them. These emerging deities may represent the patron gods of the *k'atun*. Alternatively, rulers are often pictured in Period Ending scenes in the guise of certain deities. It is possible that these are the patron deities of the *k'atun*.

THE MYTHOLOGICAL PERIOD ENDING EVENT OF 4 AJAW 8 KUMK'U

The ancient era event was the last *k'atun* ending of the previous era. Although numerous inscriptions refer to the era event and the actions conducted by certain deities on this Period Ending, most of these references give limited information (Freidel et al. 1993; Freidel and MacLeod 2000; Looper 2003; Carrasco 2005; Callaway 2011; Stuart 2011). Some facts can be gleaned from the calendar itself. As noted above, each *tzolk'in* day was ruled by a number god and day name god. In the case of the date 4 Ajaw, the number god is the deity K'inich Ajaw (the sun god) and the day lord is the deity One Ajaw. The patron for the month Kumk'u is a zoomorphic creature whose name has not been deciphered yet and little can be said about him. The Yearbearer in power on 4 Ajaw 8 Kumk'u was Ben.

Although most of the era-event notations are succinct, some passages expand on the details. Several texts indicate that one of the activities carried out on 4 Ajaw 8 K'umku was the changing or renewal of three primordial hearthstones (Freidel and MacLeod 2000; Carrasco 2005). The Quiriguá Stela C text states that the three hearthstones were specifically set up by the Paddler Gods, a deity with an undeciphered name and Itzamnaaj, respectively. When traditional Maya build a new home, the building is prepared for occupancy by a series of ritual actions including the positioning of the three-hearthstone fireplace. The house is ritually defined and made into a safe space by a procession around its quadrilateral perimeter with offerings being made at each of the corner posts and at the center. So whose fireplace (and by extension household) was set up or renewed on 4 Ajaw 8 Kumk'u?

According to the Popol Vuh narrative, the three Heart of Sky thunderbolt gods and the Heart of Earth creator grandparents (who were the embodiment of complementary opposition) wanted to make beings who would worship them (Christenson 2003a:78). Their first act was to make a place for humans to live. They made the earth rise up from the waters of the Place of Duality and established its quadrilateral nature. The first household on the surface of the earth was that of the creator grandparents and their offspring (Bassie-Sweet 2008:64–67). In Maya worldview, the quadrilateral world is metaphorically referred to as a house. The household of the creator deities was the quintessential home and role model for these metaphors. The creator deities' household represented the Place of Duality, which was the ideal state of existence in Mesoamerica. Every time the Maya created a house or a community they were replicating the Place of Duality. It seems reasonable to conclude that the primordial fireplace of the 4 Ajaw 8 Kumk'u Period Ending was that of the creator deities. Humans replicated the mythological actions of the deities in their historical Period Ending ceremonies. When the ruler renewed the creator deities' house during the Period Ending ceremonies, he was also renewing his community as a safe place to live and renewing the larger world as well.

On Quiriguá Stela C, the act of setting the hearthstones was said to be "under the authority" of the lord or lords of the location Six Sky. As discussed in chapter 1, *Six Sky* is one of the names for Itzamnaaj's celestial court (Boot 2008). It is hard to know whether this statement refers specifically to Itzamnaaj or to his entire court.

Although never mentioned on public monuments, 4 Ajaw 8 Kumk'u events that occurred at the cave home of God L are featured on two pottery vessels (K2796 and K7750). In contrast to the celestial court of the paternal grandfather Itzamnaaj, the maternal grandfather God L sits within his Underworld cave enclosure in these two scenes. Two tiers of deities are seated before him. K2796 features eight deities while K7750 depicts ten. The role of God L and these deities in the 4 Ajaw 8 Kumk'u event is unclear. The main text on both vessels is parallel, and it lists what Stuart believes are six categories of deities that were put into order on this date. Two of these names (sky gods and earth gods) appear to form a couplet. The phrase "sky gods and earth gods" also appears in lists of god names in historical Period Ending texts such as the 9.0.10.0.0 Period Ending on Tikal Stela 31.

PERIODS OF 900 DAYS

There is evidence that the Maya performed rituals at the end of every *tun* period within a *k'atun*, but that emphasis was placed on the endings of fifth *tun* (1,800th day), tenth *tun* (3,600th day), and fifteenth *tun* (5,400th day), in addition to the all-important twentieth *tun* (7,200th day). As noted by Stuart (2005a), there is also evidence that the Maya celebrated every 900th day of a *k'atun*. Eight such events would happen within a *k'atun* at 900 days, 1,800 days, 2,700 days, 3,600 days, 4,500 days, 5,400 days, 6,300 days, and 7,200 days. As can be seen from this calculation, four of those dates fall on *tun* endings. At Palenque, the intermediate 900-day Period Endings were celebrated by junior members of the court.

THE NARRATIVE TIME FRAME

Most Maya monumental texts include a series of events that form a narrative. Like any great literature, Maya narratives move both forward and backward in time. After the initial date and event of the narrative, a change in the time frame can be indicated by a new Calendar Round date and/or a convention nicknamed Distance Numbers. A Distance Number is simply a notation that gives the amount of time between two dates. It is given in the order of *k'ins*, *winals*, *tuns*, *k'atuns*, and *bak'tuns*. In some cases, a Distance Number notation is preceded by a glyph which has been nicknamed the Distance Number Introductory Glyph (DNIG). As discussed in chapter 1, the DNIG can include complementary opposite pairings (Hopkins 1996, Hull 1997, 2003; Knowlton 2002; Stuart 2003a). The DNIG appears to function as a way of highlighting a particular event (see the following chapter).

When a narrative introduces a time-frame change without the use of a Distance Number, the Long Count position of the new Calendar Round date is the next occurrence of that Calendar Round date unless some other information intervenes. An example of this is found on the three lintels of Structure 33 at Yaxchilán that form a continuous narrative. This story is related to events in the life of the ruler Bird Jaguar and begins on Lintel 1 with the statement that on 11 Ajaw 8 Tzek Bird Jaguar performed a dance (Grube 1992; Looper 2009:35). He is illustrated holding a scepter in the form of the deity GII (figure 3.1). As we know from other monuments, 11 Ajaw 8 Tzek was the day of Bird Jaguar's accession, but the Lintel 1 text refers only to his dancing. His wife stands adjacent to him, clutching a bundle. She is specifically named (at J1–J3) as "the mother of Shield Jaguar." Bird Jaguar's son was Shield Jaguar IV, who on this date would have been only three months old (note that here Shield Jaguar IV is given his royal name, taken from his grandfather, although he is referred to by his pre-accession name Chel Te' on the next lintel in the narrative). On the second lintel (Lintel 2), the time frame of the story moves forward five *tuns* to 4 Ajaw 3 Sootz' (9.16.6.0.0), and states that five *tuns* of his lordship had finished on this date. In addition to changing the time frame of the story, this statement alerts the reader to the fact that the preceding dance was part of Bird Jaguar's accession ceremonies. On Lintel 2, Bird Jaguar is again illustrated dancing, but in this dance he holds a bird scepter and is accompanied by his now five-year old son, Chel Te', who also wields a bird scepter (figure 3.2). On the third lintel, Lintel 3, the time frame of the narrative backs up one *tun* to 8 Ajaw 8 Sootz' (9.16.5.0.0), and the image shows Bird Jaguar and his *sajal* (a subordinate lord) performing yet another GII dance (figure 3.3).

FIGURE 3.1. *Yaxchilán Lintel 1, after Ian Graham.*

The narrative on the Structure 33 lintels does not contain a Long Count notation to place the Calendar Round dates in linear time nor does it include Distance Numbers leading from one date to the next. The scribe employed a more subtle reference by using a Supplementary Glyph G with the Calendar Round dates on Lintel 1 and Lintel 3. Simply because of the mathematics, a specific Calendar Round date can only occur with the same Glyph G once every 468 years. Hence, the use of a Glyph G in the date indirectly establishes the appropriate Long Count position.

VARIATION

As we have noted, the manners in which the Classic Maya could represent a syllable or word are quite varied, and this variation is used to infuse another layer

FIGURE 3.2. *Yaxchilán Lintel 2, after Ian Graham.*

of meaning into the text. The literal meaning of the variants (say, an abstract glyph or its personified head variant) may be the same, but their unread nature can carry subtle meanings to the reader that are surely not unintended. In the same fashion, the dates and events presented on two monuments may be the same, but their manners of presentation may give quite different slants on history. Furthermore, the most prescribed set of facts—the elements of a date or the titles of a lord—could be arranged in such a way as to give the recitation of the information a literary structure that expressed its importance.

A comparison of Bird Jaguar's nominal phrases on the Structure 33 lintels illustrates the variation in style and format that the artists employed. On Lintel 1, Bird Jaguar's personal name (glyph A5) is followed by the title "he of 20 captives," three couplets referring to additional titles, and the title West Kaloomte' (figure 3.1). The poetic structure of his nominal phrase is A-BB-CC-DD-A (see the chart on the lintels of Structure 33 below). It opens with "he of 20 captives" (theme A, at A6), followed by the first couplet, theme B (A7–B9), which states he was "the captor of Aj Uk" and "the captor of Jeweled Skull." Each of these constructions is a possessive phrase that begins with the

102   THE CALENDAR AND THE NARRATIVE TIME FRAME

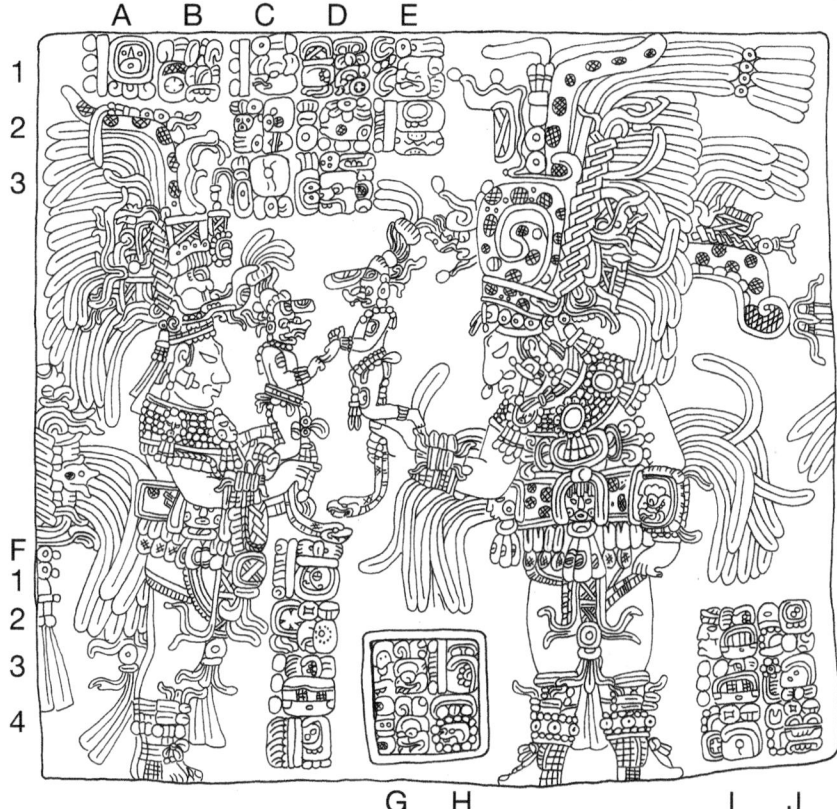

FIGURE 3.3. *Yaxchilán Lintel 3, after Ian Graham.*

pronoun *u* "his." In the first captor title, the pronoun "his" is represented by a head variant that takes the form of a skull, while the second title uses the standard abstract T1 *u* sign. This variation does not change the pronunciation or the function of the pronoun.

The second couplet, theme C (A10–C10), is formed by the paired titles "3 *k'atun* [?]" and "3 *k'atun Yajaw Te'*." (The first of these titles is undeciphered and the meaning of the second one is opaque.) The number three in both cases is represented by the wind god, who was the god of the number three. Again, the use of a head variant does not alter the pronunciation of the word. The third couplet, theme D (H9-I9), is composed of another paired set of titles known as Emblem Glyphs. While most sites have only one emblem glyph, both Yaxchilán and Palenque have two. The first Yaxchilán emblem glyph has not been deciphered, but appears to represent an earflare. The second is *Pa'chan*, "split sky"

THE CALENDAR AND THE NARRATIVE TIME FRAME 103

(Martin 2004). Each Emblem Glyph includes the phrase "holy lord." The *k'u* (or *ch'u*) "holy" sign consists of liquid (drops) juxtaposed with various other signs. In the first *k'u* sign, the liquid falls onto a shell sign, while in the second the liquid falls onto a *k'an* "yellow, precious" sign. The shell and *k'an* cross elements of the *k'u* sign do not affect the pronunciation of the title, but they visually emphasize its sacred nature (the droplets represent sacrificial substances in images of ceremonial activity). The West Kaloomte' title is found at H1–I2.

On Lintel 2, Bird Jaguar's nominal phrase is less elaborate: two of the couplets are reduced to single titles (figure 3.2). His personal name (at glyph M) is followed by the titles "he of 20 captives" (theme A, glyph N) and "the captor of Aj Uk" (theme B, O1–O2), and "three *k'atun ajaw*" (theme C, O3). The Emblem Glyph couplet, theme D, follows: "holy lord of [earflare]" (O4), "holy lord of Pa'chan" (glyph P), and the nominal phrases end with theme A, the title *Bakab* "ruler" at glyph Q.

Bird Jaguar's nominal phrases on Lintel 3 return to the poetic format of Lintel 1, but with a twist (figure 3.3). His name (E1) is followed by theme A, "he of 20 captives" (E2), and proceeds to the theme B couplet "the captor of Aj Uk" (G1–H1), "the captor of Jeweled Skull" (G2–H2). This is followed by the theme C couplet, "3 *k'atun ajaw*" (I1–J1), "3 *k'atun ch'ajom*" (I2–J2). The first occurrence of the number three is expressed as a head variant, while the second is represented by the standard three dots. The last couplet, theme D (I3–J3) is composed of the paired Emblem Glyphs of Yaxchilán. In the first *k'u* "holy" sign, the liquid falls onto the *k'an* cross; in the second, it falls from the shell sign. In the vast majority of examples of the *k'u* sign, the liquid falls from the variable element, which suggests that the placement of the element below the liquid was a deliberate attempt to create variation within the couplet itself.

Bird Jaguar's nominal phrases on the lintels of Structure 33:

Lintel 1	Lintel 2	Lintel 3
Bird Jaguar,	Bird Jaguar,	Bird Jaguar,
A¹: he of 20 captives	A¹: he of 20 captives	A¹: he of 20 captives
B¹: captor of Aj Uk	B¹: captor of Aj Uk	B¹: captor of Aj Uk
B²: captor of Jeweled Skull	B²:—	B²: captor of Jeweled Skull
C¹: 3 *k'atun yajawte'*	C¹: 3 *k'atun* lord	C¹: 3 *k'atun* lord
C²: 3 *k'atun* lord	C²:—	C²: 3 *k'atun ch'ajom*
D¹: Emblem Glyph 1	D¹: Emblem Glyph 1	D¹: Emblem Glyph 1
D²: Emblem Glyph 2	D²: Emblem Glyph 2	D²: Emblem Glyph 2
A²: West *kaloomte'*	A²: *bakab* (ruler)	A²:—

An alternative analysis of the structure of these phrases might link Bird Jaguar's name and the unchanging appellation "he of 20 captives" as a unit and match it as a framing element with the last term or couplet in each nominal phrase. The frames would then read:

Bird Jaguar, he of 20 captives, West Kaloomte'.

Bird Jaguar, he of 20 captives, *Bakab*.

Bird Jaguar, he of 20 captives, Lord of Yaxchilán.

Similar variations of presentations are found on the three "tablets" (*tableros*, i.e., wall panels) found in the Palenque Cross Group that form a continuous narrative (Bassie-Sweet 1991:201–210) (see chapter 8 for further discussion). Their overall structures are parallel, but the presentation of their contents varies. Each of the main texts of the three Cross Group wall panels is composed in a slightly different format. For instance, each presents its initial calendrical information in a different order (see the chart of calendrical notations of the Cross Group, below).

All three tablets begin in deep time with the birth of mythological beings. The initial date of the main text on the Tablet of the Cross (figure 8.5) lists, in order, the Long Count notation 12.19.13.4.0 (A1–B7) (December 7, 3121 BC), the *tzolk'in* date (8 Ajaw, A8–B8), the *haab* date (18 Tzek, A9–B9), the complete Supplementary Series (glyphs G/F, "Lord of the Night" [A10] and the Lunar Series [B10–A13]), and then the 819-day count Distance Number (B13), the 819-day count event (A14–B15), and the 819-day count Calendar Round (A16–B16). This is followed by the Initial Series event verb, the birth of Muwan Mat (A17–C1). The narrative then continues with a series of mythogical and historical events joined together by Distance Numbers.

The main text of the Tablet of the Sun (figure 8.6) begins with the Long Count of 1.18.5.3.6 (A1–B7) (October 25, 2360 BC) and is followed by the *tzolk'in* date (13 Kimi, A8–B8), the combined glyphs G/F of the Supplementary Series (A9), the *haab* date (19 Keh, B9), and then the Lunar Series (A10–B12). The 819-day count information follows in the format of the Tablet of the Cross, with the Distance Number, the event, and the Calendar Round date of the count (A13–A16). The following event, the birth of the deity GIII, is preceded by an introductory glyph (B16) that places emphasis on his birth (Josserand 1991:22). Like the Tablet of the Cross, the narrative then continues with a series of mythological events before turning to historical actions.

The main text of the Tablet of the Foliated Cross (figure 8.7) returns to the format of the Cross tablet and gives, in order, the Long Count 1.18.5.4.0 (A1–B7)

(November 8, 2360 BC), *tzolk'in* date (1 Ajaw, A8–B8), *haab* date (13 Mak, A9), and the complete Supplementary Series (G/F at B9, Lunar Series at A10–A12). But then, there follows, in order, the 819-day count Distance Number (B12–A13), Calendar Round (B13–A14), and event (B14–B15). The following event, the birth of the deity GII, is preceded by the notation "the third time" (A16), again a device for emphasizing the event. The narrative moves from this birth to the mythological Period Ending of Muwan Mat and then to historical actions.

Calendrical notations on the panels of the Cross Group (CR, Calendar Round; DN, Distance Number) can be summarized as follows:

Temple of the Cross	Temple of the Sun	Temple of the Foliated Cross
Long Count	Long Count	Long Count
tzolk'in date	*tzolk'in* date	*tzolk'in* date
haab date	G/F	*haab* date
G/F	*haab* date	G/F
Lunar Series	Lunar Series	Lunar Series
819-day count DN	819-day count DN	819-day count DN
819-day count event	819-day count event	819-day count CR
819-day count CR	819-day count CR	819-day count event
birth of Muwan Mat	then: birth of GIII	3rd time: birth of GII

The style of glyphs on each tablet is also varied. As noted, the ISIG has a reference to the patron deity of the *haab* embedded in it. The patron god of the ISIG on the Tablet of the Cross and Tablet of the Foliated Cross is expressed using logograms, while that on the Tablet of the Sun is a head variant. The numerical coefficients of the Long Count, *tzolk'in*, and *haab* on the Tablet of the Cross employ head variants that add to the formality of the date. The same dates are found on the balustrades (*alfardas*), where the numbers are recorded in bars and dots. On the Tablet of the Sun, the numerical coefficients and Long Count–period glyphs corresponding to the deity GIII's birth are presented as head variants, as is the numerical coefficient of the *tzolk'in* date (but not that of the *haab*). Likewise, while the Long Count of the Tablet of the Foliated Cross again uses head variants for the numerical coefficients and period glyphs, only the *tzolk'in* date, not the *haab*, uses head variants. The 1 Ajaw birth date of the deity GII employs the portrait of the deity One Ixim for the number 1 and the deity One Ajaw's portrait for the word *ajaw*. These head variants are not just fancy writing. Rather, the use of One Ajaw's portrait brings visual emphasis to this date. The artist was likely drawing attention to the fact that the deity GII was born on the same *tzolk'in* date as One Ajaw.

SUMMARY

The patron deities for the various time periods and astronomical synodic periods indicate the close affiliation and direct influence the deities were thought to have in the everyday life of the Maya. There were patron deities for each month, year, *k'atun* cycle, lunar half-year, and Venus phase in addition to the number gods and day lords of the *tzolk'in* cycle. In fact, there was a dizzying array of deities that were in power at any given moment. This situation highlights an essential purpose of the Maya calendar systems, which was to monitor these many deities and make proper offerings and petitions to them at the appropriate time. Obviously, the calendar specialists in charge of these supernatural intercessions had enormous influence and power over the actions of the community. In Classic period art, the ruler and his secondary lords are depicted performing priestly functions during these periodic festivals. Landa's description of the *k'atun*, Wayeb, and New Year festivals of the Postclassic period indicates that the priests took front and center roles during these events.

The formal narratives found on Classic period monuments frequently feature a Period Ending event and such events are most often the initial date of the story. These dates certainly function to anchor the various Calendar Round dates of the narrative into the time frame of the Long Count, and thus linear time, but the elaboration of these initial Period Ending dates through the use of the Supplementary Series, full-figure glyphs, and so on places great emphasis on the Period Ending event itself, and by extension, the deities that these Period Ending events honored. The hundreds of examples of Period Ending events documented in monumental art speak to how these ceremonies reinforced the power, status, and prestige of the elite. The *k'atun* ceremonies continued to be performed in the Postclassic period, and the Classic period emphasis on the role of the king in the *k'atun* cycle is still evident in these later ceremonies. For example, Roys (1933:192) noted that at the beginning of each *k'atun*, young lords underwent a ritual examination by the ruler to ascertain whether they had the qualifications to be rulers themselves.

NOTES

1. In highland Guatemala where the *tzolk'in* calendar and divination system are still in use, there are numbered locations in the community landscape where the ritual specialists go to make offerings on specific calendar dates (Tedlock 1992:71). Numbered place names also occur in Classic period inscriptions. It is possible that the number in a location refers to a relationship between the number deity and the location. There is also some evidence that the Maya considered the sky and Underworld to

be layered, and that some numbered mythological locations refer to such layers. These concepts may not be mutually exclusive.

2. A notation nicknamed the 819-day count also appears in a small number of texts (Berlin and Kelley 1961). The count relates to the progression of GII-God K (K'awiil) through four directional quadrants, and records how long ago, for a given Long Count date, GII entered a particular quadrant, and the Calendar Round date of that entry. Progression through each quadrant takes 819 (13 × 9 × 7) days. The significance of this information is unknown.

4

The Literary Nature of Mayan Texts, Ancient and Modern

This chapter contrasts traditional and innovative approaches to the analysis and understanding of Maya literature, both Classic and contemporary, and suggests a new direction for Maya epigraphy. Epigraphic and linguistic fields of study have undergone paradigm shifts over the span of their history. The concepts of paradigm and paradigm shift were developed to characterize progress in scientific research (Kuhn 1962), and they are applicable here. The first paradigm in Maya epigraphy—throughout the nineteenth and early twentieth centuries—accomplished the identification and classification of the graphic variants of hieroglyphic writing. With rare exceptions, no meanings were assigned to the glyphs, although potential meanings were discussed at length (e.g., Barthel 1967).[1] In the terms of semiotics, the study of signs and sign systems (Morris 1946), this approach would be called *syntax*, the study of signs apart from their meanings (a sense distinct from that given the term in linguistic research). By the middle of the twentieth century, most hieroglyphs could be recognized and classified into variable categories, only some of which were known to have specific meanings (other than those in the domains of calendrics and mathematics). The situation at this point was similar to having discovered a large trove of ancient historical texts, but being able to read only the dates. Time periods that corresponded to external systems, such as astronomy, could be accounted for, but nothing more.

DOI: 10.5876/9781607327424.c004

The shift to the second paradigm of Maya epigraphy began with the seminal works of Tatiana Proskouriakoff, Heinrich Berlin, and Yuri Knorosov, and in semiotic terms can be called *semantics*, the study of what the signs and their combinations mean. Proskouriakoff (1960, 1963, 1964) deciphered the hieroglyphs for birth, accession, and death, identified royal names, both male and female, and discussed the structure of sentences, demonstrating the presence of history in the inscriptions. Berlin (1959, 1963) added to this history, and Knorosov (1958, 1967, 1982) provided the key to deciphering phonetic writing. Identified hieroglyphs could now be "read" and their combinations translated, so that the historical content of the inscriptions could be extracted and the nature of the language being written could be subjected to analysis. An early manual for this sort of research was published by David Kelley (1976), who introduced the "structural method" that became the standard methodology for decipherment. Dozens of articles detailing the history of individual sites followed.

Kelley pleaded with linguists for more information on the Mayan languages and their earlier forms, but this information was not yet available. However, beginning in the late 1960s, progress was made in the linguistics of Mayan languages, ultimately including Epigraphic Maya, the hypothetical language of the hieroglyphs. Descriptive structural linguistics predominated until the late twentieth century, with the production of grammars and dictionaries of languages in all branches of the Mayan family (see McQuown 1967 for a mid-century summary of work in Mesoamerica, and Hopkins and Josserand 1994 for a later summary of work in Mayan). Historical linguistics classified the languages and sketched their prehistory, with seminal works by Terrence Kaufman (1964, 1976, 1978) and J. Kathryn Josserand (1975). A more theoretical approach replaced structuralism in the latter part of the twentieth century, and articles in linguistics journals regularly treat Mayan languages, but have little relevance for epigraphy. With regard to Epigraphic Maya, the somewhat contentious state of the art is exemplified by the papers in Søren Wichmann's *The Linguistics of Maya Writing* (2004a; see also the review by Hopkins 2006b).

It is here proposed that it is time for a third paradigm in Maya epigraphy, one that corresponds to the semiotic category of *pragmatics*, the study of the uses of a sign system. The analogy of such a shift in linguistics would be a shift from historical and theoretical linguistics to sociolinguistics—that is, from language to the social uses of language. Now that we can read most inscriptions in a semblance of their original language—and extract their historical content—we should now turn to investigating just how scribes manipulated the variables of written text in order to achieve social ends. Such an approach would bring Classic Maya writing into its deserved position among the world's literatures. The Classic Maya were not only great astronomers and mathematicians, iconographers and architects, but they were skilled writers as well, and it is high time their literary arts were appreciated.

CATEGORIES OF SPEECH

It has long been known that Mayan societies have a keen interest in and understanding of the difference between genres of speech. Gary Gossen (1974a), in his study of the Tzotzil of San Juan Chamula, revealed a folk taxonomy of the kinds of speech (*k'op*), ranging from the least structured, conversation, to the most structured, prayer, or, as the Tzotzil saw it, speech styles from the least to the most "heated," or sacred, with language games and formal oratory as intermediate categories:

I. *Lo'il K'op*, ordinary or conversational language

II. *K'op Sventa Xk'ixnah Yo'nton*, language for people with heated hearts
    k'op sventa tahimol h'olol, children's improvised games
    k'ehoh sventa h'olol, children's improvised songs
    sk'op h'opisyal, oratory for cargoholders
    k'op sventa kavilto, court language
    k'op sventa chopol kirsano, emotional or bad language

III. *Puru K'op*, pure words, oral tradition
    a. *'ach' k'op*, recent words
        batz'i 'ach' k'op, true recent narrative
        'ach' lo'il, recent talk
        chubah lo'il, crazy talk
        'ixtol k'op, frivolous language
        hut k'op, lies, untrue prose jokes
        batz'i 'ixtol lo'il, truly frivolous talk, verbal dueling
        mukul k'op, baba k'op, buried or superficial language
        k'ehel k'op, obscure words, proverbs
        hak'om k'op, hidden words, riddles
        tahimol, traditional games
        sventa muk'ta kirsano, adult games
        sventa h'olol, children's games
    b. *"antivo k'op*, ancient words
        batz'i 'antivo k'op, true ancient narrative

sventa ba'yel banamil, First Creation narratives
sventa xcha'lomal banamil, Second Creation narratives
sventa yoxibal banamil, Third Creation narratives
k'op ta xak' riox, language for rendering holy
sventa bisob satik, for measuring the face, crossing oneself
sventa xich' Ho' h'olol, for baptism
sventa nupunel, for marriage
sventa muklumal, for burial
sventa kirsano, for laymen
sventa h'abtel xchi'uk h'ilol, for cargoholders and shamans
resal, prayer
sventa kirsano, for laymen
sventa 'anima, for the dead
sventa h'abtel, for cargoholders
sventa h'ilol, for shamans
sventa pale, for the priest
sventa chopol kirsano, for evil people (Protestants, witches, etc.)
k'ehoh, song
sventa yahval h'ch'uleletik, for the patron of our souls
sventa htotiketike, for the saints

The essential element of structure that gives speech its "heat" (the metaphor for holiness) is the *couplet*, parallel lines that differ minimally. The use of couplets marks a text as formal speech, something greater than ordinary conversation. The opening segment of a Ch'ol Maya prayer (Vásquez 2001) exemplifies a highly structured text. Prayers consist almost entirely of couplets; they also employ metaphorical language: "I come before your hands, I come before your feet," means "I come into your presence." Couplets (AA, BB, CC, etc.) can be manipulated to form more complex structures such as *alternating couplets*, ABAB, or *nested couplets*, ABBA; they can be extended to *triplets*, AAA, and so on. These manipulations give a Mayan text its literary quality, its "heat," its holiness:

A	*Wäle, Kyum Jesucristo*	Now, My Lord Jesus Christ,
A	*ksanto tyaty*	my Holy Father,
A	*kselestial tyaty*	my Celestial Father,
B	*la'me kpasel tyi yeb'al 'awok*	I come beneath your feet,
B	*tyi yeb'al 'ak'äb'.*	beneath your hands.
A	*Wäle, Kyum,*	Now, My Lord,

A	wäle kmilagroso tyaty,	now, my Miraculous Father,
B	wä tyi 'iyeb'al 'awok,	here beneath your feet,
B	wä tyi 'iyeb'al 'ak'äb	here beneath your hands.
A	Wäle, Señor,	Now, Lord,
C	tyi tyäliyoñ 'wä' tyi 'iyeb'al 'awok,	I came here beneath your feet,
C	tyi tyäliyoñ jk'atyiñ beñtyixoñ yik'oty gracia.	I came to ask for blessing and grace.

These same markers of formality are found in modern Maya narrative, where they tend to occur most frequently around peak events in a narrative. In a Ch'ol story about the Lightning God, Chajk (also known as *Lak Mam*, Our Grandfather), some fishermen come upon Chajk straddling a branch that hangs out over the water, his foot caught by some "water animal." Chajk sends the fishermen to his house to fetch his hat and shirt, without which he cannot throw lightning. On their return, he puts on his clothes and blasts the animal with a lightning bolt, the peak event of the narrative of Lak Mam (Arcos Alvarez, Alvaro López, and Cruz Guzmán 2016:69–76):

A	*Che jale 'ora,*	And then,
A	*k'iñlaw 'ab'i,*	crashing!, they say,
A	*ñup'law 'ab'i,*	flashing!, they say,
B	*Tza' tyojmi jiñ Chajki,*	Lightning struck,
C	*b'a tzi ñijka 'ib'ä jiñ Lak Mami*	when he shook himself.
C	*Tza' jach 'i ñijka 'ib'ä,*	He just shook himself
B	*tza' tyojmi jiñ Chajki*	and Lightning struck.
D	*Tza' tyiki jiñ ja'.*	The water dried up.
D	*Tza' säjp'i jiñ ja',*	The water went down,
D	*ma che' ku 'añix ja'.*	there wasn't any water.
A	*K'iñlaw,*	Crashing,
A	*ñup'law 'ab'i 'añ.*	flashing, they say it was.
E	*'Añ 'i chäñil ja',*	That water animal,
E	*tza' chämi.*	it died.

The peak event is framed by the expressions of noise and flashing, *k'iñlaw, ñup'law* (AA . . . AA). The event itself is expressed in a nested couplet or chiasmic structure, BCCB. The results of the thrown lightning are related in a triplet, DDD. Following the closing frame, the action of throwing the lightning is contrasted to its other result, the death of the offending animal (E).

POETRY IN A MODERN MAYA TEXT

With this introduction, let us proceed to the presentation of a modern Maya text and show how it has been handled in the past, and how we would suggest handling it in the future. The text in question is the Lacandón Maya "Song of the Jaguar," recorded by the missionary couple Philip and Mary Baer and published in Mexico in 1948. As published in the Mexican journal *Tlalocan*, the text is as follows (Baer and Baer 1948:376):

> 1. *jujuntsit in jitik in wok.* 2. *jujuntsit in jitik in k'äb* 3. *tan u pek in nej* 4. *tin wu'uyaj u tar a k'ay ch'iknach* 5. *netak in wenen* 6. *tin kästaj u pachtäkih che?* 7. *oken tin wenen yokor jenen che?* 8. *tu yek'er in nok' tu yek'er in k'äb* 9. *tu yek'er in shikin.*

Following the presentation of the text in Lacandón, the Baers added an analysis in the form of a literal translation:

> 1. Each I lift-up my back-feet 2. Each I lift-up my front-feet 3. Continually it moves my tail 4. I heard it come your voice very-far 5. Very-almost I sleep 6. I looked-for its back-fell tree 7. Went-I I slept on fallen tree 8. Its stripes my hide its stripes my front-feet 9. Its stripes my ears.

They then finished with a free translation:

> I pick up each of my feet and let them fall on the trail. My tail moves. I heard your voice come from a distance. I am sleepy. I searched for a fallen tree to go to sleep. I went to sleep on the fallen tree. My hide and feet and ears are striped.

A modern linguistic treatment would present the text in a multiline format, with a line for the original text, an abstract morpheme-by-morpheme analysis, a line of grammatical identification of the morphemes, phrase structure, and a literal and free translation. For example, the analysis of the first line of the Lacandón text:

Jujun tsit 'in jitik 'in wok.	Transcription
ju-jun tsit 'in-jit-ik-ø 'in(w)-'ok.	Underlying morphemes
rep-num-numcl 1A-VTR-trans-obj 1A-n	Morphological analysis
AdvPhrase + Subject-VTR-Object + Object	Syntactic analysis
one-one step I-move-it my-foot	Literal translation
Step by step I move my feet.	Free translation

Each of these analyses contributes to the understanding of the text, in the sense that we know what has happened in the narrative. A jaguar, moving his feet and twitching his tail, has heard a song coming from a distance, gotten sleepy, and gone to sleep on a log.

Now, however, let us consider the structure of the text and see if that adds any meaning to it. There are parallel lines, alternating themes, and tripletted phrases. If we format the Lacandon *Song of the Jaguar* in such a way as to show that structure, the text appears as in the following table (Hopkins 2008):

A	*Jujun tsit in jitik in wok.*	Step by step I move my feet.
A	*Jujun tsit in jitik in k'äb'.*	Step by step I move my paws.
B	*Tan 'u pek 'in nej.*	My tail is twitching.
C	*Tin wu'uyaj 'u tar 'a k'ay ch'iknach.*	I heard your song come from afar.
D	*Netak in wenen.*	I'm getting sleepy.
C	*Tin käxtaj u pachtäkih che'.*	I look for a fallen log to sleep on.
D	*'Oken tin wenen yokor jenen che'.*	I'm going to sleep on the fallen log.
E	*Tu yek'er 'in nok'.*	My hide is spotted.
E	*Tu yek'er 'in k'äb'.*	My paws are spotted.
E	*Tu yek'er 'in xikin.*	My ears are spotted.

Now we can appreciate that this Lacandón song is a magical formula for putting stalking jaguars to sleep. In the first stanza (with a structure of a couplet versus a singlet, AAB) the jaguar is stalking the human. The rhythm of the language imitates the steady footsteps of the stalking animal, pausing only to twitch his tail. In the second stanza (alternating couplets, CDCD) the jaguar hears the song, gets sleepy, looks for a log, and goes to sleep. The text alternates between hearing the song and responding to it (C . . . C) and the onset of sleepiness (D . . . D). In the final stanza (a triplet, EEE), the jaguar is dreaming, and the repetitive structure corresponds to the snores of the sleeping animal. If you haven't seen it before, welcome to Maya poetry.

The point of this exercise is that for all the analytic effort put into recognizing the parts of speech and classifying them—a worthy and necessary enterprise for some kinds of work—there is still much to be learned by looking at the structure of the text itself. These patterns cannot be accidental. They represent deliberate manipulation of the language in order to achieve an effect.

NARRATIVE STRUCTURE OF MODERN TEXTS

Apart from the elaborations around peak events, there are many more elements of structure in narrative texts. In the Ch'ol repertory, for example

(Josserand 2016: 15–31), a traditional folktale (as opposed to a recent narrative) begins with an "evidentiality statement," telling the listener(s) where and from whom the narrator learned the story (Altman 1996). A revered ancient tale will be attributed to the ancestors: "a long time ago, our ancestors used to tell this story" (or a much more elaborated introduction). The evidentiality statement and the formal closing that ends the tale ("That's the way that ended") constitute a framework that delimits the beginning and the end of the narrative. Other Mayan languages employ similar framing devices (e.g., Hofling 2012:404–405).

The body of the narrative begins with the establishment of background, the physical setting of the story, its chronological era, and so on., and introduces some of the main characters. This scene-setting is composed in non-completive verbal aspect (e.g., incompletive aspect, the equivalent of Spanish imperfect, an ongoing action) and may be glossed "they used to do such-and-such" or "so-and-so used to do that." Background information is commonly marked with the reportative particle *'ab'i*, glossed "they say," emphasizing the fact that the storyteller is reporting events he or she did not personally witness: "the time came, they say, that there were fishermen, they say. Three fishermen."

Once the scene is set, the event line begins with the first use of a completive verbal aspect (the equivalent of English past tense or Spanish preterit): "they saw Lak Mam, straddling a branch." Subsequent events that are part of the narrative line are told in completive forms. Occasional side remarks, in non-completive forms, may add necessary context. Events are not necessarily related in chronological order. One mechanism for signalling a new event is a break in the timeline, a backstep in time. Another is the use of introductory phrases like "and then," or "ah, but no!" These markers break up the narrative into paragraph-like sections, and within a section (or episode) there is a constant topic, the person whose identity may be suppressed once it has been established. That is, there are rules for participant tracking, for identifying the subject referred to by an ambiguous pronoun (Josserand 1995).

The peak event of a narrative is marked by the use of what Robert Longacre (1985) referred to, in an essay on Mesoamerican narratives, as "the zone of turbulence surrounding the peak." This may be an increased use of couplets and their manipulations, unusual syntax, the suppression of normally accessible information, and other devices. The peak event of the Lightning God story, above, exemplifies this "turbulence." Alfonso Lacadena (2012), discussing hieroglyphic texts in terms of literary analysis, classifies extreme examples of turbulence as a kind of *hyperbaton* (syntactic inversion) called *sychysis*, "alternation of the order . . . carried to the extreme to produce syntactic obfuscation" (2012:46), which "forces greater engagement and thought on the part of the reader" (2012:47).

Following the peak event, in a modern Ch'ol narrative, there is a denouement that takes the form of a repetition of critical events in the preceding narrative. In jaguar transformation tales (Josserand et al. 2003), following a harrowing series of events that culminates in the peak event, the tension breaks, and the fortunately surviving protagonist is discovered by others and asked to explain to them what has happened. A woman who has spent the night in a tree fighting off a climbing jaguar is, when the jaguar departs at dawn, approached by neighboring villagers and asked, "What was all that noise we heard last night?" She then relates the series of events that brought her to her current state. This retelling of the story is also the place where listeners can chime in and show they were paying attention by relating some of the events themselves. It also offers an opportunity for the expression of the moral of the story: "That's why you don't travel late at night."

When the audience has exhausted its interventions, the storyteller closes the narration with a traditional ending: *Che' tza' 'ujtyi b'ajche jiñi.* "That's the way that ended."

The point of this rather extensive discussion of narrative texts is to emphasize that there are norms for how a narrative should be told. The genre of narratives is a kind of formal speech, and speakers are judged by how well they attend to the traditional norms. These norms are not set in stone; a good storyteller plays with them as well as he or she plays with the elements of the event line. But they are the standard against which storytellers are judged, and we have witnessed novice storytellers being put in their place by the audience when they ignored the rules—starting, for example, with the event line, without an evidentiality statement or sufficient background information (see the story *The Jaguar Man*, in Hopkins and Josserand 2016:129–138).

A detailed analysis of a number of contemporary Ch'ol folktales has been published as part of the volume *Chol (Mayan) Folktales* (Hopkins and Josserand 2016). While the model applied to these texts was developed from observation of the performances of contemporary storytellers, there are striking parallels in the Classic period texts recorded in hieroglyphics. These issues were discussed by Kathryn Josserand in workshops as early as 1984 (Josserand 1991:31), in a brief article in 1990 (Hopkins and Josserand 1990), and in an extensive article published in 1991 (Josserand 1991, followed by a Spanish translation in 1997). More recently, narrative analysis was combined with text and image analysis in a study of the Palace Tablet of Palenque (Bassie-Sweet et al. 2012), and applied to the Temple of the Inscriptions sarcophagus text as well (Hopkins and Josserand 2012).

Here, rather than repeat these analyses, we will reexamine the Sarcophagus Rim inscription with a focus on its poetic structure, and contrast this treatment with earlier epigraphic analyses, in a manner parallel to the discussion of the modern oral text, the Lacandón *Song of the Jaguar*, above. The point of this exercise is that looking at the literary structure of the song gives a far greater understanding of the intent of the author—the pragmatics—than the simple listing of its content. We will argue that the same is true for Classic texts, and that this is what we need to base the next paradigm of Maya epigraphy on. In this endeavor, we can draw on the literary structures of modern Maya texts for inspiration, because they employ many of the same rhetorical devices we can detect in the Classic inscriptions.

THE SARCOPHAGUS LID TEXT OF THE PALENQUE TEMPLE OF THE INSCRIPTIONS

The Temple of the Inscriptions sarcophagus is composed of a block of stone set on six support legs and a stone lid. The top of the lid features a portrait of K'inich Janaab Pakal I framed by a sky band that includes portraits of three secondary lords (figure 7.1). The four sides of the lid are carved with a continuous text of 71 glyph blocks. The sides of the box are decorated with portraits of four Early Classic Palenque rulers as well as a female and two males. As is discussed in chapter 7, these latter figures are the mother, father, and maternal grandfather of K'inich Janaab Pakal I.

Merle Greene Robertson's drawing of the lid text constitutes a transcription of the text (Robertson 1985:258). As drawn, the text began on the south side and proceeded around the east and north sides, ending on the west side. This order responded to the fact that the south side of the sarcophagus faces viewers as they complete the descent down through a flight of stairs inside the pyramid of the Temple of the Inscriptions to peer into the chamber where the sarcophagus lies. For many years this was thought to be the proper reading order of the inscription, but as we see below, this was in fact incorrect.

The drawing of the inscription constitutes a transcription of the text, parallel to the transcription of the Lacandón oral text discussed above. Operations parallel to the kinds of analysis practiced on the Lacandón text are the conventional next steps in an epigraphic study. The first step is to identify the hieroglyphs in terms of the entries in Thompson's *Catalog* and later modifications to the numbering system. William Ringle and Thom Smith-Stark published such an analysis in *A Concordance to the Inscriptions of Palenque, Chiapas, Mexico* (1996:104–105). Following Ringle and Smith-Stark, the first nine glyphs of the south-side text, for example, are identified and partially glossed as follows (commas separate the transcriptions of each glyph block, colons and periods represent the relative placement of glyphic elements: above, below, to the side, etc.):

VIII.500a[533a], XIII.551:130, 740.88.(181a:125a)E,
8 Ajaw 13 Pop from birth
VI.500a[527], XI.16:528, IV.1c:(644+528)M:116,
6 Etz'nab 11 Yax 4-his-seating-of-*tun* (*chan u chum tun*)
679aA.207b:585a, 184.(583a:932)M, 36j.168:747a?.
i och bi to death *kina* Shield *Pacal ch'ul Ajaw* holy lord.

In recent years, it has become popular to render the text in Epigraphic Maya, a hypothetical construct of the language spoken during the Classic period by the authors of the texts. Stuart and Stuart (2008:178) present the following transcription of the glyphs just classified, along with a literal translation to English:

Waxak Ajaw Uxlajunte' K'anjalaw [Pop] Sihyaj
(On) Eight Ajaw the Thirteenth of K'anjalaw he is born.

Wak Etz'nab Buluchte' Yaxsihoom Chan-u-chumtuun
Six Etz'nab the Eleventh of Yaxsihoom [Yax] Four are the stone-seatings,

i-ochbih K'inich Janab Pakal, K'uhul Ajaw.
then K'inich Janab Pakal, the Divine Lord, entered the path.

An alternative approach would subject the Epigraphic Maya to the same kinds of morphological and syntactic analysis practiced on the Lacandón text. An approximation of such an analysis is shown in the following analysis of the south-side text:

Transcription: *waxak Ajaw ux-lajun-te' K'anjalaw sihy-aj-ø*
Morphology: num dayname num-numcl monthname VTR-pas-B3
Syntax: AdvPhrase (calendric) VTR-passive-Subject
Gloss: 8 Ajaw 13 K'anjalaw [Pop] was-born-he

wak Etz'nab buluch-te' Yaxsihoom chan u-chum-tun
num dayname num-numcl-monthname num-ø A3-VPO-n
AdvPhrase (calendric) num-Subj Poss-NP
6 Etz'nab 11 Yax[sihoom] four-were his-stone seatings

i och-bih-ø K'inich Janab Pakal k'uhul ajaw
conj VIN-n-B3 n n n (name) adj-n
Conj VINphrase SubjectPhrase
and then [was] the road-entering [of] K'inich Janab Pakal, Divine Lord.

However, none of these detailed treatments of the inscription pays any attention whatsoever to the overall structure of the text, and it is our contention that such attention is necessary if we are more fully to understand the intentions of the authors. In fact, considering its structure in the light of the structure of contemporary oral texts, Kathryn Josserand (1989, 1991) pointed out that the text did not begin on its south side, as assumed by everyone who had dealt with it up until then, but on the east side (as Stuart and Stuart, following Josserand, present the text). It follows Maya ritual order, in imitation of the movements of the sun. The text begins on the east side (where the sun rises), moves to the north (where the sun is at zenith), then to the west (where the sun sets), and concludes on the south (where the sun passes through the Underworld). In modern Maya rituals the next movement is to the center. An example is the *Hoye K'u* (Five Day) ceremonies of the Chuj in San Mateo Ixtatán, corresponding to the ancient period of the Wayeb (Hopkins 2012b:108). After circumambulating San Mateo to perform rituals at the crosses marking the four sides of the town on the first four days, celebrants proceed to the church, in the center of the town, for the fifth-day ceremonies. By that analogy, the final move here should be to the scene on the top surface of the sarcophagus lid, where K'inich Janaab Pakal I is, in fact, shown in after-death experience.

Josserand's reanalysis cleared up a number of troublesome questions, which is what an appropriate analysis is supposed to do. Particularly problematic were a series of glyphs at the end of the south side and another series at the beginning of the east side. The translation of these adjacent segments of text remains a problem, as suggested by Stuart and Stuart's (2008:178) translation: [east side] "The burden of the maize (god) formed (so?) . . . [south side] The ancestors of the ? Great Serpent arrange it, they oversee it."

Likewise, there was confusion about how to interpret the end of the west side, the supposed end of the text. The death dates of a royal couple were followed immediately by a parentage statement naming them as parents, but no name was given for the child (although the logical person was K'inich Janaab Pakal I, named in the supposed opening segments of the adjacent text on the south side). In fact, Stephen Houston (1997:302) used this apparent disconnect to argue that texts were not always readable as they stood, but needed to be interpreted by knowledgeable readers: "The connection to speech becomes opaque, for the reader would have to know in advance whether a particular pronoun referred to a name appearing some 44 glyph blocks earlier. Such features indicate that oral interpretation was sometimes necessary to reduce ambiguity in written text."

A proper analysis transformed these problems into literary devices. Like modern Chol narratives the text is framed by a formal opening and a formal closing, the problematic glyphs on the east and south sides. Within the text, various events are emphasized through the use of couplets and other elaborations, including inserting one event inside another. A major break in the text is signaled by a backstep in time, a frequent device marking major sections of a hieroglyphic text as well as contemporary narratives. The peak event, the death of K'inich Janaab Pakal I, is signaled by moving a phrase that normally would follow his name to the first of the sentence (fronting) and marking the death verb with a special emphatic conjunction. Without entering into issues of just how to transcribe the text in Epigraphic Mayan, let us look at the inscription on the slides of the sarcophagus lid in terms of an English gloss of its language. The following analysis reveals the two themes of the text: the death of rulers and the Period Endings some of them celebrated (implied Long Count dates are in brackets). The content of the inscription is historical, but its presentation is both narrative and poetic:

East

—	Opening phrase.
[9.4.10.4.17]	On 5 Kaban 5 Mak died Ahkal Mo' Nahb I.
[9.6.11.0.16]	On 7 Kib 4 K'ayab died K'an Joy Chitam I.
[9.6.16.10.7]	On 9 Manik 5 Yaxk'in died Ahkal Mo' Nahb II.
[9.7.0.0.0]	On 7 Ajaw 3 K'ank'in was the Period Ending of Kan Bahlam I.
[9.7.9.5.5]	On 11 Chikchan 3 K'ayab died Kan Bahlam I, holy Palenque lord.
[9.8.11.6.12]	On 2 Eb *ti' haab* Keh died Lady Yohl Ik'nal.

North

[9.8.19.4.6]	On 2 Kimi 14 Mol died Ajen Yohl Mat, holy Palenque lord.

West

[9.8.18.14.11]	On 3 Chuwen 4 Wayeb died Janaab Pakal, holy Palenque lord.
—	On 4 Chikchan
[9.10.0.0.0]	On 1 Ajaw 8 K'ayab was the Period Ending of Sak K'uk',

[9.10.7.13.5]	13 Yax died Sak K'uk'.	
[9.10.10.1.6]	On 13 Kimi 4 Pax died K'an Mo' Hix, holy Palenque lord.	
—	The son of K'an Mo' Hix and Lady Sak K'uk'	
South		
[9.8.9.13.0]	on 8 Ajaw 13 Pop was born	
[9.12.11.5.18]	On 6 Etz'nab 11 Yax, 4 his Period Endings, and then died K'inich Janaab Pakal I, holy lord of lords.	
—	Closing phrase.	

Note that two ancestors (Kan Bahlam I and Lady Sak K'uk') are marked as having celebrated Period Endings. Kan Bahlam I was likely the maternal great-grandfather of K'inich Janaab Pakal I and the namesake of K'inich Janaab Pakal I's son (Bassie-Sweet 1991:206). He is also the first ruler in the lid inscription to be named with an Emblem Glyph, "Holy Lord of Palenque." K'inich Janaab Pakal I's grandfather and namesake (Janaab Pakal) and father (K'an Mo' Hix) also have Emblem Glyphs.

Lady Sak K'uk' was K'inich Janaab Pakal I's mother. A special flourish that emphasizes her importance is the insertion of her Period Ending date inside her death date. This composition is a nested couplet:

4 Chikchan (1 Ajaw 8 K'ayab was the Period Ending of Sak K'uk') 13 Yax died Lady Sak K'uk'.

In the death phrase of K'inich Janaab Pakal I, it is noted that he lived through four Period Endings (9.9.0.0.0–9.12.0.0.0), likely more Period Endings than any of the other subjects in the sarcophagus lid narrative. The first flourish that marks his death as the peak event of the text is the fronting of his parentage statement, normally found after the protagonist's name. The second and third flourishes are the notation of his birth (unique on this monument) and his age (in the form of counting Period Endings), and the prefixed emphatic conjunction *i* on the death verb, the equivalent of "and then."

The child of K'an Mo' Hix, the child of Lady Sak K'uk', on 8 Ajaw 13 Pop was born. On 6 Etz'nab 11 Yax, four were his Period Endings, and then died K'inich Janaab Pakal I, holy lord of lords.

The narrative of the sarcophagus lid text can be analyzed using its poetic structure (Bassie-Sweet 2013b). The structure of three deaths, a Period Ending, and a death (AAABA) is followed by another three deaths, a Period Ending, and a death (AAABA). These form a larger couplet structure which could be called *parallel stanzas*. A third stanza is formed by the death of K'inich Janaab Pakal I's father, the birth of K'inich Janaab Pakal I, his Period Endings, and his death (ACBA):

Stanza 1	A	Death (Ahkal Mo' Nahb I)
	A	Death (K'an Joy Chitam I)
	A	Death (Ahkal Mo' Nahb II)
	B	Period Ending (Kan Bahlam I)
	A	Death (Kan Bahlam I)
Stanza 2	A	Death (Lady Yohl Ik'nal)
	A	Death (Ajen Yohl Mat)
	A	Death (Janaab Pakal)
	B	Period Ending (Sak K'uk')
	A	Death (Sak K'uk')
Stanza 3	A	Death (K'an Mo' Hix)
	C	Birth (K'inich Janaab Pakal I)
	B	Period Endings (K'inich Janaab Pakal I)
	A	Death (K'inich Janaab Pakal I)

In addition, the sarcophagus text can also be divided into three episodes by backsteps in time from 9.8.19.4.6 to 9.8.18.14.11 (at the turn from the north to the west side), and from 9.10.10.1.6 to 9.8.9.13.0 (at the turn from the west to the south side). The first episode relates the deaths of ancestors, the second the deaths of K'inich Janaab Pakal I's namesake and parents, and the final episode the death of K'inich Janaab Pakal I. These structures are implicit in the text itself, not imposed by the analyst. The episodes are delimited by the chronological backsteps in time. The episode peak events are marked by elaboration (the addition of Period Ending dates and Emblem Glyphs), and the peak event of the text is multiply marked (fronting of the parentage statement, addition of Period Endings and the Emblem Glyph, and the use of the emphatic conjunction).

Such structures are not unique to Maya texts. While these particular examples are not mentioned, Alfonso Lacadena (2012), citing other Classic texts, notes that in the field of literary analysis, some of these rhetorical devices have been called *hyperbaton* (permutation of constituents, alteration of normal syntactical order for effect). The first kind of hyperbaton, *anastrophe* (inversion), AB to BA, includes what linguists have called simply "fronting" (Josserand

1991:19–20), the displacement to the beginning of a syntactic structure of some element, for purposes of emphasis. The fronting of K'inich Janaab Pakal I's parentage statement is an example: "K'inich Janaab Pakal I, the child of Lady Sak K'uk' and K'an Mo' Hix" has become "the child of Lady Sak K'uk' and K'an Mo' Hix . . . K'inich Janaab Pakal I." Note that this passage also employs the technique that Josserand (1991:19–20) called *promotion*, the elevation in syntactic class of an element. Thus, the parentage statement, normally an appositive attached to a noun ("K'inich Janaab Pakal I, the child of Lady Sak K'uk'"), has been promoted to the subject of a sentence: "the child of Lady Sak K'uk', the child of K'an Mo' Hix, was born."

Simple fronting abounds in Classic Maya texts (Josserand and Hopkins 1991:281–284). The normal, or unmarked, sentence order is verb-subject-temporal. But in historical texts, where the date of the event is emphasized, the order becomes temporal-verb-subject. This construction is so common in Classic texts (as above) that it is not usually considered to be a form of fronting, but work with modern speakers shows that initial temporal is not an unmarked syntactic order (Cruz Guzmán 1986; Pérez Martínez 1987).

Hyperbaton proper involves the insertion into a sequence of a new element: AB to A<X>B. The insertion of Lady Sak K'uk's Period Ending into her death statement is an example: "On 4 Chikchan (1 Ajaw 8 K'ayab was the Period Ending of Sak K'uk') 13 Yax, died Sak K'uk'." This and the fronting of the parentage statement might also be considered to be the third type of hyperbaton, *sychysis*, "alternation of the order of the constituents carried to the extreme to produce obfuscation . . . [which] forces greater engagement and thought on the part of the reader" (Lacadena 2012:46–47). This unusual order certainly did produce obfuscation, and only greater engagement and thought on the part of readers resolved the issue.

This analysis of the text has a point. While the historical paradigm extracts from the text all the dates, events, and protagonists, it does little else. It does not treat the relative weight given to events and people by the scribal program. There is more to the inscription than its historical content. Only if we look at the way the information is presented to us can we appreciate that the scribes are doing much more than listing historical events. They are *narrating* history with a *rhetorical* strategy, in a *poetic* format. The manipulations of the text cannot be unintended. They are part of the meaning of the inscription, and they can be used to infer the intentions of their creators. A *pragmatic* analysis adds much to the historical analysis. Beyond the epigraphic analysis and decipherment of the text there is still more to be learned from the relationship between the text and image.

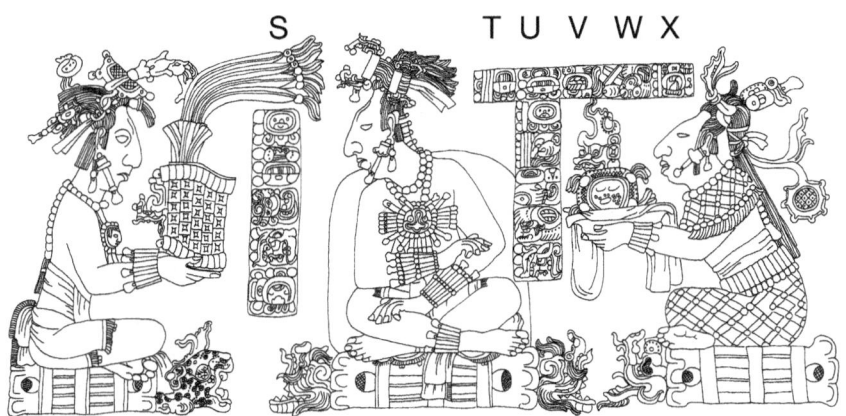

FIGURE 4.1. *Palenque Palace Tablet, scene, after Schele.*

THE PALENQUE PALACE TABLET OF HOUSE A-D

In a longer text there are still more devices that can be discerned. Here the parallels with modern oral texts are with the structure of narrative texts rather than with poetry. Thus, we should expect to find opening and closing frames, internal sections featuring common topics, delimited by specific devices, and peak events marked by some sort of turbulence (elaboration, syntactic alterations, etc.). In addition, if the text is accompanied by images, there should be notable associations between elements of the images and elements of the text (see chapter 5 for further discussion of this topic). A good example of a monument with a narrative text of moderate length is the Palace Tablet of Palenque that was housed in House A-D of the Palace (Robertson 1985:259–284) (figures 4.1, 4.2).

The Palace Tablet is a monumental wall panel that features a main text in the shape of an H. There is a scene in the upper space of the H and a blank space in the lower section. It has been suggested that the blank space (65 cm × 81 cm) had a small bench positioned below it (Robertson 1985:54). The Palace Tablet relates events in the life of K'inich K'an Joy Chitam II, who was a son of K'inich Janaab Pakal I and his wife, Lady Tz'akbu Ajaw. In the events that predate K'inich K'an Joy Chitam II's accession, he receives a pre-accession name composed of the number three, an undeciphered logogram, and the name *Mat*. The logogram is composed of an axe and earth glyph that was, at one time, thought to be read as *ch'akan*. We retain this name as Ux [Ch'akan] Mat in order to avoid the rather cumbersome form of Ux-?-Mat. In the Palace Tablet scene, Ux [Ch'akan] Mat is flanked by his father, K'inich

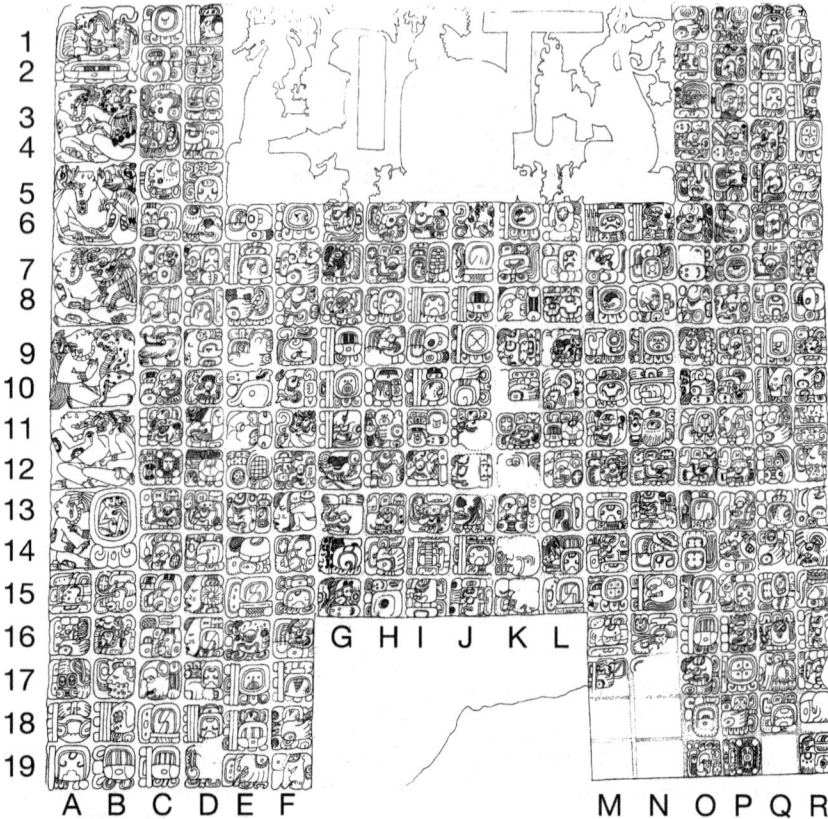

FIGURE 4.2. *Palenque Palace Tablet, main text, drawing by Linda Schele, courtesy of David Schele.*

Janaab Pakal I, and his mother, Lady Tz'akbu Ajaw. K'inich Janaab Pakal I hands his son a "drum major" headdress while his mother extends a bowl containing a flint-and-shield icon (*tok'-pakal*). The headdress was first given this nickname because it resembled the headdress of a drum major in a marching band (Schele 1976). In the caption text of the Palace Tablet, the headdress is named Ux Yop Huun (literally, "three-leaf headdress"), and the climax of the story at the end of the main text is the dedication of House A-D and the statement that this house belonged to the Ux Yop Huun (Bassie-Sweet 2008:227–228). It is likely that this headdress was not only kept in House A-D but that it was displayed on the small bench in front of the Palace Tablet. The platform of Temple XIX illustrates the Ux Yop Huun belonging to K'inich

Ahkal Mo' Nahb III (the ruler who succeeded K'inich K'an Joy Chitam II), and it shows this headdress sitting on a stand (figure 5.22). Such a storage and display method would protect the long feathers of the headdress.

The Palace Tablet caption text, which begins the narrative of the monument, is strategically placed within the scene (figure 4.1). The first event is the birth of the Ux Yop Huun in AD 598 (9.8.4.10.0 1 Ajaw 3 Wayeb), followed by the acquisition of this heirloom object by Ux [Ch'akan] Mat some 56 years later when he was nine years old (9.11.1.13.0 8 Ajaw 18 Xul) (Bassie-Sweet et al. 2012). The feathers of the headdress arch over the birth text, which is positioned between K'inich Janaab Pakal I and his son. The section of the caption text that refers to the acquisition of the headdress begins in the last glyph block in this column of text and ends in the text behind his back. This second unit of caption text overlaps the back of the throne on which Ux [Ch'akan] Mat is sitting. To read the caption text, the viewer is first taken between the action of K'inich Janaab Pakal I handing his son this headdress and then diagonally across the body of Ux [Ch'akan] Mat. While the caption text does not directly reference the *tok'-pakal* object offered by Lady Tz'akbu Ajaw, the *tok'-pakal* icon touches the right block text. It is apparent that Ux [Ch'akan] Mat will next receive this object from his mother. These two actions in the scene form a sequential, visual couplet. The framing of an action with a caption text is a well-known convention used in Maya art to identify such things as when, who, and what is being portrayed (Bassie-Sweet 1991) (see chapter 5 for further examples of this framing convention).

Stuart (2008, 2012b) has published a different interpretation of this scene. Before proceeding to a discussion of the main text, a slight digression is in order to address his arguments. Contrary to Stuart's statement that our identification of Ux Yop Huun as the name of the drum major headdress is based "in large part on the meaning of *huun* as 'headband' and on the supposed presence of a Jester God image on the front of the headdress itself," it is the framing convention that is the basis of our interpretation. Stuart claims that the caption text has no direct relationship to the actions in the scene and cannot be assigned a Long Count date, and that the Ux Yop Huun is either the personal name of the "jester god" and/or the name of a Preclassic hero-king. He ignores the framing convention and concludes that the scene illustrates the accession of K'inich K'an Joy Chitam II, which is featured in the main text. Stuart dismisses our identification for the following reasons:

1. Headdresses that are similar in shape to the drum major headdress are named in other texts as *ko'haw* "helmet," not *huun* "headdress/headband."

2. No Maya inscription elsewhere is known to refer to the birth of an object or costume element.
3. Houses (proto-Mayan *7atyooty or *7atyuuty) can only be owned by people or gods, living or deceased, not objects.

As Stuart himself noted, Three Yop Huun refers to a headdress on Tikal Stela 4:

> Stela 4 of Tikal may hold a very important reference to Ux Yop Huun in its inscription, where the glyph seems integral to a verbal expression for royal accession (Figure 13). This phrase is an elaboration on the standard *k'al huun* accession phrase—perhaps the earliest one known, in fact—and is used to record the crowning of the important Tikal ruler Nuun Yax Ahiin (the "Curl Nose" of earlier literature). In the initial **K'AL** verb glyph, in place of the usual simple **HUUN** or **SAK-HUUN** above the **K'AL** hand, we instead find a "foliated ajaw" glyph preceded by three dots. The "three" prefix with the leaves strengthens the equivalence to the Ux Yop Huun name, and the context establishes the key fact that this name refers directly to the headband or headdress that is "fastened" upon the new king. Ux Yop Huun here appears to serve as a label of a ritual paper crown. (Stuart 2012b:128)

Given that the four portraits of Nuun Yax Ahiin illustrate him in Teotihuacán-inspired attire, and not traditional Maya royal attire, it is clear that the Ux Yop Huun refers to a different office than that of the royal office of *sak huun*. This is plainly demonstrated on the Palenque Temple XIX platform, where the ruler K'inich Ahkal Mo' Nahb III is pictured with both the *sak huun* headband and the drum major headdress (figure 5.22).

Despite Stuart's statement that he doubted the word *huun* "was ever extended to include the sort of headdress held by Pakal in the scene" (Stuart 2012b:127), the Tablet of the Slaves illustrates K'inich Ahkal Mo' Nahb III receiving the drum major headdress, and the adjacent text refers to it as a *huun* "headdress" of K'inich Ahkal Mo' Nahb III (Bassie-Sweet et al. 2008:208–209) (figure 5.23). The glyphs representing K'inich Ahkal Mo' Nahb III's name overlap the feathers of the headdress, which, in turn, touch K'inich Ahkal Mo's Nahb III's shoulder (Wald 1997). Again, such conventions are used to indicate which of the main events of a text is illustrated. Additionally, the illustration of K'inich Ahkal Mo' Nahb III's drum major headdress on the Temple XIX platform includes an avian *huun* god positioned on top of it.

Furthermore, very little is known about how the Maya categorized their many different kinds of headdresses (Zender 2004b). On Piedras Negras Panel 2, a number of individuals wear helmet-like headdresses that include

Tlaloc elements (Martin and Grube 2008:143–144). It is believed that such helmets originally derived from Teotihuacán shell headdresses that arrived in the Maya region during the Early Classic period (Stone 1989). In the Panel 2 hieroglyphic text, these helmets are referenced by either a logogram of the basic helmet or a phonetic substitution that presents the word *ko'haw* (Schele, Mathews, and Lounsbury 1990). Although such a word has not survived in any of the Cholan Mayan languages, a cognate of this word (*kovov tak'in*) referring to a Spanish military helmet is found in a colonial Tzotzil dictionary (Laughlin 1988:615; Macri and Looper 2003:290). The narrative on the Temple of the Inscriptions middle tablet lists the accoutrements of the three Palenque thunderbolt gods, including their *ko'haw* headdresses (Macri 1988; Schele, Mathews and Lounsbury 1990:3–4). The name of the deity GI's *ko'haw* headdress is a logogram representing his Quadripartite Badge headdress, which he is seen wearing in numerous contexts (Hellmuth 1987). This headdress does not have the shape of a shell helmet. In other words, a *ko'haw* headdress does not necessarily take the form of the helmet headdress. Furthermore, the specific name of the deity GIII's *ko'haw* headdress includes the name *huun*. Hence, the fact that the drum major headdress has the form of a helmet-like headdress does not negate the fact that it could also have been referred to as a *huun*.

Stuart's second point is that there are no other examples where the creation of an object is couched in terms of a birth. It is true that the other texts that refer to objects and structures only refer to their dedication rituals, but absence of evidence is not evidence of absence. There is abundant proof that the Maya considered ritual objects and buildings to be spiritually alive. It is also well documented that the Maya thought that headdresses could embody ancestors and deities, and that humans could don such headdresses and become that personality (Houston and Stuart 1998). Given that these objects were thought to be alive, it is not impossible that the Maya would metaphorically refer to the creation of a headdress as its birth. In fact, it would be surprising if they didn't.

Last, the dictionaries of relevant Mayan languages provide ample evidence that the term derived from proto-Mayan **7atyooty* or **7atyuuty* (Kaufman 2003:947) is regularly used to refer to diverse containers, not just the houses of people and deities. In the Aulie and Aulie (1998:87) dictionary of Ch'ol, for example, the entry "*otot* . . . casa" lists the phrase *otot xux* "panal de avispa" (beehive) and the derivative *i yotlel ixim* "troje" (corn granary). The historical dictionary of Ch'ol (Hopkins and Josserand 2011) lists more such phrases: *yotot chab'* "beehive," *yotot machit* "machete scabbard," and *'otot 'ixim* "granary" (the latter two examples from a 1935 source), and *yotot joläl,* "cap" (literally, "container for the head," from a 1789 Ch'ol source). Further afield, in the Mayan language Chuj (Hopkins 2012b; Felipe Diego 1998), the reflex of proto-Mayan **7atyuuty* does not primarily refer to "houses" but is glossed "*vaina; lugar para guardar cosas; casa habitual*" ("scabbard; place to keep things; habitual residence"; Felipe Diego 1998:274, citing *yatut machit* "machete scabbard" as a sample usage).

Stuart himself cites examples from Classic period texts of the term *otoot* used for "owners" other than people and gods:

> Oddly enough, "house" is a fairly common label on ceramic vessels and containers of various types. Several so-called "poison bottles" are also described as "houses" in their hieroglyphic tags. For example, a small "codex style" flask bears the inscription *y-otoot u-may Ahk Mo'*. "It is the 'house' of the tobacco of Ahk Mo." We also find "house" used on plates, cylindrical vases and lided [sic] cache vessels . . . Contrary to some other interpretations, the "house" here must refer to the vessel, and not to the building in which it was deposited. (Stuart 2005d:132)

A reasonable interpretation of the evidence is that the term derived from proto-Mayan **7atyooty* or **7atyuuty* refers to containers for various objects, including—but not limited to—people. It is perhaps best understood as "residence, the place where people and things reside." Therefore, the statement that House A-D was owned by Ux Yop Huun does not provide any proof that Ux Yop Huun was not a headdress.

We now examine the narrative structure of the main text of the Palace Tablet. The following is a timeline of the events of the Palace Tablet:

Timeline of Caption Text	
9.8.4.11.0 1 Ajaw 3 Wayeb	birth Ux Yop Huun
9.11.1.13.0 8 Ajaw 18 Xul	tying Ux Yop Huun
Timeline of Main Text (backstep in time)	
9.10.11.17.0 11 Ajaw 8 Mak	birth Ux [Ch'akan] Mat
9.10.18.17.19 2 Kawak 12 Keh	first bloodletting Ux [Ch'akan] Mat
9.11.0.0.0 12 Ajaw 8 Keh	Period Ending of K'inich Janaab Pakal I
9.11.13.0.0 12 Ajaw 3 Ch'en	rope event Ux [Ch'akan] Mat
9.12.11.5.18 6 Etz'nab 11 Yax	death K'inich Janaab Pakal I
9.12.11.12.10 8 Ok 3 K'ayab	accession K'inich Kan Bahlam II
—	seating Ux [Ch'akan] Mat as *bah ch'ok*
9.13.10.1.5 6 Chikchan 3 Pop	death [K'inich Kan Bahlam II]

Backstep in time	
9.13.10.0.0 7 Ajaw 3 Kumk'u	Period Ending of K'inich Kan Bahlam II
9.13.10.1.5 6 Chikchan 3 Pop	burial K'inich Kan Bahlam II
9.13.10.6.8 5 Lamat 6 Xul	accession K'inich K'an Joy Chitam II
Backstep in time	
9.9.2.4.8 5 Lamat 1 Mol	accession K'inich Janaab Pakal I
9.13.10.6.8 5 Lamat 6 Xul	accession K'inich K'an Joy Chitam II
9.14.8.14.15 9 Men 3 Yax	dedication of Ux Yop Huun's house

Again, there are several ways to analyze this narrative. As the timeline indicates, there are three backsteps in time that can be used to divide the narrative into four episodes. The caption texts of the scene form the first episode of the narrative. The first backstep occurs when the narrative moves from Ux [Ch'akan] Mat's receiving the Ux Yop Hunn at age nine to the Initial Series date of the main text, which features his birth. This Initial Series date includes the Supplementary Series and 819-day count, and is elaborated through the use of elegant full-figure glyphs. Ux [Ch'akan] Mat's nominal phrase includes parentage statements naming him as the child of K'inich Janaab Pakal I and his wife, Lady Tz'akbu Ajaw. The narrative then moves from his birth to his first bloodletting, when he was seven years old, performed in the company of a series of gods including the three thunderbolt deities GI, GII, and GIII. From the bloodletting event, the story proceeds to the first Period Ending event (9.11.0.0.0) in the life of the young Ux [Ch'akan] Mat that occurred a year later. The text merely states that his father K'inich Janaab Pakal I made offerings on this date. It is known from the Temple of the Inscriptions narrative that the 9.11.0.0.0 event was an elaborate affair in which K'inich Janaab Pakal I adorned and honored GI, GII, and GIII.

The Palace Tablet narrative then moves to the 9.11.13.0.0 Period Ending event in which Ux [Ch'akan] Mat performed a ritual action involving a rope, and again the text indicates the ritual involved the three thunderbolt deities GI, GII, and GIII. From this Period Ending ceremony, the time frame moves forward 18 years to the death of K'inich Janaab Pakal I. Included in this death statement is K'inich Janaab Pakal I's title as a four-*k'atun* Kaloomte'. While *Kaloomte'* is most often characterized as a title of a supreme ruler, there is evidence that it specifically refers to a high priest of the war god Tlaloc (Bassie-Sweet and Hopkins 2014:142–143).

The next sentence restates K'inich Janaab Pakal I's death, but in this case it refers to the death as something that happened to his *sak huun* headdress of rulership. Regretfully, the glyph in question has not been deciphered. The timeline moves from the death of K'inich Janaab Pakal I to the accession four months later of his eldest son K'inich Kan Bahlam II, who is named as the *suku-winik ch'ok* "older brother" (Stuart 1997:5). On this occasion, K'inich Kan Bahlam II was 48 while his brother Ux [Ch'akan] Mat was 39. While K'inich Kan Bahlam II was the older brother, he also took on the role of One Ajaw when he became king, and One Ajaw was the eldest brother of the Hero Twins set.

The next passage in the narrative refers to a second event that occurred on the occasion of K'inich Kan Bahlam II's accession. This was the seating of Ux [Ch'akan] Mat as the *bah ch'ok* "first youth" heir-apparent designation. Ux [Ch'akan] Mat is named as the *itz'in winik* "younger brother." Again, this may refer not only to his role as the younger brother of the ruling king, but as the king's junior partner, just as Yax Bolon was the junior partner to his older brother, One Ajaw. The story then moves forward 18 years and refers to a death on 9.13.10.1.5 without naming the subject.

In summary, this second section of the narrative deals with events in the pre-accession life of Ux [Ch'akan] Mat (his birth, his first bloodletting, the first major Period Ending in his life, his first minor Period Ending, the death of his father, the accession of his brother, and his own designation as heir apparent, and a death). The reader can anticipate that the story is about to explain who died, and, in fact, that is what it does. However, it does so by stepping back in time to the last Period Ending event in the life of K'inich Kan Bahlam II (9.13.10.0.0), and then restates the 9.13.10.1.5 event as the burial of K'inich Kan Bahlam II. This backstep in time begins the third episode of the story, but it also forms a couplet with the previous mention of the death.

After relating the burial of K'inich Kan Bahlam II, the story restates the death date and then tells of the accession of Ux [Ch'akan] Mat and gives his royal name as K'inich K'an Joy Chitam II. The restated death uses the same undeciphered death reference regarding the *sak huun* headdress that was used in K'inich Janaab Pakal I's death statement. So the story relates three events related to the demise of K'inich Kan Bahlam II: his death, his burial, and whatever happened to his crown of rulership when he died. The date of K'inich K'an Joy Chitam II's accession is elaborated with a Supplementary Series and with a special marker that refers to the rising sun. The implication is that Ux [Ch'akan] Mat became king and took on the name K'inich K'an Joy Chitam II at sunrise on this date. He is also named for the first time with both the holy lord of Matwiil and holy lord of Palenque titles, and the west Kaloomte' title.

The narrative then makes another backstep in time and begins the fourth and final episode of the story by saying that it had been 87 years since K'inich Janaab Pakal I's accession. The accession of K'inich K'an Joy Chitam II is then restated, followed by the dedication of House A-D by K'inich K'an Joy Chitam II some 18 years later. This house dedication includes a Supplementary Series and the statement that House A-D was the house of the Ux Yop Huun.

DISTANCE NUMBER TREATMENT

The Palace Tablet narrative creates a timeline of events that are linked through the use of Distance Numbers (DN). As noted in the previous chapter, a DN simply states the number of days between two events, and occasionally a DN is preceded by a glyph called a Distance Number Introductory Glyph (DNIG). While some of the longer Palenque narratives such as the Temple of the Inscription tablets and the Cross Group narratives do not employ DNIGs, six of the 10 DNs in the Palace Tablet narrative are preceded by a DNIG. The distribution of these DNIGs suggests that they function in this narrative to create couplets and emphasis. The pattern of DNIGs and DNs in the three sections of the main text is shown in the following table:

A	ISIG	birth of Ux [Ch'akan] Mat
A	DNIG	first bloodletting of Ux [Ch'akan] Mat
A	DNIG	Period Ending of K'inich Janaab Pakal I
B	DN	Period Ending of Ux [Ch'akan] Mat
A	DNIG	death K'inich Janaab Pakal I
B	DN	accession of K'inich Kan Bahlam as king, accession of Ux [Ch'akan] Mat as *bah ch'ok*
A	DNIG	death of K'inich Kan Bahlam

In the next section of text, both events lack DNIGs:

B	DN	burial of K'inich Kan Bahlam
B	DN	accession of K'inich K'an Joy Chitam II

In the final section, both events have DNIGs:

A	DNIG	accession of K'inich K'an Joy Chitam II
A	DNIG	house dedication K'inich K'an Joy Chitam II

This usage of Introductory Glyphs does not appear to be a random pattern, but a poetic one. We return to this issue below.

TOPICAL DIVISIONS OF THE TEXT

Breaks in the timeline were used to define four episodes in the Palace Tablet text (figure 4.2). As noted, there are many different ways to analyze the text, and each may provide a distinct result. A slightly different analysis of the Palace Tablet text emerges if we take the viewpoint of participant tracking, topics, and topic change. From this vantage point, the text can be broken into six episodes rather than four, and the breaks between episodes can be moved slightly. We do not yet have enough comparative evidence to suggest which of these alternatives the scribes had in mind, and it is possible that they would have been content with a modicum of ambiguity. Formal patterns are, after all, to be played with by creative writers.

A topical analysis divides the text into segments with common topics. The first such episode is the caption text that accompanies the image (S1–X1). The topic theme here is Ux Yop Hun, the headdress; no other subject is named.

The second episode (A1–F14) begins with an elaborate full-figure Initial Series and extensive Supplementary Series (Lord of the Night, Lunar Series, and 819-day count), corresponding to the Long Count date 9.10.11.17.0 and Calendar Round 11 Ajaw 8 Mak. The Initial Series date is a backstep from the last date on the caption text. The event is the birth of Ux [Ch'akan] Mat, the topic of this episode, and his birth starts the event line of the main text. This episode is devoted to events in the early life of the protagonist. The initial event, his birth, is greatly elaborated by the addition of parentage statements, which indirectly also serve to identify the flanking figures in the scene. The second event is his first bloodletting some seven years later, in the presence of the Palenque triad gods, GI, GII, and GIII.

The third episode (E15–I14) begins with a DN that moves the chronology forward just over a year. The topic changes to K'inich Janaab Pakal I, and the text relates a series of events in the life of K'inich Janaab Pakal I that are related to his son: after K'inich Janaab Pakal I celebrated the 9.11.0.0.0 Period Ending, his son (still called Ux [Ch'akan] Mat) performed a rope-related event at the 9.11.13.0.0 Period Ending. Some 18 years later, K'inich Janaab Pakal I died.

The fourth episode (J14–N12) relates events in the reign of K'inich Kan Bahlam II, K'inich Janaab Pakal I's older son. The chronology moves forward some six months from K'inich Janaab Pakal I's death to the accession of K'inich Kan Bahlam II (called "the elder brother"), and relates the contemporary accession of Ux [Ch'akan] Mat ("the younger brother") to *bah ch'oklel*, "first prince status." Some 16 years later, K'inich Kan Bahlam II died. It is notable that in this episode, K'inich Janaab Pakal I is referred to only obliquely, with a reference to "his white headband" on a date corresponding to his death.

The same oblique reference will be used later, at N13–M14 in the next episode, to refer to the death of K'inich Kan Bahlam II.

The fifth episode (N13–R1) features the accession of K'inich K'an Joy Chitam II, now called by his royal name. The timeline moves forward less than a year after the death of K'inich Kan Bahlam II (referred to only obliquely) to the accession of his younger brother. The importance of this event—the first peak event—is emphasized by the inclusion of a Supplementary Series (Lord of the Night and Lunar Series) corresponding to the accession date of 9.13.10.6.8, 5 Lamat 6 Xul. The new ruler's name is accompanied by numerous titles, including the office of West Kaloomte'. A back reference to K'inich Janaab Pakal I's accession closes the episode and anticipates the next peak event.

The sixth and final episode (Q2–R19) returns the topic to the headdress. Counting from K'inich K'an Joy Chitam II's accession, the chronology moves forward to the dedication of the house of Ux Yop Hun, and the importance of this second peak event is stressed by the inclusion of another Supplementary Series, corresponding to 9.14.8.14.15, 9 Men 3 Yax. K'inich K'an Joy Chitam II is said to have been present, and the event took place at a location within Palenque.

DISTANCE NUMBER INTRODUCTORY GLYPHS

The timeline is moved forward (and occasionally backward) by DNs, which count time elapsed between two events. Several kinds of DN expressions are used in the Palace Tablet text, and their differential use seems to be significant. As elsewhere in Palenque (Josserand 1991), the most common form of DN expression begins with a DNIG, a verb form based on *tz'ak*, cognates of which refer to adding pieces to something (e.g., bricks to a wall, or, in medicinal reference, reuniting soul parts). These constructions have two parts, the event counted from and the event counted to. If the earlier event is understood from the context, its verbal expression can be suppressed: "so much time went by (since the last event mentioned) and . . ." The later event usually is a Calendar Round date, followed by a new sentence that expresses the event: "so much time went by, and it came to be Calendar Round date. X happened." On the other hand, the DN may lead directly to an event verb, the Calendar Round date to follow.

The second part of these constructions, the later event, is usually introduced by another verbal phrase, based on the verb *ut*, "finish, come to be," usually in its completive form u-ti, *'uti* and occasionally in a pluperfect form, suffixed with T126: u-ti-ya, *utiy*. This verb is commonly preceded by the emphatic conjunction *i* (T679a), which we gloss as "and then," that is, *i uti* "and then, it came to pass."

In the Palace Tablet inscription, there are six examples of DNIG constructions that use the emphatic conjunction to mark the event in the second sentence, and if we abstract the events from these constructions, they are the principal elements of the event line: from the birth of Ux [Ch'akan] Mat:

A1–D17	the birth of Ux [Ch'akan] Mat
C18–E9	Ux [Ch'akan] Mat's first bloodletting
E15–F7	K'inich Janaab Pakal I's Period Ending
G8–H13	Ux [Ch'akan] Mat's Period Ending
I7–I14	the death of K'inich Janaab Pakal I
L15–N8	the death of K'inich Kan Bahlam II
M13–P12	the accession of K'inich K'an Joy Chitam II
Q2–R19	the dedication of Ux Yop Hun's house

Most episodes have only one such expression; the second episode contains two instances, relating to K'inich Janaab Pakal I's Period Ending and his death. If we look in detail at the construction of the second sentences in these DNIG constructions, a pattern emerges. First a chiasmic structure:

E6 . . .	*i uti* CR Verb . . .	Ux [Ch'akan] Mat's first bloodletting
F16 . . .	*i uti* CR *k'atun#* Verb . . .	K'inich Janaab Pakal I's Period Ending
H9 . . .	*i uti* CR *k'atun#* Verb . . .	Ux [Ch'akan] Mat's Period Ending
I9 . . .	*i uti* CR Verb . . .	death of K'inich Janaab Pakal I

And then, as the text approaches the climax, a background event and two focused events:

N7 . . .	*i* Verb CR . . .	death of K'inich Kan Bahlam II
N14 . . .	*i* DAWN CR (SS) Verb . . .	accession of K'an Joy Chitam II (Peak 1)
R8 . . .	*i uti* C(SS)R Verb . . .	dedication of Ux Yop Huun's house (Peak 2)

The first peak event substitutes the "dawn" glyph (N14, the sun emerging between the earth and the sky) for the otherwise employed *uti*. This is the only instance of this glyph in the text. Note that the two peak events display slightly different treatments of the Supplementary Series. The first instance presents first both parts of the Calendar Round, and the Supplementary Series follows. The second instance splits the Calendar Round parts with the Supplementary Series, as is normally done in an Initial Series date. This event ends the main text just as an Initial Series opens it.

ELABORATION AND RELATIVE WEIGHT

A mechanism for signaling the importance of an event is the elaboration of phrases, especially the name and title phrases of the actors. Thus, when Ux [Ch'akan] Mat's birth is reported, his *ch'ok* title and name are preceded by some seven glyph blocks that appear to refer to the place of his birth, and his name is followed by parentage statements for both of his parents, with titles of their own. The subject phrase of the sentence, then, consists of 27 glyph blocks (D4–D17). In K'inich K'an Joy Chitam II's accession statement (M13–P12) not only is the date elaborated with a Supplementary Series, but after the event verb phrase (O1–P2) there follow 10 glyph blocks of supposed titles before the protagonist's name is given (with both his pre-accession name and the first use of his royal name).

These elaborations can be quantified to give an estimate of the relative weight (i.e., relative importance) of each person and object named in a text. A rough count of glyph blocks in the Palace Tablet text yields the following results:

K'inich K'an Joy Chitam II	70 (first episode), 54 (fourth episode)
	total 124 (48% of the text)
Ux Yop Hun	15 (caption text), 36 (final episode)
	total 51 (20% of the text)
K'inich Janaab Pakal I	47 (third episode)
	total 47 (18% of the text)
K'inich Kan Bahlam II	37 (fourth episode)
	total 37 (14% of the text)

In order of importance, then, the protagonists are K'inich K'an Joy Chitam II, Ux Yop Hun, K'inich Janaab Pakal I, and K'inich Kan Bahlam II.

Three events in the text are marked by the inclusion of Supplementary Series. Taking this as a sign of importance, the three most important events in the text are the birth of K'inich K'an Joy Chitam, his accession as ruler, and the dedication of the headdress house. That is, the two protagonists who receive the most text (together, 68%) are also the protagonists of the most highly marked events.

Overall, the Palace Tablet inscription conforms to the expected pattern of a Cholan narrative. It is framed by an opening and closing related to the same topic, the headdress. It proceeds in a series of episodes whose boundaries are marked (some by backsteps in time), whose topics differ from one another and whose episode peak events are introduced with the focus marker *i*. It climaxes in a peak event that is syntactically distinct, employing an otherwise unused verb (the dawn glyph), and it closes with a second peak that couplets the opening caption text and mimics the initial event of the main text. It cannot be accidental that the whole text is arranged in an H pattern, with the scene featuring the headdress in the upper cleft, and an empty space in the lower cleft that is just the right size for the headdress to be displayed there.

In summary, the first event of the Palace Tablet narrative (the birth of the Ux Yop Hun) and the last event (the dedication of the Ux Yop Hun house) concern the UxYop Hun headdress. These two events frame the historical events in the life of K'inich K'an Joy Chitam II. The illustration of K'inich K'an Joy Chitam II's acquisition of the Ux Yop Huun and *tok'-pakal* icon places great emphasis on this event, and specifically places the focus on the Ux Yop Huun. Within the main text narrative there are two peak events marked with Supplementary Series notations: K'inich K'an Joy Chitam II's accession and the house dedication. The main text focuses on the *sak huun* headdress of rulership in its recounting of the various accessions and deaths of these three Palenque kings, but the story is ultimately about the Ux Yop Huun.

While the Tablet of the Slaves and the Temple XIX platform indicate that K'inich Ahkal Mo' Nahb III received the Ux Yop Huun on the occasion of his accession as king, the Palace Tablet illustrates K'inich K'an Joy Chitam II obtaining this headdress and a *tok'-pakal* icon as a young boy of nine, many years prior to his accession as king. This is similar to the *tok'-pakal* event of K'inich Kan Bahlam II who received his *tok'-pakal* icon when he was six years of age (see chapter 7). Another pre-accession event of K'inich K'an Joy Chitam II is illustrated on the Dumbarton Oaks Tablet, and demonstrates the importance of these early rituals (see chapter 8 for an overview of this sculpture).

SUMMARY

The two sample hieroglyphic texts analyzed above—one short and poetic, the other long and narrative—illustrate the utility of analysis beyond decipherment. The crowning achievement of Maya epigraphy in the late twentieth century was the ability to read texts and extract their historical content. This was made possible by advancements in both epigraphy proper and Mayan linguistics. Using structural models and applying the scientific method, epigraphers compared and contrasted sets and sequences of glyphic variants, proposed and tested hypotheses about their phonetic and semantic values, and gradually reached near-total understanding of the writing system and the contents of inscriptions. Linguists benefited from increasing knowledge of Mayan languages and reconstructed hypothetical models of the language spoken by the Classic period scribes, using hieroglyphic evidence to test and support hypotheses. There remain many issues to be resolved in both these fields, but the questions to be answered are of increasingly smaller scope. Maya epigraphy has reached a level of maturity at which there is little disagreement about the content of inscriptions; most scholarly readers of a new inscription will arrive at the same conclusions about what is being said.

Meanwhile, relatively little attention has been paid to *how* the content is being said. It is apparent from the few monumental inscriptions that have been subjected to extensive analysis that there were Classic norms of poetic and narrative discourse. Literature should be added to the inventory of advanced arts of the ancient Maya, along with calendrics and mathematics, astronomy, architecture, and art in general. But literary norms were manipulated by the scribes. Maya texts are not standardized, cookie-cutter texts that simply fill in formulaic structures with particular data. They are highly creative works of literature, well-told stories, well-crafted poems, and artful mixtures of the two.

In the midst of a recitation of history, inscriptions may break into what has to be seen as prayer or poetry, as on the south side of Stela A at Copán. The text suddenly goes into sets of contrasting words or phrases that appear to be a dedication blessing: *chan te chan, chan na chan, chan ni chan, chan mi chan;* Holy Lord of Copán, Holy Lord of Tikal, Holy Lord of Calakmul, Holy Lord of Palenque . . . east, west, south, north, and so on. Incidentally, the chronology of that monument is chiasmic, beginning with its erection date on a day (A) 12 Ajaw, stepping back to the erection of Stela H on a (B) 4 Ajaw, forward to a Period Ending on (B) 4 Ajaw, and finally three months forward to the dedication date on a (A) 12 Ajaw. Similar prayer-like structures are found on Tikal's Stela 31 (initial-text columns) and elsewhere.

A common pattern on monuments is to compare and contrast ancient mythology to contemporary history, as is famously done on Palenque's Cross Group wall panels. A beautiful example of this is the creation text on Quiriguá's Stela C, where the events of setting up the world are related in nested couplets on one side (ABCCBA) as background to the historical events on the other side.[2] Another use of nested couplets is the edge text of Yaxchilán's Lintel 23, where the distinguished pedigree of the owner of the building is recited in chiasmic form (ABCCBA). This text is interesting in that it was first grossly misunderstood. Schele and Freidel (1990:269) derived from it a confusing genealogical chart. Not until Josserand (2007) recognized the nested couplets in it was the text read properly.

The case of Yaxchilán's Lintel 23 illustrates the need to understand literary structures in order to advance our understanding of Classic texts. Being able to ascribe confusing structures to style rather than mistakes clears up a lot of troublesome inscriptions. When we told Linda Schele about the "zone of turbulence surrounding the peak" in Mesoamerican narratives, she was greatly relieved that what epigraphers had thought were either mistakes or deliberate obfuscation could now be seen as deliberate rhetorical strategies (Lacadena's [2012:46–47] *sychysys*).

Similar arguments can be made about the placement of text with respect to images (Bassie-Sweet 1991). An example discussed above is the caption texts of Palenque's Palace Tablet. Segments of text are placed in such a way as to aid the viewer in identifying the objects and people depicted: the feathers of the headdress drape over the inscription that tells of its origin, the inscription relating its holding impinges on the back of the throne where the protagonist is sitting. Another obvious example is Yaxchilán's Stela 11, where Bird Jaguar's headdress touches his name in the inscription that frames his head, and Shield Jaguar III's foot touches his name in the inscription below. On Quiriguá's Stela J, the feathers on the scepter held by the ruler curl around the corner to touch the verb in his accession statement in the inscription.

Even without accompanying images, the arrangement of text can be meaningful. On Yaxchilán's Structure 12 (Tate 1992:168–170), a series of four lintels celebrates a sequence of ten rulers, but not all are given the same weight. On the first of the series (Lintel 60, the "New Lintel") the seating in office of four rulers is recorded. On the second (Lintel 49), three rulers are seated. The third lintel (Lintel 37) records the seating of only two rulers, and the final lintel (Lintel 35) is wholly dedicated to a single ruler, no doubt the patron of these carvings. On Structure 22 (Graham and von Euw 1977:45–51), three ancient lintels (Lintels 18, 20, and 22) were reset into a rebuilt structure and a new fourth lintel (Lintel 21) was added over the central doorway. The latter lintel records the initial dedication of the building and the rededication of the building by Bird Jaguar, more than three hundred years later. The original dedicator was apparently a member of the Skull family, as was Bird Jaguar's recently married wife. A nice wedding gift.

These manipulations of text and text-and-image, and the strategic placement of inscriptions on monuments and of monuments on buildings, are not random events. They are carefully planned manipulations that add meaning to the inscriptions themselves. If we do not take these elements into account, we are missing part of the intended messages of the scribes and architects. We can move beyond decipherment, beyond the historical approach to a pragmatic one that seeks to discover these hidden meanings. In brief, it is time for a paradigm shift.

NOTES

1. This article, in the *Boletín Informativo* of the Comisión para el Estudio de la Escritura Maya, UNAM—at the center of Maya epigraphy in the late 1960s—goes through Zimmermann's glyph catalog from Z1 to Z91 and compares readings offered by Wolfgang Cordan, Yuri Knorosov, David Kelley, Günther Zimmermann, Eric Thompson, and Thomas Barthel; a one-page appendix adds additional information sent to Barthel in a letter from Thompson.

2. The mythological inscription on the east side of Stela C forms a couplet with the historical inscriptions on the west side.

5

Text and Image

The narrative structure of hieroglyphic texts has been analyzed and the various conventions used to highlight events and create climactic moments within the storyline of the text identified. The images that accompany inscriptions also have narrative structures. The relationship between text and image is reciprocal, and both methods of communication are structured in similar, complementary ways. This chapter is an overview of the poetic nature of Maya text and image with a focus on the intimate relationship between these two forms of communication. It also includes a discussion of the nature of hieroglyphic signs and how they are incorporated into the image.

SEMANTIC MARKERS IN MAYA ART

Traditionally, the largest sign in a glyph block was called the *main sign* and the other signs surrounding it were called *affix signs* (Thompson 1962). *Prefixes* were to the left of the main sign, *postfixes* were to the right, *superfixes* were above, and *subfixes* were below. In some cases, affixes are actually much larger signs that have been simply overlapped by the main sign. Only when both signs appear in separate, sequential glyph blocks is it obvious what the full form of the overlapped glyph is. Rather than overlapping two glyphs, the scribe occasionally chose to reduce the second glyph in size and place it in front of the first glyph (i.e., between the background glyph and the

DOI: 10.5876/9781607327424.c005

reader). This type of superimposing one glyph in the foreground of another is traditionally called *infixing*, since in a two-dimensional space one glyph appears to be inside the other. There are also examples of infixed signs that are not intended to represent a separate word, but rather function as semantic markers (Hopkins 1994, 2012; Hopkins and Josserand 1999; Josserand and Hopkins 2002; Mora Marin 2008). Stone and Zender (2011:13) refer to such glyphs as property qualifiers.

Semantic markers do not affect the pronunciation of the sign on which they are infixed, rather they function like visual adjectives providing additional information about the glyph itself. Some such markers indicate the inherent nature of the object(s) depicted in the hieroglyph (stone, wood, water, human, etc.). Many of these mark cognitive categories of objects and beings that relate to their natural substance; such categories are grammatically marked in the pronominal systems of Mayan languages in northwest Guatemala (as noun classifiers; Hopkins 2012c). These icons function, not to add to the meaning of the hieroglyph, but to identify it. Other semantic markers inform about qualities such as lightning and color that are not directly depicted. What distinguishes these icons from other glyphic elements is that they are not intended to be read, rather they help readers understand what they are seeing.

A common and widely recognized semantic marker identifies things made from stone. The word *tuun "stone" (Western Mayan *toonh) is represented by the T528 sign (Kaufman 2003:436; Stuart 1996). This logograph is a profile view of a limestone cave mouth with stylized stalactites hanging from the ceiling (Bassie-Sweet 1991:108–109). Caves containing such speleothems (cave deposits) are a common feature of the karst topography that characterizes much of the Maya lowlands. Given that limestone was the primary stone of the Maya region, it is predictable that the Maya would use a feature of that stone to represent the word stone. Numerous signs incorporate these *tuun* "stone" elements as semantic markers to indicate they are made of stone such as the *witz* "mountain" glyph and the logographs that represent the word *tok'* "flint" (T112, T245, T257, T354, T786) (Houston 1983; Schele and Miller 1986:46; Stone and Zender 2011:fig. 27). In Maya art, illustrations of limestone objects such as altars and stelae are often marked with the *tuun* elements. For example, a scene on a carved peccary skull from Copán shows two lords flanking a stela and altar, which are both marked with *tuun* elements (Fash 2001:fig. 24). Ritual combat scenes illustrate Chahk deities and lords using round, hand-size stones as striking weapons, and the verb *jatz'* "to strike" is represented by a logograph of a hand holding such a stone marked with *tuun* elements (Zender 2004a).

A second widely recognized semantic marker is the icon that marks "earth"; in hieroglyphs it occurs in the day name Kab ("earth") and in images it identifies the earth, as on the sides of the Palenque Temple of the Inscriptions sarcophagus box. In images, the distinctive features of the syllable sign te (from te', "tree, wood") appear as a semantic marker on wooden objects such as canoes as in the Tikal Burial 116 canoe scenes (Thompson 1950:282–284). Less widely accepted is the semantic sign for "human," a small circle inside another circle that frequently appears on the "seating" glyph (a human torso) or the "scattering" verb (a down-turned hand) (Hopkins 2012c).

"Water" is frequently marked with aquatic plants and animals such as fish and conch shells. The use of fish to indicate a watery environment is widespread in Mesoamerican art. For example, the place names at the bases of Izapa Stela 1, Stela 22, and Stela 67 feature fish swimming in water. As discussed in chapter 1, waterlilies are employed as signs for water and pools of water. Waterlilies are also a common component of headdresses. Many waterlily headdresses feature a fish nibbling at the flower (Rands 1955). These fish function as semantic markers to indicate that the flower in question is a waterlily. In a similar fashion, some birds are featured with fish in their mouths, indicating they are fish-eaters.

Another example of a common semantic marker is the T24 sign. Although T24 and its head variant T1017 have not been definitively deciphered, the T24 sign is an axehead with parallel lines drawn on the surface. Chahk thunderbolt gods are frequently illustrated swinging such an axe. When T24/T1017 is employed as an infix to mark objects and deities, it has been interpreted to refer to reflectiveness, shininess, or brightness (Stuart 2010; Stone and Zender 2011:71). There is evidence that the T24/T1017 sign represents the luminous quality of the creator deities that is directly related to the bright flash of lightning and meteors (Bassie-Sweet, in press, in review).

The T712 *ch'ab* sign is an obsidian bloodletter and it is often infixed with the T24 sign (figure 5.1A). The T24 sign does not alter the pronunciation of the T712 sign as *ch'ab*, instead it indicates the luminous nature of the obsidian bloodletter as a manifestation of a meteor. In Maya art, obsidian eccentrics, axes, spearheads, sacrificial blades, and scepters are infixed with either the T24 luminous/lightning flash sign or the T504 *ak'ab* "night, darkness" sign. Such obsidian bloodletters are often seen decorating the loincloths of Maya rulers, alluding to the duty of the king to perform personal acts of penile bloodletting. Piedras Negras Stela 7 and Stela 8 show a ruler holding a personified obsidian spear marked with the T504 *ak'ab* sign (Stuart and Graham 2003:9:39, 9:44) (figure 5.2). It has been suggested that the *ak'ab* sign is used as an infix

FIGURE 5.1. *Ch'ab–ak'ab couplet.*

on obsidian objects in order to indicate the dark color of the stone (Stone and Zender 2012:145). If so, one wonders why the scribe would not have simply used the T95 ik' "black" sign. There is a better explanation for this use of the T504 sign on obsidian objects that is related to the metonymic couplet *u ch'ab* (T712) *u ak'ab* (T504) "his creation, his darkness." This phrase, which is found in numerous hieroglyphic texts, is associated with acts of devotion and creation involving bloodletting (MacLeod and Houston cited in Stuart 1995:231; Knowlton 2002, 2010, 2012) (figure 5.1B). In some examples of the *u ch'ab–u ak'ab* couplet, the two signs are depicted in one glyph block (figure 5.1C). In these examples, the T504 sign is reduced in size and infixed on the T712 sign. This configuration makes it apparent that the *ak'ab*-marked obsidian bloodletters and weapons are direct references to the conflated *u ch'ab–u ak'ab* couplet and the role of obsidian bloodletters in acts of devotion and creation (Bassie-Sweet in press). The *ak'ab*-marked obsidian bloodletters and weapons are excellent examples of how text-based signs and metaphors are incorporated into the image.

Obsidian weapons also carry another type of semantic marker. On Piedras Negras Stela 7 and Stela 8, the distal point of the obsidian spear is tipped with a Teotihuacán-style symbol for a bleeding heart (figure 5.2). Numerous examples of obsidian have this bleeding-heart symbol, such as those found on Dos Pilas Stela 2 and Aguateca Stela 2. The bloody-heart symbol indicates the lethal nature of these obsidian objects and their association with human sacrifice.

FIGURE 5.2. *Piedras Negras Stela 7 and Stela 8 obsidian spears, after David Stuart.*

Other well-known examples of semantic markers are the signs for the colors red, yellow, black, white, and blue-green, which are often employed to indicate the color of an animal, plant, or object. As an example, hummingbirds are depicted with flowers attached to their bills in reference to their feeding habits. The flowers act as a semantic marker to indicate this bird is a nectar-sucking bird. In turn, these flowers are often marked with the *chak* "red" sign to indicate the hummingbird is sucking a red flower. Anyone who has observed hummingbirds knows that they prefer red flowers. Some illustrations of flowers include scrolls that indicate their fragrant nature (Houston and Taube 2000:269; Taube 2004:71). This is yet another case of a semantic marker.

TEXT AND IMAGE INTERCHANGE IN HEADDRESS MOTIFS

One of the most common examples of the interchange between text and image is found in the headdresses worn by various elites that contain glyphs representing either their name or that of a deity or ancestor whom they are impersonating. For instance, each of the ancestors of K'inich Janaab Pakal I that is displayed on the sides of the king's sarcophagus box is identified by an adjacent caption text (Robertson 1983:fig. 177). In addition, an element from the name of each ancestor appears in his or her headdress. The headdress of Lady Sak K'uk' "White Quetzal" contains a quetzal head. In a similar manner, her husband K'an Mo' Hix "Yellow Macaw Jaguar" has a macaw head as part of his headdress. The eye of the macaw is infixed with the ear of a jaguar. In hieroglyphic writing, this jaguar ear is used as the *pars pro toto* sign for the word *hix* "jaguar" (Stuart and Houston 1994:21). Likewise, K'inich Kan

Bahlam I "Serpent Jaguar" wears a jaguar head with the eye of a serpent. In essence, the headdress and the adjacent caption text form a couplet.

Yet another example of an ancestor wearing a headdress that represents his name is found on La Pasadita Lintel 2 (figure 5.3). In this scene, the Yaxchilán ruler Bird Jaguar performs a *chok* scattering event in the company of the La Pasadita lord Tilom on the occasion of the 9.16.15.0.0 Period Ending. Attached to the back of his belt, Bird Jaguar wears an effigy head representing his father, Itzamnaaj Bahlam. This effigy wears a headdress composed of a jaguar (*bahlam*) wearing the *ak'ab* medallion of Itzamnaaj's headdress. The *ak'ab* medallion functions as the *pars pro toto* for the name Itzamnaaj. The headdress is a rendering of the name Itzamnaaj Bahlam.

FIGURE 5.3. *La Pasadita Lintel 2, drawing after Ian Graham.*

In scenes of impersonation, lords and ladies often wear headdresses that contain the glyphic spelling of the names of deities and ancestors (Houston and Stuart 1998). La Pasadita Lintel 2 again provides one such example. In it, Bird Jaguar's headdress is composed of an owl head stacked on top of the head of a Chahk (thunderbolt) deity (figure 5.3). The shell headdress of the Chahk deity appears above the bird, while the black-tipped feather of the owl appears on the nose of the Chahk. The owl or its *pars pro toto* black-tipped feather represents the phonetic sign *'o*.[1] As read by Stuart (2013), the headdress represents the O' Chahk portion of the Yaxchilán god K'ahk' O' Chahk. It is important to keep in mind that this representation of the name of O' Chahk on Lintel 2 is not a portrait of this deity, but a full-figure representation of the elements of his name. On the underside of Yaxchilán Lintel 25, the text across the top of the lintel refers to the conjuring of K'ahk' O' Chahk, and the scene shows that the conjured deity is a Tlaloc god. While the Maya categorized Tlaloc deities as a type of thunderbolt god, these Tlaloc gods were envisioned to be quite distinct in appearance from the Chahk gods (Bassie-Sweet 2011, 2012, in press; Bassie-Sweet et al. 2015:128–144). One of the avian manifestations of Tlaloc was an owl.

TEXT AND IMAGE INTERCHANGE IN PLACE NAMES

Numerous scenes contain motifs that are, in fact, elaborate hieroglyphs. Perhaps the most obvious examples are the place names that are frequently found at the base of a scene to indicate the location of the action (Stuart and Houston 1994). Such a place name is seen on Yaxchilán Hieroglyphic Stairway 3 of Structure 44 as discussed in the section of chapter 1 regarding the role of the sun god as the god of the number four. The narrative on the center riser (Step IV) refers to the dedication of Structure 44 and calls it an *otot* "house." The name of the house is composed of four dots representing the number 4 and a portrait of the front head of the Milky Way Crocodile (Plank 2004:58). The scene on the adjacent Step III illustrates a captive lord kneeling on this house name (figure 1.13). In this version, the crocodile head has been replaced with a full-figure rendering of the beast and the number four is represented by a cartouche containing a bust of the sun god, who was the god of the number four. The cartouche is superimposed over the body of the crocodile, a very common convention in hieroglyphic writing, in which one sign is reduced in size and placed in front of another. Beneath this place name are two more glyphs that are read "within Pa' Chan," a well-known place name for Yaxchilán (Martin 2004). This phrase indicates that the "Four Crocodile" house was at Yaxchilán and that the captive was illustrated at this specific house location. Another example of a "Four Crocodile" place name is found at Palenque over the doorway leading from House E to the eastern subterranean rooms of the Palace (Robertson 1985:fig. 108–112; Plank 2004). In this example, the Milky Way Crocodile frames the doorway and the number four is simply represented by a *k'in* cartouche on the body. The rare use of a *k'in* sign to represent the number four is also found on Copán Stela 1 (D6a) where it is employed to represent the number four in the *tzolk'in* date 4 Ajaw.

These "Four Crocodile" place names are prime examples of the difficulty in determining the meaning of a polyvalent glyph. As noted in chapter 1, the T544 *k'in* sign or a portrait of the sun god (T1010b) can represent the number four, the sun, the period from sunrise to sunset, or the period from one sunrise to the next sunrise (24 hours). The T544/T1010b signs are also employed to form the word *k'inich* "sunlike." It is often only the context that allows us to determine the semantic value of a sign. For instance, a T544 *k'in* sign that is paired with an *ak'ab* "night" sign obviously contrasts diurnal and nocturnal periods. Yet when contrasted with a moon sign, the T544 sign carries the meaning of sun. Fortunately, the Yaxchilán example provides a clear understanding that the meaning was the "Four Crocodile" place, although the significance of this name may elude us.

Another difficulty in determining the meaning of this place name stems from the hieroglyphic convention of using a mythic being to represent a general class (Houston and Martin 2012). There are examples where a portrait of the Milky Way Crocodile represents the word *ahiin* "crocodile." Consequently, it is uncertain whether these Yaxchilán and Palenque place names refer to the Milky Way in some fashion or simply represent the phrase "four crocodiles." Rather than seeing the *k'in* signs on the bodies of these crocodiles as a simple case of infixing, Stuart (2005a:167–168) and Taube (2009) interpreted it to mean that the sun god resided within the womb or stomach of the crocodile. They asserted that the beast represents the sky of the Underworld, and they further argued that the motif indicates that the sun was swallowed each night by the crocodile and defecated out the next morning. In a similar fashion, Looper (2012:211) stated that "the location of a solar cartouche immediately above the glyph for Yaxchilán suggests that this entire basal register embodies the eastern horizon as viewed from the city center." Such speculations seem unjustified in these cases.

The difficulty in ascertaining the meaning of a particular place name is also apparent on Early Classic Tres Islas Stela 1 and Stela 2 that illustrate locations containing the *k'in* sign. Both stelae feature a ruler depicted in Teotihuacán-style garb, who stands above a zoomorphic creature that represents the word *witz* "mountain" (Stuart 1987). On Stela 2, a figure sits within the quatrefoil opening in the monster's forehead. To the left and right of the quatrefoil opening are portraits of the sun god and a *mo'* "macaw" (figure 5.4A). The same mountain place name is portrayed on Stela 1, but in this case, the *witz* monster is in profile view, a T544 *k'in* sign is infixed in its forehead and its mouth has been replaced with the beak of the macaw (figure 5.4B). This type of conflation of signs is common in hieroglyphic writing (Stuart 1995).[2] Although the T544 *k'in* sign in the Tres Islas place name has been transcribed as *k'inich* (Barrios and Quintanilla 2008), it is more likely that it represents the word "four" (*chan*), given that there are a number of examples of the number four prefixed to the word "macaw." On Dresden Codex page 40c, the caption text refers to a "four macaw place," using the standard four dots to represent the number four, a macaw head to represent the word *mo'*, and the standard *nal* sign that is often attached to place names. The text on the Copán Motmot floor marker also refers to a "four macaw" place. The adjacent Ballcourt I had sculptures that illustrated four full-figure macaws (Taube 2003b:fig. 11.3). In addition, each serpent-wing of these birds has four feathers that terminate in a macaw head. As noted by Taube, murals from Teotihuacán also illustrate a bird whose wings include four macaw heads. While it is unclear what this imagery represents, it

FIGURE 5.4. *Place names from Tres Islas Stela 1 and Stela 2, after Ian Graham.*

is well established that both Tres Islas and Copán had intimate contact with Teotihuacán during the Early Classic period, when these works of art were produced (Stone 1989; Stuart 2000). These place name cases exemplify the importance of context in determining the meaning of certain motifs.

The examples discussed above demonstrate that many motifs found in Maya art represent words. This lack of distinction between text and image is well demonstrated on the Early Classic panel on the façade of the Copán Margarita Structure. The right panel of the structure illustrates the doorway of a building (figure 5.5). Arching over the doorway is the double-headed Milky Way Crocodile, much like the double-headed Milky Way Crocodile that decorates the actual doorway of the adjacent Structure 22. A Chahk deity wielding a thunderbolt axe is juxtaposed with the rear head of the Margarita crocodile. The upper corners of the doorway are marked with *bak'tun* birds. The doorway itself contains a full figure rendering of the name of the Copán king K'inich Yax K'uk' Mo' as discussed in chapter 1. The words *k'uk'* "quetzal" and *mo'* "macaw" are represented by a quetzal and a macaw whose necks are intertwined. The quetzal bird has the characteristic crest, green feathers and red breast while the macaw is distinguished by its beak. Despite the difference in size between an actual quetzal (40 cm) and a macaw (96 cm), each of the Copán birds is depicted with the same-sized body. Both birds are illustrated with large talons and with wings that are conflated with a serpent head. Each bird has a *yax* sign attached to its head and a sun god representing the word *k'inich* emerging from its mouth. The birds perch on a well-known mythological place name that is found in numerous contexts in Maya art (Kubler 1977; Carlson 2007–2008). In its fullest form, the place name is composed of a zoomorphic head, the glyph for blood, and two footprints, and it is prefixed

FIGURE 5.5. *Copán Margarita Panel, after John Carlson.*

with the number nine. We refer to it by the nickname *Nine Place* because of the uncertainty of its decipherment. The Nine Place is often associated with Period Ending events such as on Copán Stela D, where it designates the location of 9.15.5.0.0 Period Ending event of the Copán ruler Waxaklajuun Ub'aah Ka'wiil. The presence of the Nine Place name, the *bak'tun* birds, and the Milky Way Crocodile on the Margarita panel suggests that the scene represents an abbreviated reference to a Period Ending event performed by K'inich Yax K'uk' Mo'. His full-figure name phrase takes the place of his portrait in a tour de force of text and image interplay.

TEXT AND IMAGE PLACEMENT: FRAMING AND BRACKETING

Maya monuments often include both large blocks of text (the main text) and a scene that includes caption texts. In her analysis of various compositions, Bassie-Sweet (1987, 1991) demonstrated that the placement of the text and image on different surfaces forced the viewer to walk around the monument, or in the case of sequential lintels, to walk from doorway to doorway within a building. The narratives on the three panels of the Palenque Cross Group form a continuous story that required the viewer to walk from building to building, and literally perform a counterclockwise circuit around the perimeter of the Cross Group plaza (see chapter 8).

When encountering a scene for the first time, the viewer sees the image first and then reads the text. While this may seem to be an obvious point, many researchers analyze hieroglyphic texts with little regard for the associated image or where the text is placed in regards to the image. The conventions used by Maya artists to indicate who is being depicted in a scene, and which of the many events of the narrative is being illustrated, have been noted (Bassie-Sweet 1987, 1991). The most common method is a convention in which the text in closest proximity to a figure or a text that frames a figure functions to qualify that figure and their actions. In many cases, the text not only frames but actually touches the figure, object, or action that it references. Examples of these techniques are ubiquitous (Bassie Sweet 1991:41–63).

Before Josserand's research, it was assumed that the most important event from a narrative relating the accession of a king was the accession of the king and that this was the event pictured in the image (Proskouriakoff 1960; Schele 1976). However, the narrative structure of the text and the placement of that text in relationship to the image demonstrate that this is not always the case. As an example, Proskouriakoff identified the birth, accession, and Period Ending events of a series of rulers in the texts of Piedras Negras. She assumed that the monuments that featured the ruler sitting in a niche represented the accession of the king. An examination of the placement of the text on the front of Stela 6 indicates that the 9.12.15.0.0 Period Ending conducted by the king frames the niche and it is the only event featured on the front of the monument (Bassie-Sweet 1987, 1991; Stuart and Graham 2003:36). The niche scene on the front of Stela 11 does not contain a text, but rather the narrative begins on the left side of the monument with the 9.15.0.0.0 Period Ending by the ruler and continues this Period Ending description on the right side (Stuart and Graham 2003:59). The right text ends with a statement referring to the ruler's birth and accession. In order to complete the reading of the Period Ending statement, the viewer is taken across the image of the ruler sitting in his niche. The king holds a small bag in his hand that is marked with the date of the Period Ending, not the accession. Furthermore, the Paris *k'atun* pages illustrate the mythological role model for human Period Ending ceremonies (Hellmuth 1987; Love 1994). The figures in these scenes sit on the same type of scaffold decorated with the Milky Way Crocodile and a headless crocodile as the Piedras Negras ruler. It is worth noting that the Piedras Negras stelae, like those of Quiriguá, were typically erected at five-year intervals, on Period Endings.

Another example of the framing convention is found on Yaxchilán Lintel 2 (figure 3.2). The image shows Bird Jaguar standing in a frontal pose, while holding two cross-shaped scepters decorated with flowers and descending birds. His five-year-old son, Shield Jaguar IV, stands to the left, holding another bird scepter of smaller size. The text begins in the upper left with the Calendar Round date of 4 Ajaw 3 Sootz' and the statement that it was the fifth anniversary of the accession (glyph block A–E).³ Although whose accession is not directly stated, other monuments indicate this was the date of Bird Jaguar's accession anniversary. The next clause is found at glyph blocks F–H and I–J, and it can be paraphrased in English as "it is the body of Shield Jaguar dancing with the bird scepter" (Houston, Stuart and Taube 2006:66; Looper 2009:35). By reading this text, the viewer is brought to the image of the young Shield Jaguar IV holding his bird scepter. The next clause (glyph blocks K–N, O1, O2, O3, O4, P, and Q) states that Bird Jaguar also danced with a bird scepter. To move from glyph block N to glyph block O, the viewer is drawn across the body of Bird Jaguar.

The Dumbarton Oaks Tablet demonstrates how the main text and caption text can both conform to the framing convention (figure 1.1). This panel is a looted monument that can be attributed to the Palenque region by style and by the historical content of its text (Coe and Benson 1966). There has been some speculation about whether the monument originated from Palenque itself or a subsidiary site to the west. What is clear is that the monument is missing parts of the seated figures and the axe of the standing figure. The fact that the surviving main text opens with a Distance Number and closes in mid-sentence indicates that part of the main text on both sides is also missing. Hopefully, the remainder of the monument will be recovered someday and its original context revealed.

The scene illustrates a dancing male dressed as a Chahk deity. He holds a water jar in his right hand and brandishes an axe in his left. The two people that flank him sit in a cross-legged fashion while holding animated god figures in their laps. The caption texts above their respective heads identify them as Lady Tz'akbu Ajaw (left) and K'inich Janaab Pakal I (right). Lady Tz'akbu holds a GII figure while K'inich Janaab Pakal I cradles the avian *huun* god. The central figure does not have an adjacent caption text so we must look to the main text for his identity.

The timeline of the surviving main text is straightforward. A distance number of 4.7.0 moves the time frame forward from the seating of the stone on the 9.11.0.0.0 12 Ajaw 8 Keh Period Ending (October 14, AD 652) to an event on 9.11.4.7.0 6 Ajaw 8 Kumk'u (February 10, 657) involving K'inich K'an Joy Chitam II and his father K'inich Janaab Pakal I. At the time of this event, K'inich K'an Joy Chitam II was almost nine years old. The timeline then proceeds to the Calendar Round date of 9 Manik' 5 Muwan, which can be assigned the Long Count position of 9.11.18.7.7 when K'inich K'an Joy Chitam II was 26. Some researchers (Coe and Benson 1966; Houston and Taube 2012:43) have suggested that the placement of this date in the Long Count is uncertain, but Bassie-Sweet noted that it is a straightforward placement if the narrative structure of the text is considered:

> Schele (1982, 1988) and Dütting (1984) place the Long Count position of 9 Manik' 5 Muwan at 9.14.11.2.7, a full Calendar Round cycle later (fifty-two years). But there is no precedent for this arbitrary jumping of a full Calendar Round cycle. As noted in chapter 1, the convention of omitting Distance Numbers or Calendar Rounds from a sentence does not create confusion in the Long Count position: the context of the preceding dates establishes the time frame which remains in effect unless other information contravenes. If the Maya jumped Calendar Round cycles arbitrarily, then we cannot reliably date *anything* that isn't directly tied to a Period Ending or Initial Series by a Distance Number. Therefore, using basic calendrical rules, this date, 9 Manik' 5 Muwan, must be given the Long Count position of 9.11.18.7.7. (Bassie-Sweet 1991:222)

Despite the decipherment of many of the glyphs involved, the meaning of the events that occurred on 6 Ajaw 8 Kumk'u and 9 Manik' 5 Muwan are difficult to comprehend. The first event involved *och* "entering" the *yotot nah tu wayibil Ux Bolon Chahk* "the house of the sleeping place of the deity Ux Bolon Chahk," and it is said to have taken place under the authority of K'inich Janaab Pakal I. Given that he was the reigning king at the time, this later statement is not surprising. Houston and Taube (2012:43) interpret the entering of the house to be a dedication act, but this is by no means clear. The narrative continues with an action of *tek'aj yok* "(was) stepped on his foot" on the mountain of a god, and ends with a statement that it was the *u tz'akbuji* "succession" of K'inich K'an Joy Chitam II. The time frame then advances 17 years to the 9 Manik' 5 Muwan event. The action on this date is said to be the *och* "entering" of GII on a mountain top, and then refers to the Ux Bolon Chahk deity again. Regrettably, this event seems to end in mid-sentence.

Houston and Taube (2012:44) argued that it was difficult to determine which of these two dates is featured in the scene, but that in either case the

Figure 5.6. *Palenque Tablet of the Cross, scene, drawing by Linda Schele, courtesy David Schele.*

scene illustrates K'inich K'an Joy Chitam II in the guise of Ux Bolon Chahk. Notwithstanding the ambiguous meaning of the main text, it is perfectly clear from the placement of the text that the featured action is the earlier 6 Ajaw 8 Kumk'u event (Bassie-Sweet 1991:222). K'inich K'an Joy Chitam II's head is tilted upwards and he gazes in the direction of the 6 Ajaw 8 Kumk'u text. The text not only frames K'inich K'an Joy Chitam II's head, but his name phrase is placed directly over his head, just as his parents' name phrases are directly over their heads. The Dumbarton Oaks Tablet is a very clear example of how Maya artists placed the text in a scene to clarify who and what was being depicted.

Yet another example of the framing convention is found on the Tablet of the Cross which illustrates two figures facing a central icon (figure 5.6). This central icon functions as both an object directly related to the deity GI and as a specific location where K'inich Kan Bahlam II made offerings to this god. The left figure is significantly shorter than the right one. The relative size of these two figures matches that of Bird Jaguar and his five-year-old son on Yaxchilán Lintel 2 (Bassie-Sweet 1991:204). The Tablet of the Cross caption text begins with an event by K'inich Kan Bahlam II when he was just six years old on 9.10.8.9.3 9 Ak'bal 8 Xul. This caption text also identifies K'inich Kan Bahlam II by referring to him by his pre-accession name and as the child of K'inich Janaab Pakal I and Lady Tz'akbu Ajaw. The 9 Ak'bal event frames the head of the short figure, and by reading it the viewer is literally brought to the short figure. The obvious conclusion to draw is that this is an illustration of the young K'inich Kan Bahlam II performing his 9 Ak'bal 8 Xul event. The narrative continues with the block of text at the feet of K'inich Kan Bahlam II that refers to an action conducted by him a year later on the Period Ending 9.10.10.0.0. From this event, the story moves to the block of text that frames the tall figure. It states that the accession of K'inich Kan Bahlam II on 9.12.11.12.10 8 Ok 3 K'ayab when he was 48 years old was followed by an event some six years later on 2 Kib 14 Mol (at age 55). The accession statement begins in the block of text in front of the tall figure's face and ends in the first glyph block behind him. In order to read the complete accession statement, the viewer is drawn across the head of the tall figure. Again, the obvious conclusion to draw is that the tall figure is K'inich Kan Bahlam II performing his accession ceremony.

The artist of the Tablet of the Cross constructed a brilliant work of art that illustrates two events that occurred at the same location and involved the same subject, but that occurred on different dates. The caption texts and the bilateral symmetry of the central icon divide the scene into two parts. The representations of K'inich Kan Bahlam II as a young prince and as a king contrast the junior and senior aspects of this individual. Complementary opposition is further seen in the bands that form the base of the scene. The young K'inich Kan Bahlam II stands on a band marked with night symbols (night, moon and star signs) while the older K'inich Kan Bahlam II's band is composed of sun and sky signs. It is interesting that on the occasion of his accession, K'inich Kan Bahlam II acquired his *k'inich* title that is related to the heat of the sun, and he is depicted standing above a *k'in* "sun" sign.

Given the persistent claims that the small figure is a portrait of the dead K'inich Janaab Pakal I (Houston and Taube 2000:271; Taube 2004:78; Eberl and Graña-Behrens 2004:103; Houston, Stuart, and Taube 2006:150), a brief digression is in order to discuss the history of this identification. In his first discussion of the Cross Group figures, George Kubler (1969) noted that all three tablets illustrated the same pair of figures. He suggested that the shorter figure may have been a foreigner from the cooler highland region to the south of Palenque, based on the thickness of his clothing. He also noted the presence of the "sun shield" (K'inich Janaab Pakal) sign in the adjacent caption texts. In a later publication, Kubler (1972) continued with his supposition that the short figure was a foreigner. He noted that the caption texts adjacent to the tall figure (on all three Cross Group Tablets) referred to a date in AD 683 (the date is January 10, 684) and that the caption text adjacent to the short figure on the Tablet of the Cross and Tablet of the Foliated Cross refers to a date 43 years earlier (actually 42.5 years earlier). He correctly identified the tall figure as "Jaguar Snake" (Kan Bahlam), based on the appearance of this nominal phrase in the caption text adjacent to the figure. Kubler argued that the clothing of the short figure was related to motifs from Teotihuacán, and he incorrectly identified this figure as "he of the pyramid" based on the pyramid glyph (T685) that follows the date in the adjacent caption text. The T685 pyramid glyph is a pictograph of a tiered structure with a staircase. Although unbeknownst to Kubler at the time, the T685 glyph in this context functions as part of a verb and has nothing directly to do with the identity of the figure per se.

Linda Schele presented an analysis of the Cross Group panels at the 1974 Mesa Redonda (Schele 1976). She noted that K'inich Janaab Pakal I's nominal phrase occasionally includes a title that contains the T685 glyph. This title is composed of the number five, T685, and the T4 *nah* "house" glyph.[4] Schele argued that the pyramid verb was a reference to K'inich Janaab Pakal I, and further noted that K'inich Janaab Pakal I's name glyph appears later in the caption text. She therefore concluded that the small figure was K'inich Janaab Pakal I. Ignoring the other three Calendar Round dates of the caption text, Schele further concluded that the scene represented one moment in time, the transfer of power from K'inich Janaab Pakal I to his son K'inich Kan Bahlam II on the occasion of K'inich Kan Bahlam II's accession. Given that K'inich Janaab Pakal I was deceased at this time, Schele speculated that the clothing worn by the small figure and his diminutive size somehow indicated death.

In 1970, Christopher Jones wrote a paper on Tikal parentage statements, and circulated it to a small group of colleagues (Jones 1977). He noted that the names of the protagonists in several Tikal texts were followed by other nominal phrases referring to a male and female, and he logically concluded that these were parentage statements. When Linda Schele first presented her analysis of the Cross Group panels, she was unaware of Jones's work. She did not realize that the subject of the Cross Group caption text narrative was

K'inich Kan Bahlam II, and that K'inich Janaab Pakal I's name only appears at that end of K'inich Kan Bahlam II's nominal phrase as part of his parentage statement.[5]

During the 1975–1976 academic year, Floyd Lounsbury conducted a Maya hieroglyphic writing seminar at Yale during which he discussed the identification of the small figure. Schele attended this seminar and made cassette recordings (digitized tape recordings made available to the author by David and Elaine Schele from the private archives of Linda Schele). In these recordings, Lounsbury noted that the T685 verb of the 9.10.8.9.3 9 Ak'bal 8 Xul event is not the "pyramid" title of K'inich Janaab Pakal I and, therefore, this verb could not be used as evidence that the small figure was this king. He further noted that K'inich Janaab Pakal I's name only occurs in the caption texts as part of K'inich Kan Bahlam II's parentage statement. He tentatively suggested that the two figures might both be portraits of K'inich Kan Bahlam II. At the time, Schele dismissed these facts and maintained that the clothing indicated death and that the scene was a transfer of power from the deceased king to his son (Lounsbury, personal communication 1986). Lounsbury's interpretation was regretfully not disseminated outside of his classroom.

In the fall of 1986, Bassie-Sweet began research for a paper on the relationship between text and image using the basic premise that the text is a narrative, and that the text in closest proximity to a figure names that figure. When she applied that premise to the Palenque monuments, it became apparent to her, just has it had been to Lounsbury, that the small figure on the Cross Group tablets was a young K'inich Kan Bahlam II. Using this simple framing convention, she also concluded that the actions on the Dumbarton Oaks Tablet and the Temple XIV panel that had been identified as postmortem events by Schele and Lounsbury were, in fact, pre-accession events (see below). In telephone conversations, she explained her premise and findings to Kathryn Josserand, Nick Hopkins, John Fought, and David Stuart, who readily accepted her new interpretations. She subsequently sent a draft paper to several researchers including Lounsbury who responded with a letter detailing his prior identification of the small figure on the Cross Group panels as a young K'inich Kan Bahlam II. Bassie-Sweet presented her arguments the following year in a session at the annual American Anthropological Association meeting organized by Josserand and Hopkins, and her work was published in 1991. Although her central argument was based on the positioning of the caption text in relation to the figures, she also pointed out that the ratio of size between the two figures matched that of the 53-year-old Bird Jaguar and his five-year-old son, Shield Jaguar IV, on Yaxchilán Lintel 2.

Although Schele resisted the identification of the short figure as the young K'inich Kan Bahlam (Schele and Freidel 1990:470), further confirmation of this identification came with a new decipherment of the initial phrase on the caption text framing the short figure on the Tablet of the Foliated Cross. This phrase identifies the short figure using the title *bah ch'ok* "first youth," which labels the heir apparent (Schele 1990). This is precisely who the six-year-old K'inich Kan Bahlam II was. Schele eventually accepted the identification of the short figure as a young K'inich Kan Bahlam II, but Houston and Taube have asserted that the small figure is the dead K'inich Janaab Pakal I, although they fail to give any evidence for their position other than citing Schele's initial work. While there are examples of a deceased ancestor interacting with the living, such as Copán Altar Q, these ancestors are identified by the caption texts adjacent to them or by the headdresses that spell out their names. Our point is that the framing convention cannot be used as a method of identifying subjects and actions by researchers when it suits their interpretation of a scene, but simply ignored when it does not. This overview of the Cross Group figures demonstrates how interpretations change in light of new decipherments and information. It also highlights the difficulties in challenging intepretations that are embedded in the literature.

VISUAL FOCUS

In scenes that contain more than one figure, a number of visual devices are used to focus attention on one of the figures and their actions. These include the frontal pose of the figure, elaboration of costume, the gaze of the other figures, or domination of the picture plane (Bassie-Sweet 1991). Similar conventions are also found in the scenes painted on ceramic vessels. Houston (1998) noted that the primary figure is often positioned on the right side of a scene, although there are many exceptions to this preference.

Elements of the scene are frequently positioned to draw attention to certain areas of text and facilitate the flow of the narrative. Yaxchilán Lintel 2 provides an excellent example of this convention (figure 3.2). Glyph block H is the name of the bird scepter, and the bird scepter held by Bird Jaguar overlaps the end of the glyph block. The scepter is held upright with the bird in a descending pattern of flight. Shield Jaguar IV's scepter and bird are positioned in a similar fashion. The birds fly in the direction of the reading order of the adjacent glyph blocks. The other scepter held by Bird Jaguar is positioned horizontally and the bird flies in the direction of the reading order of its adjacent glyph blocks.

FIGURE 5.7. *Yaxchilán Lintel 5, drawing after Ian Graham.*

A similar pattern appears on Yaxchilán Lintel 5 which also illustrates Bird Jaguar holding two bird scepters (figure 5.7). In this case, he is flanked by one of his wives, Lady Six Jalam Chan Ajaw. The narrative begins with the lower glyph block adjacent to Bird Jaguar's left leg and continues across his body to the glyph block adjacent to his right leg. This text refers to the bird scepter

160   TEXT AND IMAGE

dance performed by Bird Jaguar (Looper 2009:34). The bird on the scepter that he holds in his right hand flies towards the glyph block adjacent to his right leg. The narrative ends with the upper glyph block that is positioned between the scepter held by Bird Jaguar in his left hand and Lady Six Jalam Chan Ajaw's head. This text names her. The scepter is held vertically with the bird's body in a descending position, but the bird gazes in the direction of its adjacent glyph block, and its tail feather actually touches the top of the glyph block.

The placement of the long feathers of headdresses and back racks are often arranged to direct the reader to the next block of texts as well. For example, the feathers of Bird Jaguar's back rack on Lintel 5 are positioned in an upside-down U shape to facilitate the flow of the text from the right block of text to the left. The same convention is found on Yaxchilán Lintel 1, Lintel 2, and Lintel 3 (Bassie-Sweet 1991:56–57). The feathers of the backracks are slightly askew, which also suggests the movement of the dance.

These various examples exemplify the techniques and conventions used by Maya artists to create a narrative flow through a scene. Text and image contrast and complement each other, but they are also so often intermixed that the line between text and image is blurred.

VERBAL COUPLETS

As noted in chapter 4, the principal element that gives Mayan discourse its formality and sacredness is couplet structure (Gossen 1974a, 1977). Court language, sacred speech, prayers, and ancient stories are spoken in couplet form. The Popol Vuh is written in couplets, as are many other important indigenous documents (Edmonson 1971; Christenson 2003a, 2003b, 2012). Most monumental inscriptions are written in a grid pattern and are read in columns of two beginning in the upper left hand side of the grid. This placement of two consecutive glyphs side by side is visually reminiscent of verbal couplets and formal language.

Objects from the Late Preclassic and Early Classic periods are often inscribed with dedicatory texts or name tags. A Late Preclassic earflare excavated from a tomb at the site of Pomoná, Belize, is inscribed with couplets, suggesting that such rhetorical conventions were in use from an early date (Justeson et al. 1988; Carrasco 2005:218). Another example is found on the Leiden Plaque discussed in the Introduction. The front of the celt illustrates a Maya ruler with a captive sprawled at his feet while the inscription on the back of the celt records the Long Count date of 8.14.3.1.12 1 Eb, seating of Yaxk'in, and refers to the seating of the king using the same verb as the *haab* date. The

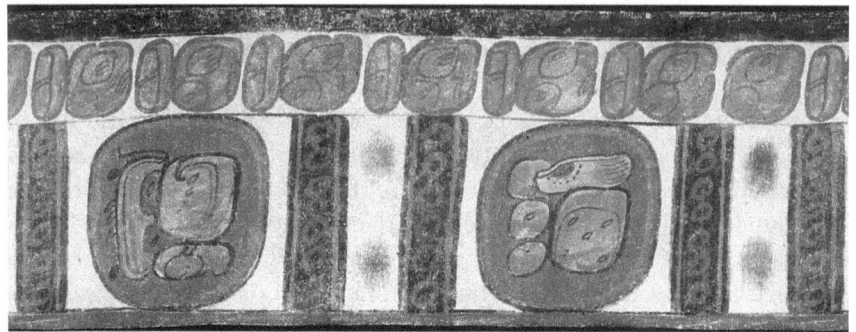

FIGURE 5.8. *Vessel K5466, photograph courtesy Justin Kerr.*

seating of the month was when the patron of the forthcoming month was put into power. The pairing of the seating of Yaxk'in and the seating of the king on the Leiden Plaque thus forms a couplet that cleverly equates the seating of the king with the seating of a month, suggesting the two are both natural, even inevitable, phenomena.

In Classic period monumental texts, Lounsbury (1980:107–115) was the first to note the use of hieroglyphic couplets in his discussion of the Tablet of the Cross text, which lists a series of accessions in couplet form. More recently, Carrasco (2012a) has discussed a variety of couplets found in Palenque inscriptions. As is discussed more fully in the next chapter, a prominent example of coupleting is seen on the Palenque Tablet of the 96 Glyphs, which records the accessions of K'inich K'an Joy Chitam II, K'inich Ahkal Mo' Nahb III, and K'inich K'uk' Bahlam II (figure 6.1). Each ruler's accession statement is paired with the statement that the accession occurred in House E of the Palace. These three couplet statements form a larger triplet construction that constitutes the event line of the narrative, anticipating the peak event.

Verbal couplets also appear on pottery vessels. The scene on vessel K5466 illustrates two oversized glyphs painted on red cartouches (figure 5.8). The glyphs read *u jaay* "his clay vessel" and *yuk'ib'* "his drinking vessel" (see Stuart 2005d for an overview of the decipherment). This couplet is an abbreviated form of the longer Primary Standard Sequence (PSS). Coe (1973) coined this PSS term for the dedicatory texts that are painted around the lips of some vessels. The PSS typically includes a dedicatory statement, the kind of vessel it is, its purpose or contents, and the owner's name (Stuart 1989; MacLeod 1990; Mora-Marín 2004). The PSS visually functions like a counterclockwise circuit around a ritual space that defines and sanctifies that space. Ultimately, the PSS transforms an ordinary vessel into one that can be used in sacred acts.

FIGURE 5.9. *Vessel K2695, photograph courtesy Justin Kerr.*

Another instance of a couplet in a pottery scene is vessel K2695, which depicts a throne within a building (figure 5.9). A lord stands in front of the throne while flanked by male and female attendants. The jambs of the building at either end of the scene are painted with three cartouches that state *tz'ib'al naah* "the writing house" and *yotot 'bakab* "the house of the Bakab." The terms *naah* and *otot* can both refer to architectural structures, but *otot* carries the connotation of ownership and home. The K2695 couplet is describing the illustrated throne room as a place where writing was produced and where the Bakab dwelled: "the house of writing, the home of the Bakab."

VISUAL COUPLETS

There are many examples of visual couplets in Maya art. The quetzal and macaw on the Copán Margarita façade with their mirror-like symmetry form a visual couplet (figure 5.5). The motif of two intertwined birds is also found on an Early Classic vessel, but in this case the birds are a macaw and a turkey (Hellmuth 1987).[6] In the Madrid Codex (page 85a), a turkey and vulture are entwined. While we might not understand the relevance of these two latter motifs, the juxtaposing of the two birds again forms a visual couplet.

More obvious examples of visual couplets are found on the hundreds of pottery vessels where two almost identical motifs or scenes are painted on either side of the vessel. A beautiful illustration is K1387; it depicts two avian manifestations of the deity One Ixim (figure 5.10). Other examples are seen

FIGURE 5.10. *Vessel K1387, photograph courtesy Justin Kerr.*

FIGURE 5.11. *Dieseldorff vase, watercolor by M. Louise Baker, courtesy of University of Pennsylvania Museum of Archaeology and Anthropology, image #165148.*

on nine vessels from Tikal Burial 116 that have two scenes separated by a column of glyphs or motifs (Culbert 1993:fig. 69–75). A Chamá vase in the Dieseldorff collection illustrates two almost identical depictions of the corn god One Ixim (figure 5.11). Adjacent to each figure is a caption text composed

FIGURE 5.12. *Chamá bat vase*, watercolor by M. Louise Baker, courtesy of University of Pennsylvania Museum of Archaeology and Anthropology, image #165052.

of two sequential *tzolk'in* day names without a corresponding numerical coefficent. The left caption is Ben (the thirteenth day in the *tzolk'in* sequence) and Ix (fourteenth day) while the right caption is Kib (sixteenth day) and Kaban (seventeenth day). Another Chamá vessel illustrates two supernatural bats with outstretched wings (figure 5.12). Adjacent to each bat is a column of glyphs consisting of Kaban and Kawak (nineteenth day) glyphs repeated three times. The Kaban glyphs are painted white while the Kawak signs are red. This coloring visually enhances the couplet structure of these glyphs. An unprovenanced vessel now in the Duke University Museum of Art (K5354) highlights the importance of couplet structure. This vessel depicts two virtually identical supernatural animals separated by columns of pseudoglyphs (figure 5.13). There is a relatively large corpus of pottery vessels that contain elements that take the form of a hieroglyph, but do not represent words (Calvin 2006). Despite the fact that the pseudoglyphs on K5354 do not signify words, they are painted in alternating white and red colors that form visual couplets. The artist of K5354 may not have known how to write proper hieroglyphs, but he clearly understood the importance of poetic structure.

There are also pottery scenes that relate a sequential series of events that form both a verbal and visual couplet, such as that found on K1183 (figure 5.14). The first column of text on the vessel begins with a dedicatory phrase and ends with the name of the object that was dedicated. This object is represented by an Ik' cartouche. To the right of the dedicatory text, Itzamnaaj is

FIGURE 5.13. *Vessel K5354, photograph courtesy Justin Kerr.*

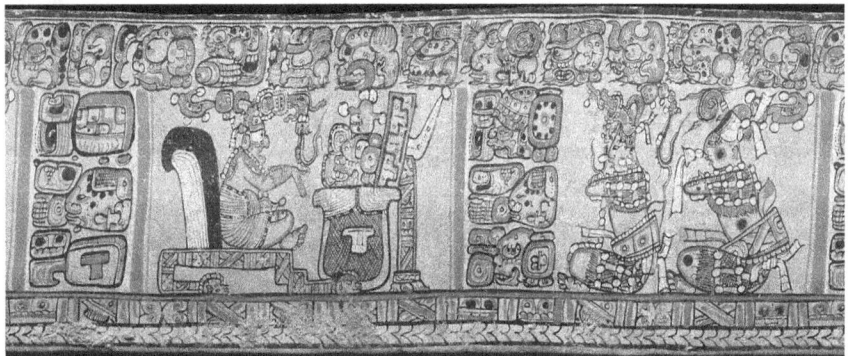

FIGURE 5.14. *Vessel K1183, photograph courtesy Justin Kerr.*

pictured sitting on his celestial throne. A large jar decorated with an Ik' sign is positioned in front of him. The jar contains a skull sitting in an unwrapped cloth bundle. The skull appears to be propped up against a back rest. Behind the skull bundle and jar is a second column of text that also begins with a dedicatory phrase and ends with the name of the object that was dedicated. In this case, the object is named as a white skull. To the right of this column of text sit One Ixim and his son One Ajaw looking in the direction of Itzamnaaj and the skull jar. The two parallel dedicatory texts form a verbal couplet that appear to refer to the Ik' jar and skull, but these two caption texts also break the scene into two parts and create a visual couplet.[7]

THE POETIC STRUCTURE OF CO-ESSENCES VESSELS

A small number of pottery scenes illustrate co-essences with adjacent caption texts that name the co-essence and the human possessor of the co-essence

FIGURE 5.15. *Vessel K793, photograph courtesy Justin Kerr.*

FIGURE 5.16. *Vessel K791, photograph courtesy Justin Kerr.*

(Houston and Stuart 1989; Grube and Nahm 1994). The standard phrase is "X is the co-essence of Y," with Y often named as the lord of a particular royal house or site. Many of the Classic-period pottery vessels that feature co-essences, such as vessel K771, present them as a sequential group of three co-essences that are depicted in a row with their caption texts in front of them. There are two unprovenanced vessels (K793 and K791) now housed in the Princeton Museum that expand on this triplet theme. As noted by Just (2012:139), it is likely that these two vessels were produced by the same artist and probably even came from the same tomb. Vessel K793 illustrates three pairs of co-essences (figure 5.15). Each pair faces one another with a caption text situated between them. The left figure sits in profile while the right figure sits in a frontal pose placing more emphasis on him. In terms of narrative structure, these images form an AB-AB-AB triplet. In contrast to the pairs of co-essences on K793, the co-essences on K791 are arranged in groups of three (figure 5.16). On the left of each group two co-essences are stacked one above the other (AB) with a third, standing co-essence to the right (C). These nine co-essences form a triplet structure of ABC-ABC-ABC. A similar poetic composition is seen on the famous Altar de Sacrificios vase where two pairs of three co-essences are illustrated that form a couplet of ABC-ABC (figure 5.17).

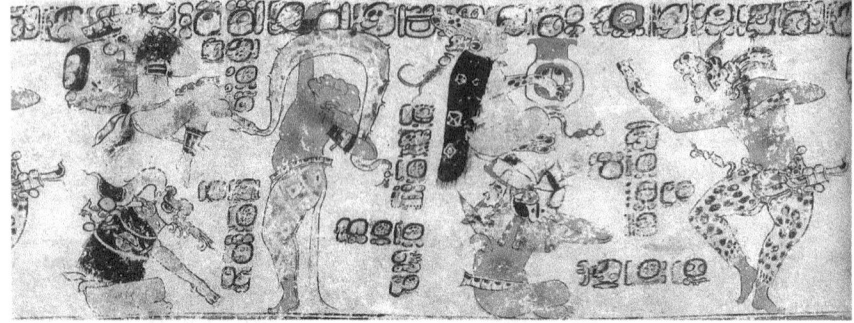

Figure 5.17. *Altar de Sacrificios vase, Vessel K30088, photograph courtesy Inga Calvin, curated by Museo Nacional de Arqueología y Etnología, Guatemala.*

In ethnographic sources, co-essences play a prominent role in social control, and are thought to be agents of certain illnesses or diseases. Stuart has suggested that the Classic-period co-essences illustrated in pottery scenes were directly related to illness:

> My contention, based on specific evidence presented at the Forum, is that the *way* beings are representations of the animated dark forces wielded by Classic Maya sorcerers in their attempts to influence other people, and perhaps other rulers. One could think of them as spells, curses, or other sorts of enchantments wielded by *brujos*. These could be manifested as diseases and afflictions of the body, or perhaps as some other misfortune, but the point always seems to be their harmful effects on others. Mesoamerican folktales are replete with such beings, and many are described in published ethnographies and other sources. (Stuart 2005)

There is considerable evidence that co-essences were intimately linked to both curses and cures (Helmke and Nielsen 2009; Hoopes and Mora-Marín 2009). In the Maya region, the curing of illness first requires the healer to ascertain the supernatural source of the illness. The incantations for the cure of certain diseases that are recorded in the Ritual of the Bacabs indicate that the healer recited the nature of the illness, including its personified form and parentage (Roys 1965). In light of this tradition, it is possible that the vessels featuring co-essences were produced for a curing ceremony or to commemorate the successful completion of a curing ceremony. In other words, they do not represent a curse directed at someone or at some community, rather they represent a successful incantation against the afflictions. Their poetic structure echoes the couplet structure of the Ritual of the Bacab incantations.

OTHER FORMS OF VISUAL COUPLETS

As noted in earlier chapters, the word *tz'ak* "completion" is often written with a metonymic glyph that contrasts two complementary opposites such as sun and moon (Hull 1997; 2003, 2012; Knowlton 2002; Stuart 2003a). These opposite signs form a visual couplet. The Yaxchilán cartouches discussed in chapter 1, which depict the father and mother of the ruler as inhabitants of the Place of the Duality in the sky, also form visual couplets. Yaxchilán Stela 4 illustrates them within cartouches that contrast the sun and moon, respectively. Although this has been interpreted to mean that the parents became the sun and moon in the afterlife, we would caution against such a literal interpretation. In fact, the mother within the moon cartouche wears the headdress of the deity GI, who is not associated with the moon. It is more likely that this visual couplet on Stela 4 was intended to display the parents of the ruler not just as members of the Place of Duality, but as the embodiment of duality.

A prime example of unusual couplet structure is found in the Temple Inscription of Copán Structure 10L-26-1. This inscription, which is composed of 24 glyphs blocks, frames a niche on the wall of the inner temple and is executed using full-figure glyphs. Stuart (2000, 2005b, 2008) observed that it is actually two parallel texts of 12 glyph blocks each that appear to repeat the same sequence of words. He noted that one text uses imagery associated with Teotihuacán while the other is in a traditional Maya script. The full figures of the Teotihuacán-style font are more accurately described as beings dressed in the guise of the deity Tlaloc. These figures have the face of Tlaloc and/or wear his distinctive headdress. The legs of at least three figures take the form of the meteor serpent avatar of Tlaloc, which is named 18 Ub'aah Chan in the Maya region, much like K'awiil is often illustrated with a lightning serpent leg. Other figures have 18 U B'aah Chan faces or take on the guise of this deity by wearing an 18 Ub'aah Chan headdress. The Teotihuacán-styled font does not at all resemble the writing system at Teotihuacán or any other Mesoamerican system. Nevertheless, Stuart characterized the inscription as being like the Rosetta Stone with the Teotihuacán-style "font" being paired with the traditional font. We offer a different explanation. From the perspective of poetic structure, the two texts form a couplet. The inscription is, in fact, a masterpiece of verbal and visual couplet structure.

CHIASMUS STRUCTURE

Carrasco (2012a:139) noted an instance of chiasmus structure in the Temple of the Inscriptions narrative that deals with the 9.11.0.0.0 and 9.12.0.0.0

Period Ending ceremonies. The 9.11.0.0.0 Period Ending actions performed by K'inich Janaab Pakal I are presented in standard order while those of the 9.12.0.0.0 Period Ending are reversed. He also discussed a chiasmus structure found in the caption texts of the Tablet of the Orator and Tablet of the Scribe (Carrasco 2012a:157–160). These two panels originally flanked a throne in the House E courtyard. They illustrate two kneeling captives in mirror-image to each other. The texts form a chiasmus structure that echoes their mirror-image portraits:

Tablet of the Orator
A The person of ? is your creation-darkness
B the vassal of Ahkal Mo' Naab, the Bakab

Tablet of the Scribe
B Seen is your person/body Lord of Matwiil
A the gift/child of your creation-darkness

The presence of an ABBA chiasmus structure has been identified on the Copán Structure 8N-11 bench (Bassie-Sweet 2013b) (figure 2.2). As noted in chapter 2, this sky band features full-figure glyphs that contrast the complementary opposites of day-night and moon-Venus. From left to right, the glyphs are portraits of One Ixim as a lunar patron (A), an *ak'bal* god representing night (B), a central axis (C) composed of the T1017 head (see below), the sun god representing day (B), and a scorpion deity as a patron of Venus (A). This is the chiasmus structure of AB-C-BA. As an aside, the Copán bench sun god is pictured in the act of emerging from his centipede cartouche, which refers to the dawn when the sun is rising. Similarly, the *ak'bal* god is seen in the reclining pose that is specifically identified with birth. So these two gods contrast, not day and night per se, but the birth of the day and the birth of the night, that is, dawn and sunset. Visually, it is a very clever and subtle opposition.

The poses of these deities are symmetrical, with the moon and Venus patrons (A) facing away from each other and the dawn and sunset gods (B) facing each other. The T1017 head that is the central axis of this bilateral symmetry is positioned between the dawn and sunset gods. A sky band with a similar kind of bilateral symmetry is seen on the back of Quiriguá Stela I, which illustrates a back rack worn by the ruler K'ak' Tiliw (figure 5.18). The back rack features a human figure framed by a sky band. The left side of the sky band is composed of a moon glyph, square-nosed beastie and crossed-band sky glyph (ABC) while the right side is a *k'in* "sun" glyph, square-nosed beastie and cross-band

FIGURE 5.18. *Quiriguá Stela I, after Matthew Looper.*

sky glyph (ABC). The individual glyphs are not positioned like a column of vertical text, but rather are turned on their sides and facing inward. The moon and sun signs (A) are complementary opposites. The square-nosed beastie (B) and cross-band sky glyphs (C) are mirror images of each other. Bilateral symmetry is a widespread convention in Maya art, and it was frequently used to create visual couplets as well as chiasmus structures as will be further discussed below.[8]

A visual chiasmus structure is found on vessel K533, which depicts the Motul de San José lord Yahawte' K'inich dancing with a lord from the site of Hix Witz. The lords who are dressed in jaguar costumes are portrayed in a frontal pose with heads turned to face each other. They are each flanked by a secondary lord. These figures form a visual chiasmus couplet of ABBA. The figures on vessel K2695 also have this chiasmus structure (figure 5.9). The central male and female face each while standing in a frontal pose. A secondary male and female stand adjacent to them in profile, again forming an ABBA structure.

TEXT AND IMAGE COUPLETS

Houston and Miller (1987) argued that monumental scenes do not portray one moment in time, but rather the totality of an event. They are correct in the

FIGURE 5.19. *Dresden Codex Wayeb pages, after J. Antonio Villacorta and Carlos A. Villacorta.*

sense that the scene is not intended to be a snapshot of the moment, but rather a stylized and ritualized record of the event. Nevertheless, there are a number of monuments where the verb in the text refers directly to the pictured action in the image. Such monuments include Yaxchilán Stela 1 and La Pasadita Lintel 2, where the verb is a logograph of a left hand with drops falling from it, representing the verb *chok* "to scatter" (Grube cited in Schele and Grube 1995:40), and the scene shows the ruler with drops falling from his hands (figure 5.3). In addition, there are many monuments where the verb is a general statement of the event and it forms a couplet with the image (Bassie-Sweet 1991:41). For instance, Period Ending narratives frequently refer to the wrapping of a stone, yet the image shows the conjuring of deities by the ruler (Stuart 1996).

Multiple actions within a scene can also form couplets such as in the four Dresden Codex Wayeb pages that illustrate four gods making offerings to the directional Yearbearer deity and his trees (pages 25–28). The adjacent caption texts refer to the placement of the four world trees, but the action depicted in each scene shows the god holding up a decapitated bird in his right hand while scattering incense in a downward motion from his left hand (figure

5.19).⁹ In the Dresden context, page 26c shows the drops falling into a burning incensario, so it is apparent that the left hand of the Dresden deity refers to the throwing of incense into a burner. In his description of the Wayeb ceremonies performed by the Postclassic Yucatec Maya, Bishop Diego de Landa gives a detailed description of the offerings given to the Yearbearer deity that were modeled after these mythological actions. He noted that, after burning incense as an offering to the deity, the priest cut off the head of a turkey hen and gave the head as an offering (Tozzer 1941:141, 144, 146, 147). This has significant implications for the Dresden action because it suggests that the action of the god holding up the decapitated hen in his right hand does not reference the act of giving a headless turkey to the Yearbearer deity and his tree, but rather the act of decapitating the turkey. The turkey in the first scene even has blood still spurting from its neck. Given Landa's description, it can be concluded that the left and right hands of the Dresden gods form a couplet referencing the sequential acts of burning incense and decapitating a turkey.

Another example of multiple actions in one scene is found on Yaxchilán Lintel 8, where the ruler Bird Jaguar and his subordinate *sajal* are illustrated in the heat of battle subduing their respective enemies (figure 5.20). The sentence stating the capture of Jeweled Skull by Bird Jaguar begins on the upper left of the scene and concludes on the upper right. By reading this capture text, the viewer is brought to the image of Bird Jaguar grasping the arm of Jeweled Skull who is further identified by his name glyph inscribed on his thigh. The smaller block of text that frames the *sajal* names him, and it states that he is the captor of another prisoner. The latter is also branded by a name glyph on his thigh. It is possible that both captures historically happen adjacent to each other, but it is more likely that they are juxtaposed to form a couplet. Both lords are dressed as Tlaloc warriors, although Bird Jaguar is more emphasized by his additional costume elements, including the headdress of the Black Witch Moth Tlaloc, and by the fact that he carries the obsidian meteor spear associated with this god. The overlap of the bodies of the two captives places Jewel Skull in the foreground and places further importance on Bird Jaguar's capture. The bilateral symmetry of their poses forms a visual chiasmus: captor, captive, captive, captor.

Other examples in which the verb of the narrative expresses the action of the image are found in scenes of dancing where the verb is *ahk'ot* "to dance" and the scene shows a figure dancing (Grube 1992). This verb is often followed by the name of the type of dance performed, and the scene shows dancers performing with objects or costume elements that refer to the type of dance (Looper 2009:16–20). Some of these dance scenes form a visual couplet, such

FIGURE 5.20. *Yaxchilán Lintel 8, after Ian Grahma.*

as the dances of the deity One Ixim that are illustrated on pottery. One Ixim is often illustrated twice, as on K517, K703, K1837, and K4464. While both depictions are usually dressed in a similar fashion, their gestures and poses are often contrasted. They also carry different supernatural animals in their back racks. In some examples, such as K3400 and K8966, a caption text accompanies each depiction of One Ixim. The two caption texts are structurally similar, and they form a verbal couplet.

Monumental works of art can also have couplet form. Both Yaxchilán Stela 35 and Lintel 25 illustrate Yaxchilán queens conjuring a female ancestor by the name of Lady Ohl, who was intimately related to the Tlaloc deity K'ahk' O' Chahk (Bassie-Sweet 2008:fig. 39, 47; 2013). On the front of Yaxchilán Stela 35, Lady Ik' Skull is seen holding the skull of Lady Ohl in her right hand and a bowl of bloodletting instruments in her left (figure 5.21A). Lady Ik' Skull wears a similar skull motif in her headdress, but this skull wears a Tlaloc

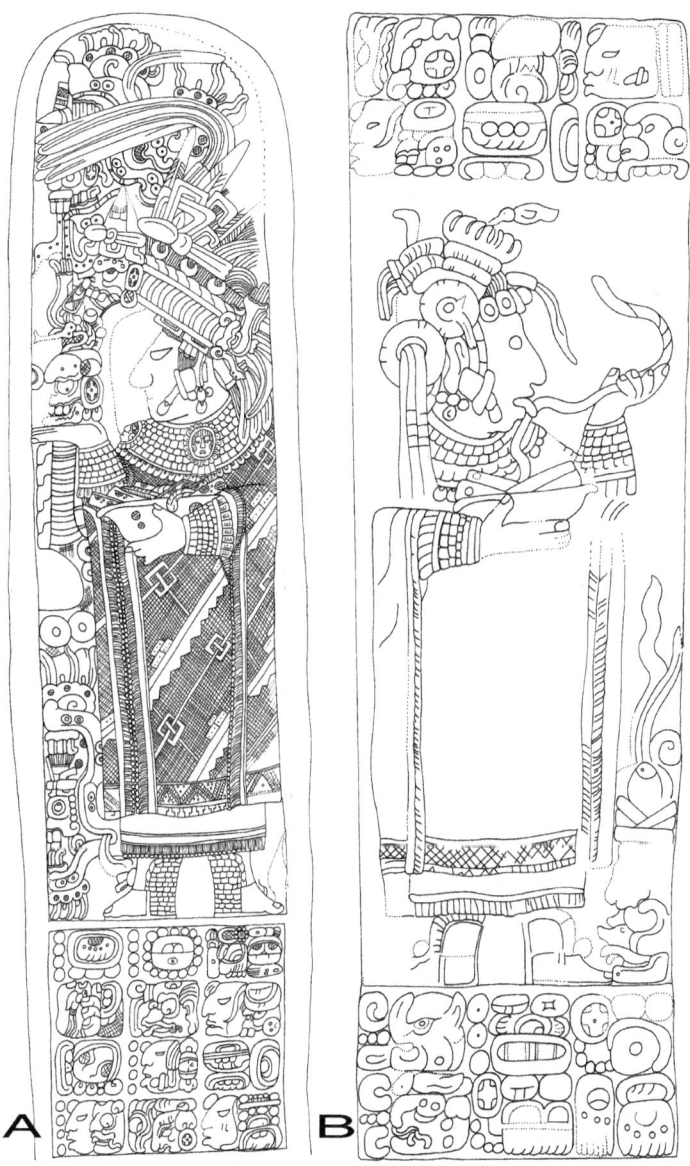

FIGURE 5.21. *Yaxchilán Stela 35, drawing by Karen Bassie-Sweet.*

headdress. In other words, the headdress skull has been dressed as Tlaloc. A double-headed 18 Ub'aah Chan serpent rises behind Lady Ik' Skull with Tlaloc deities emerging from its mouths. The text at the base of the scene begins with the date and states that the conjuring was under the authority of four females, but their name phrases are undeciphered. The text then refers to the penance of Lady Ik' Skull. The narrative continues on the back of the monument which illustrates Lady Ik' Skull pulling a sacrificial cord through her tongue (figure 5.21B). At her feet is a bowl containing burning offerings. The text begins above her head with a statement referring to her sacrifice and ends with the text beneath her feet that states she is the mother of Bird Jaguar. Thus, the narratives on the front and back of Stela 35 form a sequential couplet.

SEQUENTIAL COUPLETS ON THE PALENQUE TEMPLE XIX PLATFORM

As discussed in the previous chapter, the scene on the Palenque Palace Tablet illustrates a sequential couplet (figure 4.1). The young K'inich K'an Joy Chitam II, who is flanked by his father, K'inich Janaab Pakal I, and his mother, Lady Tz'akbu Ajaw, is pictured in the process of receiving two objects from them, the Ux Yop Huun headdress and the *tok'-pakal* icon. K'inich Janaab Pakal I and his wife Lady Tz'akbu Ajaw sit in mirror-image of each other. Both wear the headdress of the Waterlily Bird-Serpent. K'inich K'an Joy Chitam II faces towards his father and leans slightly towards him. K'inich K'an Joy Chitam II's position is structurally similar to the central icon on the Tablet of the Cross that divides the scene into two sequential events. A more complex sequential action is found in the scene carved on the side of the Palenque Temple XIX platform. This scene shows the ruler K'inich Ahkal Mo' Nahb III sitting on a throne (Stuart 2005a) (figure 5.22). On the left side of the scene are three secondary lords seated in profile. The caption texts adjacent to these lords identify them as holders of an office nicknamed the "banded-bird" because it has yet to be deciphered (Stuart 2005a:133–136). This office had priestly duties (Zender 2004b). The caption text that frames the first priest states that he is a secondary lord called Janaab Ajaw who is impersonating Itzamnaaj. He holds in his extended hand the *sak huun* headdress of rulership. K'inich Ahkal Mo' Nahb III leans forward ready to accept this crown. The caption text that names K'inich Ahkal Mo' Nahb III is divided into two blocks of text in front of him. It begins by saying that he is impersonating the deity GI. Although the area of K'inich Ahkal Mo' Nahb III's headdress has been damaged, the avian manifestation of GI that takes the form of a heron eating a fish protrudes out from the headdress area, and it is juxtaposed beside GI's name phrase in the first block of caption text. To the right of K'inich Ahkal Mo' Nahb III is a headdress perched on a stand and another set of three

FIGURE 5.22. *Palenque Temple XIX platform, after David Stuart.*

secondary lords. This headdress is similar in construction to the Ux Yop Huun headdress seen on the Palace Tablet. The first lord is seated in a frontal pose, indicating his superior status. His name phrase is juxtaposed with the Ux Yop Huun headdress, and the feathers of his headdress and that of the Ux Yop Huun overlap. It has been argued that this secondary lord was the caretaker of this headdress at the time of K'inich Ahkal Mo' Nahb III's accession (Zender 2004b:317; Bassie-Sweet, Hopkins, and Josserand 2012).

The main text of the panel is divided into two large blocks that flank the scene. It relates a series of mythological events including the accession of GI which is said to have occurred under the authority of Itzamnaaj, and the historical events of K'inich Ahkal Mo' Nahb III, including his accession and a Period Ending event. As noted by Stuart (2005a), the accession of K'inich Ahkal Mo' Nahb III as pictured in the scene was patterned after that of GI with the priest taking the role of Itzamnaaj and K'inich Ahkal Mo' Nahb III taking on the guise of GI. The juxtaposing of the secondary lords on the right side of the scene with the Ux Yop Huun headdress suggests that the next step in the day's events involved this headdress. The Tablet of the Slaves shows this to be the case. This tablet illustrates K'inich Ahkal Mo' Nahb III receiving the Ux Yop Huun and *tok'-pakal* on the day of his accession (Wald 1997) (figure 5.23). Clearly the function that the Ux Yop Huun headdress represented was of great importance to K'inich Ahkal Mo' Nahb III, as it was to K'inich K'an Joy Chitam II, yet it is not referenced in the main text of the Temple XIX platform.[10]

In brief, the left side of the Temple XIX platform illustrates the climactic moment of K'inich Ahkal Mo' Nahb III's accession just before he donned the *sak huun* while the right side alludes to his subsequent acquisition of the Ux Yop Huun. These two actions form a sequential couplet. The caption texts that name the far left and far right secondary lords are positioned adjacent to the ends of their loincloths and intrude laterally into the space of the main text. Their parallel depiction emphasizes the bilateral symmetry of the scene and its couplet composition.

FIGURE 5.23. *Palenque Tablet of the Slaves, after Linda Schele.*

THE COUPLET STRUCTURE OF THE PALENQUE TEMPLE XXI BENCH

A scene that features sequential but parallel actions is found on the front panel of the Temple XXI bench (figure 5.24). In the center of the scene, a figure sits cross-legged on a pillow throne with a jaguar-skin back rest. He extends a bloodletting perforator towards two individuals on his right. The first individual, who is wearing a cape of feathers or leaves, is pictured in an identical cross-legged pose. An animal figure kneels in profile before the caped lord and

FIGURE 5.24. *Palenque Temple XXI platform, after David Stuart.*

extends an unusual object towards him. The object appears to be composed of the same material as the cape, with five tassels coming out of the center. The right side of the scene illustrates another caped figure and animal figure performing a similar action, but the two figures have been reversed and they form a mirror-like image of the poses on the left side.

The central figure sits at a slightly higher level than the flanking figures. His throne overlaps the knee and foot of each caped figure while his bloodletter overlaps the left caped figure. This puts the enthroned figure in the foreground of the scene and places great emphasis on him. His gaze and gesture direct attention to the two individuals seated on his right. The diagonal line created by the perforator and the crossed arms of the caped figure as well as his downward gaze place emphasis on the tasseled object. The two depictions of the action involving the tasseled object differ in a subtle, but significant detail. The left figure is actively engaged in the action as he reaches out and touches the tasseled object with his left hand while the right figure sits in a more passive pose with his left hand still resting on his leg. This follows the composition on the Palace Tablet, Tablet of the Slaves, and Temple XIX platform where the left side of the scene represents an event in motion while the right shows a sequential event about to begin.

The Temple XXI narrative commences with the block of text above the head of the caped lord on the left. It is a nominal phrase that opens with the statement that *okib* is the *ch'ok* "youth" name of K'inich Ahkal Mo' Nahb III and then gives this ruler's regnal name. By using his pre-accession name, the text clearly identifies the caped figure as being the pre-regnal K'inich Ahkal Mo' Nahb III. The narrative continues with the block of text between K'inich Ahkal Mo' Nahb III and the animal figure. This caption text names the animal figure and indicates he is a secondary lord who carries the banded-bird title of priests. Why the priest takes on this unusual animal form is unknown.

The next two blocks of text frame the central figure. This text is an impersonation statement that names the enthroned figure as K'inich Janaab Pakal I in the guise of an individual whose name has not been fully deciphered and whose identity has yet to be clearly determined. The nominal phrase is composed of two parts. The first is a phonetic *ch'a* sign prefixed to the T1077 sign. T1077 is a Chahk portrait that has an element over the mouth that resembles the cartoon character Casper the Friendly Ghost. This Casper-like element often stands as the *pars pro toto* for the portrait glyph. The Tablet of the Cross lists an Early Classic king (circa AD 435) whose name is represented solely by the Casper-like element. This Palenque king was, thus, whimsically nicknamed Casper. Given that T1077 has not been deciphered, the Casper nickname is retained here.[11]

The second part of the nominal phrase in the Temple XXI caption text is a prepositional phrase that contains a pictograph of a stingray spine used for bloodletting and a serpent (*chan*). This phrase was initially deciphered as *U K'ix Chan*, but there is evidence that the correct reading is *u kokan chan* (Davletshin 2003; Stone and Zender 2011:79). In either case, the name can be glossed as "the stingray spine of the serpent." In the Temple XXI scene, K'inich Janaab Pakal I wears a headdress that includes the T93 *ch'a* sign, the T1077 Casper sign, and a serpent with a stingray spine protruding from his mouth. By reading the first block of text, the viewer is brought to the action of K'inich Janaab Pakal I holding a stingray spine bloodletter. To finish reading K'inich Janaab Pakal I's nominal phrase, the reader is drawn across his headdress that spells out the name Casper-U Kokan Chan.

The narrative continues with the block of text over the head of the right figure that names him as U Pakal K'inich, and states that he is the *bah ch'ok*. The caption text between U Pakal K'inich and the animal figure repeats the name of the priest. There is circumstantial evidence from other monuments that K'inich Ahkal Mo' Nahb III was the grandson of K'inich Janaab Pakal I (Bassie-Sweet 1991:247–248; Ringle 1996), and that U Pakal K'inich was either the son or brother of K'inich Ahkal Mo' Nahb III (Bernal Romero 2002; Stuart 2005a). K'inich Ahkal Mo' Nahb III was born in AD 678 and acceded in 722, but no death date for him is currently known. No birth, accession, or death dates survive for U Pakal K'inich, but the Temple XVI text indicates he was ruling by 742, and that he took the full name U Pakal K'inich Janaab Pakal at his accession.

In the scene on the Temple XXI bench, both K'inich Ahkal Mo' Nahb III and U Pakal K'inich have pre-accession names in their nominal phrases, which indicates that their actions with the tasseled object refer to events that happened before their respective accessions (Carrasco 2005). Like the Temple XIX platform, these caption texts contain no Calendar Round dates to indicate when the depicted actions occurred, and we must look to the main text for clarification. The main text is composed of a single line of glyphs across the front lip of the bench and two large blocks of text on the right and left sides of the bench scene. It begins with the Long Count date of 9.13.17.9.0 3 Ajaw 3 Yaxk'in (AD 709) and a Period Ending event involving the reigning king K'inich K'an Joy Chitam II. This is one of the 900-day Period Endings of the *k'atun*. The text goes on to describe the role of the *okib ch'ok* and U Pakal K'inich *ch'ok* in this event. Although it has been suggested that the name *okib ch'ok* refers to U Pakal K'inich in this passage (Stuart 2005a:86), the caption text has already indicated that the *okib ch'ok* was K'inich Ahkal Mo' Nahb III. In other words, this passage indicates that both of these *ch'ok* lords participated in this 900-day Period Ending event. At this point in time, K'inich Ahkal Mo' Nahb III was already 31, so the designation of *ch'ok* is clearly related to his junior status in the hierarchy of the court and not to age.

The glyph representing their roles in this 900-day Period Ending has not been deciphered, but this same date and Period Ending verb also appear on the Temple XIX stucco pier in reference to an action performed solely by U K'inich Pakal (Stuart 2005a:44). In this context, his Period Ending role is described as his first such participation. The Temple XIX text then refers to the wrapping of the Period Ending stone on 9.14.0.0.0, followed by U K'inich Pakal's second 900-day Period Ending on 9.14.2.9.0. Unlike U K'inich Pakal, the 9.13.17.9.0 Period Ending event was not K'inich Ahkal Mo' Nahb III's first such event. The Temple XVIII text indicates that the 16-year-old K'inich Ahkal Mo' Nahb III participated in a 900-day Period Ending event during the reign of his uncle K'inich Kan Bahlam II in AD 694. Stuart (2005a:44) noted that minor Period Ending events such as this may have been conducted by junior members of the court in preparation for their future roles as king.

The Temple XXI story next relates the dedication of shrines for GI in AD 734 and for GII and GIII in AD 736 that were conducted by K'inich Ahkal Mo' Nahb III, who, by that time, was king.[12] The time frame then moves forward a month to the 9.15.5.0.0 Period Ending ceremony conducted by K'inich Ahkal Mo' Nahb III that is said to have occurred in the company of the Palenque triad of gods. The final passage recalls an ancient event on 7.5.3.10.17 (252 BC) involving the shrine or shrines of the deities GI and GII that was conducted under the authority of an individual named with just the T1077 Casper glyph, and this individual is stated to be a lord of Palenque. The placement of this Casper figure in deep time and his Palenque emblem glyph designation suggests he was thought to be a very ancient ancestor.

The Tablet of the Cross narrative states the birth of an individual called U Kokan Chan in 993 BC and his subsequent accession as king in 967. U Kokan

Chan is said to be a lord of Matwiil. How this king relates to the character Casper–U Kokan Chan of Temple XXI is unclear. It has been suggested that K'inich Janaab Pakal I was impersonating both U Kokan Chan of Matwiil and Casper of Palenque in the Temple XXI scene (Stuart and Stuart 2008:111). It is equally possible that Casper–U Kokan Chan was the full name of the third-century Palenque lord, and that he was partially named after his illustrious Matwiil predecessor, U Kokan Chan. In this scenario, the caption text would give the full name of this character while the main text would simply use the first part of the name. Why K'inich Janaab Pakal I is pictured in the guise of Casper–U Kokan Chan may be related to the concept that a ruler was thought to be the manifestation of all the kings that preceded his rule (Bassie-Sweet 2008:10).

The only event of the Temple XXI main text that occurred before the accession of K'inich Ahkal Mo' Nahb III is the 9.13.17.9.0 3 Ajaw 3 Yaxk'in Period Ending that is juxtaposed across the top of the scene. It is logical to conclude that this 900-day Period Ending is the illustrated action, given that the main text states that U Pakal K'inich also participated in this event and he too is illustrated in the scene. However, it seems odd that U Pakal K'inich is named as just a *ch'ok* in the main text, but as the *bah ch'ok* in the caption text. As noted, the title *bah ch'ok* designates the heir apparent, and U Pakal K'inich did not acquire this title until after the AD 722 accession of K'inich Ahkal Mo' Nahb III. There is likely a simple answer to this issue. Many caption texts refer to the illustrated person using titles that refer to their status at the time of the monument's creation rather than their status during the pictured event. This appears to be the case with U K'inich Pakal (Stuart 2005a:41).

The attendance of K'inich Janaab Pakal I in the Temple XXI ceremony is more difficult to understand, given that he died some 25 years before the 9.13.17.9.0 Period Ending. It is likely that K'inich Janaab Pakal I appears as a supernatural participant who was thought to have overseen and validated the Period Ending rituals of his grandsons (Stuart and Stuart 2008:230). K'inich Janaab Pakal I's participation in this event may be similar to the narrative of the Tablet of the 96 Glyphs, which ends by stating that the 9.17.13.0.0 Period Ending during the reign of K'inich K'uk' Bahlam II was conducted under the auspices (*u kab*) of K'inich Janaab Pakal I. At that point in time, K'inich Janaab Pakal had been dead for over a hundred years. The portrait of K'inich Janaab Pakal I on the Temple XXI platform is like an illustrated *u kab* statement.

The costume elements of the Temple XXI scene are consistent with other pre-accession events. In the Cross Group panels that illustrate K'inich Kan

Bahlam II's pre-accession rituals when he acquired his *bah ch'ok* title, he wears a plain cape that is tied with the same distinctive knot as that found on the cape worn by the animal priest, and the tassels of K'inich Kan Bahlam II's headdress have the same form as the tasseled object. As noted by Carrasco (2005), the Temple XXI scene also has parallels with a scene on vessel K1440 that illustrates two elderly males dressed as the Waterlily Bird Serpent. One of these males holds the tasseled object over the head of an individual dressed in the same type of cape and headdress worn by K'inich Ahkal Mo' Nahb III and U Pakal K'inich. A further parallel is seen in the adjacent scene on K1440 that illustrates a mythological role model for the animal priest who carries the banded-bird title. He is a supernatural figure with the body of a man, but with the head and wings of a bird.

The title *ch'ajom*, which is carried by both males and females, refers to the act of offering incense to the gods and ancestors, and presumably to the making of the incense as well. This function was described by Landa as one of the duties of the Postclassic priests. A full-figure rendition of the *ch'ajom* title on the Copán Structure 9N-8-82 bench shows a male dropping incense into a burner. The inscription on Yaxchilán Throne 2 is composed of full-figure glyphs that also include a depiction of the *ch'ajom* title (Mayer 2008:fig. 8). As noted by Scherer and Houston (2015), this *ch'ajom* figure wears the same headdress, cape, and tied ponytail as those worn by K'inich Ahkal Mo' Nahb III and U Pakal K'inich in the Temple XXI scene. The implication is that K'inich Ahkal Mo' Nahb III and U Pakal K'inich are functioning as *ch'ajoms* as part of their participation in the 9.17.13.0.0 Period Ending.

What is pertinent to this discussion of couplet structure is that the actions of K'inich Ahkal Mo' Nahb III and U Pakal K'inich in the scene are presented as a parallel, sequential couplet in which K'inich Ahkal Mo' Nahb III is depicted engaged in the ritual act and U Pakal K'inich is pictured waiting to begin. The five caption texts of the scene (caped figure, priest, central figure, caped figure, priest) form a poetic structure of ABCAB while the bilateral poses of the flanking figures form a visual chiasmus structure.

REVERSED TEXTS AS CHIASMUS STRUCTURE

In the corpus of Maya monumental art, reversed or mirror-image hieroglyphs appear in limited contexts. The use of mirrors for divination purposes has led many researchers to interpret these texts as literally representing the surface of a mirror and a portal into the supernatural world of the deities (Schele and Miller 1986; Taube 1988b). However, given the tradition of bilateral symmetry and chiasmus structure in Maya art, the simplest explanation for the pairing of regular text with a reversed or mirror-image text is that the artist intended to create a visual chiasmus narrative.

As discussed above, the Nine Place is a mythological location that is associated with Period Ending events. The Nine Place is often paired with a second place name that incorporates *chiit*, *k'an*, and *nal* signs, and that is prefixed with the number seven (Kubler 1977). This Nine Place and Seven Place couplet likely represents a pair of complementary opposites that either function to name two aspects of one location or two separate locations within a specific larger space.[13] Many examples of these paired place names are depicted as mirror images. One such instance is found on the circular stone known as the Copán Motmot Marker (Stuart 2004a:fig. 11.11). The scene is divided down the middle by two columns of regular text that refer to the 9.0.0.0.0 Period Ending event. The viewer's right side of the scene is a portrait of K'inich Popol Hol sitting in profile while cradling a scepter in his left arm. He rests his feet on the Seven Place glyph, which is depicted as regular text. The left side of the scene illustrates his father, the Copán ruler K'inich Yax K'uk' Mo'. He sits in a similar but mirror-image pose, and he rests his feet on an abbreviated form of the Nine Place glyph. This glyph is in mirror-image with the bar and dots on the right side of the glyph block. The mirror-image poses of the two lords and these two place names not only form a couplet, but also a chiasmus structure.

There are many other examples of these paired place names where one of the names is in mirror-image. As discussed above, the panel on the right side of the Margarita structure includes the Nine Place glyph, and it is depicted as a regular text with the bar and dots on the left side. Given the symmetrical nature of the architectural decorations of this building complex, it was suspected that a parallel panel featuring the Seven Place location existed on the left side of the building (Barbara Fash, personal communication). Although the archaeologists chose not to excavate the left façade of the structure, they did remove a small amount of the fill to confirm the presence of the panel and the Seven Place glyph. The glyph is depicted in mirror-image. This same configuration is found on Copán Stela D which illustrates the ruler Waxaklajuun Ub'aah K'awiil performing the 9.15.5.0.0 Period Ending. The Nine Place and Seven Place glyphs are seen in the imagery adjacent to the ruler's knees. Like the Margarita panel, the Seven Place glyph is in mirror-image.

Another example of mirror-image text is found on the panels of Copán Temple 11. This building has four doorways, each oriented to a different direction, and each doorway is framed by two panels of hieroglyphs, one of which is a reversed text (Schele, Stuart, and Grube 1989). Yet another instance of this kind of reversed structure is found on the Chilib pillar, where the left column of text has been carved in mirror-image (Mayer 1981:plate 12). A similar structure is seen on an Early Classic vessel that has a two columns of text on each side (Hellmuth 1987:fig. 45, fig. 46). Although not in mirror-image, the reading order of the left text has been reversed from the traditional reading order of left to right.

Another case of mirror-image text is found on the Laxtunich wall panel (Mayer 1980:28–30; Schele and Miller 1986:226; Martin and Grube 2000:135) (figure 5.25). In this scene, the Yaxchilán ruler Itzamnaaj Bahlam IV sits on a throne with three war captives positioned beneath him. A secondary lord named Aj Chak Maax kneels on the step adjacent to the throne and extends an object to his king. Houston (1998:343) argued that Aj Chak Maax was the central figure in the scene because he is pictured on the right. Houston refers to Aj Chak Maax as the "peak" figure, apparently borrowing a term used by Josserand (1991) for the peak events of a narrative. Houston's interpretation, however, ignores the narrative structure of the text and its placement. The narrative begins with a double column of regular text positioned between Itzamnaaj Bahlam IV and Aj Chak Maax. The text states that Aj Chak Maax was the captor of these prisoners and that three days after the capture they were "adorned." This block of text ends with the statement that the captives of Aj Chak Maax were for Shield Jaguar IV (*u baak ti yajaw* "his captives for his lord"). The narrative continues with the mirror-image text carved on the edge of Itzamnaaj Bahlam IV's throne which gives his names and title. The object being handed to Itzamnaaj Bahlam IV is strategically placed between the two texts. Schele and Miller (1986:226) suggested that the throne text was reversed to deemphasize Itzamnaaj Bahlam IV, but, in fact, the reversed text forms a chiasmus structure with the upper text, and actually draws attention to Itzamnaaj Bahlam IV. By reading the mirror-image text from right to left, the viewer's attention is drawn to the ruler who leans forward to accept the object, and away from Aj Chak Maax.

Mirror-image text is also found on Site R Panel 3 (Mayer 1995:77–78, Plates 257, 258) (figure 5.26). In this scene, Bird Jaguar stands holding a parasol-like object. Kneeling before him is his secondary lord Ahkmo'. The narrative begins with a mirror-image block of text above Ahkmo' that describes an undeciphered action by him. The narrative continues with the mirror-image text behind Bird Jaguar that states Ahkmo's relationship to Bird Jaguar. Bird Jaguar is named with an exceptionally long string of titles that begins in the mirror-image text behind him and continues across the bottom row of regular

FIGURE 5.25. *Laxtunich wall panel, after Linda Schele.*

text. This juxtaposing of mirror-image and standard text is another example of visual chiasmus structure.

Yet another chiasmus text is seen on Yaxchilán Lintel 25 (figure 5.27). Lintel 25 spans the central doorway of Structure 23, and it is flanked by Lintel 24 and Lintel 26 that cover the west and east doorways, respectively. The underside of

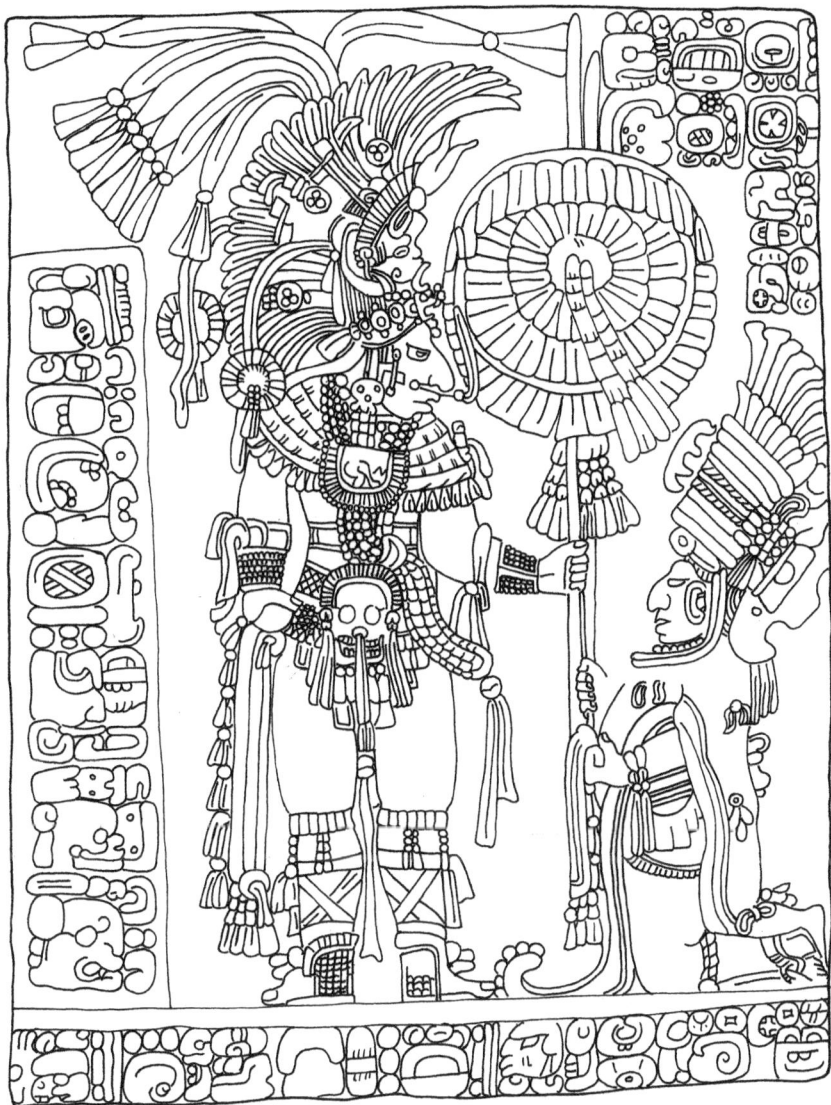

FIGURE 5.26. *Site R, Panel 3, after Berthold Riese.*

Lintel 25 contains a scene with mirror-image text that forms a continuous narrative with the regular text on the front edge of the lintel. The scene illustrates the Yaxchilán queen Lady K'abal Xook holding a bowl of bloodletting instruments in her left hand with the skull of Lady Ohl positioned on her extended

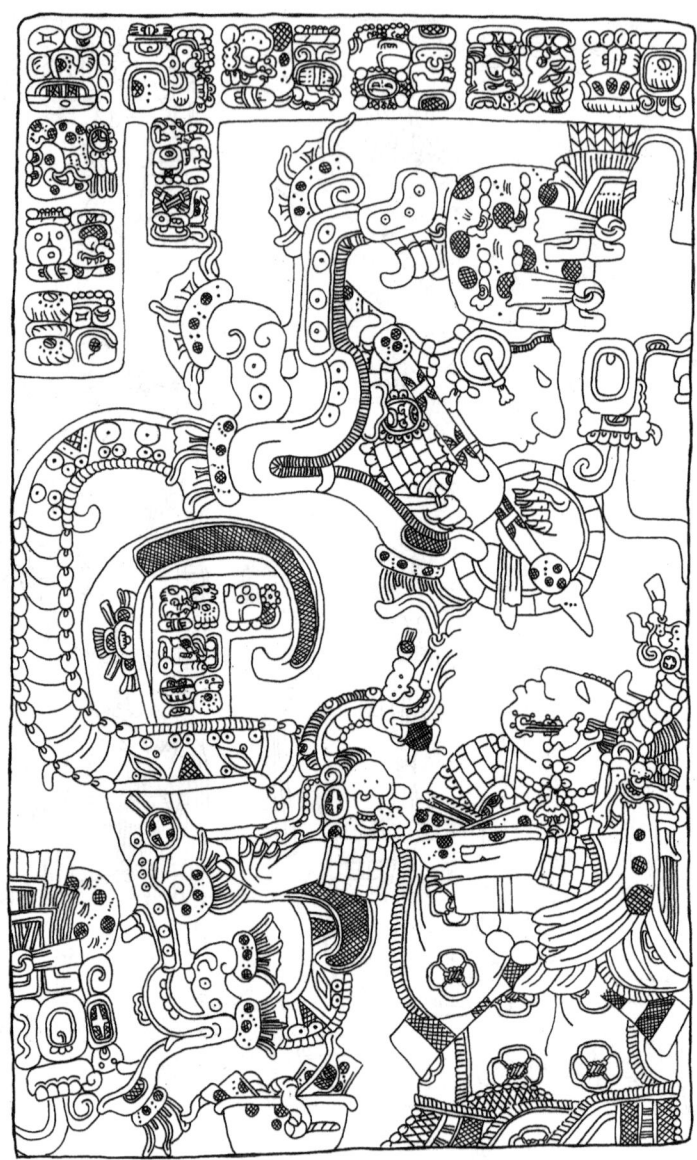

FIGURE 5.27. *Yaxchilán Lintel 25, after Graham.*

right forearm. Like Lady Ik' Skull on Stela 35, Lady K'abal Xook wears Lady Ohl's skull in her headdress. She sits before a rearing double-headed 18 Ub'aah Chan serpent that disgorges a Tlaloc deity from its lower head and a warrior wearing a Tlaloc mask and headdress from its upper head. Lady K'abal Xook's head is tilted backwards as she gazes up at the warrior. The visual focus is clearly on this warrior who emerges from the 18 Ub'aah Chan carrying a flint spear in the right hand and a shield in the left. Like Lady K'abal Xook, the warrior wears the headdress and tied ponytail of a Ch'ajom. Given that the spear is carried in the right hand, it is apparent that the scene is not reversed like the text. The narrative starts with a large, mirror-image text that runs across the top of the scene from right to left and down its upper left side. It begins with a triplet construction that refers to the conjuring and *tok'-pakal* of the deity K'ahk' O' Chahk and ends with a "holy spear" event by Shield Jaguar III. While the meaning of this latter action is unclear, Lintel 24 refers to the burning torch held by Shield Jaguar III as a "holy spear." The Lintel 25 narrative continues with two smaller blocks of mirror-image text positioned within the scene that states that Lady K'abal Xook is impersonating Lady Ohl. By reading this caption text, the viewer is brought past the image of the Ch'ajom warrior to Lady K'abal Xook. Given that the skull of Lady Ohl on Stela 35 wears a Tlaloc headdress, it seems apparent that the conjured Ch'ajom warrior who wears the Tlaloc mask on Lintel 25 is Lady Ohl.

As noted earlier, the 18 Ub'aah Chan is the meteor serpent avatar of Tlaloc. Its body is decorated with stylized Black Witch Moth wings. While its hieroglyphic name indicates it is a *chan* "snake," its segmented body indicates it is caterpillar, that is, the larval form of the Black Witch Moth (Bassie-Sweet et al. 2015; Bassie-Sweet, in press). The Maya categorize caterpillars as a type of snake. In a typical use of the framing convention, the moth wings on the upper head of the 18 Ub'aah Chan overlap the caption text naming Lady Ohl as well as the glyph block referencing the *tok'-pakal* of the deity K'ahk' O' Chahk. In other words, Lady Ohl's spear and shield is the *tok'-pakal* of the Tlaloc god K'ahk' O' Chahk.

The narrative continues on the front edge of the lintel where the text is in normal reading order. It restates the conjuring event and ends with the dedication of the building. The text states that the building belonged to Lady K'abal Xook, but that the dedication was carried out under the authority of Shield Jaguar III. Houston (1998:342) suggested that the glyphs on the underside of Lintel 25 were reversed in order to face the viewer as they entered the building and looked up. This seems highly unlikely, given that no other Yaxchilán lintels have reversed texts, including the two adjacent lintels of this building. On monuments that contained mirror-image texts, the reversal of the glyphs did not impact how the reader pronounced the words represented by these texts or their reading order, but it did create a visual chiasmus that functioned like a couplet. In a previous chapter, it was noted that disturbed syntax was employed in a narrative to bring emphasis to certain statements. Like disturbed syntax, visual chiasmus structure functions to bring emphasis or focus in a scene or to create a couplet structure.

SUMMARY

Many objects and structures (jewelry, bone tools, bloodletters, thrones, houses, etc.) include a text that indicates who owned them (Mathews 1979; Stuart 1995, 1998). In their most abbreviated form, such possessive phrases simply state the type of object and the owner's name or title such as "the earring of X" or "the bloodletter of X." More elaborate "name tags" often include a dedicatory verb and sometimes even a date. As discussed above, the Primary Standard Sequence is such a dedicatory text. Stuart (2005d) stated that the purpose of the PSS was to mark ownership of important ritual objects. While this is clearly the case, there is also another aspect to these texts. We believe that one of the purposes of couplet structure, chiasmus, mirror-image, and bilateral symmetry in Maya art was to present to the viewer a formal, ritual environment that replicated that of the Place of Duality, the ideal space necessary for proper ritual actions. In the context of a pottery scene, it is likely that couplets and paired images also changed the vessel from a mere container into a sacred one that would be suitable for ritual circumstances.

The establishment of proper sacred space was frequently accomplished by a circuit around the perimeter. Such spaces often replicated the quadrilateral world that, in turn, replicated the Place of Duality. The narrative on the panels of the Palenque Cross Group required the viewer to walk from building to building, and literally perform a circuit around the perimeter of the Cross Group plaza (Bassie-Sweet 1991) (see chapter 8). The viewing of a stela that is carved on more than one of its sides requires the viewer to walk the perimeter of the monument. Turning a vessel to view the image is also similar to conducting a circuit. Reading the PSS required the viewer to completely rotate the vessel as well, which rededicated and affirmed the sacred nature of the object and its space.

NOTES

1. Stuart's reading of this name as O' Chahk illustrates an ongoing problem in Maya epigraphy. Perhaps because practical orthographies do not write word-initial glottal stops, epigraphers take certain signs to represent vowels, when there is ample

evidence they are normal consonant-vowel (CV) syllable signs (i.e., glottal stop–vowel), in this case '*b* (Hopkins 2006b). The name should be '*O Chahk*, by orthographic convention written *O Chahk*.

2. Tres Islas Stela 3 also illustrates this place name, but the monument is too eroded to read where the *k'in* sign would likely have occurred.

3. Glyph blocks are given designations beginning on the upper left side of a scene. Rows are named alphabetically while rows are named numerically.

4. A literal translation would be "he of the five pyramid house," but what this might reference is unclear. It has been speculated that it refers to K'inich Janaab Pakal I as the builder of five pyramids.

5. K'inich Kan Bahlam II is not named in these three Cross Group passages using his regnal name. Rather, he is named using his pre-accession titles.

6. Stone and Zender (2011:fig. 93:4) and Houston (2014:157) misidentified the turkey as a quetzal. However, the bird clearly has the diagnostic wattle of a turkey.

7. Robicsek and Hales (1982:31) suggested the pair of seated figure were One Ajaw and his brother Yax Bolon, and that identification was followed by other researchers. Taube (1998:460) correctly identified the first figure as One Ixim. However, his assertion that the skull is a jester god and a hearthstone is questionable.

8. Another example of narrative chiasmus structure is found in the Lunar Series that often follows a Long Count notation. The Lunar Series states the number of days since the new moon (Glyph E), the number of the lunar half-year, the patron of the lunation, the name of the lunation, and the length of the lunar month (Glyph A). When the length of time since the new moon exceeds 20 days, the number is written with a combination of bars and dots and the T683 moon sign, which in this context represents 20 days. For instance, on Naranjo Stela 13, the number 27 of Glyph E is written with two dots, a bar, and a moon sign. This ordering of units is like a distance number where the order of units is the number of days followed by the number of *winals* (units of 20). The length of the lunar month (Glyph A) is always either 29 or 30 days. However, this is written with the moon sign first and the bars and dots second (Montgomery 2002:95, 98). This ordering of units is like a Long Count where the *winal* precedes the number of days. The reversal of the number order between Glyph E and Glyph A forms a chiasmus structure that brackets the other lunar information. This bracketing of calendar material is seen on a larger scale in Long Count dates. The Initial Series Introductory Glyph that begins Long Count dates refers to the patron of the *haab*, the Long Count numbers come next, followed by the *tzolk'in* date, the Supplementary Series (Glyphs F and G, and the Lunar Series), and finally the *haab* date itself. Thus, the *haab* patron and *haab* date bracket all of the calendrical material. The entire text of a stela is often bracketed, beginning with the Initial Series and ending with a reference to a Period Ending, often the same date.

9. The god pictured on Dresden page 25c does not appear to have drops falling from his hand. However, the Dresden Codex is damaged where the drops would have been.

10. We can also conclude that the *tok'-pakal* represented an essential role that these lords acquired. The Tablet of the Sun illustrates K'inich Kan Bahlam II attaining the *tok'-pakal* when he was six. Thus, both he and his brother K'inich K'an Joy Chitam II received this insignia as youths while K'inich Ahkal Mo' Nahb III attained his on the day of his accession.

11. Casper is also known by the nickname "the Ch'a ruler" (Stuart and Stuart 2008:110).

12. Some sections of the Temple XXI text were not recovered during excavations, but fortunately the Temple XIX narrative has parallel events, which allows for a reconstruction.

13. Grube and Stuart have suggested that the Nine Place and Seven Place might refer to the sunrise location of the winter and summer solstice sun; however, the evidence for such an interpretation is, at best, weak (Stuart 2009). On Zacpeten Altar 1, the Seven Place is associated with the birth of an individual on 9.18.19.9.17 8 Kaban, seating of Kumk'u. In the 584,285 calendar correlation used by Stuart, the back-dated Gregorian date for this event would be December 27, AD 809, six days after the winter solstice. In his conversion of the Zacpeten date, Stuart miscalculated and stated that this date occurred on December 23 and was, therefore, related to the winter solstice.

6

The Palenque Tablet of the 96 Glyphs

The Tablet of the 96 Glyphs is one of the latest surviving historical texts from Palenque, dating from the late eighth century (figure 6.1).[1] It is a poetic construction of great eloquence that was executed in an incised style that retains the beauty of Maya calligraphic brush strokes. Although it does not have an associated ritual scene like many of the Palenque monuments, it employs an extraordinary number of head-variant glyphs.[2] These head variants add considerable visual interest to the composition and display the virtuosity of its author.

THE HISTORICAL BACKGROUND OF THE PROTAGONIST

The protagonist of the Tablet of the 96 Glyphs is K'inich K'uk' Bahlam II, the great-grandson of K'inich Janaab Pakal I (Bassie-Sweet 1991:247–248, Ringle 1996). K'inich Janaab Pakal I had two sons who succeeded him, K'inich Kan Bahlam II (AD 635–702) and K'inich K'an Joy Chitam II (644–721). A third son named Tiwol Chan Mat was born in 648 and died at the age of 32 in 680 (Ringle 1996; Stuart 2005a). Tiwol Chan Mat's son, K'inich Ahkal Mo' Nahb III, who was just two years old at the untimely death of his father, came to the throne in 722, following the reigns of his father's two older brothers. There is some evidence that K'inich Ahkal Mo' Nahb III was followed in the succession by U Pakal K'inich Janaab Pakal

DOI: 10.5876/9781607327424.c006

and then another Palenque king known only from a conquest monument at Toniná (Martin and Grube 2008:174). Finally, in 764, K'inich K'uk' Bahlam II took the Palenque throne and ruled for at least twenty years. The narrative on the Tablet of the 96 Glyphs concerns itself with only K'inich Janaab Pakal I, K'inich K'an Joy Chitam II, K'inich Ahkal Mo' Nahb III, and K'inich K'uk' Bahlam II.

THE SETTING OF THE MONUMENT

The Palace of Palenque is a complex of interconnected buildings and courtyards. The earliest Palace structure currently visible is House E (circa 654), which forms the east border of a small courtyard nicknamed the Tower Court.[3] House E is unique in that its exterior façade had a white background decorated with flower motifs while most other Palace structures were painted red (Robertson 1985). On an interior wall of House E is the Oval Palace Tablet, which illustrates K'inich Janaab Pakal I receiving the Ux Yop Huun headdress from his mother. The adjacent caption texts do not give a date for this event, but merely name the two figures. Although not the crown of rulership, it is likely that K'inich Janaab Pakal I received the Ux Yop Huun headdress on the same day as his accession into kingship in 615, much like K'inich Ahkal Mo' Nahb III received his Ux Yop Huun (Bassie-Sweet and Hopkins 2012). On the wall above the Oval Palace Tablet is an eroded painted text that refers to the accession of K'inich Ahkal Mo' Nahb III. A stone seat was positioned in front of the Oval Palace Tablet that contained a hieroglyphic inscription relating the earlier accessions of K'inich Janaab Pakal I, K'inich Kan Bahlam II, and K'inich K'an Joy Chitam II. As discussed in chapter 1, House E replicated the palace of the creator grandfather Itzamnaaj where the mythological accession of the deity GI was performed (Carrasco 2015).

The Tower Court is now dominated by a tower on its north side that was built in the Late Classic period. Such constructions are exceedingly rare in the Maya region, and its purpose is open to debate. A three-step staircase abuts the south base of the tower. There may have been a painted mural on the tower wall that provided a backdrop for whoever or whatever was seated on the stairs (Robertson 1991:76). The Tablet of the 96 Glyphs was found face down between House E and the staircase, displaced from its original location (Angel Fernández 1985; Robertson 1985). The first step of the tower staircase has a recessed area that would accommodate the Tablet of the 96 Glyphs, and it is highly likely that this was where the tablet was originally situated (Robertson 1985:fig. 1).

The Tablet of the Orator and Tablet of the Scribe flanked the Tower Court staircase (Robertson 1991:76). These two panels both illustrate a captive taken under the auspices of the Palenque *yajawk'ahk'* lord Chak Suutz' during a war against Piedras Negras in 725 (Martin and Grube 2000:173). As documented on the Tablet of the Slaves, Chak Suutz' became a *yajawk'ahk'* lord at the grand age of 52 during the rule of K'inich Ahkal Mo' Nahb III. Carrasco (2012b:157) has documented the chiasmus structure of the caption texts on these monuments and the bilateral symmetry of the two captives.

The Creation Tablet and several other incised carvings in fragmentary form were found in the Tower Court. Porter (1994) believes that they were part of a throne with the Tablet of the 96 Glyphs functioning as the seat. Although Stuart and Stuart (2008:257) doubt Porter's specific placement of these fragments, it must be noted that the Long Count date of the Creation Tablet is the birth date of K'inich K'uk' Bahlam II's grandfather, Tiwol Chan Mat. Given that K'inich K'uk' Bahlam II and his father received their right to rule through their descent from Tiwol Chan Mat, this is surely not a coincidence.

THE TABLET OF THE 96 GLYPHS NARRATIVE

The text of the Tablet of the 96 Glyphs is a two-section narrative; that is, its two sections correspond to distinct time frames. The first section, composed of several episodes linked by Distance Numbers, opens with an episode that sets the initial time frame and states the narrative themes, the importance of the king K'inich Janaab Pakal I, and his relation to the building commemorated on this tablet. Although lacking the embellishment of a Long Count and Supplementary Series, the initial sentence of the Tablet of the 96 Glyphs is elaborated through the use of head variants in seven of the eight glyph blocks. The narrative begins with the statement "on 12 Ajaw 8 Keh the eleventh *k'atun* ended under the auspices (*u kab*) of K'inich Janaab Pakal I, title, Holy Palenque Lord" (A1–B4). This is the Long Count date of 9.11.0.0.0 12 Ajaw 8 Keh (October 14, AD 652), and it starts the event line.

The narrative then moves forward two years to the dedication of a building called the White Great House (A5–A8) on 9.11.2.1.11 9 Chuwen 9 Mak (November 4, 654) (Stuart 1998). It further states that this house belonged to K'inich Janaab Pakal I, the five-*k'atun* lord (B8–D1). K'inich Janaab Pakal I's title of five-*k'atun* lord refers to his age when he died, not his age at this dedication event.[4] Given the proximity of the Tablet of the 96 Glyphs to House E and the white color of its exterior, Stuart (1998:378) logically concluded

FIGURE 6.1. *Palenque Tablet of the 96 Glyphs, drawing by Linda Schele, courtesy David Schele.*

that this statement refers to the dedication of House E. "White Great House" could also be reasonably glossed "White Palace."

The second episode (A5–D1) sets the grammatical pattern for the presentation of the next three events, each of which involves seating a ruler of Palenque in kingship in the White Great House. These events are all presented using the same set phrasing, the constant pattern of statements in this segment of the text, where a Distance Number (DN) counts elapsed time between the last event (now referenced as background or "old information") and the Calendar Round (CR) date of the next ruler's seating. The Calendar Round is the grammatical subject of the special intransitive verb *uti* "came to pass," and this verb carries a focus marker (the Posterior Event Indicator, T679, read *i-*), indicating that the event on this date is on the event-line. This pattern is, roughly: "So much time passed [DN since the last event], and then it came to be Calendar Round. The next event took place."

The first sentence begins with a Distance Number Introductory Glyph (DNIG) that contrasts head variants representing Day and Night (C2). In fact, each new event on the event-line in the first section is introduced by a unique substitute for the DNIG, the verb normally used to indicate the passing of time, read *u-tz'ahk-aj* "was added or augmented" (D8, E7, G6). Instead of writing this verb in the usual way, here—as in several other known texts—the verb is replaced graphically by poetic renderings utilizing typically Mayan couplets of paired oppositions. The paired opposition occupies the position of the verbal main sign, and the verbal affixation (*u-* prefix, *-aj* suffix) is normal. The subject of this verb is the DN (composed of numbers, or adjectives, plus the names of time periods, nouns). The CR date functions grammatically as the subject of the other verb, *uht-i* "came to pass" or "occurred" (Stuart 1984).

The seating of K'inich K'an Joy Chitam II (9.13.10.6.8 5 Lamat 6 Xul, June 3 AD 702) is stated using the positional verb *chum* "to be seated" (*chum-lah*, the completive aspect of the positional verb) (D5) with its complement specifying the office (*ajawlel* "kingship") (C6a), and its subject the ruler's name (C6b–D6). K'inich K'an Joy Chitam II is also named as the holy Palenque lord (C7). The accession is then restated in a sentence that can be loosely paraphrased as "his throne-seating (was) in the White Great House" (D7–C8). The T609a *tz'am* "throne" sign represents a pillow covered in jaguar skin (Stone and Zender 2011:97). Such portable thrones are commonly seen as the seat or cushion of a ruler in palace scenes, and they are often positioned on top of a stone bench. Deities such as Itzamnaaj are also illustrated seated upon such portable thrones. For example, Itzamnaaj sits upon a jaguar pillow on K7727. On K5764, he sits on a bench with the pillow adjacent to him.

Note that the locational information that might have been expressed as a locative phrase in the first sentence (in what building, on what throne) has been promoted to an independent sentence. This promotion also reaffirms the importance of the White Great House and the jaguar throne: they are not merely props to provide a setting, but are essential to the overall theme of this text.

The next seating in the Tablet of the 96 Glyphs narrative is related in a couplet form structurally similar to K'inich K'an Joy Chitam II's accession. It begins with a *tz'ak* DNIG that contrasts head variants that are unfortunately too eroded to read in their entirety (D8), and relates the seating of K'inich Ahkal Mo' Nahb III in kingship and names him as a *Yajawte'* (E4) and holy Palenque lord (F3) (9.14.10.4.2 9 Ik' 5 K'ayab, January 3, 722).[5] The second part of the accession couplet notes his seating in the White Great House (E6–F6), but in this case uses a different verb, perhaps *buch* "to be seated." It does not refer to the *tz'am* throne directly.

The third seating begins with another *tz'ak* glyph that contrasts Star and Moon (E7). It recounts the accession of K'inich K'uk' Bahlam II, naming him with two titles (Baakel Wayal and Ajpitziil Ohl) (G3–H3) in addition to the "holy Palenque lord" designation (9.16.13.0.7 9 Manik' 15 Woh, March 8, 764). The second part of his accession couplet repeats the "his throne-seating in the White Great House" phrase (G5–H5) used in K'inich K'an Joy Chitam II's accession statement.

The last episode in this section, its peak event, is K'inich K'uk' Bahlam II's first *k'atun* (20-year) anniversary in office (9.17.13.0.7 7 Manik' seating of Pax,

November 24, AD 783). This 23-glyph block segment of text (G6–K1) constitutes almost one-quarter of the entire text, and it is the peak event of this section of text. The anniversary event begins with another *tz'ak* glyph, but this DNIG now contrasts Wind and Water (G6, in the form of the day names Ik' and Imix). K'inich K'uk' Bahlam II is named with the same two titles (I2–J2) found in his accession statement, but the narrative goes on to elaborate his titles by adding the *Yajawte'* title (I3) held by his father, the *k'atun* Ajaw title (I4), and the Bakab title (J4). His name phrase ends with a parentage statement that declares he was the child of K'inich Ahkal Mo' Nahb III and Lady Bird (J5–K1).[6]

The second section begins a new time frame (L1–K4), that is, it restarts the event-line by going back in time seven days from the anniversary date (November 24) to the 13-*tun* ending (9.17.13.0.0 13 Ajaw 13 Muwan, November 17, AD 783). It states that it had been seven days since the Period Ending had occurred and then (focus marker T679) there was the completion of the first *k'atun* anniversary of K'inich K'uk' Bahlam II's accession. The peak event of the first section now appears as the peak event of the second section as well. The narrative then makes a couplet statement that refers to the carving of a *k'an tun* "yellow stone" (*yuxuluuj k'an tuun; utapaw ? woj* "he carved the yellow stone, he inscribed glyphs upon it"; Carrasco 2012b:160). The carving of *k'an tun* stones is known from other contexts, and in this instance the carving of the *k'an tun* stone likely refers to the carving of the Tablet of the 96 Glyphs itself (Stuart 1990). The passage referring to the carving is followed by the statement that these acts were carried out under the auspices of the five-*k'atun* lord, K'inich Janaab Pakal I. As is seen in the following chapter, the participation of deceased kings and ancestors in the affairs of the living was a common belief. The narrative ends with a restatement of the one-*k'atun* anniversary event (L7-L8).

In summary, the Tablet of the 96 Glyphs narrative is divided into two sections (table 6.1). The first section begins with the Period Ending under the auspices of K'inich Janaab Pakal I, then proceeds to the dedication of House E, the accessions of K'inich K'an Joy Chitam II, K'inich Ahkal Mo' Nahb III, and K'inich K'uk' Bahlam II, and ends with the first-*k'atun* anniversary of K'inich K'uk' Bahlam II's accession. The second section repeats the initial structure of the first section by beginning with a Period Ending followed by the anniversary of the accession and the creation of the tablet under the auspices of K'inich Janaab Pakal I. It ends with a short statement referencing the first-*k'atun* accession anniversary. In each section, the anniversary event of K'inich K'uk' Bahlam II's accession is the peak event. The narrative structure draws a parallel between K'inich Janaab Pakal I's Period Ending and dedication of House E and K'inich K'uk' Bahlam II's Period Ending and the creation of the Tablet on the occasion of his first *k'atun* as ruler. The dedication of House E and the creation of the tablet are both said to be under the auspices of K'inich Janaab Pakal I.

TABLE 6.1. *Event-line chart for the Tablet of the 96 Glyphs*

SECTION I: OPENING, THEMATIC STATEMENT, NARRATIVE DEVELOPMENT AND PEAK

Episode 1 (A1–B4): Setting and Time Frame
    9.11.0.0.0 The eleventh *k'atun* ended, under the auspices of Pakal.

Episode 2 (A5–D1): Statement of Theme
    9.11.2.1.11 (2+ years later) the White Great House was dedicated, in Pakal's house.

Episode 3 (C2–C8): Narrative Development A
    9.13.10.6.8 (48+ years later), K'an Joy Chitam was seated as lord; he sat on the jaguar throne in the White Great House.

Episode 4 (D8–F6): Narrative Development B
    9.14.10.4.2 (19+ years later), Ahkal Mo' Nahb was seated as lord; he sat in the White Great House.

Episode 5 (E7–H5): Narrative Development C
    9.16.13.0.7 (22+ years later), K'uk' Bahlam was seated as lord; he sat on the jaguar throne in the White Great House.

Episode 6 (G6–K1): Peak Event
    9.17.13.0.7 (20 years later), K'uk' Bahlam completed his first *k'atun* in office, (titles and parentage statement).

SECTION II: NEW CHRONOLOGICAL FRAME, RESTATEMENT OF THE PEAK, ELABORATION, AND CLOSING

Backstep in Time (L1–K3)
    9.17.13.0.0 (7 days earlier) it had been 13 Ajaw 13 Muan, the thirteenth *tun*,

Restatement of the Peak (L3–K4)
    9.17.13.0.7 and then was completed as his first *k'atun* as lord.

Elaboration (L4–K7)
    The stone was carved, under the auspices of Pakal.

Closing (L7–L8)
    And then ended his (K'uk' Bahlam's) first *k'atun* as lord.

THE PROTAGONIST

There are potential problems presented by this text in the identification of the protagonist and the interpretation of the final episode. It may seem unusual to us to have no mention whatsoever of the protagonist in the entire last section of the text, but this is a literary device used with some frequency by the Classic Maya. Modern discourse theory provides the framework necessary for understanding how the Maya kept track of the actors and props introduced in a narrative, and how the reintroduction of old information helps reestablish a participant as the discourse topic, the grammatical antecedent for pronominal references in a text segment (Josserand 1995, 1997). In the final section of the Tablet of the 96 Glyphs, where he is not mentioned by name, the reintroduction of K'inich K'uk' Bahlam II is accomplished by the repetition of the peak event from the last section, his first *k'atun* anniversary as ruler. Although his name was deleted (he is the unnamed possessor of the one-*k'atun* phrase), he is there in the underlying structure, and now functions as the topic. When K'inich Janaab Pakal I's name appears near the end of the text, it is in a backgrounded phrase ("under the auspices of . . ."), so we know we have not had a topic shift, only another reference to a theme. A final focus marker (inset in the verb at L7) again recalls the anniversary event, and as above, although his name is deleted, K'inich K'uk' Bahlam II is again the underlying referent, the local (or current) discourse topic.

LITERARY DEVICES: FOCUS

Even though the verb preceding the Calendar Round date carries the Posterior Event Indicator (PEI, or focus marker, T679), the focused event is actually the event that took place on this date, not the date itself. In this narrative, these focus markers serve chiefly as indicators of temporal movement through the text, marking the events on a sequential event-line. It may be significant that—visually—the focus markers march steadily upward in a diagonal line to the peak event, at A6, C4, E2, and G1. The verb of the new event is given special prominence by appearing first in its own sentence, the expected initial element, the CR date, having been removed to a separate sentence. The event is then given further emphasis by a second, parallel sentence that serves as a couplet to the first statement of the event. Only two times in this text does the PEI or focus marker appear directly on the event verb rather than on the verb *uti* "came to pass." Both instances are expressions of the first *k'atun* anniversary (L3 and L7) and the climax of the story.

LITERARY DEVICES: FRONTING AND PROMOTION

Fronting and *promotion* are linguistic terms for changes in word order that move an element to the beginning of the sentence (fronting), or grammatical changes that transform a given element to a "higher" syntactic category (promotion). An example of the latter is the transformation of a CR date from the temporal phrase of one sentence to the subject phrase of an independent sentence. Instead of "on this date, this event happened," the date is promoted: "It was this date. This event happened."

The PEI (T679, *i*) represents a sentence conjunction that occurs initially in the sentence and that must be followed immediately by a verb or other predicate. Thus the use of the PEI results in the fronting of the verb, because it requires that the verb immediately follow it. The CR (temporal phrase) of such a sentence is displaced from its normal initial position and either (1) occurs at the end of the sentence or (2) is promoted and removed completely from the original sentence to form a new, independent sentence. Thus, the unmarked sentence (0) may be transformed into either (1) or (2) when the focus marker (PEI) is attached to the Verb:

(0) Temporal (CR) + Verb + Subject.
   On 12 Ajaw 8 Keh ended the eleventh *k'atun*.

(1) PEI + Verb + Subject + Temporal (CR).
   And then ended the eleventh *k'atun*, on 12 Ajaw 8 Keh.

(2) Verb + Temporal (CR). PEI + Verb + Subject.
   It came to be 12 Ajaw 8 Keh. And then ended the eleventh *k'atun*.

An alternative treatment of the CR, especially if it is old information, is to omit mention of it. Events stated without CRs can be assumed to have taken place on the last-mentioned date. A typical episode from the Tablet of the 96 Glyphs:

C2–D3	Pron-Vb DN-iy	Time passed for 17 days, 4 *winals*, 8 *tuns*, and 2 *k'atuns*
C4–5	PEI-Vb S	and then came to pass 5 Lamat 6 Xul.
D5–C7	Vb Prep-Comp S	Was seated as Lord K'inich K'an Joy Chitam II, Emblem Glyph.
D7–C8	Pron-Vb Loc	He sat on the throne in the White Great House.

The event statements in the first section of the Tablet of the 96 Glyphs illustrate the maximum options of fronting and promotion. A typical episode (C2–C8) is composed of three sentences in which both the DN and the temporal phrase (CR) are promoted to subjects of separate sentences, which are then conjoined. The focused event is presented in one sentence and then coupleted in another.

The first set of conjoined sentences (C2–C5) begins with the DNIG verb (C2), *u tz'akaj* "(time) passed," whose subject is the DN (D2–D3). This sentence is then conjoined to the second sentence with the focus marker (PEI), which is an emphatic sentence conjunction (at C4a). The second sentence has as its verb *uti* "came to pass" (C4b); its subject is the CR (D4–C5). Thus the conjoined sentences "time passed for 17 days, 4 months, 1 *tun*, and 2 *k'atuns*; and then, it came to be 5 Lamat 6 Xul" accomplish the removal of the temporal phrases from the event statement, which is then further emphasized by coupleting.

The final two sentences, which are coupleted, state the event: "Seated as Ajaw . . . was K'an Joy Chitam II, Divine Lord of Palenque. He besat the Jaguar Throne, [in the] White Great House."

VISUAL VARIATIONS

Although the Tablet of the 96 Glyphs does not contain a ritual scene, the author of the narrative used a wide variety of ways to express the same word and by doing so introduced visual interest into the story. For example, the word *ajaw* in the initial Period Ending *tzolk'in* day 12 Ajaw (A1) is represented by a portrait of the deity One Ajaw wearing his *sak huun* headdress rather than the more typical logographic *ajaw* sign (K2) that is used in the final section in reference to the 9.17.13.0.0 13 Ajaw 13 Muwan Period Ending.

The narrative contains fifteen other references to the word *ajaw*; five of these are found in the Emblem Glyphs that end the name phrases of K'inich Janaab Pakal I (B2), K'inich K'an Joy Chitam II (C7), K'inich Ahkal Mo' Nahb III (F5, I7), and K'inich K'uk' Bahlam II (H4). In these Emblem Glyph examples, the word *ajaw* is represented by the T168/T518 sign for *ajaw*.[7] The word *ajaw* also appears five times in the phrase *ta ajawlel* "in kingship." The first occurrence is in the accession statement for K'inich K'an Joy Chitam II where the word *ajaw* is again represented by the T168/T518 sign *ajaw* sign (C6b). In the next passage relating K'inich Ahkal Mo' Nahb III's accession, a vulture head variant of *ajaw* (F3) is employed. In the following accession of K'inich K'uk' Bahlam II, an anthropomorphic head variant (H2) represents the word.[8] This variation in the *ajaw* sign is continued in the two anniversary statements where the word *ajaw* in the "kingship" glyph is first expressed using a rodent head version (J1) and then the anthropomorphic head variant (K4b). The alternation between the anthropomorphic head variant and the vulture head variant of *ajaw* is also seen in the *yajaw te'* title found at E4 and T3. Last, the word *ajaw* in the five-*k'atun ajaw* title of K'inich Janaab Pakal I is first written as the logographic *ajaw* (D1) and then as the vulture variant (L6).

As discussed above, the accessions of K'inich K'an Joy Chitam II, K'inich Ahkal Mo' Nahb III, and K'inich K'uk' Bahlam II are each stated in parallel, couplet form. Despite the parallel nature of this triplet construction, there are many visual variations within these statements as well. As noted, each accession begins with a *tz'ak* DNIG, but each glyph uses a different set of contrasting elements. The DNs themselves are presented in different forms as well. The DN for K'inich K'an Joy Chitam II's accession uses head variants for the *winal*, *tun*, and *k'atun* periods as well as head variants for the numbers for the latter two time periods (C3–D3). The *u* syllable in the *uti* glyph is written with a *xoc* fish head variant (C4). In contrast, K'inich Ahkal Mo' Nahb III's accession employs head variants for its *winal* and *tun* period, but uses bars and dots for the numbers (E1–F1). Its *uti* glyph takes the form of an anthropomorphic head (E2). The accession of K'inich K'uk' Bahlam II returns to the format used in K'inich K'an Joy Chitam II's accession and uses head variants for the numbers and time periods (F7–F8) and the *xoc* fish head variant (GI).

An examination of the other occurrence of the *u* preposition sign in the narrative shows the same richness in variation. The manner in which K'inich K'uk Bahlam II's Baakel Wayal title is written also shows inventive form. In the first instance, the word *baak* "bone" is written with a logograph representing a section of a bone while the word *way* is expressed with a head variant (G3). This treatment is reversed in the second occurrence where *baak* takes its head variant form and *way* is represented by the logographic *way* sign (I2).

SUMMARY

The narrative of the Tablet of the 96 Glyphs opens with the end of the eleventh *k'atun* (9.11.0.0.0; October 14, 652) under the auspices of K'inich Janaab Pakal I and the dedication of a building owned by him (9.11.2.1.11; November 4, 654).[9] The text then relates the accessions of three Palenque rulers who are said to have been seated in the building owned by K'inich Janaab Pakal I. The last ruler mentioned is K'inich K'uk' Bahlam II, and the narrative then further relates the first *k'atun* anniversary of his rule. His nominal phrase is elaborated with the *Yajawte'* title, also carried by his father, and his parentage statement. The text closes with a reference to the Period Ending (9.17.13.0.0; November 17, 783), the creation and dedication of a monument (probably the Tablet of the 96 Glyphs itself) on the occasion of K'inich K'uk' Bahlam II's first *k'atun* anniversary of kingship, and a restatement of the anniversary.

The building referred to in the text of the Tablet of the 96 Glyphs is called the *Sak Nuk Nah* "White Great House" (A8), and appears to be the adjacent House E of the Palace complex, the only Palenque building consistently painted white (Robertson 1985:21–22). In any case, the Tablet of the 96 Glyphs was displayed in the court outside House E, it relates K'inich Janaab Pakal I to House E, and it narrates the enthronement of the direct ancestors of K'uk' Bahlam II (in K'inich Janaab Pakal I's dynasty) in that White Great House. While later monuments may eventually be uncovered at Palenque, the Tablet of the 96 Glyphs currently stands as the latest monumental inscription of Palenque. Neither the eloquence of its narrative nor the beauty of its carving hints at the decline that Palenque was experiencing at the end of the Classic period.

The various examples of Maya art discussed in chapter 5 demonstrate that visual and literary forms often had the same poetic structure. The following chapter is an examination of the Palenque Temple of the Inscriptions tomb. It focuses on the poetic structure of the tomb art and the intimate relationship between its texts and images, and explores how those relationships can enhance our understanding of Palenque history.

NOTES

1. This chapter is based on a section of a 1991 research report, "The discourse analysis of Maya hieroglyphic texts from the Western Lowlands," by J. Kathryn Josserand and Nicholas A. Hopkins, in *A Handbook of Classic Maya Inscriptions, part 1: The Western Lowlands*, pp. 425–445. Final Performance Report, National Endowment for the Humanities, Grant RT-21090-89.

2. Statistically, 83 percent of the glyph blocks on the Tablet of the 96 Glyphs incorporate some kind of head variant. In comparison, just 38 percent of the glyph blocks in the main text of the Temple XIX platform use head variants.

3. The Palace has never been fully excavated, hence, the earlier buildings beneath it are not yet properly documented.

4. The placement of the five-*k'atun* title after K'inich Janaab Pakal I's personal name is curious. In all other examples, including the one at the end of this narrative, the title precedes his personal name.

5. The meaning or function of the title *Yajawte'* title is unclear.

6. The name of K'inich K'uk' Bahlam II's mother is composed of the logograph used to represent the day name *Men*. As discussed in chapter 1, the logogram represents a supernatural bird and may carry the value *tz'ikin* "bird."

7. In most examples of Emblem Glyphs, the logographic *ajaw* sign is placed behind the main sign and only the top portion of the sign is visible, as is the case in the Tablet of the 96 Glyphs (Stuart 1995:192). In the Thompson catalogue, this visible portion was erroneously given its own designation of T168 and the lower portion assigned the number T518.

8. It is interesting that the *ta* "in" glyph paired with the vulture *ajaw* is the animal version of this sign (T51) and not the logographic version (T113) used in the other two statements.

9. The Tablet of the 96 Glyphs has been the subject of various attempts to read its text in a Mayan language, beginning in 1984. During the workshop phase of the Maya Meetings at Texas that year, it occurred to Hopkins, who together with Josserand had been working on Ch'ol for several years, that it might now be possible to render the Classic text in a semblance of the original language. That initial attempt looks crude 30 years later, but it stunned the workshop audience when it was first performed, and the presentation was repeated with similar effect in 1990 at the Metropolitan Museum of Art (Josserand 1990). Schele was so taken by the dramatic effect of putting the text into a real language that translations into modern Mayan languages became a fixture in her workshops.

7

The Narrative of the Palenque Temple of the Inscriptions Sarcophagus

The main focus of this chapter is on the narrative text on the Palenque Temple of the Inscriptions sarcophagus lid and its relationship to the scenes on the top of the lid and on the sides of the box. It is our contention that the artist/artists of the sarcophagus used the juxtaposing of text and image to convey genealogical and political information that was pertinent not only to K'inich Janaab Pakal I but also to his son and successor, K'inich Kan Bahlam II.

THE SETTING

The Temple of the Inscriptions is a multichambered building that sits atop a large pyramid (Ruz 1973). Three panels that form a continuous text are located on the interior walls of the building. This text provides information that is not only relevant to the sarcophagus narrative but complements it. The first panel (east tablet) of the temple recounts the accession and Period Ending events for K'inich Janaab Pakal I and a series of rulers who preceded him:

Protagonist	Accession (AD)	Period Ending (AD)
Ahkal Mo' Nahb I	501	9.4.0.0.0 (514)
K'an Joy Chitam I	529	9.5.0.0.0 (534), 9.6.0.0.0 (554)
Ahkal Mo' Nahb II	565	9.6.13.0.0 (567)
Kan Bahlam I	572	9.7.0.0.0 (573), 9.7.5.0.0 (578)

DOI: 10.5876/9781607327424.c007

Lady Yohl Ik'nal	583	9.8.0.0.0 (593)
Ajen Yohl Mat	605	9.8.13.0.0 (606)
Muwan Mat	612	9.9.0.0.0 (613)
K'inich Janaab Pakal I	615	9.10.0.0.0 (633)

The first six of these rulers also play a role in K'inich Janaab Pakal I's sarcophagus narrative.

The temple narrative incorporates pivotal events in Palenque's history, including the sacking of Palenque by the powerful state of Calakmul in AD 611, and the apparent failure of Ajen Yohl Mat and Muwan Mat to properly honor the deities on their Period Endings as a consequence (Martin and Grube 2000; Carrasco 2005, 2012a). The second panel (middle tablet) details the subsequent successful Period Ending events of K'inich Janaab Pakal I on 9.11.0.0.0 (652) and 9.12.0.0.0 (672) and gives an account of his actions regarding the deities GI, GII, and GIII. It specifies the accoutrements of these three gods, including the fact that the Quadripartite Badge motif is the headdress of GI. The final panel (west tablet) moves forward to the 9.13.0.0.0 (692) Period Ending after the king's death and references two Period Endings in the distant future. The timeframe of the narrative then backs up to the birth (603) and accession (615) of K'inich Janaab Pakal I and makes references to both ancient and future accessions and Period Ending events. Many of these passages are difficult to understand, but the text highlights the arrival at Palenque of the defeated king of Santa Elena, Nuun Ujol Chahk, in 659 (an important Palenque conquest that is also featured in a Palace narrative; see below). At this point in time, K'inich Janaab Pakal I was 56 years old and his son K'inich Kan Bahlam II was 25. The narrative again backs up in time with references to K'inich Janaab Pakal I's marriage to Lady Tz'akbu Ajaw (626) and her death (672), his own death (683), and the subsequent accession of their son four months later. The narrative ends with a statement that on the day of his accession K'inich Kan Bahlam II performed some kind of ritual action related to his father's tomb.

As comprehensively discussed by Carrasco (2005, 2012a), the achievements of K'inich Janaab Pakal I in honoring the gods form rhetorical contrast to the earlier failures of his immediate predecessors. He also noted in regard to the temple narrative:

> Much of the text of the Temple of the Inscriptions, in addition to its political rhetoric, is really a formula for the proper treatment of icons and other sacra. In fact, it is among the most important documents for understanding the

core devotional practices of a royal cult of the image, which was widespread throughout the Classic Maya world. We can extract from it that the Ajaw (kings/queens) of Palenque had presented bundles and offerings to material manifestations of the patron gods before the war and that, after Calakmul destroyed these icons, the city was left without the presence of these deities for a sufficient period of time that offerings could not be made. However, Janaab Pakal restored order and appropriate ritual protocol by again initiating a series of devotional acts focused on the icons of Palenque's patron deities. (Carrasco 2012a:132–133)

The importance of successful Period Ending ceremonies also plays a role in the sarcophagus narrative as discussed below.

THE TOMB

In 1949, workers under the direction of the Mexican archaeologist Alberto Ruz discovered a rubble-filled staircase under the floor of the temple (Ruz 1973). The excavation of that staircase took the archaeologists deep within the bowels of the pyramid to the burial chamber of K'inich Janaab Pakal I and its sarcophagus. Given its size, it is apparent that the sarcophagus was constructed first, and then the crypt room, interior staircase, and pyramid were built around it. In the initial construction of the box, a key-shaped cavity to house the body was chiseled out of the middle of the large stone block. A step-shaped recess was carved around the lip of the cavity to hold a matching rabbet lid that would be flush with the top of the box. A pair of holes was drilled at both ends of the rabbet lid for the insertion of guide ropes. Once the body and its accompanying grave goods were placed inside the cavity and the proper ceremonial actions performed, the rabbet lid was lowered into place, the ropes were removed, and the holes were filled with stone plugs. At this point, the body was effectively sealed in stone. A massive lid that covered the entire top of the box was then placed on top of it.

The doorway between the stairs and the tomb occupies the south wall. Nine stucco figures decorate the east, west, and north walls of the tomb: four on the east, four on the west, and one on the north (Robertson 1983:fig. 234–331). Water-seepage from above has coated these stuccos in layers of lime and badly damaged them. Still there is enough detail left to indicate that they all wear similar headdresses and costumes, and they hold a GII lightning-bolt axe and a shield decorated with a portrait of GIII. All the figures on the east and west walls sit or stand in a frontal pose, but their heads are turned towards the north end of the tomb. The first figure is encountered on the east wall just inside the doorway. He is seated facing to his right and carries the GII axe in his right hand and the GIII shield in his left. Opposite to him on the west wall is a similar, seated male who is turned to his left and carries the axe in his left hand and the shield in his right. In other words, the west figure is a mirror-image composition of the east. The east and west walls each contained two niches. The first niche on the east wall contains a standing figure. Although he faces in the same direction as the first east figure, he holds the axe in his left hand and the shield in his right. His counterpart on the west wall niche is in mirror-image to him. The second niche on the east wall contains two standing figures that both look to their right and hold their axes in their right hands and their shields in the left. In the western niche across from these two figures are two more figures. They stand in mirror-image to the figures in the eastern niche. The last figure is on the northern wall. It is another seated figure who looks to his right.

The identification of these figures is hampered by the lack of adjacent caption texts and the damage caused by the water seepage. Eight of the figures wear short, fringed skirts, but the third figure on the east side wears a long skirt. The headdress of this figure contains glyphic elements that spell out the name of the ruler Lady Yohl Ik'nal (Schele and Mathews 1998:128). Although there has been much speculation about who these other eight figures represent, it is impossible to know with certainty. These tomb figures are not unique. The walls of an early Classic tomb in Temple XX were painted with similar standing figures holding GII lightning bolt axe and round shield (Morales 1999).

THE SARCOPHAGUS LID SCENE

Before discussing the narrative structure of the sarcophagus text, a brief overview of the scene on the top of the lid is in order. K'inich Janaab Pakal I is depicted sitting in a reclining pose atop the Quadripartite Badge motif with a stylized tree positioned behind him (figure 7.1). A supernatural bird perches on the top of tree and a double-headed serpent is entwined in its branches. A K'awiil god and Jester God emerge from the mouths of the serpent. K'inich Janaab Pakal I and the Quadripartite Badge motif are framed by the open jaws of the centipede-snake. As noted in chapter 1, such zoomorphic creatures are thought to represent the cave exit from the Underworld.

The Temple of the Inscriptions narrative states that the Quadripartite Badge motif is the headdress of the thunderbolt deity GI, and indicates the intimate relationship that GI had with this icon. The Quadripartite Badge motif and

FIGURE 7.1. *Palenque Temple of Inscriptions, sarcophagus lid, after Merle Greene Robertson.*

tree also appear as the central icon on the Tablet of the Cross. As discussed in chapters 1 and 8, the narratives of the Tablet of the Cross and the building that houses it are dedicated to GI.

K'inich Janaab Pakal I is dressed in the jade costume of One Ixim, but he is also shown with the flaming forehead celt of the thunderbolt deity GII (K'awiil) emerging from his forehead. Stone and Zender (2011:19, 31) concluded that this indicated he was transformed into GII. However, this depiction of K'inich Janaab Pakal I as a thunderbolt is parallel to modern Maya beliefs concerning deceased ancestors (Bassie-Sweet 2008; Bassie-Sweet et al. 2015). It is believed that people have co-essences that share their soul but that take a form outside of their bodies. While the majority of co-essences are animals, the most powerful people such as the leaders of the community have co-essences that take the shape of thunderbolts, whirlwinds, and meteors. Leaders use their co-essences to protect the community from outside forces. These co-essences live on after the death of the individual and continue their guardian duties. Thunderbolt deities and the force of thunderbolts were and still are central allegories for power. One of the most common images on monumental sculpture is a lord holding the GII scepter that represents a thunderbolt. Therefore, the image of K'inich Janaab Pakal I as a thunderbolt may not be intended to indicate that he specifically became GII, but rather that his soul was a thunderbolt and that he controlled this powerful force.

There are several examples of One Ixim with a GII celt in his forehead, such as those on K5126 and K8714. Obviously, they are directly related to the image of K'inich Janaab Pakal I on the sarcophagus lid. As discussed in chapter 2, the word *ajan* refers to unripe corn and this word is represented by the portrait of a corn deity that is thought to be a manifestation of One Ixim (Boot 2009; Zender 2014). The name *Ajan K'awiil* appears in a number of hieroglyphic contexts, and it is likely the name of this thunderbolt aspect of One Ixim.

The scene on the sarcophagus lid is encircled by a sky band. Sky bands were often used in Maya art to represent a pathway across the sky such as the Milky Way and ecliptic, but they were also employed as a framing device to define a celestial-related event. Palenque examples are seen on the piers of House A of the Palace and the four outer piers that flank the main doorway of the Temple of the Inscriptions (Robertson 1983, 1985). Each Temple of the Inscriptions pier shows an individual holding a baby K'awiil (GII) that is in a reclining pose. Although these stuccos are badly eroded and their caption texts destroyed, enough remains on Pier B and Pier E to show that the figure stands on the Quadripartite Badge motif with a sky band encircling the scene. Analogous compositions are also found on pottery vessels. A large, square-shaped vessel with four feet was found in the royal Burial 30 at Dos Pilas, which is thought to be that of the Dos Pilas king Itzamnaaj K'awiil (Just 2012:105). The interior of the vessel is decorated with a Quadripartite Badge

FIGURE 7.2. *Dos Pilas Burial 30 vessel.*

motif that is surrounded by both a sky band and a PSS text (figure 7.2).¹ The sky band of the sarcophagus lid creates a similar celestial, quadrilateral space in which K'inich Janaab Pakal I is depicted.

The sky bands on the east and west sides of the sarcophagus contain cartouches formed by a bar on either side. Within these rectangular cartouches are *k'in*, *ak'ab*, star, and moon signs as well other glyphs that have not yet been deciphered, such as the square-nosed beastie and shields. There are two clear examples of complementary opposition between the east and west cartouches. A *k'in* "sun, day" sign is positioned on the northeast corner of the sky band while a "night" glyph is found on the northwest corner. Adjacent to K'inich Janaab Pakal I's head on the east side is another *k'in* sign and the glyph in the opposite position on the west side is a moon sign. A similar complementary opposition of sun and moon is found on K4681 and K1892 (figures 1.7, 1.8). As discussed in chapters 1 and 2, these two pottery scenes show One Ixim at the center of the world, flanked by his sons One Ajaw (sun) and Yax Bolon (full moon) on the horizons. On K4681, One Ixim's outstretched arms echo the stylized tree behind K'inich Janaab Pakal I.

The first scholarly interpretations of K'inich Janaab Pakal I's reclining pose focused on the fact that he appears to be falling, and it was thought that he was descending into the centipede-snake's mouth (Ruz 1973; Robertson 1983; Schele and Miller 1984). However, it has been demonstrated that the reclining pose is a convention specifically referencing birth, emergence, or transformation (Taube 1994; Stuart, Houston, and Robertson 1999; Martin 2002; Stuart 2005a). As an example, One Ixim is pictured in the reclining pose on the vessel K2713, and the adjacent caption text refers to birth. In hieroglyphic writing, the *k'in* bowl of the Quadripartite Badge motif is used to represent the word *el* "go out, emerge" (Stuart 2005a:65), which further reinforces the emergence theme. K'inich Janaab Pakal I's afterlife, thus, involved the same kind of transformation as that of One Ixim, and he is rising from this location not falling into it.

It has been suggested that the depiction of K'inich Janaab Pakal I was not intended to represent his physical body (which the Maya most certainly knew was rotting away inside the box), but rather the apotheosis of his soul as a deity (Ruz 1973; Robertson 1983; Schele and Miller 1984:306; Schele and Freidel 1990; Freidel, Schele, and Parker 1993; Schele and Mathews 1998; Stuart 2005a; Stuart and Stuart 2008; Bassie-Sweet 2008; Taube 2004; Stone and Zender 2011). There has been much debate concerning what god he was thought to become and what this deity represented. This issue is discussed at the end of the chapter.

THE SARCOPHAGUS LID TEXT

A number of authors have noted that the minimal distance between the sarcophagus and the wall of the crypt would make it difficult for anyone to circumnavigate the sarcophagus and read its lid text. It has been suggested, therefore, that this narrative was intended for viewing by the gods. Perhaps a more credible explanation is that the sarcophagus text is an example of a narrative that encircles the perimeter of a sculpture and functions to define a ritual space around the sarcophagus box that sanctifies it for all eternity, much like the PSS encircles and sanctifies pottery vessels. In any case, the text would have been visible by humans until the chamber was built around the sarcophagus. The following is an overview of the narrative structure of the lid text, and how the juxtaposing of this text with the images on the lid and box provides significant information about the life and death of K'inich Janaab Pakal I.

A continuous text is carved on the four sides of the sarcophagus lid, often referred to as the Sarcophagus Rim text. On the sides of the box are portraits of four of the rulers mentioned in the temple narrative as well as an additional female and two males. The sarcophagus narrative complements the temple

FIGURE 7.3. *Palenque sarcophagus lid text, after Merle Greene Robertson.*

narrative. Like the PSS on pottery vessels, the sarcophagus text is read in a counterclockwise fashion. As first noted by Josserand (1989, 1991), the lid narrative begins on the east side with an opening text that Stuart (Stuart and Stuart 2008:178) reads as "the burden of maize was formed" although the meaning of this phrase is opaque (figure 7.3). From top to bottom, figure 7.3 shows the east, north, west, and south rim, respectively. The narrative continues with succinct statements giving the death dates for the first three kings from the temple text: Ahkal Mo' Nahb I (524), K'an Joy Chitam I (565), and Ahkal Mo' Nahb II (570), followed by the 9.7.0.0.0 Period Ending of Kan Bahlam I (573) and his subsequent death (583). This pattern of three deaths followed by a Period Ending and death is repeated in the next section of the text. It relates the death of Lady Yohl Ik'nal (604) (east side), Ajen Yohl Mat (August 612) (north side), and Janaab Pakal (March 612), and then the 9.10.0.0.0 Period Ending (633) and death (640) of Lady Sak K'uk' (west side).[2]

In essence, these two sections of text form parallel verses as discussed in chapter 4. However, the second section differs from the first in several aspects. While the dates in the first section proceed in a chronological order, those of the second section do not. The death of Ajen Yohl Mat in August of 612 in the second section is stated before that of Janaab Pakal, who died the previous March. In addition, the Period Ending and death of Kan Bahlam I stated in the first section are presented as sequential events, but those parallel events of Lady Sak K'uk' in the second section begin with the *tzolk'in* date of her death, then give the Period Ending Calendar Round date and Period Ending statement, and end with the *haab* date of her death and death statement. As observed by Josserand (1991), this is an example of a nested couplet and disturbed syntax, which is one of the devices employed to bring focus on a particular event or person. This places great emphasis on the death of Lady Sak K'uk'. Another contrast between these two couplets is that Kan Bahlam I's Period Ending repeats the information in the temple text that he was the officiant at the 9.7.0.0.0 Period Ending ceremony. In contrast, the temple text states that K'inich Janaab Pakal I was the officiant at the 9.10.0.0.0 Period Ending, not Lady Sak K'uk'. This again place emphasis on this woman.

The narrative continues with the death of K'an Mo' Hix (643) and then reaches the climax of the story. It states the parentage of K'inich Janaab Pakal I and his birth (603), then makes a reference to the four Period Endings that occurred during his lifetime (9.9.0.0.0, 9.10.0.0.0, 9.11.0.0.0, and 9.12.0.0.0), and finally climaxes with his death (683). His parentage statement, which begins this climax section, states that he was the child of K'an Mo' Hix and Lady Sak K'uk'. The story ends with a closing statement that the events happened under the supervision of a grandfather (or grandfathers) of a great serpent. The uniqueness of this serpent name prevents us from knowing who this might be.

TWO ALTERNATIVE ANALYSES

As befits an elegant work of literature, there is more than one way to analyze the structure of this text, and the two authors (Bassie-Sweet and Hopkins) hold slightly different views. Bassie-Sweet, as discussed earlier, sees the text as being structured as follows (leaving aside the opening and closing statements):

First Section	Second Section	Peak Episode
Death Ahkal Mo' Nahb I	Death Lady Yohl Ik'nal	Death K'an Mo' Hix
Death K'an Joy Chitam	Death Ajen Yohl Mat	Birth K'inich Janaab Pakal I
Death Ahkal Mo' Nahb II	Death Janaab Pakal	PE K'inich Janaab Pakal I
PE Kan Bahlam I	PE Lady Sak K'uk	Death K'inich Janaab Pakal I
Death Kan Bahlam I	Death Lady Sak K'uk'	

This analysis stresses the poetic parallelism of the two stanzas and the peak episode. Hopkins would hold to the formal structure created by the two backsteps in time in the chronological sequence and see the text as:

First Section	Second Section	Peak Episode
Death Ahkal Mo' Nahb I	Death Janaab Pakal	Birth K'inich Janaab Pakal I
Death K'an Joy Chitam	PE Lady Sak K'uk'	PE K'inich Janaab Pakal I
Death Ahkal Mo' Nahb II	Death Lady Sak K'uk'	Death K'inich Janaab Pakal I
PE Kan Bahlam I	Death K'an Mo' Hix	
Death Kan Bahlam I		
Death Lady Yohl Ik'nal		
Death Ajen Yohl Mat		

This analysis shows parallel, but not identical, verse structure that resembles, in a way, the lintels of Yaxchilán Structure 12. The first section lists remote ancestors, the second lists only immediate ancestors, and the final, peak, section, lists only the featured protagonist. The final section also replaces Death with Birth in its structure.

THE SARCOPHAGUS BOX

Beneath the sarcophagus lid text on each side of the box are portraits of figures emerging from cracks in the earth. A fruit tree is juxtaposed behind each figure. The caption texts beside each individual clearly name them as the historical figures of the lid text (Berlin 1959). In addition, a number of these historical figures wear headdresses that contain the glyphic elements from their names (Kelley 1976:6). For instance, the central element in the headdress of Lady Sak K'uk' ("White Quetzal") is a quetzal head. The central element in the headdress of her husband K'an Mo' Hix ("Yellow Macaw Jaguar") is a macaw head with a jaguar glyph infixed in its eye. In a similar fashion, K'inich Kan Bahlam I ("Serpent Jaguar") wears a jaguar headdress with the spiral eye of a serpent. Although it seems to be redundant to name these individuals with both a caption text and a headdress, such duplication can also be interpreted to be another case of a text and its adjacent image forming a couplet. Given that these are afterlife portraits, the redundancy may be a way of highlighting that these individuals were identified even in the afterlife with these particular animals. Some of the nominal phrases in the caption texts on the sarcophagus sides differ from the ones in the narrative on the lid. For example, the caption text referring to Kan Bahlam I includes the title *K'inich*, while his nominal phrase in the temple narrative and lid narrative merely refer to him as *Kan Bahlam*. With the exception of K'inich Janaab Pakal I and his son K'inich Kan Bahlam II, K'inich Kan Bahlam I is the only other individual who carries this important title in any of the Temple of the Inscription texts.

The torso of each figure on the sarcophagus box is in a frontal pose. On the east side, the first two figures face to the viewer's left while the third faces to the right (figure 7.4). The north side has two figures facing each other (figure 7.5). The west side repeats the pattern of the east side with two figures facing to the left and the third facing to the right (figure 7.6). The south side then repeats the pattern of the north side with two figures again facing each other (figure 7.7). The compositions of the east, north, west, and south sides thus form a visual pattern of alternating couplets, ABAB.

FIGURE 7.4. *Palenque sarcophagus box, east side, after Merle Greene Robertson.*

FIGURE 7.5. *Palenque sarcophagus box, north side, after Merle Greene Robertson.*

A ritual circuit conducted around a quadrilateral space defines and encases the space, but also forms a protective boundary. The sarcophagus box is a cosmogram of the quadrilateral world with K'inich Janaab Pakal I's ancestors defining the borders. This is similar to modern beliefs that the souls of the ancestors live in the landscape surrounding the community and protect it from harmful forces (Bassie-Sweet 2008). As an aside, if the stucco figures on the walls of the tomb also represent the subjects of the sarcophagus lid text, then this guardian function is further reinforced by these stucco sculptures.

The relationship between the subjects named in the text of the lid and the figures on the box is obvious on the east and south sides, but less so on the north and west sides. For example, below the east text that relates the deaths of Ahkal Mo' Nahb I, K'an Joy Chitam I, Ahkal Mo' Nahb II, Kan Bahlam I,

FIGURE 7.6. *Palenque sarcophagus box, west side, after Merle Greene Robertson.*

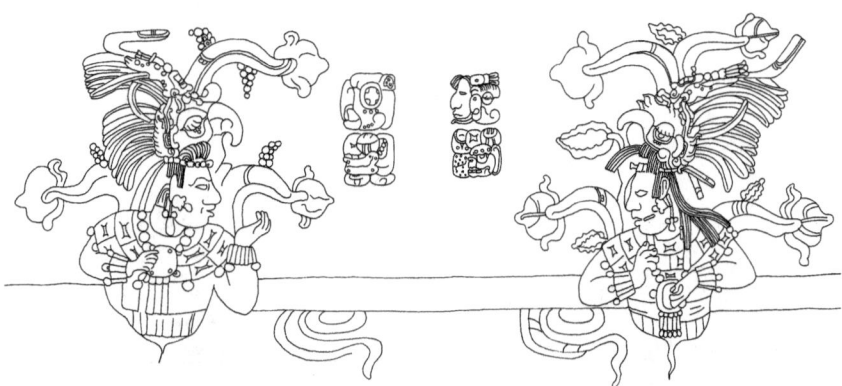

FIGURE 7.7. *Palenque sarcophagus box, south side, after Merle Greene Robertson.*

and Lady Yohl Ik'nal are portraits of Ahkal Mo' Nahb I, Kan Bahlam I, and Lady Yohl Ik'nal (figure 7.3).

Kan Bahlam I is highlighted in the lid text by the elaboration of his Period Ending event and the statement that he was a holy lord of Palenque. The *tzolk'in* and *haab* dates of his Period Ending event are presented in separate glyph blocks, which places visual emphasis on this event. In the scene on the box, all three rulers are accorded the "holy lord" title in their respective caption texts, but Kan Bahlam I's caption text is composed of four glyph blocks and it uses a head variant of the "holy" title for further emphasis. He is also named with the *K'inich* title. The birthdates of Ahkal Mo' Nahb II (523) and Kan Bahlam I (524) mentioned in the Tablet of the Cross narrative indicate that they were of the same generation. It is likely that a portrait of Ahkal Mo' Nahb II was not included on the sarcophagus box and that Kan Bahlam I was highlighted because K'inich Janaab Pakal I (the protagonist of the story) was a direct descendant of Kan Bahlam I.

The lid text and image on the south side of the box also have a direct relationship. The south lid text relates the birth and death of K'inich Janaab Pakal I (figure 7.3). What immediately precedes this statement on the west side of the lid is the clause that says K'an Mo' Hix and Lady Sak K'uk' were his parents. The south side of the box illustrates these two parents (figure 7.7). The image functions like an illustrated parentage statement beneath the text of K'inich Janaab Pakal I. Lady Sak K'uk' is the highlighted figure in the scene as it is she, not her husband, who carries the "holy Palenque lord" title. Although Lady Sak K'uk' may never have ruled, it has been argued that she was the child of the ruler Lady Yohl Ik'nal, and that K'inich Janaab Pakal I acquired the right to rule through her (Bassie-Sweet 1991).

The juxtaposing of K'inich Janaab Pakal I with his parents on the south side of the sarcophagus provides some insight into the configuration on the north side of the box that illustrates another portrait of K'an Mo' Hix and Lady Sak K'uk' (figure 7.5). Once again, Lady Sak K'uk' is highlighted with the "holy Palenque lord" title. Despite ample room for a lengthy text, the north lid inscription surprisingly only states the death of Ajen Yohl Mat. While this may seem a strange juxtaposition, there is likely a simple explanation. Ajen Yohl Mat ruled for seven years during a turbulent time in Palenque's history. He was succeeded by Muwan Mat who lasted less than three years as king. He, in turn, was succeeded by K'inich Janaab Pakal I who took the throne at the tender age of twelve. The fate of Muwan Mat is unknown because the sarcophagus lid does not address his death, and he does not appear in other inscriptions at Palenque. The brief time interval between these three accessions, however, suggests the strong possibility that these three kings were of the same generation. The most obvious reason for the juxtaposing of Ajen Yohl Mat with the parents of K'inich Janaab Pakal I is that they were also his parents (Bassie-Sweet 1991:206, 245).

The relationship between the text and image on the west side of the sarcophagus is also related to genealogy. The west lid text relates the death of Janaab Pakal, Lady Sak K'uk', and K'an Mo' Hix (figure 7.3). As noted above, the lid text highlights Lady Sak K'uk's Period Ending and death. However, the image below this text illustrates Janaab Pakal, Lady Yohl Ik'nal again, and K'an Joy Chitam I (figure 7.6). With the exception of the father of K'inich Janaab Pakal I, Janaab Pakal is the only male mentioned in the sarcophagus text who was not a ruler. Nevertheless, he was accorded a Palenque emblem glyph and he was the namesake of the great K'inich Janaab Pakal I. The text on a Group IV incensario stand indicates that Janaab Pakal oversaw the accessions of a number of Palenque court officials during the reign of Ajen Yohl Mat, which indicates he played a strategic role in the court of this young king who came to the throne after the death of the ruler Lady Yohl Ik'nal (Martin and Grube 2008:161; Zender 2004:293b). The most logical conclusion is that Janaab Pakal was Lady Yohl Ik'nal's husband and, thus, the grandfather of Ajen Yohl Mat and K'inich Janaab Pakal I (Bassie-Sweet 1991:206, 241–246). The west lid text, therefore, relates the death of Janaab Pakal and his daughter Lady Sak K'uk', and it is juxtaposed with his image and that of his wife, Lady Yohl Ik'nal. This is a very reasonable explanation of why Lady Yohl Ik'nal is depicted twice on this monument.

The final segment of text on the west side relates the death of Lady Sak K'uk's husband K'an Mo' Hix and makes the statement that K'an Mo' Hix and Lady Sak K'uk' were the parents of K'inich Janaab Pakal I. This places emphasis on K'an Mo' Hix in that he is the only subject of this section of text and his name precedes that of Lady Sak K'uk' in the parentage statement. Oddly enough, the image juxtaposed with this text is a portrait of K'an Joy Chitam I. What are we to make of this pairing? It may be that K'an Mo' Hix and K'an Joy Chitam I are juxtaposed because K'an Mo' Hix descended from this early Palenque king, although obviously not in the direct descent line of rulership. The lid text does state that K'an Mo' Hix was a holy lord of Palenque (although this status could be due to his marriage to a royal). K'an Mo' Hix did not die until the twenty-fourth year of his son K'inich Janaab Pakal I's reign, and one can only assume that he played a prominent role in his son's court.

THE SECONDARY LORDS OF THE SARCOPHAGUS LID

As noted, the apotheosis of K'inich Janaab Pakal I on the sarcophagus lid is framed by a sky band (figure 7.1). In contrast to the celestial signs on the east and west sides, the north and south bands each contain portraits of three individuals (Zender 2004b; Chinchilla Mazariegos 2006). Each portrait is presented as a bust within a half-quatrefoil shape. The caption texts adjacent to these portraits indicate that both the north and south sides illustrate the same three men: Jewel Bird, Chak Chan, and Yuhk Mak'abajte'. The caption texts on the north and south bands name both Jewel Bird and Chak Chan with the sacerdotal title *Ajk'uhuun*. On the north band, Yuhk Mak'abajte' is named as *sajal* (a lord with both military and priestly duties). It is likely that the titles accorded these three secondary lords represent their highest status office at the time of their own deaths. Although these double portraits create a visual couplet, there are differences between the two. While the south side portraits of these secondary lords as well as the celestial cartouches on the east and west sides are separated by double bars, all three men on the north side are pictured within one long and undivided cartouche. This long cartouche is flanked on each end by cartouches containing the complementary opposite signs of night and day, as noted above.

Chinchilla Mazariegos (2006) argued that these secondary lords were portrayed in celestial cartouches because they took on celestial identities in the afterlife similar to the Central Mexican concept that warriors joined the sun as celestial beings in the afterlife. Be that as it may, this interpretation does not explain why these three secondary lords are each illustrated twice. These dual portraits on the north and south sides of the sarcophagus lid are thematically parallel to the dual portraits of Lady Sak K'uk' and K'an Mo' Hix on the north and south sides of the box. As noted above, the section of the lid text that is juxtaposed with these images refers to the rulers Ajen Yol Mat and K'inich Janaab Pakal I, respectively. The implication is that, like Lady Sak K'uk' and K'an Hix Mo', these three secondary lords were specifically associated with both of these rulers.[3] Although references to secondary lords are limited in the corpus of Palenque art, there is an inscription on a stone bust from Group IV that indicates that Yuhk Mak'abajte' was a member of Ajen Yol Mat's court (Zender 2004b). It also states that Yuhk Mak'abajte' acquired the title of *Yajawk'ahk'* ("Fire Priest") on December 28, 610, during the reign of Ajen Yol Mat. References to the other two lords are found on fragments of a Temple IV panel that unfortunately do not contain dates. The text does indicate that Chak Chan and Jewel Bird participated with K'inich Janaab Pakal I in a war event (Zender 2004b:306–310). Given the dual groupings of these three secondary lords on the sarcophagus lid, it is not unreasonable to propose that all three lords had courtly careers during the reign of Ajen Yol Mat and continued those duties during the reign of K'inich Janaab Pakal I.[4]

THE DEATH AND AFTERLIFE OF K'INICH JANAAB PAKAL I

There are a number of verbs used to describe different aspects of an individual's death and funeral. The most straightforward actions are the verbs *cham* "to die" and *muhkaj* "to be buried." Other actions are metaphorical, such as a phrase that appears to refer to the departure of the soul from its body at the time of death (Proskouriakoff 1963:162–163; Hopkins 2014). It is this phrase that is used to describe the death of K'inich Janaab Pakal I in the Palace Tablet narrative (J10–I11). On Tikal Stela 31, another term deciphered as *ochha'* "to

FIGURE 7.8. *Vessel K6547, after Kerr.*

enter the water" relates the death of the Tikal king Chak Tok Ich'aak I in 378 while the passing of the Tikal king Sihyaj Chan K'awiil II (456) is noted by the term *ochb'ih* "to enter the road" (Stuart 1998:388). The death-related phrase *ochb'ih* is used in the Temple of the Inscription tablet text and sarcophagus text to describe the deaths of not only K'inich Janaab Pakal I, but his wife, his mother, his father, his paternal grandfather, and the rulers that preceded him. It also appears in the Palace Tablet narrative in reference to K'inich Kan Bahlam II's death in 702.

Vessel K6547 also includes the death phrase *ochb'ih* (figure 7.8). This vessel illustrates two sequential events related to the death and burial of a lord. The first event depicts the deceased lord wrapped in a bundle and placed on top of a stone burial bier. The left leg of the bier is inscribed with the *ochb'ih* verb. Six mourners standing in shallow water flank the lord. This scene suggests that entering the road involved the preparation of the deceased body beside a body of water. The second scene illustrates the lord's now skeletal body within a tomb at the base of a pyramid. Three personified trees grow above the skeleton. In short, these two scenes show acts related to the lord entering the road and the final state of his body within its tomb. It is thematically parallel to the sarcophagus, which states that the Palenque lords and ladies entered the road, and then illustrates them as fruit trees (Schele and Mathews 1998:122).

On vessels K1202 and K6979, both the *ochb'ih* and *ochha'* phrases are found in association with the dressing and transformation of the deity One Ixim after his demise. It is, therefore, highly likely that the process that these elite humans were thought to undergo after death was parallel to that of One Ixim. The fate of One Ixim is directly pertinent to the sarcophagus lid scene because K'inich Janaab Pakal I is dressed in One Ixim's jade costume and has clearly taken on this deity's persona. Furthermore, K'inich Janaab Pakal I was buried in a jade costume including a jade mask that covered his face.

The caption text on vessel K6979 describes the scene as One Ixim entering the water. One Ixim is illustrated standing in waist-high water while dressing in his jade costume with the assistance of his two sons and four Underworld goddesses. The washing of a body after death is customary in almost all cultures, and it is also a common Mesoamerican tradition to wash a deity and his or her clothing before an important event. The nakedness of the goddesses and their unbound hair suggest this is a bathing and dressing scene (Bassie-Sweet 2008:292–294). The vessel K1202 illustrates a similar scene. In this case, One Ixim is being dressed by six goddesses and his son One Ajaw. The phrase in the caption text used to describe One Ixim's action is *ochb'ih* "to enter the road." The caption text also indicates where this event happened and calls it "the Seven Water place." As noted in chapter 1, the Maya metaphorically refer to rivers as roads of water. The description of One Ixim's aquatic location as both a road and water suggests that the Seven Water place specifically refers to a river.

The road of the *ochb'ih* expression is most often interpreted by researchers to be either the path of the sun or one of the roads of the Underworld. There is another possibility. The ecliptic is an imaginary line that marks the annual path of the sun across the night sky. The moon and planets always appear on or adjacent to this path. The Maya viewed the Milky Way as a celestial river inhabited by a crocodile, and the mouth of that crocodile was the black rift of the Milky Way (see Bassie-Sweet 2008:37 for overview). When the black rift is directly overhead, marking the Place of Duality in the night sky, the path of the ecliptic crosses it just to the south, forming a crossroads in the sky. Consequently, it is plausible that the water and road referenced in the death phrases is the Milky Way. Evidence to support this interpretation is found in the numerous examples of the Milky Way Crocodile that illustrate the Quadripartite Badge motif on its tail.

The juxtaposing of One Ixim and the Quadripartite Badge motif is found in a number of contexts. On vessel K1270, One Ixim is shown emerging from the open mouth of a serpent which, in turn, is rising from the personified *k'in* bowl. The head of One Ixim rests in the *k'in* bowl on vessel K2849 (figure 8.8). These appear to be *pars pro toto* representations of the same theme as the sarcophagus lid. But what does this action represent? In Mesoamerica, birth, emergence, and transformation were often metaphorically tied to the cycles of corn and the sun. Moreover, there is a theme of deities being reborn or transformed through the act of burning. This is also associated with the corn cycle, for the field is first burnt and then planted with corn seed that germinates and sprouts with the first rains. The immolation of deities is found in a Popol Vuh episode in which the Hero Twins undergo such a fire transformation during their trials in the Underworld before they take on their final roles as sun and full moon (Christenson 2003a:177–79). In Central Mexico, the gods Nanahuatl and Tecuciztecatl sacrifice themselves by leaping into a pyre, and in doing so become the sun and moon (Sahagún 1959–1963:7:4–6). Particularly pertinent to this discussion is an account of the transformation of the cultural hero Quetzalcoatl. According to the Annals of Cuauhtitlan, Quetzalcoatl transformed into the morning star through fire:

> Now this year, 1 Reed, is when he got to the ocean, the seashore, so it is told and related. Then he halted and wept and gathered up his attire, putting on his head fan, his turquoise mask, and so forth. And as soon as he was dressed, he set himself on fire and cremated himself . . . And as soon as his ashes had been consumed, they saw the heart of a quetzal rising upward. And so they knew he had gone to the sky, had entered the sky. The old people said he changed into the star that appears at dawn. Therefore they say it came forth when Quetzalcoatl died, and they called him Lord of the Dawn. (Bierhost 1992:36)

A number of researchers have interpreted the sarcophagus scene as K'inich Janaab Pakal I's apotheosis as the sun based on his position above the bowl of the Quadripartite Badge motif, which is marked with a *k'in* "sun" sign (Robertson 1974, 1983; Schele and Miller 1984:306). Given that this motif is the headdress of GI, it has been further argued that GI was the dawning sun and that K'inich Janaab Pakal I was identified with this alleged solar deity in the afterlife (Taube and Houston 2015; Stuart 2005a; 2007b:219; 2009; Stuart and Stuart 2008:198). On the other hand, Bassie-Sweet has argued that after One Ixim–One Hunahpu's resurrection, his final celestial destiny was to become the morning star while that of his son One Ajaw–Hunahpu was to become the sun (Bassie-Sweet 2008; Bassie-Sweet et al. 2015). This archetypical model can be applied to the fates of K'inich Janaab Pakal I and his son and successor K'inich Kan Bahlam II. In this scenario, K'inich Janaab Pakal I rose as the morning star One Ixim–One Hunahpu after death, and when his son K'inich

Kan Bahlam II subsequently replaced him in his role as king, K'inich Kan Bahlam II then took on the guise of One Ajaw–Hunahpu and acquired his *k'inich* title. This apotheosis of the dead king as the morning star follows the afterlife fate of Quetzalcoatl, whose avian manifestation was thought to be a male quetzal bird just like One Iximʼs avian manifestation.

It is difficult to determine conclusively whether K'inich Janaab Pakal I was identified in death with the morning star or with the sun. The discussion concerning the roles of these deities and the meaning of the sarcophagus lid will not end any time soon, nor should it. There needs to be a constant reevaluation and ongoing examination of the interpretations and issues. What is directly relevant to this discussion is that the Temple of the Inscriptions narratives state that all deceased members of K'inich Janaab Pakal I's family and all the previous rulers with the exception of Muwan Mat entered the road.

SUMMARY

The Palenque sarcophagus provides a unique view of how the Palencanos envisioned the death and afterlife of the ruling elite. By examining the narrative structure of the sarcophagus text and its relationship to the adjacent scenes it is possible to draw some conclusions regarding the genealogy of the Palenque ruling elite. The layout of the text and scenes of the sarcophagus box draw a direct parallel between Ajen Yol Mat and K'inich Janaab Pakal I. This pairing is likely based on more than just the fact that they were brothers. The site of Santa Elena is situated on the Río San Pedro Mártir approximately halfway between Palenque and Calakmul. The river provided easy access from the central Petén to the lower Usumacinta, the Tabasco coast, Veracruz, and Central Mexico, and it was, thus, of strategic economic advantage to control. An eroded and undated monument from Santa Elena appears to indicate that Ajen Yol Mat held sway over Santa Elena at some point, and may have overseen the accession of one of its rulers (Grube, Martin, and Zender 2002:II:16–17). Calakmul was also obviously interested in this waterway. As noted above, the Temple of the Inscriptions temple text refers to two key events in Palenque's history: the sacking of Palenque in 611 by Calakmul, which occurred during the reign of Ajen Yol Mat and presumably at a time when he was in control of Santa Elena, and the arrival at Palenque of the defeated Santa Elena lord Nuun Ujol Chahk under the victorious K'inich Janaab Pakal I in 659. The inference appears to be that K'inich Janaab Pakal I was able to restore Palenque's regional control, and at least temporarily regain this strategic advantage.

K'inich Janaab Pakal I's triumph over Santa Elena is also featured in the inscription on the Palace House C staircase (Grube, Martin, and Zender 2002; Martin and Grube 2000:165). House C was dedicated on December 25, 661, so, unlike the Temple of the Inscriptions narrative, this account was created shortly after the war event.[5] The House C time frame begins with the birth (603) and accession (615) of K'inich Janaab Pakal I. It then moves back in time, not to the Calakmul defeat during Ajen Yol Mat's reign, but to an earlier conquest of Palenque by Calakmul on 9.8.5.13.8 (AD 599) when Lady Yohl Ik'nal (K'inich Janaab Pakal I's grandmother) was in power. The last event of the House C narrative ties this loss to the successful capture of Nuun Ujol Chahk and a series of lesser lords that occurred just six days before his arrival at Palenque. The implication appears to be that the defeats in 599 and 611 that likely limited Palenque's control or influence in the Santa Elena region were rectified by K'inich Janaab Pakal I in 659. The House C narrative states that the Palenque thunderbolt gods GI, GII, and GIII were "thrown down" by Calakmul during the sacking of Palenque. This had to have been seen not only as a physical defeat of Palenque, but as a great spiritual failure by Lady Yohl Ik'nal and her court to summon the protection of the Palenque patron gods. It is not surprising then that the later Temple of the Inscriptions narrative focuses on the ability of K'inich Janaab Pakal I to appease these deities during the Period Endings of his tenure, and obtain their benevolence throughout his reign.

Four months after the death of K'inich Janaab Pakal I, his eldest son K'inich Kan Bahlam II took the throne. The Temple of the Inscriptions was dedicated seven years after K'inich Janaab Pakal I's death on July 6, 690 (Stuart and Stuart 2008:171). While finishing the Temple of the Inscriptions, K'inich Kan Bahlam II also constructed the three buildings of the Cross Group, one for each member of the triad of thunderbolt deities. This complex was dedicated a year and a half later (January 10, 692), just in time for the 9.13.0.0.0 Period Ending (March 12) when K'inich Kan Bahlam II again honored these gods. The topic of the next chapter is the Cross Group narrative.

NOTES

1. The PSS text is on the interior wall of the vessel and does not appear in our illustration (see Just 2012:fig. 40).

2. In their gloss and translation of the sarcophagus lid text, Stuart and Stuart (2008:178) inadvertently left out the death of Lady Sak K'uk'.

3. The grouping of a ruler with three secondary lords who act together during a ceremony is seen on the Temple XIX platform where three lords who hold the

"banded-bird" title conduct the accession ceremony of K'inich Ahkal Mo' Nahb III. Another set of three lords, led by a Yajawk'ahk' ("Fire Priest"), sit to the left of the ruler and wait to perform a second ceremony.

4. These three secondary lords also appear on the legs of the sarcophagus box. Chak Chan and Jewel Bird face each other on the southwest and southeast legs, respectively, while Chak Chan and Yuhk Mak'abajte' face each other on the northwest and northeast legs. Chak Chan appears to be the senior of the three secondary lords, given his dual portrait on the legs. In an early study, Bassie Sweet (2008:310) incorrectly suggested these three secondary lords might have officiated at K'inich Janaab Pakal I's funeral.

5. Stuart (Stuart and Stuart 2008:159) claimed that this dedication (9.11.9.5.19 4 Kawak 2 Pax) occurred on the winter solstice. However, using the 584,285 correlation constant favored by Stuart, this date would be December 25, four days past the solstice.

8

The Palenque Cross Group Narrative

The inscriptions found in the three buildings of the Palenque Cross Group form a continuous narrative that provides a wealth of examples regarding narrative structure and the relationship between text and image. This chapter explores these remarkable works of art.

THE SETTING

Don Juan Mountain is a massive ridge that erupts out of the coastal plain and marks the northern boundary of the highlands in this region. It is named after a Ch'ol deity called Don Juan who is thought to inhabit the mountain. An unexcavated site on the east peak contains buildings in the style of Palenque and the major Ch'ol ceremonial cave on its north cliff once contained Palenque-style tiered incensarios (Bassie-Sweet et al. 2015). On the north base of Don Juan Mountain are a series of foothill ridges. The site of Palenque is situated on a ridge that runs parallel to the eastern end of the mountain and the valley of the Chacamax River.

The highest point of the Palenque ridge is about 600 m in elevation, and it is labeled as Cerro El Mirador ("Viewpoint Hill") on the 1:50,000 INEGI maps of Mexico. Cerro El Mirador provides a 360-degree view of the coastal plain to the north and the Chacamax Valley to the south. Approximately 1 km west along the ridgeline from Cerro El Mirador, a

DOI: 10.5876/9781607327424.c008

steep ravine drops down the north slope of the ridge. This ravine is the source of the Otolum River. In the rainy season, water flows down the ravine until it reaches a small natural plateau at the 185-m mark of the ridge. This plateau is where the major Late Classic buildings of Palenque were constructed. The Otolum crosses the Palenque plateau through an aqueduct built by the Maya and then plunges further down the near-vertical grade to the plain below.

The spur from the ridgeline that forms the east slope of the Otolum ravine ends in a hill that rises some 146 m above the site plateau. Although it has never been excavated, a small pyramid (Group D) graces the top of this hill. It provides an exceptional view of the plain in front of Palenque. Some sources (Robertson 1991:8; Stuart and Stuart 2008:192) refer to this hill as El Mirador, and Stuart has argued that in the Palenque inscriptions the place name Yemal K'uk' Lakam Witz "Descending Quetzal Big Mountain" refers to this hill. This may be the case, but we prefer the neutral designation of the Group D hill.

The Cross Group is located on a terrace between the base of the Group D hill and the aqueduct. It is composed of a plaza with a small radial platform at its center and temple-pyramids on its west, north, and east sides. The doorways to all three Cross Group buildings are oriented to the center of the plaza. The Temple of the Sun, which delineates the west side of the plaza, is a freestanding structure. The Temple of the Foliated Cross borders the east side of the plaza, and its substructure was built on the slope of the Group D hill. The Temple of the Cross demarcates the north side of the plaza. Its superstructure is only slightly larger than that of the other two buildings, but its substructure is significantly larger and taller. Although its substructure has not been comprehensively excavated, it is likely that it, or another earlier version of this building, was built over a natural hillock that abuts the Group D hill. This was a common construction technique that saved materials and manpower. The southeast corner of its substructure joins the northwest corner of the Temple of the Foliated Cross substructure. On the south side of the Cross Group plaza is a higher terrace with more buildings. These are located on the slopes of the Group D hill (Temples XVII, XVIII, XVIIIA) and at its base (Temples XIX, XX, XXI). On the south side of this terrace are perennial springs that feed the Otolum River and turn it into a reliable, dry-season water source.

Each Cross Group building was devoted to one member of the Palenque triad of thunderbolt gods and was richly adorned with stucco decorations. In addition, low-relief panels decorated the balustrades, walls, sanctuary piers, and doorjambs. The remains of the outer building piers indicate that they also contained significant information but, regrettably, most of them have been destroyed. The inscriptions of the buildings state that all three structures were dedicated on 9.12.19.14.12 5 Eb 5 K'ayab (January 10, AD 692), some eight years after K'inich Kan Bahlam II's accession when he was 56 years old (Stuart 1998:392). A small sculpture found near the Temple of the Foliated Cross also repeats the dedication date of the buildings and ends with a reference to the 9.13.0.0.0 Period Ending that occurred 88 days later (Stuart 1998:401).

PERIPHERAL CROSS GROUP TEXTS

The Cross Group texts indicate that the sanctuary within each building represented the birth location of its respective god, and that these sanctuaries were called *pib nah*, which Houston (1996) interpreted to mean "sweatbath." Each sanctuary also had a proper name. The Temple of the Cross sanctuary name is composed of the number six, an undeciphered element, and a sky sign (Six-?-Sky) (Stuart 2006). The name of the Temple of the Sun sanctuary has two parts. The first is a "fire/smoke" sign and an inverted water vase that appears quite frequently in hieroglyphic writing and art, although the vase sign has yet to be definitively deciphered. The vase sign is thought to be related to rainmaking because inverted water vases are used as metaphors for rain (see Dresden Codex pages 39 and 74, and Madrid Codex page 30a). In the context of the Temple of the Sun, the vase is conflated with a mountain sign and prefixed by the number nine. This "Nine Fire/Smoke-Vase Mountain" name is followed by the phrase K'inich Paskab ("Sunlike Dawn"). The Temple of the Foliated Cross sanctuary name is composed of a nah "house" glyph, a *k'an* sign, and a T214 sign that represents a clump of some kind of foliage. It can also include a square-nosed serpent prefixed to the *k'an* sign. The square-nosed serpent appears in a variety of contexts where it serves as a visual flourish and does not appear to represent a separate word. Boot (2006) noted that the Nah K'an T214 house name also appears on Tortuguero Monument 6, but in this example the T214 foliage sign is replaced with phonetic signs representing the word *jal*. Like the Temple of the Foliated Cross, the Tortuguero Nah K'an Jal is also called a *pib nah*. In Cholan languages, the term *jal* is used to describe reeds, and as a verb it references weaving. The Maya wove both *Cyperus canis* (flatsedge) and *Typha* (cattail) into mats (Osborne 1965:283), and there is a logographic sign composed of strips of woven material that has the value of *jal* "to weave" (Stone and Zender 2011:81). Given that Stuart (2000) has identified the glyph for *puh* "cattail," it seems reasonable to suggest that the T214 *jal* sign refers to flatsedge.

In summary, the name of the Temple of the Cross refers to a sky location, the Temple of the Sun to a mountain, and the Temple of the Foliated Cross to a house associated with reeds. These names appear at other sites, which suggest that they were part of the standardized Classic Period mythology and not specific to Palenque.[1]

It has long been known that the Maya viewed their temple-pyramids as mountains, and that mountains were thought to be manifestations of deities (see Bassie-Sweet 2008 for overview). The logical conclusion to draw from these beliefs is that each Cross Group building was metaphorically thought to be the manifestation of its respective deity. In addition, several researchers have suggested that the triad building arrangement of the Cross Group represents the three hearthstones (Hansen 1992; Freidel, Schele, and Parker 1993; Taube 1998), and Bassie-Sweet (2008) has extended that argument and identified the triad of thunderbolt gods as manifestations of the three hearthstones. This follows a Mesoamerican tradition in which the hearthstones are thought to be identified with specific gods. The identification of the three hearthstones with thunderbolt gods accords with the fact that lightning is a source of fire in nature.

The latest date referenced in the Cross Group buildings is the Period Ending on 9.13.0.0.0 8 Ajaw 8 Woh (March 18, AD 692), but it is given in the future tense. This Period Ending was to be the first major calendrical event of K'inich Kan Bahlam II's reign. It is likely that the Cross Group was built not just to represent these deities, house their images, and honor them, but to provide a venue where offerings could be made to these gods on this specific Period Ending, much like the Tikal twin pyramid complexes were built to accommodate major Period Endings at that site. The badly eroded stela found at the base of the Temple of the Cross likely commemorated this Period Ending event, since it appears to bear a single glyph reading 8 Ajaw, below a standing figure.

The historical events of K'inich Kan Bahlam II that are stated in the Cross Group texts are his pre-accession event designating him as the heir apparent (*bah ch'ok*) at age six, his first participation in a Period Ending on 9.10.10.0.0 at age seven, his accession (the tying of the *sak huun* headdress) at age 48, and a series of events at age 55 that spanned two days (2 Kib 14 Mol to 3 Kaban 15 Mol), about six months before the dedication of the buildings. The nature of these later events is still somewhat unclear. The verb of the 2 Kib 14 Mol event is pul "to burn" (Stuart 1994). Houston (1996) believes it refers to the firing of a *pib nah* "sweatbath" (the sanctuary structure), while Stuart (2006) thinks the actions are related to effigies of the three deities. The 3 Kaban 15 Mol event refers to a house named as that of K'inich K'uk' Bahlam, and includes the conjuring of gods by a priest named Nuk Yajaw Chan (Stuart 2006:97–98). Nuk

Yajaw Chan carries the "banded-bird" title, and he is named as the individual who tied the headband of rulership onto the head of K'inich Kan Bahalm. This is parallel to the scene on the Temple XIX platform where the secondary lord carrying the "banded-bird" title hands the new king K'inich Ahkal Mo' Nahb III his *sak huun* headdress.

As discussed in the previous chapter, the tablets of the Temple of the Inscriptions indicate that K'inich Janaab Pakal I performed actions directed at the triad of thunderbolt gods. The Cross Group sanctuary panels illustrate K'inich Kan Bahlam II performing rituals at shrines that were dedicated to the thunderbolt triad during the reign of his father, when he was six years old, and again on the occasion of his own accession. Given these circumstances, it is apparent that prior to the completion of the Cross Group buildings in 692 there had to have been another set of places identified with this triad of gods where both K'inich Kan Bahlam II and his father K'inich Janaab Pakal I performed their ceremonies. Whether there was an earlier set of shrines on the Cross Group site, on the terrace to the south, on Don Juan Mountain, or in some other location is unknown. Hopefully future excavations will resolve this issue.

THE ALFARDAS

The first inscription encountered on each Cross Group building was located on the alfardas (balustrades) of its staircase, and it refers to the dedication of the shrine (*pib nah*) within the temple (Houston 1996). The Temple of the Cross alfardas narrative begins on the left-hand side of the staircase with the mythological birth of GI at a supernatural location called Matwiil (1.18.5.3.2 9 Ik' 15 Keh, October 21, 2360 BC) (figure 8.1). The birth verb is a metaphorical phrase "to touch the earth," perhaps a word play involving the (near) homophones täl "to touch" (Aulie and Aulie 1998:114) and tal "to come" (Hopkins, Josserand, and Cruz 2011:214). A huge Distance Number then moves the time frame forward some three thousand years to the Calendar Round date 5 Eb 5 K'ayab (January 10, AD 692). The narrative continues on the right alfarda with the dedication verb, the proper name of the Temple of the Cross sanctuary, and a clause that states that GI was the god of K'inich Kan Bahlam II (Stuart 1998). K'inich Kan Bahlam II's name phrase is elaborated with his Baakal Waywal title (the meaning of this term is unclear) and a parentage statement indicating he was the child of K'inich Janaab Pakal I and Lady Tz'akbu Ajaw. The text ends with the statement that the shrine was built at the Lakamha' Chan Ch'een place (Stuart 2006). Lakamha' is a place name

FIGURE 8.1. *Palenque Temple of the Cross, alfarda inscription, after Merle Greene Robertson.*

that has been identified as the ancient name for the Otolum River and for Palenque in general (Stuart and Houston 1994). The Distance Number that joins the birth date to the dedication date in effect gives the age of the deity when the building was dedicated. This Distance Number is given in the order of an Initial Series date (*bak'tun*, *k'atun*, *tun*, *winal*, and *k'in*). Reversing the order of a Distance Number notation is a rhetorical device that is used to place emphasis on an event.

The Temple of the Sun alfarda texts are badly damaged and are missing sections of text (figure 8.2). Enough remains, however, to indicate that the end of the narrative was not parallel to the Temple of the Cross text. The text begins on the left side with the birth ("to touch the earth") at Matwiil of GIII (1.18.5.3.6 13 Kimi 19 Keh, October 25, 2360 BC), but the next eight glyph blocks are missing. Given that the right alfarda begins with the name of the building, implying a dedication date, it seems likely that the missing glyph blocks recorded the Distance Number between these two events. The time frame then moves forward to the 9.13.0.0.0 Period Ending. The next two glyph blocks are only partially preserved, but can be reconstructed as the

FIGURE 8.2. *Palenque Temple of the Sun, alfarda inscription, after Merle Greene Robertson.*

tzolk'in date of the Period Ending and K'inich Kan Bahlam II's name. The last four glyphs of the text are completely destroyed. They probably contained either K'inich Kan Bahlam II's parentage statement or his titles and the Lakamha' Chan Ch'een place name.

The Temple of the Foliated Cross alfardas return to the structure of the Temple of the Cross alfardas and give the birth ("to touch the earth") of GII at Matwiil (1.18.5.4.0 1 Ajaw 13 Mak, November 8, 2360 BC), the dedication event, and the proper name of GII's building, and state that GII was the god of K'inich Kan Bahlam II (figure 8.3). The Baakal Waywal title, the parentage statement, and the Lakamha' Chan Ch'een place name are also repeated.

If we view these three alfarda texts from the viewpoint of poetic structure, they form a chiasmus pattern of ABA:

A	TC alfarda	birth, dedication event
B	TS alfarda	birth, dedication event, Period Ending
A	TFC alfarda	birth, dedication event

In short, the alfarda texts introduce the triad of thunderbolt gods of Matwiil, give the proper name for their shrines, and declare them to be the gods of

FIGURE 8.3. *Palenque Temple of the Foliated Cross, alfarda inscription, after Merle Greene Robertson.*

K'inich Kan Bahlam II, the Baakal Waywal. It seems obvious that the Cross Group buildings were intended to replicate Matwiil. According to the Popol Vuh, the creator deities made the earth rise up from the waters of the Place of Duality, and then established their household on the surface of the earth. It is likely that Matwiil names their household, that is, the Place of Duality on the surface of the earth.

THE SANCTUARY JAMBS

Each sanctuary of the Cross Group buildings had a text on one of its jambs, although only that of the Temple of the Foliated Cross has survived in its entirety (figure 8.4). This text begins with the Calendar Round date of the building dedication and includes a Supplementary Series and an 819-day count notation. The dedication verb is repeated, but this time the dedication refers to a different structure called the *kunul* of GII, which Stuart (2006) interprets as referring to some kind of platform within the building. GII is named with his *ch'ok* and Na Ho Chan titles and as the "cherished one" of K'inich Kan Bahlam II (see below for discussion of this phrase). A Distance

FIGURE 8.4. *Palenque Temple of the Foliated Cross, jamb, after Merle Greene Robertson.*

Number then links the dedication event to the future Period Ending on 9.13.0.0.0. It ends with the statement that this structure was built at Lakamha'. The alfarda text and the sanctuary jamb text form a couplet referring to the dedication of the GII shrine. The fragmentary texts from the other two sanctuary jambs include calendrical information that indicates these texts also referred to the dedication event. It is likely that they too formed couplets with their respective alfarda texts.

Given their fragmentary state, it is difficult to make a comparison between the three sanctuary jamb texts except that each text ends with a place name that denotes different aspects of the same general location. The Temple of the Cross jamb location is Lakamha' Chan Ch'een, that of the Temple of the Sun is Descending Quetzal Mountain, Lakamha', and the location named on the Temple of the Foliated Cross is simply Lakamha'. These place names also occur in the temple tablets and are discussed below.

THE SANCTUARY PIERS

Each temple had a set of two sculptured sanctuary piers (Robertson 1991). None of the piers has survived in its entirety, but the piers appear to illustrate the ceremonies that were performed on the occasion of the building dedications. The best preserved are those of the Temple of the Cross. The left pier illustrates the adult K'inich Kan Bahlam II holding the Quadripartite Badge icon in an inverted position with liquid pouring from it (Robertson 1991:fig. 34). The caption text indicates he is impersonating the mythical ancestor U Kokan Chan and possibly another ancestral figure, and he wears a headdress that incorporates the names of these ancestors (Stuart 2006). A small Yopaat Chahk figure swings from his hip. K'inich Kan Bahlam II faces the right pier, which illustrates God L, the maternal grandfather of the Hero

Twins and patron god of obsidian merchants, smoking a cigar. The inscription above the two piers repeats the name of the building and that GI was the "cherished one" of K'inich Kan Bahlam II, holy lord of Palenque. In contrast, what remains of the shattered sanctuary piers on the Temple of the Sun and Temple of the Foliated Cross all appear to illustrate adult portraits of K'inich Kan Bahlam II. These piers differ from the Temple of the Cross sanctuary piers in that each scene is framed by a band that literally spells out the name of its respective sanctuary.

The Temple of the Sun right jamb illustrates K'inich Kan Bahlam II carrying a Tlaloc incense bag and holding a spear. Although a major piece of the panel is now missing, a 1787 drawing by Armendáriz shows that the spear was a flint blade with obsidian chips protruding from the blade base (Stuart 2006:157). The Armendáriz drawing also indicates that there was a caption text that framed the top of the spear. This text began with the Calendar Round date 10 Chuwen 4 Sak (9.12.15.7.11, September 12, 687) that also occurs on the Temple XVII panel (Mathews, cited in Stuart 2006:157). The Temple XVII caption text refers to a war event with Toniná on this date, just three years into K'inich Kan Bahlam II's reign. The Temple XVII scene illustrates K'inich Kan Bahlam II dressed as the Kaloomte' (Tlaloc warrior priest) and holding a similar spear.[2] The military theme of the sanctuary pier matches the subject matter of the adjacent Tablet of the Sun, which features war-related iconography.

Another interesting feature of the Temple of the Sun right jamb is the parentage statement that frames the lower body of K'inich Kan Bahlam II. It notes that he was the child of the five-*k'atun* lord K'inich Janaab Pakal I and Lady Tz'akbu Ajaw. It then states that he was also the grandson of a lord from the site of Uxte'k'uh, the home site of his mother (Stuart 2000). This Uxte'k'uh lord was K'inich Kan Bahlam II's maternal grandfather. The intimate relationship between Palenque and Uxte'k'uh is also documented in the marriage of K'inich Kan Bahlam II's younger brother, Tiwol Chan Mat, to Lady Kinuw of Uxte'k'uh (González and Bernal 2004:267). Although the specific location of Uxte'k'uh is unknown, numerous inscriptions indicate it played a role in the military conflicts of the region (Grube, Martin, and Zender 2001). It seems reasonable to speculate that K'inich Kan Bahlam II acknowledged his maternal grandfather and his ties to Uxte'k'uh because this site participated in the Toniná conflict.

Both of the Temple of the Foliated Cross sanctuary piers illustrate K'inich Kan Bahlam II holding an obsidian bloodletter. What is left of the right pier indicates that his pose is a mirror image of his portrait on the Temple of the Cross left pier. He wears the same ancestral headdress and costume, including a small Yopaat Chahk figure swinging from his hip. The adjacent caption text names him as the child of K'inich Janaab Pakal I and Lady Tz'akbu Ajaw. She is further named in this caption text with the title Lady of Matwiil.

THE SANCTUARY TABLETS

A large panel is found on the back wall of each sanctuary (figures 5.6, 8.5–8.7). Each of these Cross Group tablets illustrates two actions carried out by the same person at the same location, but on different dates. The short figure is the six-year-old K'inich Kan Bahlam II performing a pre-accession event while the tall figure is K'inich Kan Bahlam II on the occasion of his accession at age 48 (Bassie-Sweet 1991; see also chapter 5, this volume). A block of main text flanks each side of the scene. The Initial Series dates for the three Cross Group main texts begin in mythological times:

Tablet of the Cross	12.19.13.4.0 8 Ajaw 18 Tsek	December 7, 3121 BC
Tablet of the Sun	1.18.5.3.6 13 Kimi 19 Keh	October 25, 2360 BC
Tablet of the Foliated Cross	1.18.5.4.0 1 Ajaw 13 Mak	November 8, 2360 BC

THE TABLET OF THE CROSS

The Tablet of the Cross main text opens with the birth of an enigmatic figure called Muwan Mat and proceeds to his first bloodletting at age eight (13.0.1.9.0 11 Ajaw 18 Mak, February 3, 3112 BC) (Carrasco 2005:452; 2010:607–608; 2012a) (figure 8.5). The birth verb is the standard *siyaj* "birth." The story then backs up in time to the 13.0.0.0.0 Period Ending (August 13, 3114 BC), which is described as the changing or renewal of the three hearthstones and joins this event to the dedication of the Six-?-Sky Place, which occurred just two days after Muwan Mat's bloodletting (13.0.1.9.2 13 Ik' *ti' haab* Mol, February 5, 3112 BC). The text states that GI descended from the sky on this occasion, and it names the Six-?-Sky Place as a north house. Clearly this is the mythological model for the Temple of the Cross.

The narrative then moves from this event to the arrival (*huli*) of GI at Matwiil (1.18.5.3.2 9 Ik' 15 Keh, October 21, 2360 BC). The text then restates the arrival, but uses the same "touch the earth" phrase found on the alfardas to describe his birth at Matwiil, and states that he was the creation-darkness (*ch'ab-ak'ab*) of Muwan Mat. The *ch'ab–ak'ab* phrase refers to the fact that GI was manifested by Muwan Mat (Stuart 2005a:81; Knowlton 2012). The fact that GI participated in events prior to this date means that his arrival/

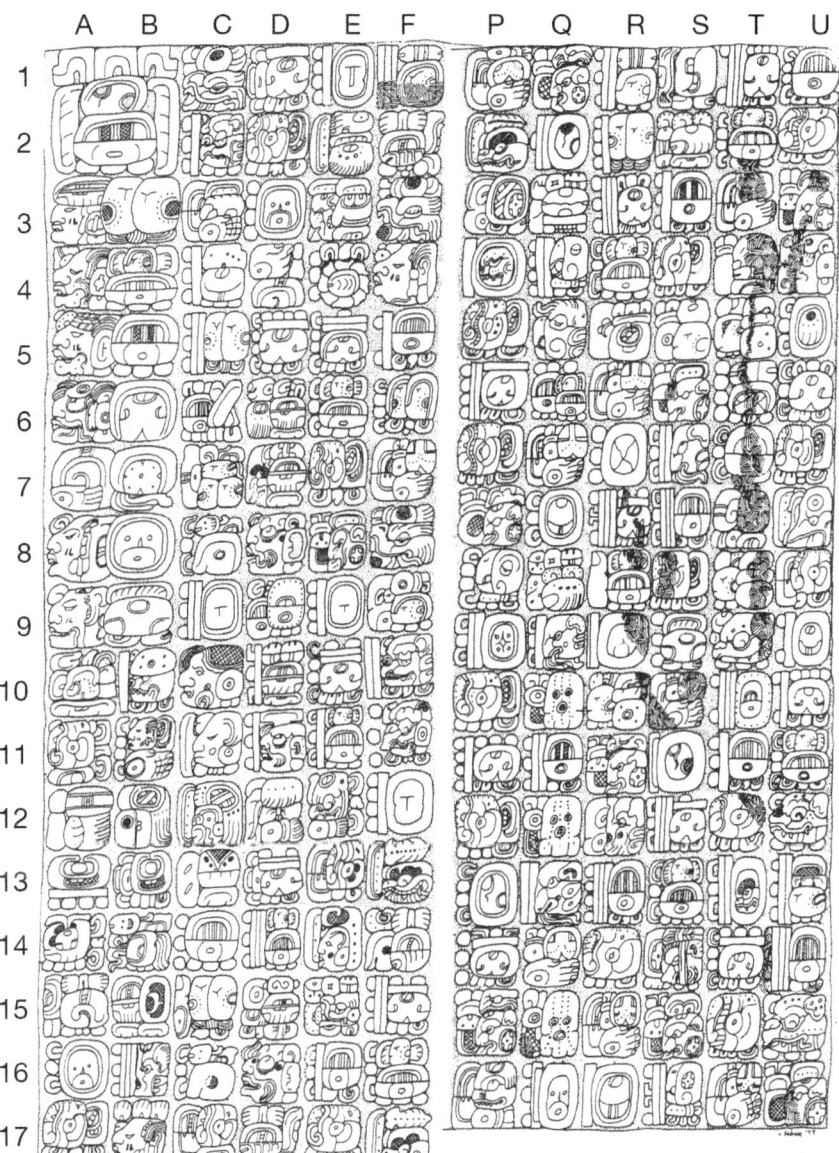

FIGURE 8.5. *Palenque Tablet of the Cross, main text, drawing by Linda Schele, courtesy David Schele.*

touching earth/creation did not represent the concept of a human birth, which is a once-in-a-lifetime event, but appears to refer to a newly manifested form of GI at Matwiil (Stuart 2005a).

The story returns to the birth of Muwan Mat and states his accession on 2.0.0.10.2 9 Ik' seating of Sak (September 7, 2325 BC), an astonishing 796 years later. From his accession, the text relates a series of births (*siyaj*) and accessions (tying of the *sak huun*) beginning with another enigmatic figure called U Kokan Chan and ending with the ruler K'inich Kan Bahlam I. The episode concerning U Kokan Chan begins on the left main text, but concludes on the right. By moving from mythological time on the left to historical time on the right, the tablet repeats the structure of the alfarda texts, where the left text states the mythological birth of the god and the right the historical dedication of the building.

Both the Tablet of the Sun and the Tablet of the Foliated Cross repeat this structure. They both open with the birth of their respective god at Matwiil on the left and then move to historical events in the life of K'inich Kan Bahlam II on the right. The Tablet of the Sun begins with the Long Count date of GIII's birth (*siyaj*) including the Supplementary Series and 819-day count (figure 8.6). The narrative then backs up in time to the 13.0.0.0.0 4 Ajaw 8 Kumk'u Period Ending event and restates GIII's birth as his arrival (*huli*) at Matwiil. It notes that, like GI, GIII is the creation of Muwan Mat, who is now also named as the holy lord of Matwiil. The next sentence gives the Distance Number from the Period Ending to the historical 2 Kib 14 Mol event. In contrast, the timeline of the Tablet of the Foliated Cross begins with the birth (siyah) of GII and moves forward from his birth to the 2.0.0.0.0 Period Ending, then returns to the birth and proceeds to the historical 2 Kib 14 Mol event.

The mythological section of the Tablet of the Foliated Cross main text is an excellent example of how important narrative structure is in analyzing texts (figure 8.7). It begins with the Long Count notation, *tzolk'in* date (1 Ajaw), *haab* date (13 Mak), Supplementary Series, and 819-day count for the birth of GII. It names GII as the third-born (siyah) god and lists his various titles. The next sentence gives a Distance Number (given in the order of the Long Count notation) that leads from his birth, now stated as his *huli* "arrival" at Matwiil, to the completion of the second *ba'ktun* on 2 Ajaw 3 Wayeb. The placement of the Period Ending Calendar Round date at the end of the sentence rather than the beginning is a common convention in the Cross Group texts. The next sentence begins with the conjuring (*tz'ak*) of GII by Muwan Mat that is said to have happened at a location named with

FIGURE 8.6. *Palenque Tablet of the Sun, drawing by Linda Schele, courtesy David Schele.*

three toponyms (Yaxhal Witznal, Sak flower Juub'nal, Nah K'an Jal), and it ends with the Calendar Round date of GII's birth, 1 Ajaw 13 Mak. Although Stuart (2006:140) has identified this conjuring as occurring on the Period Ending, the placement of the Calendar Round date at the end of the sentence clearly indicates that the conjuring occurred on the date of GII's birth, as Carrasco (2012a:149) has noted.[3]

The initial statements of GII's birth and Muwan Mat's conjuring of GII bracket the statement referring to the 2.0.0.0.0 Period Ending, and form a poetic structure of ABA. Additionally, the initial birth statement begins with the Calendar Round date while the conjuring statement ends with the same Calendar Round birth date, which creates a chiasmus structure (Carrasco 2012a:149).

In summary, the alfarda texts refer to the births of all three thunderbolt gods as "touching the earth." In the Tablet of the Cross text, the birth of GI is described as "touching the earth," arriving at Matwiil, and as the creation (*ch'ab–ak'ab*) of Muwan Mat. The Tablet of the Sun characterizes GIII's birth as *siyaj* (being born), arriving (*huli*) at Matwiil, and as the creation (*ch'ab–ak'ab*) of Muwan Mat, the holy Matwiil lord. GII's birth on the Tablet of the

FIGURE 8.7. *Palenque Tablet of the Foliated Cross, drawing by Linda Schele, courtesy David Schele.*

Foliated Cross is also described as *siyaj* (being born) and arriving (*huli*) at Matwiil, but then he is said to have been conjured (*tz'ak*) by Muwan Mat, the holy Matwiil lord. In essence, the Cross Group narrative is equating *ch'ab-ak'ab* with conjuring. This pairing of conjuring and *ch'ab-ak'ab* is also found as a couplet in the text of Lintel 3 of Tikal Temple I (*tz'ak k'uh tu ch'ab ti yak'abil*) where the Tikal ruler Jasaw Chan K'awiil I is said to have conjured and created a deity (Knowlton 2012:261).

THE MAIN TEXT OF THE TABLET OF THE CROSS

The backbone of any long narrative text is its chronology, some of it overtly marked and some of it left to be discovered by the reader. Chronology was apparently a concern of the authors, because most events are linked by specific measures of lapsed time (Distance Numbers), and these are generally tied to anchor dates that are often expressed as Period Endings. On the other hand, at several points in the Cross Group texts the exact placement of events is deliberately obscured, and there are Distance Numbers that lead to unspecified events. Likewise, there are several instances of incorrect use of Distance Numbers—for example, adding where subtraction was called for, counting from the wrong anchor date, entering the wrong numbers to connect two dates, and other indications of haste and absence of competent editing (however, apparent mistakes have occasionally been revealed later to be rhetorical devices).

There are only three Long Count positions actually stated in the Tablet of the Cross main text: the Initial Series Long Count, 12.19.13.4.0, a date almost seven years prior to the Era Event (3114 BC); the Era Event itself, 13.0.0.0.0; and the 9.0.0.0.0 Period Ending in AD 435 (figure 8.5). The last dated event in the text took place at 9.6.18.5.1, in 572, near the end of the Early Classic period. The text thus spans some 3,700 years, from the birth of gods in mythological time to legendary rulers: remote history and recent history.

Eighteen events in the Cross text are on the event line, but another dozen are present as background to these events. While many of the background events are undated, their dates are retrievable from the Distance Numbers. For instance, at R3–S7: "It was 1.8.1.18 from the birth of Manik' to his accession on 3 Etz'nab 11 Xul." The accession date is bracketed by other dates and can be placed at 9.2.12.6.18. This allows the backgrounded birth date to be calculated: 9.1.4.5.0, 12 Ajaw 13 Sak.

Five large sections of the Tablet of the Cross text are defined by their chronological anchors: (1) The text opens with an Initial Series that dates the birth of Muwan Mat (at C1). (2) Distance Numbers then link the following events to the Era Event 13.0.0.0.0 (C5), including the featured birth of Muwan Mat's offspring at F4. (3) The timeline then backs up to the initial birth (of Muwan Mat), which becomes the time anchor for Muwan Mat's accession to office and the birth and accession of the mythological U Kokan Chan (966 BC), ending at Q3 (as the text shifts to the right-hand panel). The dates of the following birth and accession of K'uk' are floating, the birth falling somewhere between 799 BC and AD 397. (4) At P10 a new linked series begins with "Casper" (born 8.19.6.8.8, AD 422) and continues through three more rulers, ending with the accession of Ahkal Mo' Nahb II. (5) The text now shifts to a new pattern, linking the birth of Ahkal Mo' Nahb II (a new time anchor) to that of Kan Bahlam, and continues to the latter's accession (U6–U17). This last section of text is highly disrupted by displaced dates and Distance Numbers that lead to unstated events, a zone of turbulence appropriate for the peak event of the text.

In terms of rhetorical style, Muwan Mat establishes the model for accessions (E5–F9) that is followed by the next eight rulers. These brief statements are an example of the "same but different" parallelisms that characterize Maya formal discourse. The only two statements that have exactly the same structure

TABLE 8.1. *Selected birth and accession statements from the Cross Tablet text*

E5–F9	DN from birth and then accession of Muwan Mat on CR.
E10–E15	DN from when it was CR (*tzolk'in* only) and then birth of U Kokan Chan, EG
F15–P3	DN from birth of U Kokan Chan and then accession on CR, EG.
O4–P9	CR birth of K'uk'
	DN from birth (to unstated event) and then accession on CR. EG.
P10–Q11	CR birth of Casper.
P15–S2	DN from accession of Casper to when it was CR, 9.0.0.0.0 at Toktan.
R3–S7	DN from birth of Manik' and then accession on CR.
R8–R13	DN from birth on CR of Ahkul Mo' Nahb I and then accession on CR.
S13–S17	DN from birth of K'an Joy Chitam and then accession on CR.
T1–T6	DN from birth and then accession of Ahkul Mo' Nahb II on CR.

Abbreviations: CR, Calendar Round; DN, Distance Number; EG, Emblem Glyph; "and then" = prefixed conjunction *i-*; "when it was" = *uti(y)*.

TABLE 8.2. *The peak event of the Tablet of the Cross:*

U6–T10	DN from birth of Ajkal Mo' Nahb II to birth of Kan Bahlam I. CR [of Ajkal Mo' Nahb' II's birth]
T11–U14	DN from birth of Kan Bahlam on CR [to unspecified event]
T15–U17	DN from birth of Kan Bahlam and then accession.

are the first and the last, the opening and closing that frame this section of text (table 8.1).

Following this series of births and accessions, the text moves into the Peak Episode and is filled with turbulence. The first statement links the birth of Ajkal Mo' Nahb II to that of his younger brother Kan Bahlam I, with a Distance Number of 1.1.1 (a year, a month, and a day). But the Calendar Round that follows Kan Bahlam I's name is not that of his birth, but that of the birth of his elder brother! The text continues with a Distance Number from the birth of Kan Bahlam I on its Calendar Round date to an unspecified event, and then ends with a Distance Number from the birth of Kan Bahlam to his accession (table 8.2).

THE MAIN TEXTS OF THE TEMPLES OF THE SUN AND FOLIATED CROSS

The main text of the tablet of the Temple of the Sun can be divided into three large sections by reference to its time frames. (1) The first section begins with the Initial Series Long Count date of 1.18.5.3.6, the birth of GIII. A Distance Number then leads back to the Era Event at 13.0.0.0.0 as background to the restated birth, this time with the parentage statement that identifies GIII as the child of Muwan Mat. (2) The second section ties back to the Era Event as its time anchor and moves forward to the right-hand side of the panel and the 2 Kib 14 Mol event (on 9.12.18.5.16) and events over the next three days. (3) The third section harks back to the heir designation of K'an Joy Chitam I (9.3.1.15.0) as background to that of K'inich Kan Bahlam II (9.10.8.9.3), and continues to the *ochte'* event of the latter. Finally, a Distance Number relates the birth of K'inich Kan Bahlam to his heir recognition and another ties that event to the Period Ending 9.10.10.0.0.

The episodes in the Tablet of the Foliated Cross text also begin in mythological time, with an Initial Series date of 1.18.5.4.0, shortly after the initial date of the Tablet of the Sun tablet. (1) The opening event is the "third birth," that of GII. A Distance Number leads to the Period Ending 2.0.0.0.0 and a conjuring performed on the occasion by Muwan Mat. (2) The second section begins with a Distance Number ordered like an Initial Series (7.7.7.3.16) that should lead to the right-hand panel, the 2 Kib 14 Mol event again, involving the triad gods. But if this Distance Number leads from the preceding date, it is in error, as noted by Schele (1981:79); it should be 7.14.13.1.16. The following days end with an event that parallels that of Muwan Mat. (3) Opening the third section, a new Distance Number moves the text to the "hot corner," the upper right-hand corner of the panel, and expresses the time between the birth of K'inich Kan Bahlam and his accession. Another Distance Number ties this accession to the 2 Kib 14 Mol event, mentioning the banded-bird lord Nuk Yajaw Chan. A final Distance Number (1.12.4) ties the 2 Kib 14 Mol event to the future Period Ending 9.13.0.0.0, but the usual syntax is reversed, and the "and then it was 2 Kib" phrase follows the phrase "it will be 8 Ajaw 8 Wo, the thirteenth *k'atun*."

The final sentence, "*i patlaj u juntan K'inich Kan Bahlam, Ch'uh Bak Ajaw*" is also difficult to interpret. The possessive phrase read here as *u juntan* was long known to substitute for other terms meaning "child (of mother)" (Cholan kin terms distinguish the sex of the parent rather than that of the child; Hopkins 1991:255). Schele (1981:87) took the possessive phrase to be an allegorical reference to the aforementioned triad gods as "the children of [mother] Chan Bahlum." In a 1989 presentation published much later, David Stuart (1997:8) related the term to entries in the earliest colonial dictionary of Yucatec Maya, the Motul Dictionary (Martínez Hernández 1929:415), for example:

huntan lah; huntale: servir a uno solo, o tener cuidado de una sola cosa, o hazer esto con mucho cuidado y diligencia embevenciéndose en ello.

(*huntan lah; huntale:* to serve only one, or to have the care of only one thing, or to do this with much care and diligence, becoming absorbed in it.)

While finding no kin term, Stuart speculated that "*Hun tan* as a term of relationship may hold the sense of 'object of care or devotion.'" This interpretation was quickly adopted. For instance, in a Cleveland workshop in 1990 (Wanyerka 1991:91), Peter Matthews said of the phrase "it is now read as U Hun Tan or her cherished one," and Schele (1992:44) added, "In Yukatek, *huntan* means 'to care for something.' The child of the god is, then, 'the cherished one.'" In the epigraphic literature, the verb based on *hun*, the number "one," and referring to single-mindedness, quickly morphed into a noun with the meaning "the cherished one."

The verb *pat(laj)*, used in what are called "dedication" phrases, has been taken to mean "construct(ed)," on the basis of the Ch'ol entry in the dictionary of Aulie and Aulie (1994:90): *pät, hacer (casa)*, and the corresponding proto-Cholan reconstruction (Kaufman 2003:952). But the meaning of the verb is not strictly "to build," as indicated by the Ch'ol expressions *pät wa'täl kuxtäl* "to carry out a pledge (to a saint)," where the couplet "to stand up, to live" refers to a commitment to perform penances, or *pät ch'ujel* "to celebrate mass," where *ch'ujel* is "holiness" (Josserand and Hopkins 1996:45), or the Tzeltal greeting *pat o'ntan*, where *o'ntan* is "heart" (Kaufman and Norman 1984:128). So what is the root meaning of this puzzling verb?

Ignoring the meanings based on *pat* "back of the torso," entries in a Tzotzil dictionary (Laughlin 1975:268) have a common sense of making individual units of something: clay pots, bean tamales, tiles, and chicken eggs. But they also include *patbe yo'on* "to gratify someone('s heart)," *patet 'o'on* "happy (is one's heart)," and *patebal* "moment before finishing being made." Throughout Tzotzil and Tzeltal, *patan* refers to the contributions one makes, be they taxes or civic service. A common sense emerges of something being brought to completion by bringing all the pieces together. Happiness may be expressed as "one is my heart," that is, all the pieces of my heart are unified, and some curing involves restoring all one's soul parts to the body, making one complete.

If we apply this notion to the final sentences of the Foliated Cross text, take the *i uti 2 Kib* phrase ("and then it was 2 Kib") to begin the last segment rather than ending the former, and recognize that oblique phrases are not always marked as such, the closing statement of the Foliated Cross text may be something like the following:

N16   And then, it was 2 Kib;
O16–N17   and then, brought together were his "cherished ones"
O17   (by) K'inich Kan Bahlam, Divine Lord of Palenque.

THE READING ORDER OF THE THREE CROSS GROUP TABLETS

Although the inscriptions of the three Cross Group tablets form a continuous narrative, there has been some debate about the sequence of the reading order (Bassie-Sweet 1991; Robertson 1991; Stuart 2006; Stuart and Stuart 2008; Carrasco 2012a). It is our contention that the reading order is readily apparent from the narrative structure and that this order reflects the birth order of the deities: Temple of the Cross (GI), Temple of the Sun (GIII), and Temple of the Foliated Cross (GII) (Bassie-Sweet 1991). The following is a brief overview of the narrative structure of the Cross Group tablets that supports the conclusion that this reading order is correct.

The reading sequence of the panels begins with the scene and its caption text and then moves to the main text (Josserand 1991). The caption text on the Tablet of the Cross starts on the left side of the scene and relates K'inich Kan Bahlam II's pre-accession event (age six) followed by the 9.10.10.0.0 Period Ending (age seven) (figure 5.6). The story then proceeds to the right side and states his accession (age 48), followed by the ceremony on 2 Kib 14 Mol (age 55). The narrative additionally states that the banded-bird lord named Nuk Yajaw Chan conjured the deities on this occasion. As noted above, the historical section of the main text does not address any of the events of the caption texts. Rather, it gives a list of birth, accession, and Period Ending events for a series of K'inich Kan Bahlam II's predecessors: K'uk' Bahlam I, Casper, Butz'aj Sak Chiik, Ahkal Mo' Nahb I, K'an Joy Chitam I, Ahkal Mo' Nahb II, and ending with his namesake K'inich Kan Bahlam I.

The various events of the Tablet of the Cross caption texts are repeated on the other two tablets, but with different emphasis, elaboration, and placement. The Tablet of the Sun has the same composition as the Tablet of the Cross, with the young prince K'inich Kan Bahlam II on the left and the king K'inich Kan Bahlam II on the right. The caption texts again confirm this identification. The left text begins with the pre-accession event and the 9.10.10.0.0 Period Ending. Unlike the Tablet of the Cross caption text, which gives the many titles of the young K'inich Kan Bahlam II and his parentage statement, this text succinctly refers to the pre-accession event and then moves on to expand on the events of the Period Ending and refers to K'inich Kan Bahlam II as the son of the holy Palenque lord. The second block of caption text gives the accession of K'inich

Kan Bahlam II and his complete parentage statement as the son of the five-*k'atun* lord K'inich Janaab Pakal I and Lady Tz'akub Ajaw, holy lord of Palenque. It does not mention the 2 Kib 14 Mol events. However, the historical section of the main text greatly embellishes the 2 Kib 14 Mol event and relates a second event that happened the next day (3 Kaban 15 Mol). This event involves a structure called the K'inich K'uk' house, which Stuart (2006) believes refers to the Group D structure. It is followed by the conjuring of the deities. The main text backs up in time and focuses on K'inich Kan Bahlam II's pre-accession event, which was conducted in the presence of GI, and compares it to a similar event conducted by the six-year-old K'inich K'an Joy Chitam I at the site of Toktan in AD 496. The story then backs up in time again to the birth of K'inich Kan Bahlam II and restates his pre-accession event. The distance number that joins these two dates together, in effect, gives the age of K'inich Kan Bahlam II when he conducted this ceremony (age six). The story concludes with a reference to the 9.10.10.0.0 Period Ending. Most important, the main text does not mention K'inich Kan Bahlam II's accession or the 9.13.0.0.0 Period Ending.

The scene on the Tablet of the Foliated Cross again illustrates the prince and the king, but now the king (and his associated accession text) has been moved to the left side. This is a literary device called fronting, in which important information is moved to the front of a sentence to place emphasis on it (Josserand 1991:14; Bassie-Sweet 1991:208). The Tablet of the Foliated Cross caption text is very succinct. Unlike the other two accession statements on the Tablet of the Cross and Tablet of the Sun, this accession statement does not include any titles or parentage statement. Without directly referring to a change in the time frame, the caption text continues with information regarding the house of K'uk Balam. The caption text adjacent to the prince on the right side of the tablet does not repeat the pre-accession date and event, but simply names the prince as the *bah ch'ok*, heir apparent. Much of the text has not been deciphered, but it ends with the statement that he is the child of the five-*k'atun* lord, K'inich Janaab Pakal I, holy lord of Matwiil. Neither the 9.10.10.0.0 Period Ending nor the 2 Kib 14 Mol–3 Kaban 15 Mol events are mentioned in the caption text. The historical section of the main text does, however, highlight the 2 Kib 14 Mol and 3 Kaban 15 Mol events, and again mentions the role of Nuk Yajaw Chan. It then steps back in time to the birth and accession of K'inich Kan Bahlam II. Again, the Distance Number that joins these two dates indicates the age (48) at which K'inich Kan Bahlam II acceded to the throne. The narrative repeats the accession and then mentions the 2 Kib 14 Mol event again, this time giving a list of the many deities involved in this event. For the first time in the narrative, the three thunderbolt gods are named together. The narrative then climaxes with a reference to the upcoming 9.13.0.0.0 Period Ending and the statement that the cherished ones (the gods) of K'inich Kan Bahlam II were patlaj "brought together" during the 2 Kib 14 Mol event. The main text of the Tablet of the Foliated Cross does not make any reference to the pre-accession or 9.10.10.0.0 Period Ending event.

From the viewpoint of narrative structure, the reading order of the Cross Group narrative is the Tablet of the Cross (the introduction of the story), the Tablet of the Sun (emphasis on the pre-accession event and 9.10.10.0.0 Period Ending), and the Tablet of the Foliated Cross (climax and emphasis on the accession and reference to the 9.13.0.0.0 Period Ending). That is, the narrative relates to the triad gods in the order GI, GIII, and GII. Moving in a counterclockwise fashion from north (Temple of the Cross) to west (Temple of the Sun) to east (Temple of the Foliated Cross) also follows the counterclockwise reading order found on the Temple of the Inscriptions sarcophagus lid and other edge inscriptions at Palenque such as Bench 1 of the Palace.[4] Furthermore, by reading the Cross Group texts in this order, the reader is taken on a ritual circuit that concludes at the base of the Group D hill, which Stuart contends is the Descending Quetzal Mountain location of the text.

We believe that the narrative structure of the Cross Group texts takes precedence over all other factors when establishing reading order. However, when named together in a hieroglyphic clauses, the triad of thunderbolt gods is always named in the sequence GI, GII, and GIII, and Stuart (2006, Stuart and Stuart 2008) has argued that the Cross Group tablets were read according to this order, starting with the Tablet of the Cross (GI), moving to the Tablet of the Foliated Cross (GII), and ending with the Tablet of the Sun (GIII). He also believes that this reading order is indicated by the alleged hierarchy and height of the three temples. He proposes that the Temple of the Cross represents the heavens, the Temple of the Foliated Cross the earth, and the Temple of the Sun the Underworld. Be that as it may, this does not constitute evidence for a reading order of the text. According to Stuart's model, the climax and end of the story would be with the minor 9.10.10.0.0 Period Ending of K'inich Kan Bahlam II when he was seven years old, rather than his first major Period Ending of 9.13.0.0.0 when he was king. It simply makes no sense for the story to be read in this order.

THE PLACE NAMES IN THE CROSS GROUP NARRATIVE

In addition to illustrating the shrines where K'inich Kan Bahlam II performed his pre-accession and accession events in honor of the Palenque triad of thunderbolt gods, the Cross Group narrative mentions specific place names where various actions were conducted. For example, the main text on the Tablet of the Sun states that the ancestral ruler K'an Joy Chitam I performed his pre-accession event at Toktan, a place associated with other early Palenque rulers (Stuart and Houston 1994:31). While the specific location of Toktan has not been ascertained, the narrative is careful to distinguish this location from Lakamha', where K'inich Kan Bahlam II's pre-accession and accession events occurred.

As noted above, the Lakamha' place name is found in combination with the Descending Quetzal Mountain place name as well as the couplet phrase Chan ("sky") Ch'een ("cave"). Other geographically related metonyms found in the hieroglyphic corpus include Kab Ch'een "earth-cave" and Chan Kab "sky-earth." The "sky-earth" metonym is also found in colonial indigenous writing and modern languages, where it refers to the world as a whole (Hull 2003, 2012). The meaning of "earth-cave" and "sky-cave" are less clear. They have been characterized as metonyms referencing a town, a region, a territory, a polity, a domain, or the universe as a whole. There are very rare triplet constructions composed of "sky-earth-cave" or "cave-earth-sky" found in two pottery texts and on Tikal Stela 31 (Helmke 2009:83). Stuart interprets the Cross Group buildings as an architectural expression of these triplet expressions (sky, Temple of the Cross; earth, Temple of the Foliated Cross; cave, Temple of the Sun). He further identifies the cave as a reference to the Underworld. The following is an overview of the three locations illustrated in each Cross Group tablet. As this discussion indicates, there is not sufficient evidence to warrant Stuart's conclusion.

THE LOCATION OF THE TABLET OF THE CROSS SCENE

Each Cross Group tablet illustrates a location specifically identified with its respective deity. As discussed above, the Tablet of the Cross illustrates some aspect of the Six-?-Sky Place. The central icon of the scene is composed of a stylized flowering tree with a supernatural bird perched on top (figure 5.6). At the base of the tree is the Quadripartite Badge, the headdress of GI. As discussed in the last chapter, this is the motif also found on K'inich Janaab Pakal I's sarcophagus lid. The inference is that K'inich Kan Bahlam II underwent a transformation or initiation at the age of six and again on the occasion of his accession, at a location that replicates the mythological place where K'inich Janaab Pakal I was thought to have undergone his transformation after death.

While the Quadripartite Badge is a common motif in Maya art, the cross-shaped tree is rarely depicted. Like the sarcophagus tree, the Tablet of the Cross tree is marked with T24/T1017 luminous/lightning flash glyphs and te' "wood" signs. The trunk and its bilateral branches terminate in stylized flowers and square-nosed serpents.[5] It has long been thought that the cross-shape of the tree refers to the four directional world roads. In such a model, the branches represent the east-west axis while the trunk represents the north-south road.[6]

The Quadripartite Badge is flanked by sky bands on either side, with the left side featuring nocturnal glyphs and the right side containing diurnal glyphs. The young K'inich Kan Bahlam II stands on the Nine Place that is positioned on top of the left skyband while the king K'inich Kan Bahlam II stands directly on the right skyband. As previously noted, the Quadripartite Badge is most often seen on the tail of the Milky Way Crocodile, such as on the Palace Bench 1 (Carlson and Landis 1985; Stuart 2003b). It is hard to escape the conclusion that the tree and Quadripartite Badge motif represent a mythological location on this celestial pathway. The use of the Quadripartite Badge as an indication of a particular location is found on a cache vessel excavated at Tikal (Culbert 1993:fig.108d). This scene illustrates a Quadripartite Badge motif juxtaposed with One Ixim conjuring the Paddler Gods from a serpent. The glyphs under One Ixim's chin identify him as a man of the Six-?-Sky Place. The intimate relationship between the Milky Way and GI is demonstrated by the fact that the Quadripartite Badge is also GI's headdress. An interesting carved vessel in the Kerr archives (K6626) juxtaposes a portrait of GI with a Milky Way Crocodile that has a Quadripartite Badge on its tail (see Bassie-Sweet 2008:269–273 for a further discussion of the celestial nature of this location).

The Milky Way was associated with rain, and the Milky Way Crocodile is frequently depicted with water pouring from its snout (Bassie-Sweet 2008:36–38). As a Chahk thunderbolt deity, GI was also directly identified with the rains. The north orientation of his building suggests that he was specifically associated with the northern rains that descend on the Maya lowlands even during the dry season (Bassie-Sweet 2008:113). The sky on the Tablet of the Cross is decorated with yax "blue-green" signs and with jade ornaments that represent shells and flowers. These symbols likely allude to the lush, moist environment associated with the rains of the Milky Way, and not just in a general way to the qualities of the Place of Duality.

The central element of the Quadripartite Badge is a stingray spine, which is a well-known bloodletter, and it is usually flanked by a cross-band element

FIGURE 8.8. *Vessel K2849, after Justin Kerr.*

and Spondylus shell. The close association of the Quadripartite Badge with sacrifice is seen on K2849, where the stingray spine is flanked by an obsidian bloodletter and flint eccentric (figure 8.8). Stingray spines, obsidian, and flint are the primary cutting tools used in bloodletting.[7] The Quadripartite Badge depicted in the headdress on Piedras Negras Stela 3 takes the form of an obsidian bloodletter with a blade extending out of the mouth of the personified motif. On the left side of the Tablet of the Cross scene, the young K'inich Kan Bahlam II holds a Quadripartite Badge with liquid flowing from it that is similar to the one that the adult K'inich Kan Bahlam II holds on the sanctuary pier (figure 5.6).[8] Such poses are typically associated with genital bloodletting. It seems reasonable to conclude that the six-year-old K'inich Kan Bahlam II is bloodletting in honor of GI, and that it was possibly his first act of sacrifice. Such childhood acts were also recorded at Dos Pilas (Houston 1993:115).

The caption text that frames the young K'inich Kan Bahlam II refers to his *okte'* ritual, although the specific nature of the *okte'* office is unclear. The caption texts adjacent to the young K'inich Kan Bahlam II on the other two Cross Group tablets also refer to this *okte'* ritual. The last four glyphs of the Tablet of the Cross *okte'* text repeat the parentage statement from the alfardas text that K'inich Kan Bahlam II was the child of K'inich Janaab Pakal I and

Lady Tz'akbu Ajaw. The leaf element from the young K'inich Kan Bahlam II's headdress extends upward and almost touches the *tzolk'in* date of the *okte'* event while his left hand, which is positioned on this chest, almost touches his mother's name phrase. Below the flow of liquid from the Quadripartite Badge is a block of text referring to the 9.10.10.0.0 Period Ending. It is likely that K'inich Kan Bahlam II's bloodletting ritually prepared him to participate in the subsequent Period Ending ceremony that included the honoring of the Palenque triad of thunderbolt gods.

On the right side, the king K'inich Kan Bahlam II holds a reclining jester god effigy, the personification of *huun* "paper" (Stuart 2014). The jester god rests on an unwrapped cloth that likely covered the effigy when it was not on display (Robertson 1991:29). Effigy bundles are well-known in Mesoamerica, and the tradition continues today (Christenson 2006). The king wears a loincloth with a simple fringe as well as a necklace, earrings, wristlets, and anklets of jade. A wide band is tied around his forehead. Although it does not look like the *sak huun* handed to the king K'inich Ahkal Mo' Nahb III on the Temple XIX platform and it lacks the jester god ornament, it does resemble the *sak huun* worn by One Ajaw on K1183 (figure 5.14).

The caption text that frames the head of K'inich Kan Bahlam II continues the narrative with the Calendar Round date of his accession (8 Ok 3 K'ayab) and specifically refers to the tying of the *sak huun* headdress of kingship (figure 5.6). In fact, all three Cross Group tablets repeat exactly the same accession phrase in their caption texts. The glyph block that contains the phrase k'al *sak huun* "binding of the white headband" is positioned immediately over the reclining jester god and almost touches it. As noted in chapter 5, K'inich Kan Bahlam II's name phrase, which ends the accession statement, begins in the last glyph in the block of text in front of his face and ends in the first glyph in the block of text behind his head.

K'inich Kan Bahlam II displays his jester god effigy to the supernatural bird perched in the tree. The yax symbol on the forehead of the bird arches over the *tzolk'in* date of K'inich Kan Bahlam's accession. The bird has a ribbon woven into a *jal* motif hanging from its mouth. Such woven motifs are ubiquitous in Maya art (Proskouriakoff 1950), and the young K'inich Kan Bahlam wears one as a pendant, as does God L. How this ribbon relates to the interaction between the king and the bird is unclear, but the end of the ribbon touches K'inich Kan Bahlam's hand. These framing devices place visual emphasis on the king's action of holding the jester god.

The bird on the Tablet of the Cross also appears on K'inich Janaab Pakal I's sarcophagus lid, and it is most often identified as the Itzamnaaj bird although it lacks the diagnostic *ak'ab* headdress element of this avian manifestation of Itzamnaaj.[9] If this is the case, then K'inich Kan Bahlam II may be receiving some kind of validation from the creator grandfather Itzamnaaj, or the Itzamnaaj bird functions as a witness to the event. An obvious parallel is the scene on the Temple XIX platform where the banded-bird lord dressed as the Itzamnaaj bird hands K'inich Ahkal Mo' Nahb III his *sak huun* headdress on the occasion of his accession (figure 5.22). The association of Itzamnaaj with the tree motif is seen on a fragment of pottery excavated at Buenavista del Cayo (Reents-Budet et al. 2000:104), where Itzamnaaj sits cross-legged on a jaguar pillow. To his right is a bone bench upon which sits a variant of the Quadripartite Badge and the tree.[10]

The block of caption text positioned behind the king K'inich Kan Bahlam II moves from his accession to the 2 Kib 14 Mol events and introduces Nuk Yajaw Chan, the banded-bird lord who officiated at K'inich Kan Bahlam II's accession (Stuart 2006:97–98). Zender (2014) has discussed the role of secondary lords as the curators of sacred objects, and one has to wonder if Nuk Yajaw Chan's duties included the curation of the *sak huun* headdress.

In all three Cross Group scenes, the king K'inich Kan Bahlam II wears the same wide band of cloth around his head with a rectangular motif protruding out of the top of the band. This motif is a standard component from the headdress worn by the deity Tlaloc. Bassie-Sweet (2012, in press) has presented evidence that the Tlaloc motif represents the office of Kaloomte', and that the Kaloomte' was the high priest or priestess of Tlaloc who took on the guise of this deity in various ceremonies. Several texts at Tikal refer to the seating of the ruler in the office of the Kaloomte', and numerous rulers are known to be simultaneously both Ajaw "king" and Kaloomte' (Martin and Grube 2000:17). Such is the case with K'inich Kan Bahlam II's father, K'inich Janaab Pakal I, and his younger brother, K'inich K'an Joy Chitam II. There is a looted panel from the Palenque region that also names K'inich Kan Bahlam II as a Kaloomte', and it likely illustrates his accession into this particular office (Bassie-Sweet 2012; in press). The origins of this panel are unknown, but it can be attributed to the Palenque region by style. It now exists in several fragments located in private collections, the Houston Museum of Fine Art, and the Museo Nacional de Antropología in Mexico City (Schaffer 1987). The scene shows K'inich Kan Bahlam II dressed in the costume of Tlaloc, although only the lower portion of the figure is intact. He is flanked on either side by secondary lords. The lord on the left, who is dressed as God L, hands K'inich Kan Bahlam II a Tlaloc effigy that is itself wearing a Black Witch Tlaloc headdress. Again we see God L (by proxy) playing an active role in the ceremonies of K'inich Kan Bahlam

II. It seems apparent that the Tlaloc element found in the Cross Group headdress is a subtle reference to his role as Kaloomte', although the Cross Group focuses and emphasizes his role as Ajaw.

THE LOCATION OF THE TABLET OF THE SUN SCENE

In contrast to the celestial Milky Way imagery of the Tablet of the Cross, the base of the Tablet of the Sun is formed by a band that alternates earth signs and T1017 luminous/lightning flash signs (the head variant of the T24 sign) (figure 8.6). Each end of the band terminates in a deity head that has the T24 luminous/lightning flash sign infixed in his forehead and cheek. Although these two deities have the square eyes and Roman noses of GI, GIII, and the sun god, they lack the diagnostic elements of these gods. The Popol Vuh describes the creator deities as bright, luminous beings, and the T24/T1017 sign appears to signify that this is not merely the ordinary surface of the earth, but the luminous world of the creator deities.

In this second pre-accession *okte'* and accession portrayal, K'inich Kan Bahlam II is featured at both events standing on the back of a diminutive supernatural figure that is, in turn, positioned on the earth band. The body of the left figure is marked with T24 signs while the right figure is infixed with Ajaw signs. The left figure is in a kneeling pose with both hands touching the earth band. The right figure is pictured in a cross-legged pose but is bent over in a prostrate position. The contrast between a kneeling pose and a cross-legged pose is seen on the Temple XIX platform where the secondary lords on the left kneel before the king to present him with his *sak huun* headdress while those on the right sit cross-legged and await their subsequent event with the king. The kneeling pose seems to characterize an event in action, and places emphasis on this event. The prostrate pose itself is most frequently seen as a sign of submission by military captives such as the prisoners who are seated in a prostrate and kneeling pose in front of K'inich Ahkal Mo' Nahb III on the Tablet of the Slaves (figure 5.23). It is unclear what the two figures on the Tablet of the Sun signify, but they do not appear to represent toponyms per se.

On the other hand, there are place names written on either side of the central icon of the Tablet of the Sun. These are the well-known pair nicknamed the Seven Place and Nine Place that was discussed in chapter 5. These place names also appear on the façade of the building, flanking a portrait of a cross-legged figure sitting on a throne (Robertson 1991:fig. 74). In Robertson's reconstruction, the figure is flanked by secondary lords holding up the same two icons held by K'inich Kan Bahlam II on the tablet. The appearance of the

FIGURE 8.9. *Palenque Temple XVII panel, after Linda Schele.*

Nine Place on both the Tablet of the Cross and the Tablet of the Sun indicates that these place names are not specific to each shrine, but possibly refer to the larger geographical space that the Cross Group as a whole represents.

The central icon on the Tablet of the Sun consists of a war shield emblazoned with the face of GIII and two crossed spears. The flint spearheads protrude from the open mouth of a centipede-snake, a common motif in Maya art (Boot 1999; Taube 2003; Kettunen and Davis 2004). Below the centipede-snake is a base of rectangular mosaics that seems to have fang-like protrusions. These mosaics are reminiscent of the platelet motifs associated with Tlaloc as seen in the portrait of K'inich Kan Bahlam on the Temple XVII panel, where he wears a platelet headdress that takes the form of the Jaguar Tlaloc (figure 8.9). The base of his flint spear is formed by a zigzag pattern of obsidian chips like his spear on the Tablet of the Sun sanctuary pier. Similar flint spears embedded with obsidian chips are also seen on Yaxchilán Lintel 8, which illustrates Bird Jaguar dressed as the Black Witch Tlaloc while capturing a foe (figure 5.20). On a practical level, such additions of obsidian increased the lethal nature of these flint weapons. Flint was thought to be a manifestation of the Chahks while obsidian was identified with Tlaloc (Bassie-Sweet, in press). A weapon that combined flint and obsidian incorporated the spiritual forces of these powerful gods.

Shields that feature the face of GIII are common in scenes of warfare across the Maya realm (Proskouriakoff 1950:93), and such shields are also found in association with Tlaloc-related imagery. An example is found on Aguateca Stela 2, where the ruler is dressed as the obsidian deity Tlaloc and carries an atlatl and spear in his right hand and has a GIII shield on his left forearm. The ruler wears an obsidian mask in the form of Tlaloc and his costume is bedecked with obsidian, the face of the 18 Ub'aah Chan meteor form of Tlaloc, the paws and face of the Jaguar Tlaloc, and the moth wings of the Black Witch Moth Tlaloc (Bassie-Sweet et al. 2015; Bassie-Sweet, in press). As discussed in the Introduction, GIII is illustrated on a Palenque incensario wearing a headdress that represents his office of Yajawk'ahk' and the central element of his headdress is a portrait of Tlaloc. These contexts demonstrate GIII's intimate relationship with Tlaloc. Both of these gods were associated with military conflicts and meteors, which were omens of war (Bassie-Sweet et al. 2015:123–144).

It is likely that the flint spears and GIII shield on the Tablet of the Sun were thought to specifically belong to GIII. If such is the case, a lord carrying these weapons would be, in effect, taking on the guise of that deity and acquiring his supernatural powers in a manner similar to donning the mask or costume of the god. There are numerous examples of lords in the guise of GIII, such as Naranjo Stela 30, where the ruler wears the twisted cord of GIII over his face much like the Aguateca ruler wears a Tlaloc mask (Houston and Stuart 1996:300).

The Tablet of the Sun central icon sits upon a bench decorated with a jaguar head and serpent heads at either end. Two cross-legged deities in mirror-image poses are bent over, holding up the bench with one hand while touching the earth band with the other. The left figure is God L who wears his owl headdress and jaguar-skin cloak. This deity is also intimately associated with obsidian in his role as the patron god for obsidian merchants. The right side of the Temple of the Sun bench is held up by the old Jaguar Paddler God, who wears a headdress in the form of the banded-bird. The Paddler Gods carry the banded-bird title on Sacul Stela 1, and it seems likely that these gods were models for the secondary lords who held this office. The appearance of the Jaguar Paddler God in his role as a banded-bird lord is very interesting in light of the function of the banded-bird lords on the Temple XIX platform (figure 5.22). There, as discussed in chapter 5, K'inich Ahkal Mo' Nahb III is flanked on the left by three banded-bird lords, and the first of these lords (Janaab Ajaw) hands him his *sak huun* headdress. The juxtaposition on the Tablet of the Sun of the old Jaguar Paddler God with the accession of K'inich Kan Bahlam II appears to allude to this function of the banded-bird lords.

There is a pottery scene (K1560) that illustrates One Ixim and his dwarf and hunchback assistants despoiling God L and the two Paddler Gods, who are stripped of their clothing and insignia (Martin 2016). Other pottery scenes also show additional episodes of what is clearly an epic story of God L's subordination (Hull, Carrasco, and Wald 2009). The pairing of God L and the Paddler God in a submissive pose on the Tablet of the Sun suggests that their coupling is related to this story, and to K'inich Kan Bahlam II's ability to conduct war and overcome opponents, including supernatural opponents.

On the left side of the Tablet of the Sun, the six-year-old K'inich Kan Bahlam II holds up a *tok'-pakal* "flint-shield" icon that touches the feathers of the GIII shield. Given that the seven-year-old K'inich K'an Joy Chitam II is illustrated on the Palace Tablet receiving a *tok'-pakal* icon just ten years after his older brother K'inich Kan Bahlam II's *tok'-pakal* event, it seems reasonable to conclude that each lord had his own individual icon.[11] A number of texts refer to the *tok'-pakal* of a lord, a deity, or an ancestor. In the context of war events, the *tok'-pakal* of an enemy lord was said to be jubuy "lowered or brought down" or chuk "captured" (Grube cited in Stuart 1995:311; Schele and Grube 1994; Hull 2012).[12] Yaxchilán Lintels 45 and 46 illustrate Shield Jaguar III before his accession in the act of capturing an enemy lord (Stuart 1995:303). The caption text on Lintel 46 indicates Shield Jaguar was the successor of the *tok'-pakal* of his ancestor Knot Jaguar.[13] The Yaxchilán examples indicate that *tok'-pakal* icons could be inherited from predecessors. It is possible that the Tablet of the Sun main text links the pre-accession event of K'inich K'an Joy Chitam I in AD 496 with the K'inich Kan Bahlam II pre-accession *tok'-pakal* event because K'inich Kan Bahlam II was specifically acquiring his ancestor's icon.

Stuart (1995:303) suggested that K'inich Kan Bahlam II's *tok'-pakal* event refers to his first acquisition of war duties. It is likely that a lord's ability to conduct successful warfare was thought to be linked to his proficiency in obtaining the spiritual support of the gods. The *tok'-pakal* icon may refer to this sacred ability, and the left side of the Tablet of the Sun scene may represent K'inich Kan Bahlam II's first step in attaining that support. Given that deities are known to possess *tok'-pakal* icons, it is possible that the crossed spears and GIII shield represents a *tok'-pakal* icon specifically linked to GIII.

On the right, the king K'inich Kan Bahlam II is pictured in a costume similar to the one he wears on the Tablet of the Cross, but now he holds a GII effigy, the deity who is manifested as a thunderbolt axe and the very essence of flint.[14] K'inich Kan Bahlam holds the GII effigy in such a way that his hand and the cloth of the effigy touch the feathers of the GIII shield and the right flint spear, respectively. As discussed in the previous chapter, K'inich Janaab Pakal I's tomb is lined with portraits of figures holding axe scepters in the form of GII and wearing the GIII shield on their forearms. This is similar to the Yaxchilán Lintel 1 portrait of Bird Jaguar on the occasion of his accession, where he also holds the GII scepter in his right hand and wears the GIII shield on his left forearm. Many scenes illustrate the ruler holding a GII scepter that we believe is a reference to his ability to command the power of thunderbolts (Bassie-Sweet et al. 2015).

THE LOCATION OF THE TABLET OF THE FOLIATED CROSS SCENE

Unlike the wide bands on the Tablet of the Cross and Tablet of the Sun, the base of the Tablet of the Foliated Cross scene is formed by a very narrow band representing water, surely an allusion to the sacred waters of the Place of Duality and the waters on the surface of the earth that replicate that location (figure 8.7). The location of GII's birth is stated in the Cross Group texts using three place names: the first of these is Yaxhal Witz. On the left side of the scene, the king K'inich Kan Bahlam II stands upon a head variant of the *witz* "mountain" glyph with a split open head that is placed in front of the water band. Within the eyes of this zoomorphic mountain sign are two glyphs representing the place name Yaxhal Witznal. In Maya mythology, the corn seed used to create the first humans was found hidden in a cliff at Paxil Mountain. The creator deities could not access this corn, so they employed a thunderbolt deity to strike open the cliff with his bolt of lightning and extract the corn. GII is the personification of that thunderbolt. Paxil Mountain was the quintessential mountain, and the zoomorphic form of the generic *witz* "mountain" sign usually incorporates a split motif in reference to this primordial act. However, additional signs are then added to the generic *witz* sign to indicate which specific mountain the zoomorphic place name represents, such as the Nine Fire-Vase Mountain place name illustrated on the Balamk'u stucco façade and on the walls of Río Azul Tomb 2 (Stuart 2006). Researchers often equate the Yaxhal Witznal of GII's birth with Paxil. While it is clearly the mountain of GII birth, and by extension a manifestation of GII, there is little direct evidence that Yaxhal Witznal is also the mountain of sustenance (Bassie-Sweet 2008:115).

The second place name referring to GII's birth is composed of a *sak* "white" sign conflated with a flower sign of unknown value and a logogram of a shell with corn foliage on top. On the right side of the Tablet of the Foliated Cross, the young K'inich Kan Bahlam II stands on a gastropod that is the full-figure rendering of this name (Stuart 2006:145). The *sak* flower sign is represented by the supernatural figure emerging from the shell while holding corn foliage and a personified corn ear. The shell itself represents the shell logogram. In addition, the shell is labeled with glyphs that read K'an Juub Matwiil; the word juub means "shell" (Stuart 2005a:169, 2006:140). As noted by Stuart, other shell motifs from the building façade are also labeled with the place name Matwiil.

The third place name from the main text describing the birth location of GII is Nah K'an Jal. As discussed above, the foliage of this T214 *jal* sign likely represents flatsedge that the Maya used to make mats. Such plants only grow in or beside water, and the base of the Tablet of the Foliated Cross is a band of water.

The central icon on the Tablet of the Foliated Cross is a highly stylized, personified corn plant. At the base of the plant is a zoomorphic head (the T1017 personified form of the T24 luminous/lightning flash sign with a *k'an* sign in its forehead). The corn stalk rises from this head and terminates in another T1017 sign from which grows the tassel of the plant. On each side of the plant are two more T1017 signs. Corn leaves grow out of the T1017 heads and terminate in a personified ear of corn. Each of these T1017 signs, thus, represents a node of the corn stalk. Note that the leaves are atypical; maize leaves alternate on the stalk, and opposing leaves do not grow from the same node.

In the context of colors, *k'an* refers to yellow, but it also has connotations associated with abundance and richness that are likely based on the yellow color of a milpa ready for harvest. In scenes where the surface of the earth is metaphorically represented as the turtle shell of the creator grandfather Itzamnaaj, the *k'an* cross is used to mark the center. The four arms of the *k'an* cross likely reference the four world roads. The multiple appearances of the *k'an* sign in these various Cross Group place names likely refers to the center.

Before they departed for their confrontation with the lords of the Underworld, the Hero Twins of the Popol Vuh each planted an unripe ear of corn inside their house at the center of the world as omens of their fate. The creator grandmother subsequently deified the ears of corn and gave them names (Center House, Center Ancestral Plot) (Christenson 2007a:188–189).

It is likely that the Tablet of the Foliated Cross corn plant with its *k'an* cross and twin ears of corn is thematically related to this concept (Bassie-Sweet 2008:222). Twin ears of corn are thought to be essential to the success of the corn harvest (Bassie 2008:20–22).

In this third and last portrayal of K'inich Kan Bahlam's pre-accession and accession, the king K'inich Kan Bahlam II is now dressed more elaborately, including the skirt and loincloth of One Ixim, and a jade pectoral. This is similar to K'inich Janaab Pakal I, who wears this costume on the sarcophagus. K'inich Kan Bahlam II again holds up a jester god similar to the one he held on the Tablet of the Cross. In this case, the jester god is seated upright, as though the god has been awakened. Unlike the bird on the Tablet of the Cross, the bird that sits atop the tassel of the corn plant has an upturned beak and a long piece of foliage-like material coming out of its mouth. He faces the king, and the material touches the jester god effigy. Juxtaposed below this is the same glyph seen adjacent to the king on the Tablet of the Cross. It is composed of the number five, a T24 luminous/lightning flash, and a house sign. What it refers to is unclear.

On all three tablets, the young K'inich Kan Bahlam II wears the same outfit of a loincloth and a shawl-like piece of cloth with knotted ends draped over his shoulders. He also has a twisted strip of material that is tied around his neck and hangs down his back. Such twisted material is also worn by the secondary lords on the west panel of the Temple XIX platform (Stuart 2005a:29). K'inich Kan Bahlam II's headdress has the same configuration as the tassel object held by the banded-bird lords on the occasion of the pre-accession events of K'inich Ahkal Mo' Nahb III and U Pakal K'inich on the Temple XXI platform (figure 5.24). This makes the three Cross Group depictions consistent with other pre-accession events. This parallel with the Temple XXI platform suggests that part of K'inich Kan Bahlam's pre-accession event was his indoctrination into the office of *ch'ajom* (a term derived from *ch'aj* "incense"). In the K'iche' region, the first office attained in the hierarchy of ritual duties is the burning of incense for the gods (Tedlock 1992).

On the Tablet of the Foliated Cross, the young K'inich Kan Bahlam II holds an obsidian bloodletter in his hand. These personified bloodletters are composed of a supernatural figure wearing a headdress of three knots and long feathers (Joralemon 1974:66). The obsidian lancet extends out of the mouth of the figure like a tongue. A particularly graphic depiction of gods performing penis perforation using the personified bloodletter is found on a vase in the University of Pennsylvania Museum (Joralemon 1974:fig. 12). A number of deities squat over bowls containing strips of paper used to catch the blood.

While he is not pictured in the actual act of penis perforation, K'inich Kan Bahlam II's wrists and ankles have paper-like material tied to them. Such cuffs appear in a variety of setting on both human and deities. As an example, a Chahk deity wears such cuffs on the Palace Creation Tablet, as do God L and the Paddler God on the Tablet of the Sun and the Temple of the Cross alfardas (Robertson 1991:fig. 267). It is quite possible that these cuffs were intended to catch the blood from autosacrifice that would certainly stain the hands and legs of a person performing such an act. This same type of cuff is found tied to the base of a flint spear on Yaxchilán Lintel 45, and may have had a similar function, that is, to catch the blood of the foe. Across Mesoamerica, blood was offered to the gods as sustenance.

On the Tablet of the Sun, the raised arms of the young K'inich Kan Bahlam II reveal that he is wearing what appears to be a series of knotted cloth strips around his torso. Schele (1974), who identified this figure as the deceased K'inich Janaab Pakal I, suggested that his unusual clothing was a marker of death. There is a Classic period vessel (K6547) that shows the burial of a lord wearing similar knotted cloth (Eberl 2001:312). On one side of the vessel, a lord is laid out on a funeral bier beside of a body of water, surely a reference to the death-related phrase "to enter the water." Mourners, who stand in the water in a state of grief, flank the bier. It is likely that this scene relates to the preparation of a body before its burial that included the washing of the deceased, a common worldwide funeral practice (Bassie-Sweet 2008:308–309). On the opposite side of the vessel, the ruler is pictured within the tomb of a pyramid in a skeletal state. Three figures that take the form of fruit trees grow about the tomb, similar to the depictions of K'inich Janaab Pakal I's ancestors on the sides of his sarcophagus box. In short, K6547 illustrates two sequential events that form a couplet: the preparation of the body for burial and its final interment. The body of the lord is encased by a row of knotted cloth. The preparation of bodies for burial varied in the Maya region, and in some areas such as Calakmul they wrapped the body. However, the physical remains of K'inich Janaab Pakal I indicate he was not swathed in such a fashion (Tiesler and Cucina 2006:34). Therefore, the wrapped body of the K6547 lord cannot be used as evidence that the short Cross Group figure is the deceased K'inich Janaab Pakal I dressed in his burial costume. In addition, if the short figure were the deceased K'inich Janaab Pakal I, he would be portrayed in the Cross Group as someone with proportionate dwarfism, and we find that highly unlikely.

The two events depicted on the Tablet of the Foliated Cross represent the climaxes of K'inich Kan Bahlam II's pre-accession and accession events. The caption text that frames the young K'inich Kan Bahlam II declares he is the *bah ch'ok*, the heir designate, and the son of K'inich Janaab Pakal I. The king K'inich Kan Bahlam II has acquired the costume of One Ixim in addition to the *sak huun* headdress. He has, in effect, become the living embodiment and replacement of his father K'inich Janaab Pakal I.

The settings of three Cross Group scenes group together and contrast the three essential elements of the quadrilateral world: sky, earth, and water. The Tablet of the Sun and what remains of the sanctuary piers have an obvious warfare theme, while that of the Tablet of the Foliated Cross and associated piers relate to agriculture and autosacrifice. The message of the Cross Group is that K'inich Kan Bahlam performed ceremonies in honor of the Palenque triad of thunderbolt gods, starting with his indoctrination into ritual life at age six and continuing through to the eve of the first important Period Ending of his reign. While he is not illustrated in the scenes, the Tablet of the Cross and Tablet of the Foliated Cross main texts specifically refer to the actions of the banded-bird lord Nuk Yajaw Chan, who tied the headband on K'inich Kan Bahlam II and who conjured the gods on 3 Kaban 15 Mol. There are numerous examples of texts that identify secondary lords as the authors and artists of various works of art (Stuart 1987, 1995). While the Cross Group was certainly created under the patronage of K'inich Kan Bahlam, the inclusion of Nuk Yajaw Chan in the Cross Group narrative hints at the possibility that this secondary lord may have been the composer of the Cross Group narrative in addition to being the main priest of the ceremonies.

GII AND THE JESTER GOD

As discussed above, the king K'inich Kan Bahlam II holds a GII effigy on the Tablet of the Sun and a Jester God effigy on the Tablet of the Cross and Tablet of the Foliated Cross. On the sarcophagus lid, there is a double-headed serpent suspended above the limbs of the tree (figure 7.1). Emerging from the left and right mouths are GII and the Jester God, respectively. Materializing from the mouth of a serpent is a common convention used in Maya to represent the conjuring of a god. This motif contrasts GII (the power of the thunderbolt) with the Jester God (the power of wisdom and knowledge), and likely represents a visual metonym for royal power.

This juxtaposing of GII and the Jester God may explain the costume and role of the two lords found on the west side of the Temple XIX platform. In this scene, three secondary lords sit in frontal poses (Stuart 2005a:128–132). The center figure is identified by the adjacent caption text as the lord Salaj Bolon of Uxte'k'uh, the home site of K'inich Ahkal Mo' Nahb III's mother.

He is flanked by two secondary lords named as *ch'ok* "youths." As noted by Stuart (2015a:102), the scene likely illustrates an event from the main text that occurred on 9.15.2.9.0 7 Ajaw 3 Wayeb during the reign of K'inich Ahkal Mo' Nahb III. Each lord wears a tall miter-like hat that Zender (2004b) has identified as that of a priest. The hat of the left *ch'ok* is bedecked with a Jester God while that of the right lord is decorated with GII. One assumes that these headdresses relate in some specific way to the priestly offices held by these men. Zender argued that one of the roles of secondary lords was as custodians of royal attire. It seems reasonable to suggest that these secondary lords may have been the curators of the royal Jester God and GII effigies.

While these secondary lords certainly played critical roles in royal ceremonial life, it should be kept in mind that the parents of the future king also appear to have had custodial functions directly related to these power objects. For example, it is K'inich K'an Joy Chitam's mother, Lady Tz'akbu Ajaw, who hands him his *tok'-pakal* icon on the Palace Tablet. One can well imagine Lady Tz'akbu Ajaw handing K'inich Kan Bahlam II his own *tok'-pakal* icon just before he performed his *tok'-pakal* action as illustrated on the Tablet of the Sun.

SUMMARY

The Cross Group narrative highlights and details the pre-accession events of the six-year-old K'inich Kan Bahlam II (June 17, 641) and his subsequent accession at the age of 48 (January 10, 684). These historical events are presented within a story that focuses on honoring and supplicating the three thunderbolt gods GI, GII, and GIII. As the Cross Group documents, K'inich Kan Bahlam II began his pastoral duties related to these patron gods at a very early age. Temple XIV is located on the northwest corner of the Cross Group plaza, and K'inich Kan Bahlam II's youthful participation in the maintenance of deities is also documented on a wall panel in that temple. The Temple XIV Tablet illustrates him at the age of 13 performing a dance with his mother as a reenactment of an ancient event (Bassie-Sweet 1991:223–128). His mother is pictured rising from her kneeling position while extending a GII effigy towards him. The main text of the tablet also records a second event at the age of 18, in which he honored a series of deities. Such early childhood events are also noted for his brother K'inich K'an Joy Chitam II and his nephew K'inich Ahkal Mo' Nahb III on other monuments.

As discussed in chapter 5, the Temple XIX platform illustrates the accession of K'inich Ahkal Mo' Nahb III in which he has taken on the guise of

FIGURE 8.10. *Chichén Itzá cenote pectoral, after Tatiana Proskouriakoff.*

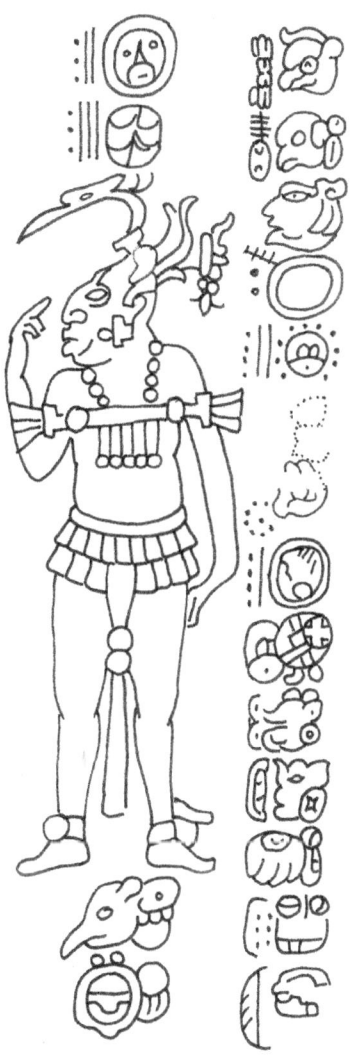

the deity GI. Although the three illustrations of K'inich Kan Bahlam II's accession in the Cross Group do not feature such an impersonation, there is a portrait of K'inich Kan Bahlam II on a jade pectoral recovered from the Chichén Itzá cenote (figure 8.10). Such pectorals, consisting of a long jade tube with various embellishments on the ends, are common in Maya art and are often recovered from tombs. They were worn horizontally across the chest such as those worn by K'inich Janaab Pakal I on the Temple XXI platform and K'inich Ahkal Mo' Nahb III on the Temple XIX platform. On the upper surface of the Chichén Itzá cenote pectoral, K'inich Kan Bahlam II is pictured wearing the bird headdress of the deity GI as well as a stylized form of GI's Quadripartite Badge headdress (Proskouriakoff 1974:110–111). The caption text begins above K'inich Kan Bahlam II's head with the Calendar Round date 13 Ajaw 18 K'ank'in and continues below his feet before moving to the front side of the pectoral with a single long column of glyphs. As noted by Proskouriakoff, the initial date is the 9.10.10.0.0 13 Ajaw 18 K'ank'in (AD 642) Period Ending prominently mentioned in the Cross Group. The narrative time frame then moves forward to the 2 Kib 14 Mol event (690) and ends with a reference to an event that occurred on 9.13.2.17.7 9 Manik seating of Pop (695). It is curious that the last event of the pectoral is not the 9.13.0.0.0 Period Ending that one would expect, given its prominence in the Cross Group narrative. The final pectoral date is, however, still an important Period Ending. The seating of Pop was the last day of the 365-day *haab*. While such events are rarely documented on Classic-period monuments, Postclassic evidence indicates the last day of the year was an intense period of ritual activity in preparation for the coming New Year.

The fact that the image of K'inich Kan Bahlam II on the pectoral is framed by the 9.10.10.0.0 Period Ending suggests that year-end ritual is the depicted action. The pectoral thus provides a glimpse of the young K'inich Kan Bahlam II's participation in the Period Ending event that is only textually referenced in the Cross Group. On the pectoral, K'inich Kan Bahlam II is pictured in a common dance pose with his right hand held beside his face and his left arm at his side with the hand turned inward (see Xcalumkín Jamb 5 for a similar dance pose; Looper 2009:fig. 5.33). The implication is that K'inich Kan Bahlam II not only honored GI on the Period Ending, but actually took on GI's persona during a dance performance. An obvious parallel is featured on the Dumbarton Oaks Tablet where his 12-year-old brother, K'inich K'an Joy Chitam, dances in the guise of another Chahk deity (figure 1.1).

As discussed above, the first mention of the 9.10.10.0.0 Period Ending in the Cross Group narrative is in the scene on the Tablet of the Cross where it follows the six-year-old K'inich Kan Bahlam II's first bloodletting in honor of GI, which occurred the year before. What can be inferred from the pectoral scene is that the Cross Group narrative does not mention the Period Ending merely as a time anchor for the bloodletting event—rather, one is a consequence of the other. This can be compared to the Palace Tablet narrative in which the first bloodletting of K'inich K'an Joy Chitam I is followed by his father's Period Ending event on the major *k'atun* ending of 9.11.0.0.0 and his own minor Period Ending event in honor of the triad of gods on 9.11.13.0.0.

The completion of the Cross Group (January 10, 692) and the subsequent celebration of the 9.13.0.0.0 ending (March 18, 692) occurred when K'inich Kan Bahlam II was approaching his third *k'atun* of life. While he would live another ten years, this building complex represented the pinnacle of his artistic accomplishments. The complex attests to K'inich Kan Bahlam II's devotion to the Palenque triad of deities throughout his life and the importance placed on the maintenance of gods by the ruling elite.

NOTES

1. As discussed in chapter 1, a looted vessel, which is not from the Palenque region, illustrates Itzamnaaj's sky court and includes the name Six-?-Sky Place (Boot 2008). The Nine Fire-Vase Mountain portion of the Temple of the Sun name is also found on the east wall of Río Azul Tomb 2 and a Balamk'u stucco façade, where it functions to name a particular mountain (Stuart 2006). In the Río Azul example, the name

is composed of a head-variant *witz* "mountain" glyph with the nine fire-vase sign positioned on top of the head (Adams 1999:fig.3–20). The Balamk'u example is also a head variant of the mountain sign, but the nine fire-vase glyph is infixed on it. The placement of the elements of the Balamk'u nine fire-vase glyph is also different. The number nine is positioned on top of the vase, and the fire glyph is under the mouth of the jar, as though the jar were emitting fire or smoke. The Nah K'an Jal place name from the Temple of the Foliated Cross occurs in a dedication phrase at Copán, where it names Structure 11 of that site (Stuart 2006).

2. Although the main text of this panel refers to events early in the history of Palenque, the caption text adjacent to the warrior figure identifies him as K'inich Kan Bahlam II.

3. Stuart (2006:145) inadvertently left out the Calendar Round date in his transcription of the Tablet of the Foliated Cross main text.

4. In the Dresden Codex, the four Chahk deities identified with the four directions are repeatedly named in the counterclockwise fashion of east–north–west–south (pages 29–31).

5. These square-nosed serpents also appear on another example of the tree and the Quadripartite Badge motif on Pier C of the Palenque Palace House D.

6. Four glyphs flank the Tablet of the Cross tree, each one prefixed with the number five. The main sign of the lower-right glyph is the square-nose serpent followed by the te' "tree" sign. This sign also appears in the Temple of the Inscriptions narrative in a couplet statement where it is paired with a reference to another tree (Stuart 2006:116). One assumes that the other three glyphs that flank the Tablet of the Cross tree also name it in some way. However, these same names also appear in the Tablet of the Foliated Cross, which does not feature the tree.

7. Taube (2009) has argued that the bowl of the Quadripartite Badge was specifically used for heart offerings. In the Popol Vuh, the three primary thunderbolt gods collectively are called Heart of Sky. Given that flint is specifically identified with GII, and GIII has obsidian associations, it is possible that the three bloodletting objects in the K2849 bowl reference the three thunderbolt deities. If so, the Quadripartite Badge might be a motif that incorporates allusions to all three thunderbolt gods.

8. The Quadripartite Badge of the young K'inich Kan Bahlam differs in that the bowl of the motif is a sky sign, not a sun sign. The meaning of this substitution is unknown.

9. Because of the lack of the *ak'ab* element, Bassie-Sweet (2008:123) proposed that the bird might instead be parallel to Wok, the swift-flying messenger bird of the thunderbolt deity Huracan that is described in the Popol Vuh. Huracan was the senior member of the Heart of Sky thunderbolt gods, and he was parallel to GI. However, the secondary lord in the guise of the Itzamnaaj bird on the Temple XIX platform

does not wear the diagnostic *ak'ab* element either, and the Itzamnaaj bird is juxtaposed with the Six-?-Sky Place name on the Boot vase. In light of this, it seems the Tablet of the Cross bird probably is an Itzamnaaj bird.

10. Another tree cross that shares thematic parallels with the Palenque trees is illustrated on Yaxchilán Lintel 2. In this scene, the ruler Bird Jaguar and his five-year-old son each hold cross-shaped trees with a descending quetzal positioned on the top (figure 3.2).

11. It is curious that these two Palenque brothers apparently received their *tok'-pakal* icons as young men while their nephew K'inich Ahkal Mo' Nahb III was given one on the occasion of his accession as king, as seen on the Tablet of the Slaves. K'inich Ahkal Mo' Nahb III was born in AD 678, during the reign of K'inich Janaab Pakal I. His father, Tiwol Mat, who was the youngest son of K'inich Janaab Pakal I, died just two years later, and Ahkal Mo' Nahb III's uncle, K'inich Kan Bahlam II, succeeded K'inich Janaab Pakal I three years after that. There is no evidence to indicate in whose household the young K'inich Ahkal Mo' Nahb III was raised, but he was ritually active during his uncle's reign, undergoing a first-bloodletting event at age 14, as stated in the Temple XVIII alfardas text. His uncle, K'inich K'an Joy Chitam II, succeeded K'inich Kan Bahlam II in 702 and K'inich Ahkal Mo' Nahb III is recorded performing a 900-day Period Ending during his reign. Although no known Palenque inscriptions record a death date for him, K'inich K'an Joy Chitam II's last recorded event (the dedication of House A-D) was in 720. Two years later, K'inich Ahkal Mo' Nahb III took the *sak huun* headdress of rulership as seen on the Temple XIX platform, and additionally was given both a *tok'-pakal* and the Ux Yop Huun headdress that same day, as illustrated on the Tablet of the Slaves.

12. As noted by Hopkins (1996), the metonym *tok'-pakal* pairs an offensive weapon with a defensive one, and it is likely a metonym for all weapons, including those composed of flint, obsidian, limestone, and bone. In a broader sense, the term *tok'-pakal* may have been used in war contexts as a metaphorical reference to all the armaments of a lord or even to the warriors under his command.

13. A number of scenes illustrate a ruler wearing an icon on his waist that refers to an ancestor (Martin 2000:60). On Yaxchilán Lintel 45, Shield Jaguar III wears a skull tied around his hip, and it is juxtaposed with the phrase referring to the *tok'-pakal*. This skull may represent Knot Jaguar.

14. Of the six depictions of K'inich Kan Bahlam II on the sanctuary tablets, this is the only time he wears sandals. The meaning of this is unknown, although scenes of warfare invariably show the warriors wearing sandals.

9

Conclusions

This volume has explored the intimate and reciprocal relationship between text and image with a focus on the public monuments of Palenque. While couplet structure has long been noted in many texts, the examples that we have identified, such as the Copán Structure 8N-11 bench, illustrate that couplet structure often goes beyond the verbal and includes visual couplets as well. Bilateral symmetry and mirror-image are frequently employed to create visual forms that parallel the chiasmus structure of the verbal text. Numerous examples of visual couplets occur in pottery scenes and in monumental art such as the Palenque Temple XXI platform, which illustrates the parallel events of K'inich Ahkal Mo' Nahb III and U K'inich Pakal, or the Cross Group tablets, which illustrate the pre-accession and accession events of K'inich Kan Bahlam II.

The placement of the text in relationship to the image is a key factor in understanding the intent of the narrative. An important but often overlooked example of this convention is seen in the Piedras Negras scaffold niche scenes (as discussed in chapter 5). Despite Proskouriakoff's initial assessment that such scenes represent accession ceremonies, the only text adjacent to the scene on Stela 6 is the Period Ending (Bassie-Sweet 1991:50). This is not to say that all scaffold scenes must, therefore, also be Period Ending scenes, given that there are thematic parallels between accession scenes and Period Ending events (Houston et al. 2006). An example of a scaffold accession scene is on a carved

DOI: 10.5876/9781607327424.c009

bone currently owned by the Dallas Museum of Art (Stuart 2007d; 2012b:132). The scene shows a figure seated upon a scaffold structure with a secondary figure holding up an avian headdress in front of him. The caption text begins with the Calendar Round date of 5 K'an *ti'* Yaxk'in and refers to the *k'ahlaj* "wrapping" of a *huun* "headdress" on a particular individual. Therefore, this scene illustrates an accession, although what office the avian headdress represents is unclear. (Stuart's assertion that the scene is one of accession into kingship is based on his belief that this avian headdress is a variation of the *sak huun* headdress of rulership. We doubt this equivalence.)

At issue here is that the framing text identifies when, what, and who is being illustrated. Despite this simple framing convention, epigraphers still often ignore the placement of text in favor of their own arbitrary assertions about what event from the narrative is being illustrated (Houston and Taube 2000:271; 2012:44; Taube 2004:78; Houston, Stuart, and Taube 2006:150; Stuart 2012b). Such assertions and assumptions have significant impact on their subsequent interpretations. For example, the Preclassic San Bartolo murals have been analyzed using parallels with Classic images (Taube et al. 2010). The west mural illustrates a scaffold scene that has similarities to both the Piedras Negras Period Ending niche scenes and the Dallas bone scene. Taube et al. concluded it represents an accession scene, based on their assertion that the Piedras Negras scenes represent accession. Given that the San Bartolo caption text has yet to be deciphered, it cannot be conclusively demonstrated whether this represents an accession or a Period Ending event. At some future point when more Preclassic texts have been discovered and their decipherment attained, it may turn out that this is, indeed, an accession. However, for the time being, researchers should err on the side of caution and at least consider alternative interpretations.

In the decades following Proskouriakoff's discovery of the historical nature of hieroglyphic texts, researchers interpreted Maya works of art as propaganda-based narratives, focusing on the legitimacy of the elites and the exploits of particular rulers. Research tended to emphasize the historical content and intersite relationships. Occasionally debate centered on the historical accuracy of the texts. In contrast, Stuart (1995, 1998) argued that monumental inscriptions were primarily elaborate name tags that function to label the monument much like texts on portable objects.

In 1979, Mathews deciphered six glyph blocks on a pair of Early Classic obsidian earrings from Altun Ha as the possessive phrase *u tup* "his earplug" followed by a nominal phrase identifying the owner of the earplug (Mathews 2001). Justeson (1983) documented another example of the *u tup* name phrase on a pair of rectangular earring pieces originally associated with a lord from Xcalumkin but deposited into the Chichén Itzá cenote at some point in time. He demonstrated that the term *tup* had a wider reference to earring ornaments in general. Another example of name-tagging on objects was noted by Stuart in 1983 on a set of carved bones excavated from Tikal Burial 116 that reads *u baak* "his bone" (Stuart 1996:151). These insights were followed by discoveries of similar possessive phrases referring to a variety of things such as pottery, bloodletting implements, sculpture, and buildings. Ownership phrases ("his drinking vessel") are a regular part of the ceramic inscriptions known as the Primary Standard Sequence. The majority of Classic-period stelae document Period Ending ceremonies (Schele 1982), and Stuart (1998) has noted that the stone often referenced in these Period Ending ceremonies likely refers to the stela itself. He noted, "I would go so far as to say that sacred or important objects are the principal concern of most of the extant Maya texts, rather than the deeds and histories of royal figures" (Stuart 1996:151). However, simply because a monument includes a self-referential statement does not necessarily indicate that the purpose of the narrative was merely name-tagging. While the Period Ending text may be a succinct statement regarding the erection or the wrapping of the stone, the image invariably shows the ruler performing devout actions of sacrifice and deity conjuring. The point of a Period Ending ceremony was not to simply mark the end of a time period, but to worship the deities who maintained the order of the world.

In the case of K'inich Janaab Pakal I, it was initially thought that his narratives and those of his descendants were attempts to justify the fact that his right to rule came through his mother (Schele and Freidel 1990). As Carrasco (2005, 2012) has eloquently argued, the theme of K'inich Janaab Pakal I's and K'inich Kan Bahlam II's narratives are neither succession nor name-tagging, but rather the restoration of the three Palenque patron gods after a turbulent period of warfare and their continuing role during the subsequent *k'atun* periods. In the Cross Group narrative, K'inich Kan Bahlam II is pictured performing his first ritual actions as a young child and then again on the occasion of his accession. Both events are set within the context of rituals involving the three Palenque thunderbolt gods.

The Cross Group narrative also presents the mythological charter for K'inich Kan Bahlam II's actions. These narratives and their accompanying images are presented as formal, proper ritual environments that replicate the ideal environment of the Place of Duality. On a more simple level, the same kind of space is defined on the Copán Structure 8N-11 bench (discussed above), which has a chiasmus couplet structure carved on its front edge. The carving defines a formal, proper space on which the owner can sit and address whomever comes to his compound. It replicates the ideal space of the Place of Duality, the court of the creator grandparents.

Certainly the presence of secondary lords in various scenes can be and has been interpreted in a variety of ways. While it is quite possible that the motivation for including secondary lords was based on the political necessity of rewarding, placating, and validating these allies, these lords played the role of ritual assistant to the king just as his wife and mother did. These secondary lords were the junior complementary opposite to the king. Their partnership with the king echoed that of the senior/junior roles of the creator deities. Again there is a duplication of the courtly life of the deities as the role model for human elite behavior.

The motivations for creating narrative works of art were likely diverse and complex. Whatever the motivations, in this volume we have pointed out that in the process of creating these works, an important factor was the incorporation of conventional narrative structures in both the visual and the verbal media. In the literary texts, these conventions employ verbal couplets on a sentence level as well as on the level of overall text structure, playing sentence against sentence for emphasis, playing text segments against each other to evoke deeper meanings. In the accompanying images, visual couplets and structural oppositions perform similar functions. Furthermore, the two sets of narratives are played against each other in creative ways. Our principal argument is that the full meaning of the monuments, including not only the intentions of their creators but their historical content as well, cannot be appreciated unless these factors are taken into account. Neither the image nor the text can be fully understood as an isolated phenomenon. The texts and images were not composed independently but as an integrated whole, and must be understood as such.

In the interpretation of a work of narrative art—visual and verbal—a knowledge of native iconography, on the one hand, and native language, on the other, is essential. Furthermore, the iconography must be understood in terms of the mythological and political frameworks within which it communicates its message. The language of the texts must likewise be understood in terms of the narrative tradition that shapes it. Further afield, the monuments must be seen as creations that took place within social, political, religious, and historical contexts.

In arguing for a more holistic treatment of Classic Maya narrative arts, we are following in the footsteps of the father of American anthropology, Franz Boas, who in his Introduction to the *Handbook of American Indian Languages* stressed the need to be as informed about native cultures as the student of Old World cultures is expected to be with respect to them:

> Nobody would expect authoritative accounts of the civilization of China or Japan from a man who does not speak the languages readily, and who has not mastered their literatures. The student of antiquity is expected to have a thorough mastery of the ancient languages . . .
>
> When the question arises, for instance, of investigating the poetry of the Indians . . . the form of rhythm, the treatment of the language, the adjustment of the text to music, the imagery, the use of metaphors, and all the numerous problems involved in any thorough investigation of the style of poetry, [it] can be interpreted only by the investigator who has equal command of the ethnographical traits of the tribe and of their language. The same is true in the investigation of rituals, with their set, more or less poetic phrases, or in the investigation of prayers and incantations. (Boas 1911:60, 62)

In this volume we have attempted to show how our knowledge of Mayan languages and oral literature as well as Maya imagery, use of metaphors, and other factors cited by Boas can contribute to better-informed interpretations of Maya monuments. Scholars have been principally concerned with the extraction of historical data from the inscriptions (e.g., Martin and Grube 2000), and rightly so. But the artful presentation of such data has occasionally confounded the historians. A prime example of confusion that was resolved by consideration of narrative structure was Josserand's (2007) correction of the genealogy of a Yaxchilán queen as proposed by Schele and Freidel (1990:269). That correction was made possible by the application of Classic Maya literary norms to the inscription (Yaxchilán Lintel 23), showing it to consist of a set of parallel, chiasmic, phrases, not a continual string of phrases. Likewise, Houston's (1997:302) claim that texts were not self-contained coherent narratives (based on his reading of Palenque's Sarcophagus Rim text) was shown to be specious when an analysis of the text in terms of Maya literary norms revealed the proper starting point for a reading of the text (Josserand 1989, 1991).

Similar arguments have been made above regarding the interpretation of visual scenes. In particular, understanding the placement of text with respect to image (Bassie-Sweet 1991) clarifies the intentions of the creators of many monuments. The lesson to be learned is that neither the text nor the images on a monument (or, for that matter, a portable object) should be analyzed in isolation. While each can first be subjected to the particular methodology appropriate to its medium, the ultimate understanding of the work must involve the integration of the media and a holistic interpretation. We hope that the many examples we have presented in this volume will inspire a more comprehensive approach to the understanding of Classic Maya narrative arts.

Che' tza 'ujtyi b'ajche jiñi.
("So it ended like that," the traditional ending to a Chol folktale.)

References

Adams, Richard E.W. 1999. *Río Azul: An Ancient Maya City*. Norman: University of Oklahoma Press.

Altman, Heidi M. 1996. "Evidentiality and Genre in Chol Mayan Traditional Narrative." MA thesis, Florida State University, Tallahassee.

Arcos Alvarez, Nicolás, Mateo Alvaro López, and Ausencio Cruz Guzmán. 2016. "The Jaguar Man." In *Chol (Mayan) Folktales: A Collection of Stories from the Modern Maya of Southern Mexico*, ed. Nicholas A. Hopkins and J. Kathryn Josserand, with the assistance of Ausencio Cruz Guzmán, 129–138. Boulder: University Press of Colorado.

Aulie, H. Wilbur, and Evelyn W. de Aulie. 1998. *Diccionario ch'ol de Tumbalá, Chiapas, con variaciones dialectales de Tila y Sabanilla*. Coyoacán, DF: Instituto Lingüístico de Verano.

Avendaño y Loyola, Andrés. 1987. *Relation of Two Trips to Peten*. Culver City, CA: Labyrinthos.

Aveni, Anthony F. 1980. *Skywatchers of Ancient Mexico*. Austin: University of Texas Press.

Aveni, Anthony F. 1990. "The Real Venus-Kukulcan in the Maya Inscriptions and Alignments." In *Sixth Palenque Round Table, 1986*, ed. Merle Greene Robertson and Virginia Fields, 309–321. Norman: University of Oklahoma Press.

Baer, Phillip, and Mary Baer. 1948. "The Lacandón Song of the Jaguar." *Tlalocan* 2(4):376.

Bardawil, Lawrence. 1976. "The Principal Bird Deity in Maya Art: An Iconographic Study of Form and Meaning." In *The Art, Iconography, and Dynastic History*

DOI: 10.5876/9781607327424.c010

of Palenque, ed. Merle Greene Robertson, 181–194. Pebble Beach, CA: Pre-Columbian Art Research, Robert Louis Stevenson School.

Barrera Vásquez, Alfredo, ed. 1980. *Diccionario Maya Cordemex*. Mérida: Ediciones Cordemex.

Barrios, Edy, and Claudia Quintanilla. 2008. "Tres Islas: un pequeño centro de comercio de las Tierras Bajas en el Río Pasión, Sayaxché, Petén." In *XXI Simposio de Investigaciones Arqueológicas en Guatemala, 2007*, ed. J. P. Laporte, B. Arroyo, and H. Mejía, 214–238. Guatemala: Museo Nacional de Arqueología y Etnología.

Barthel, T. S. 1967. "Intentos de lectura de los afijos en los jeroglíficos de los manuscritos mayas, con un apéndice con datos de J.E.S. Thompson." *Escritura maya: Boletín informativo* 1(2):4–13.

Bassie-Sweet, Karen. 1987. "Illustrated Stories: The Relationship between Text and Image." Paper presented to the 86th Annual Meeting of the American Anthropological Association, Chicago.

Bassie-Sweet, Karen. 1991. *From the Mouth of the Dark Cave; Commemorative Sculpture of the Late Classic Maya*. Norman: University of Oklahoma Press.

Bassie-Sweet, Karen. 1996. *At the Edge of the World: Caves and Late Classic Maya World View*. Norman: University of Oklahoma Press.

Bassie-Sweet, Karen. 1997. "Human Diviners and Their Supernatural Counterparts." Paper presented to the University of Pennsylvania Maya Weekend, University of Pennsylvania, Philadelphia.

Bassie-Sweet, Karen. 2002. "Maya Creator Gods." http://www.mesoweb.com/features/bassie/CreatorGods/CreatorGods.pdf.

Bassie-Sweet, Karen. 2008. *Maya Sacred Geography and the Creator Deities*. Norman: University of Oklahoma Press.

Bassie-Sweet, Karen. 2011. "Change Your God, Change Your Luck." Paper presented to the 2011 Chacmool Conference, University of Calgary, Calgary, AB, Canada.

Bassie-Sweet, Karen. 2012. "Thunderbolt and Meteor War Gods of the Maya." Paper presented to the 2012 Chacmool Conference, University of Calgary, Calgary, AB, Canada.

Bassie-Sweet, Karen. 2013a. "Mythological Charters: The Role of God L as a Patron Deity for Merchants and Traders of Obsidian, Jade and Quetzal Feathers." Paper presented to the 2013 Chacmool Conference, University of Calgary, Calgary, AB.

Bassie-Sweet, Karen. 2013b. "Ancient Maya Creator Gods." Lecture presented to the Maya Society of Minnesota, St. Paul, MN.

Bassie-Sweet, Karen. in press. "Maya Gods of Flint and Obsidian." In *Seeking Conflict: Understanding Ancient Maya Hostilities through Text and Image*, ed. Shawn G. Morton and Meaghan M. Peuramaki-Brown. Boulder: University Press of Colorado.

Bassie-Sweet, Karen. in review. "Maya Gods of War and Commerce." Manuscript submitted to the University Press of Colorado.

Bassie-Sweet, Karen, Nicholas A. Hopkins, and J. Kathryn Josserand. 2012. "Narrative Structure and the Drum Major Headdress." In *Parallel Worlds: Genre, Discourse, and Poetics in Contemporary, Colonial, and Classic Maya Literature*, ed. Kerry Hull and Michael Carrasco, 195–219. Boulder: University of Colorado Press.

Bassie-Sweet, Karen, Robert M. Laughlin, Nicholas A. Hopkins, and Andrés Brizuela Casimir. 2015. *The Ch'ol Maya of Chiapas*. Norman: University of Oklahoma Press.

Baudez, Claude. 1994. *Maya Sculpture of Copán: The Icongraphy*. Norman: University of Oklahoma Press.

Berjonneau, Gerald, Emile Delataille, and Jean-Louis Sonnery. 1985. *Rediscovered Masterpieces of Mesoamerica: Mexico-Guatemala-Honduras*. Boulogne: Editions Arts.

Berlin, Heinrich. 1959. "Glifos nominales en el sarcófago de Palenque: Un ensayo." *Humanidades* 2(10):1–8.

Berlin, Heinrich. 1963. "The Palenque Triad." *Journal de la Société des Américanistes* n.s. 52:91–99.

Berlin, Heinrich, and David Kelley. 1961. *The 819 Day Count and Color-Direction Symbolism among the Classic Maya*. Middle American Research Institute, Pub. 26:9–20. New Orleans, LA: Tulane University.

Berlo, Janet. 1983. *Text and Image in Pre-Columbian Art*. BAR International Series 180. Oxford, UK: British Archaeological Reports.

Bernal Romero, Guillermo. 2002. "U Pakal K'inich Janahb' Pakal, el nuevo gobernador de Palenque." *Lakamha'* 1(4):4–9.

Bierhorst, John. 1992. *History and Mythology of the Aztecs: The Codex Chimalpopoca*. Tucson: University of Arizona Press.

Blom, Frans. 1924. *Report on the Ruins of Uaxactún and Other Ruins in the Department of Peten, Guatemala*. Washington, DC: Carnegie Institution of Washington.

Bloomfield, Leonard. 1933. *Language*. New York: Holt, Rinehart and Winston.

Boas, Franz. 1911. *Handbook of American Indian Languages*. Washington, DC: US Government Printing Office.

Boot, Eric. 1990. *Of Serpents and Centipedes: The Epithet Wuk Chapaht Chan K'inich Ahaw*. Notes on Maya Hieroglyphic Writing 25. Rijswijk, Netherlands.

Boot, Eric. 2006. "On the Proper Name of Buildings at Copan, Tortuguero, Palenque, and Río Azul." Unpublished paper in possession of the authors.

Boot, Eric. 2008. "At the Court of Itzam Nah Yax Kokaj Mut: Preliminary Iconographic and Epigraphic Analysis of a Late Classic Vessel." http://www.mayavase.com/God-D-Court-Vessel.pdf.

Braakhuis, H. E. M. 2005. "Xbalanque's Canoe: The Origin of Poison in Q'eqchi' Mayan Hummingbird Myth." *Anthropos* 100(1):173–191

Braswell, Geoffrey. 2003. *The Maya and Teotihuacan: Reinterpreting Early Classic Interaction.* Austin: University of Texas Press.

Breedlove, Dennis E., and Nicholas A. Hopkins. 1970–1971. "A Study of Chuj (Mayan) Plants, with Notes on Their Uses. I–III." *The Wasmann Journal of Biology* 28(2):275–298, 1970; 29(1):107–128, 1971; 29(2):189–205, 1971.

Bricker, Victoria. 1997. "The Structure of Almanacs in the Madrid Codex." In *Papers on the Madrid Codex*, ed. Victoria Bricker and Gabrielle Vail, 1–25. Middle American Research Institute, Pub. 64. New Orleans: Middle American Research Institute.

Brown, Cecil H. 1977. "Folk Botanical Life Forms: Their Universality and Growth." *American Anthropologist* 79:317–342.

Callaway, Carl. 2011. "A Catalogue of Maya Era Inscriptions." PhD diss., La Trobe University, Melbourne, Australia.

Calvin, Inga. 2006. "Between Text and Image: An Analysis of Pseudo-Glyphs on Late Classic Maya Pottery from Guatemala." PhD diss., University of Colorado, Boulder.

Cancian, Frank. 1965. *Economics and Prestige in a Maya Community: The Religious Cargo System in Zinacantan.* Stanford, CA: Stanford University Press.

Carlson, John B. 1982. "Double-Headed Dragon and the Sky: A Pervasive Cosmological Symbol." In *Ethnoastronomy and Archaeoastronomy in the American Tropics*, ed. A. F. Aveni and G. Urton, 135–163. New York: New York Academy of Sciences.

Carlson, John B. 1988. "Skyband Representations in Classic Maya Vase Painting." In *Maya Iconography*, ed. E. P. Benson and G. G. Griffin, 277–293. Princeton, NJ: Princeton University Press.

Carlson, John B., and Linda C. Landis. 1985. "Bands, Bicephalic Dragons, and Other Beasts: The Skyband in Maya Art and Iconography." In *Fourth Palenque Round Table, 1980*, ed. E. P. Benson, 115–140. San Francisco, CA: Pre-Columbian Art Research Institute.

Carrasco, David. 1982. *Quetzalcoatl and the Irony of Empire: Myths and Prophecies in the Aztec Tradition.* Chicago, IL: University of Chicago Press.

Carrasco, Michael. 2005. "The Mask Flange Iconographic Complex: The Art, Ritual and History of a Maya Image." PhD diss., University of Texas at Austin.

Carrasco, Michael. 2010. "From Field to Hearth: An Earthly Interpretation of Maya and Other Mesoamerican Creation Myths." In Pre-Columbian Foodways: Interdisciplinary Approaches to Food, Culture, and Markets in Mesoamerica, ed. J. Staller and M. D. Carrasco, 601–634. New York: Springer.

Carrasco, Michael. 2012a. "The History, Rhetoric, and Poetics of Three Palenque Narratives." In *Parallel Worlds: Genre, Discourse, and Poetics in Contemporary, Colonial, and Classic Maya Literature*, ed. Kerry Hull and Michael Carrasco, 123–160. Boulder: University of Colorado Press.

Carrasco, Michael. 2012b. "Performance, Presence and Genre in Maya Hieroglyphs." In *Agency in Ancient Writing*, ed. Joshua Englehardt, 139–163. Boulder: University Press of Colorado.

Carrasco, Michael. 2015. "Portals, Turtles, and Mythic Places." In *Maya Imagery, Architecture, and Activity: Space and Spatial Analysis in Art History*, ed. Maline D. Werness-Rude and Kaylee R. Spencer, 374–411. Albuquerque: University of New Mexico.

Carrasco, Michael D., and Kerry M. Hull. 2002. "The Cosmogonic Symbolism of the Corbeled Vault in Maya Architecture." *Mexicon* 24(2):26–32.

Chinchilla Mazariegos, Oswaldo. 2006. "The Stars of the Palenque Sarcophagus." *Res* 49/50:40–58.

Chinchilla Mazariegos, Oswaldo. 2011. *Imágenes de la mitología maya*. Guatemala: Museo Popol Vuh, Universidad Francisco Marroquín.

Christenson, Allen. 1988. "The Use of Chiasmus by the Ancient Maya-Quiché." *Latin American Indian Literatures Journal* 4:125–150.

Christenson, Allen. 2003a. *Popol Vuh: The Sacred Book of the Maya*. New York: O Books.

Christenson, Allen. 2003b. *Popol Vuh: Literal Poetic Version*. New York: O Books.

Christenson, Allen. 2006. "Sacred Bundle Cults in Highland Guatemala." In *Sacred Bundles: Ritual Acts of Wrapping and Binding in Mesoamerica*, ed. Julia Guernsey and F. Kent Reilly, 226–246. Barnardsville, NC: Boundary End Archaeology Research Center.

Christenson, Allen. 2012. "The Use of Chiasmus by the Ancient K'iche' Maya." In *Parallel Worlds: Genre, Discourse, and Poetics in Contemporary, Colonial, and Classic Maya Literature*, ed. Kerry Hull and Michael Carrasco, 311–338. Boulder: University of Colorado Press.

Closs, Michael. 1989. "Cognitive Aspects of Ancient Maya Eclipse Theory." In *World Archaeoastronomy*, ed. A. F. Aveni, 389–415. New York: Cambridge University Press.

Coe, Michael. 1973. *The Maya Scribe and His World*. New York: Grolier Club.

Coe, Michael. 1977. "Supernatural Patrons of Maya Scribes and Artists." In *Social Process in Maya Prehistory*, ed. Norman Hammond, 327–347. London: Academic Press.

Coe, Michael. 1989. "The Hero Twins: Myth and Image." In *The Maya Vase Book*, vol. 1, ed. Justin Kerr, 161–184. New York: Kerr Associates.

Coe, Michael, and Elizabeth Benson. 1966. *Three Maya Relief Panels at Dumbarton Oaks*. Washington, DC: Dumbarton Oaks.

Coe, Michael, and Justin Kerr. 1998. *The Art of the Maya Scribe*. New York: Harry Abrams.

Colas, Pierre. 2003. "K'inich and King. Naming Self and Person among Classic Maya Rulers." *Ancient Mesoamerica* 14(2):269–283.

Cruz Guzmán, Ausencio. 1986. "ALIM [Archivo de Lenguas Indígenas de México] Syntax Questionnaire [Tumbalá Ch'ol]." Mayan Languages Collection. The Archive of the Indigenous Languages of Latin America. www.ailla.utexas.org . CTU001R002.

Cruz Guzmán, Ausencio. 2016. "Our Grandfather." In *Chol (Mayan) Folktales: A Collection of Stories from the Modern Maya of Southern Mexico*, ed. Nicholas A. Hopkins and J. Kathryn Josserand, with the assistance of Ausencio Cruz Guzmán, 69–76. Boulder: University Press of Colorado.

Culbert, Patrick T. 1993. *The Ceramics of Tikal: Vessels from the Burials, Caches, and Problematic Deposits*. Tikal Report no. 25, part A. Philadelphia, PA: University Museum.

Davletshin, Albert. 2003. "Glyph for Stingray Spine." http://www.mesoweb.com/features/davletshin/Spine.pdf.

Day, Christopher. 1971. *Diccionario jacalteco-español*. Computer printout from database, University of Rochester, NY. Manuscript in possession of the authors.

Durán, Diego. 1971. *Book of the Gods and Rites and the Ancient Calendar*. Norman: University of Oklahoma Press.

Eberl, Markus. 2001. "Death and Conceptions of the Soul." In *Maya: Divine Kings of the Rainforest*, ed. Nikolai Grube, 310–321. Cologne, Germany: Könemann Verlagsgesellschaft.

Eberl, Markus, and Daniel Graña-Behrens. 2004. "Proper Names and Throne Names: On the Naming Practice of Classic Maya Rulers." In *Continuity and Change: Maya Religious Practices in Temporal Perspective*, ed. Daniel Graña-Behrens, Nikolai Grube, Christian M. Prager, Frauke Sachse, Stefanie Teufel, and Elizabeth Wagner, 101–120. Markt Schwaben, Germany: Verlag Anton Saurwein.

Edmonson, Munro. 1971. *The Book of Counsel: The Popol Vuh of the Quiche Maya of Guatemala*. New Orleans, LA: Middle American Research Institute.

Edmonson, Munro, and Victoria Reifler Bricker. 1985. *Supplement to the Handbook of Middle American Indians: Literatures*. Austin: University of Texas Press.

Fash, William. 1991. *Scribes, Warriors and Kings: The City of Copán and the Ancient Maya*. New York: Thames and Hudson.

Fields, Virginia M. 1991. "The Iconographic Heritage of the Maya Jester God." In *Sixth Palenque Round Table, 1986*, ed. Merle Greene Robertson, 167–174. Norman: University of Oklahoma Press.

Filamore, Daniel, and Stephen Houston. 2010. *The Fiery Pool: The Maya and the Mythic Sea*. New Haven, CT, and London: Yale University Press.

Förstemann, Ernst. 1886. *Erläuterungen zur Mayahandschrift der Königlichen Öffentlichen Bibliothek zu Dresden*. Dresden, Germany: Warnatz und Lehmann.

Fought, John. 1985. "Cyclical Patterns in Chorti (Mayan) Literature." In *Supplement to the Handbook of Middle American Indians: Literatures*, 135–146. Austin: University of Texas Press.

Fox, James, and John Justeson. 1984. "Polyvalence in Mayan Hieroglyphic Writing." In *Phoneticism in Mayan Hieroglyphic Writing*, ed. John Justeson and Lyle Campbell, 17–76. Institute for Mesoamerican Studies, pub. 9. Albany: State University of New York at Albany.

Freidel, David, and Barbara MacLeod. 2000. "Creation Redux: New Thoughts on Maya Cosmology from Epigraphy, Iconography, and Archaeology." *PARI Journal* 1(2):1–8, 18.

Freidel, David, and Linda Schele. 1988. "Kingship in the Late Preclassic Maya Lowlands: The Instruments and Places of Ritual Power." *American Anthropologist* 90:547–567.

Freidel, David, Linda Schele, and Joy Parker. 1993. *Maya Cosmos: Three Thousand Years on the Shaman's Path*. New York: William Morrow.

García Barros, Ana. 2008. "Chaahk, el dios de la lluvia, en el periodo clásico maya: Aspectos religiosos y políticos." PhD diss., Universidad Complutense de Madrid, Spain.

Genet, Jean. 1934. "Les glyphes symboliques dans l'écriture maya-quichée. Le glyphe symbolique de la guerre." *Revue des Études Mayas-Quichées* 1:23–32

González Cruz, Arnoldo, and Guillermo Bernal Romero. 2004. "The Throne Panel of Temple 21, Palenque." In *Courtly Art of the Ancient Maya*, ed. Mary Miller and Simon Martin, 264–267. New York: Thames and Hudson.

Gossen, Gary H. 1974a. "To Speak with a Heated Heart: Chamula Canons of Style and Good Performance." In *Explorations in the Ethnography of Speaking*, ed. Richard Bauman and Joel Sherzer, 389–413. London: Cambridge University Press.

Gossen, Gary H. 1974b. *Chamulas in the World of the Sun: Time and Space in a Maya Oral Tradition*. Cambridge, MA: Harvard University Press.

Gossen, Gary H. 1977. "Chamula Genres of Verbal Behavior." In *Verbal Art as Performance*, ed. Richard Bauman, 81–116. Austin: University of Texas Press.

Graham, Ian, and Eric von Euw. 1977. *Corpus of Maya Hieroglyphic Inscriptions*, vol. 3, part 1: *Yaxchilan*. Cambridge, MA: Peabody Museum of Archaeology and Ethnology, Harvard University.

Grube, Nikolai. 1990. "Die Errichtung von Stelen: Entzifferung einer Verbhieroglyphe auf Monumenten der klassischen Mayakultur." In *Circumpacifica: Festscrift für Thomas S. Barthel*, ed. Bruno Illius and Matthias Laubscher, 189–215. Frankfurt am Main, Germany: Peter Lang.

Grube, Nikolai. 1992. "Classic Maya Dance: Evidence from Hieroglyphs and Iconography." *Ancient Mesoamerica* 3(2):201–218.

Grube, Nikolai. 2002. "Onomástica en los gobernantes mayas." In *La organización social entre los mayas, Memoria de la Tercera Mesa de Palenque*, vol. 2, ed. V. Tiesler, R. Cobos, and M. Greene Robertson, 323–353. México, DF: CONACULTA, Instituto Nacional de Antropología e Historia.

Grube, Nikolai, Simon Martin, and Marc Zender. 2002. "Palenque and Its Neighbors." In *The Proceedings of the Maya Hieroglyphic Workshop: Palenque and Its Neighbors, March 9–10, 2002, University of Texas at Austin*, ed. Phil Wanyerka, 1–119. Austin: University of Texas at Austin.

Grube, Nikolai, and Werner Nahm. 1994. "A Census of Xibalba: A Complete Inventory of *Way* Characters on Maya Ceramics." In *The Maya Vase Book*, vol. 4, ed. Justin Kerr, 686–715. New York: Kerr Associates.

Hansen, Richard. 1992. "Archaeology of Ideology: A Study of Maya Preclassic Architectural Sculpture at Nakbe, Peten, Guatemala." PhD diss., University of California, Los Angeles.

Hellmuth, Nicholas. 1975. *Escuintla Hoards: Teotihuacán Art in Guatemala*. Guatemala: Foundation for Latin American Anthropological Research.

Hellmuth, Nicholas. 1987. "The Surface of the Underwaterworld." PhD diss., Karl-Franzens-Universitaet, Graz, Austria. Culver City, CA: Foundation for Latin American Anthropological Research.

Helmke, Christophe. 2009. "Ancient Maya Cave Usage as Attested in the Glyphic Corpus of the Maya Lowlands and the Caves of the Roaring Creek Valley, Belize." PhD diss., University College, London.

Hill, Jane. 1992. "The Flower World of Old Uto-Aztecan." *Journal of Anthropological Research* 48(2):117–144.

Hofling, Charles Andrew. 1991. *Itzá Maya Texts with a Grammatical Overview*. Salt Lake City: University of Utah Press.

Hofling, Charles Andrew. 2012. "A Comparison of Narrative Style in Mopan and Itzaj Mayan." In *Parallel Worlds: Genre, Discourse, and Poetics in Contemporary, Colonial, and Classic Maya Literature*, ed. Kerry Hull and Michael Carrasco, 401–448. Boulder: University of Colorado Press.

Hofling, Charles Andrew, with Félix Fernando Tesucún. 1997. *Itzaj Maya-Spanish-English Dictionary*. Salt Lake City: The University of Utah Press.

Hoopes, John, and David Mora-Marín. 2009. "Violent Acts of Curing: Pre-Columbian Metaphors of Birth and Sacrifice in the Diagnosis and Treatment of Illness 'Writ Large.'" In *Blood and Beauty: Organized Violence in the Art and*

Archaeology of Mesoamerica and Central America, ed. H. Orr and R. Koontz, 161–220. Los Angeles, CA: Cotsen Institute of Archaeology Press.

Hopkins, Nicholas A. 1969. "A Formal Account of Chalchihuitán Tzotzil Kinship Terminology." *Ethnology* 8(1):85–102.

Hopkins, Nicholas A. 1980. "Chuj Animal Names and their Classification." *Journal of Mayan Linguistics* 2(1):13–39.

Hopkins, Nicholas A. 1988. "Classic Mayan Kinship Systems: Epigraphic and Ethnographic Evidence for Patrilineality." *Estudios de Cultura Maya* 17:87–121.

Hopkins, Nicholas A. 1991. "Classic and Modern Relationship Terms and the 'Child of Mother' Glyph (T I:606.23)." In *Sixth Palenque Round Table, 1986*, ed. Merle Greene Robertson, 255–265. Norman: University of Oklahoma Press.

Hopkins, Nicholas A. 1994. "Review of Joyce Marcus, *Mesoamerican Writing Systems: Propaganda, Myth, and History in Four Ancient Civilizations*." *Anthropological Linguistics* 36(3):382–385.

Hopkins, Nicholas A. 1996. "Metonym and Metaphor in Chol (Mayan) Ritual Language." Paper presented to the 95th Annual Meeting of the American Anthropological Association, San Francisco, CA.

Hopkins, Nicholas A. 2006a. "The Place of Maize in Indigenous Mesoamerican Folk Taxonomies." In *Histories of Maize: Multidisciplinary Approaches to the Prehistory, Biogeography, Domestication, and Evolution of Maize*, ed. John E. Staller, Robert H. Tykot, and Bruce F. Benz, 611–622. San Diego, CA: Elsevier/Academic Press.

Hopkins, Nicholas A. 2006b. "Review of Søren Wichmann, editor, *The Linguistics of Maya Writing*." *Anthropological Linguistics* 48(4):405–412.

Hopkins, Nicholas A. 2008. "The Lacandón Song of the Jaguar." *Tlalocan* 15:111–113.

Hopkins, Nicholas A. 2009. "The Place of Maize in Indigenous Mesoamerican Folk Taxonomies." In *Histories of Maize in Mesoamerica: Multidisciplinary Approaches*, ed. John E. Staller, Robert H. Tykot, and Bruce F. Benz, 223–234. Walnut Creek, CA: Left Coast Press.

Hopkins, Nicholas A. 2012a. "The Art of the Scribes: A Style Sheet for Classic Inscriptions (Antigua 2012)." PowerPoint and paper presented to the Texas Maya Meetings, Casa Herrera, La Antigua Guatemala, March 10, 2012. https://independent.academia.edu/NickHopkins.

Hopkins, Nicholas A. 2012b. "A Dictionary of the Chuj (Mayan) Language, as Spoken in San Mateo Ixtatán, Huehuetenango, Guatemala." http://www.famsi.org/mayawriting/dictionary/hopkins/dictionaryChuj.html.

Hopkins, Nicholas A. 2012c. "The Noun Classifiers of Cuchumatán Mayan Languages: A Case of Diffusion from Otomanguean." *International Journal of American Linguistics* 78(3):411–427. [A corrected Table 2 was published in *IJAL* 78(4):595.]

Hopkins, Nicholas A. 2014. "On a Wing and a Prayer: A Reconsideration of a Glyphic Reading (T77)." https://www.academia.edu/6413833.

Hopkins, Nicholas A., and J. Kathryn Josserand. 1987. "Discourse Structure in Maya Hieroglyphic Inscriptions." Paper presented to the Cleveland Conference on Mayan Text and Discourse, Cleveland State University, Cleveland, OH.

Hopkins, Nicholas A., and J. Kathryn Josserand. 1990. "The Characteristics of Chol (Mayan) Traditional Narrative." In *Homenaje a Jorge A. Suárez; Lingüística Indoamericana e Hispánica*, ed. Beatriz Garza Cuarón and Paulette Levy, 297–314. México, DF: El Colegio de México.

Hopkins, Nicholas A., and J. Kathryn Josserand. 1994. "Pasado, presente y futuro en la lingüística maya." In *Panorama de los estudios de las lenguas indígenas de México*, ed. Leonardo Manrique, Yolanda Lastra, and Doris Bartholomew, vol. 1:269–333. Colección Biblioteca Abya-Yala, 16. Quito, Ecuador: Ediciones Abya-Yala.

Hopkins, Nicholas A., and J. Kathryn Josserand. 2012. "The Narrative Structure of Chol Folktales: One Thousand Years of Literary Tradition." In *Parallel Worlds: Genre, Discourse, and Poetics in Contemporary, Colonial, and Classic Maya Literature*, ed. Kerry Hull and Michael Carrasco, 21–42. Boulder: University Press of Colorado.

Hopkins, Nicholas A., and J. Kathryn Josserand, with the assistance of Ausencio Cruz Guzmán. 2011. "A Historical Dictionary of Chol (Mayan): The Lexical Sources from 1789 to 1935." http://www.famsi.org/mayawriting/dictionary/hopkins/dictionaryChol.html.

Hopkins, Nicholas A., and J. Kathryn Josserand, with the assistance of Ausencio Cruz Guzmán. 2016. *Chol (Mayan) Folktales; a Collection of Stories from the Modern Maya of Southern Mexico*. Boulder: University Press of Colorado.

Houston, Stephen D. 1983. "A Reading for the Flint-Shield Glyph." *Contributions to Maya Hieroglyphic Decipherment* 1:13–25.

Houston, Stephen D. 1984. "An Example of Homophony in Maya Script." *American Antiquity* 49(4):790–805.

Houston, Stephen D. 1992. "A Name Glyph for Classic Maya Dwarfs." In *The Maya Vase Book*, vol. 3, ed. Justin Kerr, 526–531. New York: Kerr Associates.

Houston, Stephen D. 1996. "Symbolic Sweatbaths of the Maya: Architectural Meaning in the Cross Group at Palenque, Mexico." Latin American Antiquity 7(2):132–151.

Houston, Stephen D. 1997. "The Shifting Now: Aspect, Deixis, and Narrative in Classic Texts." *American Anthropologist* 99(2):291–305.

Houston, Stephen D. 1998. "Classic Maya Depictions of the Built Environment." In *Function and Meaning in Maya Architecture*, ed. Stephen Houston, 333–372. Washington, DC: Dumbarton Oaks.

Houston, Stephen D., and Simon Martin. 2012. "Mythic Prototypes and Maya Writing." https://decipherment.wordpress.com/2012/01/04/mythic-prototypes-and-maya-writing/.
Houston, Stephen D., and Mary Miller. 1987. "The Classic Maya Ballgame and Its Architectural Setting." *Res* 14:46–65.
Houston, Stephen D., and David Stuart. 1989. "The *Way* Glyph: Evidence for 'Co-Essences' among the Classic Maya." *Research Reports on Ancient Maya Writing* 30. Washington, DC: Center for Maya Research.
Houston, Stephen D., and David Stuart. 1990. "T632 as Muyal, 'Cloud.'" *Central Tennessean Notes in Maya Epigraphy* 1. Nashville.
Houston, Stephen D., and David Stuart. 1996. "Of Gods, Glyphs and Kings: Divinity and Rulership among the Classic Maya." *Antiquity* 70:289–312.
Houston, Stephen D., and David Stuart. 1998. "The Ancient Maya Self: Personhood and Portraiture in the Classic Period." *Res:* 33:73–101.
Houston, Stephen D., David Stuart, and Karl Taube. 1989. "Folk Classification of Maya Pottery." *American Anthropologist* 91(4):720–726.
Houston, Stephen D., David Stuart, and Karl Taube. 2006. *The Memory of Bones: Body, Being, and Experience among the Classic Maya*. Austin: University of Texas Press.
Houston, Stephen D., and Karl Taube. 2000. "An Archaeology of the Senses: Perception and Cultural Expression in Ancient Mesoamerica." *Cambridge Archaeological Journal* 10(2):261–294.
Houston, Stephen D., and Karl Taube. 2011. "The Fiery Pool: Fluid Concepts of Water and Sea among the Classic Maya." In *Ecology, Power, and Religion in Maya Landscapes*, ed. Christian Isendahl and Bodil Liljefors-Persson, 17–37. Möckmuhl, Germany: Anton Saurwein.
Houston, Stephen D., and Karl Taube. 2012. "Carved Panel." In *Ancient Maya Art at Dumbarton Oaks*, ed. Joanne Pillsbury, Miriam Doutriaux, Reiko Ishihara-Brito, and Alexandre Tokovinine, 39–47. Washington, DC: Dumbarton Oaks.
Hull, Kerry. 1993. "Poetic discourse in Maya Oral Tradition and in the Hieroglyphic Script." MA thesis, Department of Linguistics, Georgetown University, Washington, DC.
Hull, Kerry. 2000. "Cosmological and Ritual Language in Ch'orti'." FAMSI Research Report. www.famsi.org/reports/99036/index.html.
Hull, Kerry. 2002. "A Comparative Analysis of Ch'orti' Verbal Art and the Poetic Discourse Structures of Maya Hieroglyphic Writing." FAMSI Research Report.
Hull, Kerry. 2003. "Verbal Art and Performance in Ch'orti' Verbal Art and the Poetic Discourse Structure of Maya Hieroglyphic Writing." PhD diss., Department of Anthropology, University of Texas at Austin.

Hull, Kerry. 2005. "An Abbreviated Dictionary of Ch'orti' Maya." http://www.famsi.org/reports/03031/index.html.

Hull, Kerry. 2012. "Poetic Tenacity: A Diachronic Study of Kennings in Mayan Languages." In *Parallel Worlds: Genre, Discourse, and Poetics in Contemporary, Colonial, and Classic Maya Literature*, ed. Kerry M Hull and Michael D. Carrasco, 73–122. Boulder: University Press of Colorado.

Hull, Kerry M., and Michael D. Carrasco. 2012. *Parallel Worlds: Genre, Discourse, and Poetics in Contemporary, Colonial, and Classic Maya Literature*. Boulder: University Press of Colorado.

Hull, Kerry M., Michael Carrasco, and Robert Wald. 2009. "The First-Person Singular Independent Pronoun in Classic Ch'olan." *Mexicon* 31(2):36–43.

Ishihara, Reiko, Karl Taube, and Jaime Awe. 2006. "The Water Lily Serpent Stucco Masks at Caracol, Belize." *Research Reports in Belizean Archaeology* 3:213–23. Belmopan, Belize: Institute of Archaeology, National Institute of Culture and History.

Jones, Christopher. 1977. "Inauguration Dates of Three Late Classic Rulers of Tikal, Guatemala." *American Antiquity* 42(1):28–60.

Joralemon, David. 1974. "Ritual Blood-Sacrifice among the Ancient Maya." In *Primera Mesa Redonda,* part II, ed. Merle Greene Robertson, 59–76. Pebble Beach, CA: Pre-Columbian Art Research, Robert Louis Stevenson School.

Josserand, J. Kathryn. 1975. "Archaeological and Linguistic Correlations for Mayan Prehistory." *Actas del XLI Congreso Internacional de Americanistas, México, 2 al 7 de septiembre de 1974*, vol. 1:501–510.

Josserand, J. Kathryn. 1989. "A New Reading for the Palenque Sarcophagus Lid Inscription." Paper presented to the Seventh Palenque Round Table, Palenque, Chiapas, June 1989.

Josserand, J. Kathryn. 1990. "The Literary Heritage of the Kings of Palenque." Paper presented to the Symposium on Tradition and Innovation in Ancient Mexico, Metropolitan Museum of Art, New York City, October 1990.

Josserand, J. Kathryn. 1991. "The Narrative Structure of Hieroglyphic Texts at Palenque." In *Sixth Palenque Round Table, 1986*, ed. Merle Greene Robertson, 12–31. Norman: University of Oklahoma Press.

Josserand, J. Kathryn. 1995. "Participant Tracking in Hieroglyphic Texts: Who Was That Masked Man?" *Journal of Linguistic Anthropology* 5(1):65–89.

Josserand, J. Kathryn. 1997. "La estructura narrativa en los textos jeroglíficos de Palenque." In *Mesas Redondas de Palenque,* ed. Silvia Trejo, 445–481. México, DF: Instituto Nacional de Antropología e Historia.

Josserand, J. Kathryn. 2007. "The Missing Heir at Yaxchilán: Literary Analysis of a Maya Historical Puzzle." *Latin American Antiquity* 18(3):295–312.

Josserand, J. Kathryn. 2016. "The Narrative Structure of Chol Folktales." In *Chol (Mayan) Folktales: A Collection of Stories from the Modern Maya of Southern Mexico*, ed. Nicholas A. Hopkins and J. Kathryn Josserand, with the assistance of Ausencio Cruz Guzmán, 15–31. Boulder: University Press of Colorado.

Josserand, J. Kathryn, and Nicholas A. Hopkins. 1991. *A Handbook of Classic Maya Inscriptions*, part I: *The Western Lowlands*. Final Performance Report, National Endowment for the Humanities, Grant RT–21090–89, July 1991.

Josserand, J. Kathryn, and Nicholas A. Hopkins. 1996. "Chol Ritual Language; A Research Report to the Foundation for the Advancement of Mesoamerican Studies, Inc." http://www.famsi.org/reports/94017/94017Josserando1.pdf.

Josserand, J. Kathryn, and Nicholas A. Hopkins. 2011. "Directions and Partitions in Maya World View." www.famsi.org/research/hopkins/directions.html.

Josserand, J. Kathryn, with Nicholas A. Hopkins, Ausencio Cruz Guzmán, Ashley Kistler, and Kayla Price. 2003. "Story Cycles in Chol (Mayan) Mythology: Contextualizing Classic Iconography." Report of a Project Sponsored by the Foundation for the Advancement of Mesoamerican Studies, Inc. (FAMSI), Crystal River, FL. FAMSI grant number 01085. www.famsi.org/reports/01085/index.html.

Just, Bryan R. 2012. *Dancing into Dreams: Maya Vase Painting of the Ik' Kingdom*. New Haven, CT: Yale University Press.

Justeson, John. 1983. "Mayan Hieroglyphic Name-Tagging on a Pair of Rectangular Jade Plaques from Xcalumkin." In *Contributions to Maya Hieroglyphic Decipherment* I, ed. Stephen D. Houston, 40–43. New Haven, CT: HRAFlex Books.

Justeson, John, William M. Norman, and Norman Hammond. 1988. "The Ponoma Flare: A Preclassic Maya Hieroglyphic Text." In *Maya Iconography*, ed. E. P. Benson and G. G. Griffin, 94–151. Princeton, NJ: Princeton University Press.

Kaufman, Terrence S. 1964. "Materiales lingüísticos para el estudio de las relaciones internas y externas de la familia de idiomas mayas." In *Desarrollo cultural de los mayas*, ed. Evon Z. Vogt and Alberto Ruz L., 82–136. México, DF: Universidad Nacional Autónoma de México.

Kaufman, Terrence S. 1976. "Archaeological and Linguistic Correlations in Mayaland and Associated Areas of Meso-America." *World Archaeology* 8:101–118.

Kaufman, Terrence S. 1978. "Meso-American Indian Languages." *Encyclopaedia Britannica*, 15th ed., 11:956963.

Kaufman, Terrence, with the assistance of John Justeson. 2003. "A Preliminary Mayan Etymological Dictionary." http://www.famsi.org/reports/01051/index.html.

Kaufman, Terrence, and William Norman. 1984. "An Outline of Proto-Cholan Phonology, Morphology and Vocabulary." In *Phoneticism in Mayan Hieroglyphic Writing*, ed. John Justeson and Lyle Campbell, 77–166. Institute for Mesoamerican Studies Publication 9. Albany: State University of New York at Albany.

Kelley, David H. 1962. "Glyphic evidence for a dynastic sequence at Quirigua, Guatemala." *American Antiquity* 27:323–335.
Kelley, David H. 1976. *Deciphering the Maya Script*. Austin: University of Texas Press.
Kirchhoff, Paul. 1943. "Mesoamerica; Sus límites geográficos, composición étnica y carácteres culturales." *Acta Americana* 1:92–107.
Knorosov, Yuri. 1958. "The Problem of the Study of Maya Hieroglyph Writing." Translated by Sophie Coe. *American Antiquity* 23:284–291.
Knorosov, Yuri. 1967. *Selected Chapters from The Writing of the Maya Indians*. Translated by Sophie Coe. Russian Translation Series of the Peabody Museum of American Archaeology and Ethnology, vol. 4. Cambridge, MA: Harvard University.
Knorosov, Yuri. 1982. *Maya Hieroglyphic Codices*. Translated by Sophie Coe. Institute for Mesoamerican Studies Publication 8. Albany: State University of New York.
Knowlton, Timothy. 2002. "Diphrastic Kennings in Mayan Hieroglyphic Literature." *Mexicon* 24(1):9–13.
Knowlton, Timothy. 2010. *Maya Creation Myths: Words and Worlds of the Chilam Balam*. Boulder: University Press of Colorado.
Knowlton, Timothy. 2012. "Some Historical Continuities in Lowland Maya Magical Speech Genres." In *Parallel Worlds: Genre, Discourse, and Poetics in Contemporary, Colonial, and Classic Maya Literature*, ed. Kerry Hull and Michael Carrasco, 253–269. Boulder: University Press of Colorado.
Kroeber, Alfred L. 1909. "Classificatory Systems of Relationship." *Journal of the Royal Anthropological Society* 39:77–84.
Kubler, George. 1969. *Studies in Classic Maya Iconography*. Memoirs of the Connecticut Academy of Arts and Sciences. Hamden, CT: Archon Books.
Kubler, George. 1972. "The Paired Attendants of the Temple Tablet at Palenque." In *Religión en Mesoamérica, XII Mesa Redonda*, 42. México, DF: Sociedad Mexicana de Antropología.
Kubler, George. 1977. *Aspects of Classic Maya Rulership on Two Inscribed Vessels*, Studies in Pre-columbian Art and Archaeology, 18. Washington, DC: Dumbarton Oaks.
Kuhn, Thomas. 1962. *The Structure of Scientific Revolutions*. Chicago: University of Chicago Press.
Lacadena, Alfonso. 2004. "On the Reading of Two Glyphic Appellatives of the Rain God." In *Continuity and Change: Maya Religious Practices in Temporal Perspective*, ed. Daniel Graña Behrens, Nikolai Grube, Christian M. Prager, Frauke Sachse, Stefanie Teufel, and Elizabeth Wagner, 87–100. Markt Schwaben, Germany: Anton Saurwein.
Lacadena, Alfonso. 2012. "Syntactic Inversion (Hyperbaton) as a Literary Device in Maya Hieroglyphic Texts." In *Parallel Worlds: Genre, Discourse, and Poetics in*

Contemporary, Colonial, and Classic Maya Literature, ed. Kerry Hull and Michael Carrasco, 45–71. Boulder: University Press of Colorado.

Laughlin, Robert M. 1975. *The Great Tzotzil Dictionary of San Lorenzo Zinacantan*, Smithsonian Contributions to Anthropology, vol. 19. Washington, DC: Smithsonian Institution Press.

Laughlin, Robert M. 1977. *Of Cabbages and Kings*. Smithsonian Contributions to Anthropology, vol. 23. Washington, DC: Smithsonian Institution Press.

Laughlin, Robert M. 1988. *The Great Tzotzil Dictionary of Santo Domingo Zinacantan*. Smithsonian Contributions to Anthropology, vol. 31. Washington, DC: Smithsonian Institution Press.

Lévi-Strauss, Claude. 1949. *Les structures élémentaires de la parenté*. Paris: Presses Universitaires de France.

Linden, John. 1996. "Deity Head Variants of Glyph C." In *Eighth Palenque Round Table, 1993*, ed. Martha J. Macri and Jan McHargue, 343–356. San Francisco, CA: Pre-Columbian Art Research Institute.

Longacre, Robert. 1985. "Discourse Peak as Zone of Turbulence." In *Beyond the Sentence: Discourse and Sentential Form*, ed. Jessica R. Wirth, 81–98. Ann Arbor, MI: Karoma.

Looper, Mathew. 2001. "Dance Performances at Quirigua." In *Landscape and Power in Ancient Mesoamerica*, ed. Rex Koontz, Kathryn Reese-Taylor, and Annabeth Headrick, 113–135. Boulder, CO: Westview Press.

Looper, Mathew. 2003. *Lightning Warrior: Maya Art and Kingship at Quiriguá*. Austin: University of Texas Press.

Looper, Mathew. 2009. *To Be Like Gods: Dance in Ancient Maya Civilization*. Austin: University of Texas Press.

Looper, Mathew. 2012. "Dance, Power, and Ideology in Ancient Maya and Aztec Society." In *Power and Identity in Archaeological Theory and Practice: Case Studies from Ancient Mesoamerica*, ed. Eleanor Harrison-Buck, 8–20. Salt Lake City: University of Utah Press.

Lopes, Luis. 2004. "The Water-Band Glyph." http://www.mesoweb.com/features/lopes/Waterband.pdf.

López Bravo, Roberto. 2002. "La veneración de los ancestros en Palenque." *Arqueología mexicana* 8(45):38–43.

López Bravo, Roberto. 2004. "State and Domestic Cult in Palenque Censer Stands." In *Courtly Art of the Ancient Maya*, ed. Mary Miller and Simon Martin, 256–258. New York: Thames and Hudson.

López Cogolludo, Diego. 1955. *Historia de Yucatán*. Campeche: Comisión de Historia, Gobierno del Estado de Campeche.

Lounsbury, Floyd. 1976. "A Rationale for the Initial Date of the Temple of the Cross at Palenque." In *The Art, Iconography, and Dynastic History of Palenque*, ed. Merle

Greene Robertson, 5–20. Pebble Beach, CA: Pre-Columbian Art Research, Robert Louis Stevenson School.

Lounsbury, Floyd. 1980. "Some Problems in the Interpretation of the Mythological Portion of the Hieroglyphic Text of the Temple of the Cross at Palenque." In *Tercera Mesa Redonda de Palenque, 1978*, ed. Merle Greene Robertson, 99–115. Austin: University of Texas Press.

Lounsbury, Floyd. 1989. "The Ancient Writing of Middle America." In *The Origins of Writing*, ed. Wayne Senner, 203–238. Lincoln: University of Nebraska Press.

Love, Bruce. 1994. *The Paris Codex*. Austin: University of Texas Press.

MacLeod, Barbara. 1990. "Deciphering the Primary Standard Sequence." PhD diss., University of Texas at Austin.

Macri, Martha. 1988. "A Descriptive Grammar of Palenque Mayan." PhD diss., Department of Anthropology, University of California, Berkeley.

Macri, Martha, and Mathew Looper. 2003. *The New Catalog of Maya Hieroglyphs*. Norman: University of Oklahoma Press.

Marcus, Joyce. 1993. *Mesoamerican Writing Systems: Propaganda, Myth, and History in Four Ancient Civilizations*. Princeton, NJ: Princeton University Press.

Martin, Simon. 2002. "The Baby Jaguar: An Explanation of Its Identity and Origins in Maya Art and Writing." In *La organización social entre los mayas: Memoria de la Tercera Mesa Redonda de Palenque*, vol. 1, ed. Vera Tiesler Blos, Rafael Cobos, and Merle Greene Robertson, 49–78. México, DF: Instituto Nacional de Antropología e Historia.

Martin, Simon. 2004. "A Broken Sky: The Ancient Name of Yaxchilan as Pa'Chan." *PARI Journal* 5(1):1–7.

Martin, Simon. 2005. "Caracol Altar 21 Revisited: More Data on Double Bird and Tikal's Wars of the Mid-Sixth Century." *PARI Journal* 6(1):1–9.

Martin, Simon. 2016. *The Old Man of the Universe*. San Francisco, CA: Mesoweb Press.

Martin, Simon, and Nikolai Grube. 2000. *Chronicle of the Maya Kings and Queens: Deciphering the Dynasties of the Ancient Maya*. London: Thames and Hudson.

Mathews, Peter. 1979. "Altun Ha Jade Plaque: Deciphering the Inscription." *Studies in Ancient Mesoamerica*, ed. John A. Graham, 197–214. Berkeley: University of California Press.

Mathews, Peter. 2001. "The Inscriptions on the Back of Dos Pilas Stela 8." In *The Decipherment of Ancient Maya Writing*, ed. Stephen Houston, Oswaldo Chinchilla Mazariegos, and David Stuart, 368–393. Norman: University of Oklahoma Press.

Mayer, Karl Herbert. 1980. *Maya Monuments: Sculptures of Unknown Provenance in the United States*. Ramona, CA: Acoma Books.

Mayer, Karl Herbert. 1981. *Classic Maya Relief Columns*. Ramona, CA: Acoma Books.

Mayer, Karl Herbert. 1995. *Maya Monuments: Sculptures of Unknown Provenance Supplement 4*. Graz, Austria: Academic Publishers.

Mayer, Karl Herbert. 2008. "Throne 2 of Yaxchilan, Chiapas, Mexico." *Mexicon* 30(3):55–58.

McQuown, Norman A., ed. 1967. *Handbook of Middle American Indians*, vol. 5, *Linguistics*. Austin: University of Texas Press.

Metzger, Duane, and Gerald E. Williams. 1963. "Procedures and Results in the Study of Native Categories: Tzeltal 'Firewood.'" *American Anthropologist* 68(2), part 1:389–407.

Milbrath, Susan. 1999. *Star Gods of the Maya: Astronomy in Art, Folklore, and Calendars*. Austin: University of Texas Press.

Miller, Mary Ellen, and Simon Martin. 2004. *Courtly Art of the Ancient Maya*. New York: Thames and Hudson.

Montgomery, John. 2002. *How to Read Maya Hieroglyphs*. New York: Hippocrene Books.

Mora-Marín, David. 2004. "The Primary Standard Sequence: Database, Compilation, Grammatical Analysis, and Primary Documentation." Report of a Project Sponsored by the Foundation for the Advancement of Mesoamerican Studies, Inc. (FAMSI), Crystal River, FL. Grant number 02047. http://www.famsi.org/reports/02047/index.html.

Morales, Alfonso. 1999. "Temple XX and the Tomb." http://www.mesoweb.com/palenque/dig/report/report_99_07.html.

Morris, Charles W. 1946. *Signs, Language, and Behavior*. New York: Prentice-Hall.

Norman, William. 1980. "Grammatical Parallelism in Quiche Ritual Language." In *Proceedings of the Sixth Annual Meeting of the Berkeley Linguistics Society*, 387–399.

Osborne, Lilly de Jongh. 1965. *Indian Crafts of Guatemala and El Salvador*. Norman: University of Oklahoma Press.

Pasztory, Esther. 1974. *Iconography of the Teotihuacan Tláloc*. Washington, DC: Dumbarton Oaks.

Pérez Martínez, Bernardo. 1987. "The Syntax Questionnaire of ALIM (Archivo de las Lenguas Indígenas de Mexico) [Tila Ch'ol]." Mayan Languages Collection. The Archive of the Indigenous Languages of Latin America: www.ailla.utexas.org. CTU002R009.

Pitarch, Pedro. 2013. *La Palabra Flagrante: Cantos Chamánicos Tzeltales*. México, DF: Aretes de México.

Plank, Shannon. 2004. *Maya Dwellings in Hieroglyphs and Archaeology: An Integrative Approach to Ancient Architecture and Spatial Cognition*. BAR International Series 1324. Oxford, UK: British Archaeological Reports.

Powell, Christopher. 1997. "A New View on Maya Astronomy." MA thesis, University of Texas at Austin.

Proskouriakoff, Tatiana. 1950. *A Study of Classic Maya Sculpture*. Carnegie Institution of Washington, Publication 593. Washington, DC: Carnegie Institution.

Proskouriakoff, Tatiana. 1960. "Historical Implications of a Pattern of Dates at Piedras Negras, Guatemala." *American Antiquity* 25(4):454–475.

Proskouriakoff, Tatiana. 1963. "Historical Data in the Inscriptions of Yaxchilan." Part I. *Estudios de cultura maya* 3:149–167.

Proskouriakoff, Tatiana. 1964. "Historical Data in the Inscriptions of Yaxchilan." Part II. *Estudios de cultura maya* 4:177–201.

Proskouriakoff, Tatiana. 1974. *Jades from the Cenote of Sacrifice*. Cambridge, MA: Peabody Museum of Archaeology and Ethnology, Harvard University.

Proskouriakoff, Tatiana. 1993. *Maya History*. Austin: University of Texas Press

Ramírez Pérez, José, Andrés Montejo, and Baltazar Díaz Hurtado. 1996. *Diccionario del idioma Jakalteko*. La Antigua, Guatemala: Proyecto Lingüístico Francisco Maroquín.

Reents-Budet, Dorie, Joseph Ball, Jennifer Taschek, and Ronald L. Bishop. 2000. "Out of the Palace Dumps: Ceramic Production and Use at Buenavista del Cayo, Belize." *Ancient Mesoamerica* 11(1):99–121.

Riese, Berthold. 1984. "Hel Hieroglyphs." In *Phoneticism in Mayan Hieroglyphic Writing*, ed. John Justeson and Lyle Campbell, 263–286. Institute for Mesoamerican Studies, pub. 9. Albany: State University of New York at Albany.

Ringle, William M. 1996. "Birds of a Feather: The Fallen Stucco Inscriptions of Temple XVIII, Palenque." In *Eighth Palenque Round Table*, ed. Martha Macri and Jan McHargue, 45–62. San Francisco, CA: Pre-Columbian Art Research Institute.

Ringle, William M., and Thomas C. Smith-Stark. 1996. *A Concordance to the Inscriptions of Palenque, Chiapas, Mexico*. Middle American Research Institute, Publication 62. New Orleans, LA: Tulane University.

Robertson, Merle Greene. 1974. "Quadripartite Badge; A Badge of Rulership." In Primera Mesa Redonda de Palenque, part 1, 1973, ed. Merle Greene Robertson, 77–93. Pebble Beach, CA: Pre-Columbian Art Research, Robert Louis Stevenson School.

Robertson, Merle Greene. 1983. *The Sculpture of Palenque*, vol. I: *The Temple of the Inscriptions*. Princeton, NJ: Princeton University Press.

Robertson, Merle Greene. 1984. *The Sculpture of Palenque*, vol. II: *The Early Buildings of the Palace*. Princeton, NJ: Princeton University Press.

Robertson, Merle Greene. 1985. *The Sculpture of Palenque*, vol. III: *The Late Buildings of the Palace*. Princeton, NJ: Princeton University Press.

Robertson, Merle Greene. 1991. *The Sculpture of Palenque*, vol. IV: *The Cross Group, the North Group, the Olvidado, and Other Pieces*. Princeton, NJ: Princeton University Press.

Robicsek, Francis, and Donald Hales. 1981. *The Maya Book of the Dead: The Ceramic Codex*. Norman: University of Oklahoma Press.

Robicsek, Francis, and Donald Hales. 1982. *Maya Ceramic Vases from the Classic Period: The November Collection of Maya Ceramics*. Charlottesville: University Museum of Virginia.

Romney, A. Kimball. 1967. "Kinship and Family." In *Handbook of Middle American Indians*, vol. 6: *Social Anthropology*, ed. Manning Nash, 207–237. Austin: University of Texas Press.

Roys, Ralph. 1933. *The Book of Chilam Balam of Chumayel*. Carnegie Institution of Washington, pub. 523, contribution 31. Washington, DC: Carnegie Institution.

Roys, Ralph. 1965. *Ritual of the Bacabs: A Book of Maya Incantations*. Norman: University of Oklahoma Press.

Ruppert, Karl. 1940. "A Special Assemblage of Maya Structures." In *The Maya and Their Neighbors*, ed. C. Hay, 222–231. New York: Appleton-Century.

Ruz, Alberto. 1973. *Palenque: El Templo de las Inscripciones*. México, DF: Instituto Nacional de Antropología e Historia.

Sahagún, Fray Bernardino de. 1959–1963. *Florentine Codex: General History of the Things of New Spain*, trans. Charles E. Dibble and Arthur J.O. Anderson. Monographs of the School of American Research and the Museum of New Mexico. 13 vols. Salt Lake City: University of Utah and School of American Research.

Saturno, William A., David Stuart, Anthony F. Aveni, and Franco Rossi. 2012. "Ancient Maya Astronomical Tables from Xultun, Guatemala." Science 336(6082):714–717.

Saturno, William, Karl Taube, and David Stuart. 2005. *The Murals of San Bartolo, El Petén, Guatemala*, part 1: *The North Wall*. Barnardsville, NC: Center for Ancient American Studies.

Schaffer, Anne Louse. 1987. "Recent Acquisitions: Art of the Americas, Maya Art." *Bulletin of the Museum of Fine Arts* 10(2):14–15.

Schele, Linda. 1974. "Observations on the Cross Motif at Palenque." In *Primera Mesa Redonda de Palenque*, part 1, 1973, ed. Merle Greene Robertson, 41–62. Pebble Beach, CA: Robert Louis Stevenson School.

Schele, Linda. 1976. "Accession Iconography of Chan Bahlam in the Group of the Cross at Palenque." In *The Art, Iconography and Dynastic History of Palenque*, part 3, ed. Merle Greene Robertson, 9–34. Pebble Beach, CA: Pre-Columbian Art Research, Robert Louis Stevenson School.

Schele, Linda. 1981. *Notebook for the Maya Hieroglyphic Writing Workshop at Texas*. Austin: University of Texas at Austin, Institute of Latin American Studies.

Schele, Linda. 1982. *Maya Glyphs: The Verbs*. Austin: University of Texas Press.

Schele, Linda. 1990. *Ba as "First" in Classic Period Titles*. Texas Notes on Pre-Columbian Art, Writing and Culture, 5. Austin: University of Texas.

Schele, Linda. 1992. *Notebook for the Sixteenth Maya Hieroglyphic Workshop at Texas*. Austin: University of Texas at Austin, Institute of Latin American Studies.

Schele, Linda, and David Freidel. 1990. *Forest of Kings: The Untold Story of the Ancient Maya*. New York: William Morrow.

Schele, Linda, and Nikolai Grube. 1995. *Notebook for the XIX Maya Hieroglyphic Workshop at Texas: The Last Two Hundred Years of Classic Maya History*. Austin: University of Texas at Austin.

Schele, Linda, and Peter Mathews. 1998. *The Code of Kings: The Language of Seven Sacred Maya Temples and Tombs*. New York: Simon and Schuster.

Schele, Linda, Peter Mathews, and Floyd Lounsbury. 1990. *Untying the Headband*. Texas Notes on Precolumbian Art, Writing, and Culture, 4. Austin: University of Texas at Austin, Center of the History and Art of Ancient American Culture.

Schele, Linda, and Mary Miller. 1986. *The Blood of Kings; Dynasty and Ritual in Maya Art*. Fort Worth, TX: Kimbell Art Museum.

Schele, Linda, David Stuart, and Nikolai Grube. 1989. *A Commentary on the Restoration and Reading of the Glyphic Panels from Temple 11*. Copan Notes, 64. Austin, TX: Copan Mosaics Project and Instituto Hondureño de Antropología e Historia.

Schellhas, Paul. 1904. *Representation of Deities of the Maya Manuscripts*. Papers of the Peabody Museum of American Archaeology and Ethnology, vol. 4, no. 1. Cambridge, MA: Harvard University.

Scherer, Andrew, and Stephen Houston. 2015. "Blood, Fire, Death: Covenants and Crises among the Classic Maya." Paper presented to the Dumbarton Oaks Symposium, "Smoke, Flames, and the Human Body in Mesoamerican Ritual Practice." Washington, DC: Dumbarton Oaks Symposium.

Slocum, Marianna, and Florencia L. Gerdel. 1965. *Vocabulario tzeltal de Bachajón: Castellano-tzeltal, tzeltal-castellano*. México, DF: Instituto Lingüístico de Verano

Starr, Frederick. 1902. "Notes upon the Ethnography of Southern Mexico." *Proceedings of the Davenport Academy of Sciences* 9:63–172. Davenport, IA: Davenport Academy of Sciences.

Stone, Andrea. 1989. "Disconnection, Foreign Insignia, and Political Expansion: Teotihuacán and the Warrior Stelae of Piedras Negras." In *Mesoamerica after the Decline of Teotihuacan, AD 700–900*, ed. Richard A. Diehl and Janet C. Berlo, 153–172. Washington, DC: Dumbarton Oaks Research Library and Collection.

Stone, Andrea, and Mark Zender. 2011. *Reading Maya Art: A Hieroglyphic Guide to Ancient Maya Painting and Sculpture*. London: Thames and Hudson.

Stuart, David. 1987. *Ten Phonetic Syllables*. Research Reports on Ancient Maya Writing, 14. Washington, DC: Center for Maya Research.

Stuart, David. 1989. "Hieroglyphs on Maya Vessels." In *The Maya Vase Book*, ed. Justin Kerr, vol. 1:149–160. New York: Kerr Associates.

Stuart, David. 1993. "Breaking the Code: Rabbit Story." In *Lost Kingdoms of the Maya*, ed. Gene Stuart and George Stuart, 170–171. Washington, DC: National Geographic Society.

Stuart, David. 1995. "A Study of Maya Inscriptions." PhD diss., Vanderbilt University, Nashville, TN.

Stuart, David. 1996. "Kings of Stone." *Res* 29/30:148–171.

Stuart, David. 1997. "Kinship Terms in Maya Inscriptions." In *The Language of Maya Hieroglyphs*, ed. Martha J. Macri and Anabel Ford, 1–11. San Francisco, CA: Pre-Columbian Art Research Institute.

Stuart, David. 1998. "'The Fire Enters His House': Architecture and Ritual in Classic Maya Texts." In *Function and Meaning in Maya Architecture*, ed. Stephen D. Houston, 373–426. Washington, DC: Dumbarton Oaks.

Stuart, David. 2000. "The Arrival of Strangers." In *Mesoamerica's Classic Heritage: From Teotihuacan to the Aztecs*, ed. David Carrasco, Lindsay Jones, and Scott Sessions, 465–514. Boulder: University Press of Colorado.

Stuart, David. 2001. *A Reading of the Completion Hand as TZUTZ*. Research Reports on Ancient Maya Writing, 49. Washington, DC: Center for Maya Research.

Stuart, David. 2003a. "On the Paired Variants of Tz'ak." www.mesoweb.com.

Stuart, David. 2003b. "A Cosmological Throne at Palenque." www.mesoweb.com.

Stuart, David. 2004a. "The Beginnings of the Copan Dynasty: A Review of the Hieroglyphic and Historical Evidence." In *Understanding Early Classic Copan*, ed. Ellen E. Bell, Marcello A. Canuto, and Robert J. Sharer, 215–248. Philadelphia: University of Pennsylvania Museum of Archaeology and Anthropology.

Stuart, David. 2004b. "The Entering of the Day: An Unusual Date from Northern Campeche." http://mesoweb.com/stuart/notes/enteringday.html.

Stuart, David. 2004c. "New Year Records in Classic Maya Inscriptions." *PARI Journal* 5(2):1–6. San Francisco, CA: Pre-Columbian Art Research Institute.

Stuart, David. 2005a. *The Inscriptions from Temple XIX at Palenque: A Commentary*. San Francisco, CA: Pre-Columbian Art Research Institute.

Stuart, David. 2005b. "A Foreign Past: The Writing and Representation of History on a Royal Ancestral Shrine at Copán." In *Copán: History of a Maya Kingdom*, ed. Ellen E. Bell, Marcello A. Canuto, and Robert J. Sharer, 373–394. Santa Fe, NM: School for American Research.

Stuart, David. 2005c. "Ideology and Classic Maya Kingship." In A Catalyst for Ideas: Anthropological Archaeology and the Legacy of Douglas Schwartz, ed. Vernon L. Scarborough, 257–286. Santa Fe, NM: School for American Research.

Stuart, David. 2005d. "The Way Beings," *Sourcebook for the 29th Maya Meetings at Texas*. Austin: University of Texas at Austin.

Stuart, David. 2006. *Sourcebook for the 30th Maya Meetings at Texas*. Austin: University of Texas at Austin.

Stuart, David. 2007a. "Reading the Water Serpent as Witz'." https://decipherment.wordpress.com/?s=witz.

Stuart, David. 2007b. "Gods and History: Mythology and Dynastic Succession at Temple XIX and XXI at Palenque." In *Palenque: Recent Investigations at the Classic Maya Center*, ed. Damien B. Marken, 207–232. Lanham, MD: AltaMira Press.

Stuart, David. 2007c. "Old Notes on the Possible ITZAM Sign." https://decipherment.wordpress.com/2007/09/29/old-notes-on-the-possible-itzam-sign/.

Stuart, David. 2007d. "The Dallas Bone." https://decipherment.wordpress.com/2007/12/27/the-dallas-bone/.

Stuart, David. 2008. *Sourcebook for the 32nd Maya Meetings at Texas*. Austin: University of Texas at Austin.

Stuart, David. 2009. "The Symbolism of Zacpetén Altar 1." In *The Kowoj: Identity, Migration, and Geopolitics in Late Postclassic Petén, Guatemala*, ed. Prudence M. Rice and Don S. Rice, 317–326. Boulder: University Press of Colorado.

Stuart, David. 2011a. "Some Working Notes on the Text of Tikal Stela 31." www.mesoweb.com/stuart/notes/Tikal.pdf.

Stuart, David. 2011b. *The Order of Days: Unlocking the Secrets of the Ancient Maya*. New York: Harmony Books.

Stuart, David. 2012a. "The Varieties of Ancient Maya Numeration and Value." In *The Construction of Value in the Ancient World*, ed. John K. Papadopoulos and Gary Urton, 497–515. Los Angeles: Costen Institute of Archaeology, University of California.

Stuart, David. 2012b. "The Name of Paper: The Mythology of Crowning and Royal Momenclature on Palenque's Palace Tablet." In *Maya Archaeology 2*, ed. Charles Golden, Stephen Houston, and Joel Skidmore, 116–141. San Francisco, CA: Precolumbia Mesoweb Press.

Stuart, David. 2013. "Two Inscribed Bones from Yaxchilan." https://decipherment.wordpress.com/2013/05/16/report-two-inscribed-bones-from-yaxchilan/.

Stuart, David, and Ian Graham. 2003. *Corpus of Maya Hieroglyphic Inscriptions*, part 1: *Piedras Negras*. Cambridge, MA: Peabody Museum of Archaeology and Ethnology, Harvard University.

Stuart, David, and Stephen Houston. 1994. *Classic Maya Place Names*. Washington, DC: Dumbarton Oaks.

Stuart David, Stephen Houston, and John Robertson. 1999. *Notebook for the 24th Maya Hieroglyphic Forum at Texas*. Austin: Department of Art and Art History, University of Texas at Austin.

Stuart, David, and George Stuart. 2008. *Palenque: Eternal City of the Maya*. London: Thames and Hudson.

Stuart, George, and Gene Stuart. 1993. *Lost Kingdoms of the Maya*. Washington, DC: National Geographic Society.

Tate, Carolyn E. 1992. *Yaxchilan: The Design of a Ceremonial City*. Austin: University of Texas Press.

Taube, Karl. 1985. "The Classic Maya Maize God: A Reappraisal." In *Fifth Palenque Round Table, 1983*, ed. Merle Greene Robertson and Virginia Fields, 171–181. San Francisco, CA: Pre-Columbian Art Research Institute.

Taube, Karl. 1988a. "A Prehispanic Maya Katun Wheel." *Journal of Anthropological Research* 44(2):183–203.

Taube, Karl. 1988b. "Iconography of Mirrors at Teotihuacan." In *Art, Ideology, and the City of Teotihuacán*, ed. Janet C. Berlo, 169–204. Washington, DC: Dumbarton Oaks.

Taube, Karl. 1989. "Ritual Humor in Classic Maya Religion." In *Word and Image in Maya Culture: Explorations in Language, Writing, and Representation*, ed. William F. Hanks and Don S. Rice, 351–382. Salt Lake City: University of Utah Press.

Taube, Karl. 1992a. *The Major Gods of Ancient Yucatan*. Washington, DC: Dumbarton Oaks.

Taube, Karl. 1992b. "The Temple of Quetzalcoatl and the Cult of Sacred War at Teotihuacan." *Res* 21:53–87.

Taube, Karl. 1994. "The Birth Vase: Natal Imagery in Ancient Maya Myth and Ritual." In *The Maya Vase Book*, vol. 4, ed. Justin Kerr, 650–685. New York: Kerr Associates.

Taube, Karl. 1998. "The Jade Hearth: Centrality, Rulership, and the Classic Maya Temple." In *Function and Meaning in Classic Maya Architecture*, ed. Stephen D. Houston, 427–478. Washington, DC: Dumbarton Oaks.

Taube, Karl. 2000. "The Turquoise Hearth: Fire, Self-Sacrifice, and the Central Mexican Cult of War." In *Mesoamerica's Classic Heritage: From Teotihuacan to the Aztecs*, ed. David Carrasco, Lindsay Jones, and Scott Sessions, 269–340. Boulder: University Press of Colorado.

Taube, Karl. 2003a. "Maws of Heaven and Hell: The Symbolism of the Centipede and Serpent in Classic Maya Religion." In *Antropología de la eternidad: La muerte en la cultura maya*, ed. Andrés Ciudad Ruiz, Mario Humberto Ruz Sosa, and María Josefa Iglesias Ponce de León, 405–442. Madrid: Sociedad Española de Estudios Mayas.

Taube, Karl. 2003b. "Tetitla and the Maya Presence at Teotihuacan." In *The Maya and Teotihuacan: Reinterpreting Early Classic Interaction*, ed. G. E. Braswell, 273–314. Austin: University of Texas Press.

Taube, Karl. 2004. "Flower Mountain: Concepts of Life, Beauty, and Paradise among the Classic Maya." *Res* 45:69–98.

Taube, Karl. 2009. "Womb of the World." In *Maya Archaeology 1*, ed. Charles Golden, Stephen Houston, and Joel Skidmore, 86–106. San Francisco, CA: Precolumbia Mesoweb Press.

Taube, Karl, and Stephen Houston. 2015. "Masks and Iconography." In *Temple of the Night Sun: A Royal Tomb at El Diablo, Guatemala*, ed. Stephen Houston, Sarah Newman, Edwin Román, and Thomas Garrison. San Francisco, CA: Precolumbia Mesoweb Press.

Taube, Karl, William A. Saturno, David Stuart, and Heather Hurst. 2010. *The Murals of San Bartolo, El Pétén, Guatemala*, part 2: *The West Wall*. Ancient America, 10. Barnardsville, NC: Boundary End Archaeology Research Center.

Tedlock, Barbara. 1985. "Hawks, Meteorology and Astronomy in Quiché-Maya Agriculture." *Archaeoastronomy* 8:80–88.

Tedlock, Barbara. 1992. *Time and the Highland Maya*. Albuquerque: University of New Mexico Press.

Tedlock, Dennis. 1983. *The Spoken Word and the Work of Interpretation*. Philadelphia: University of Pennsylvania Press.

Tedlock, Dennis. 1996. *Popol Vuh: The Definitive Edition of the Mayan Book of the Dawn of Life and the Glories of Gods and Kings*. New York: Simon and Schuster.

Thompson, J. Eric S. 1932. "The Hummingbird and the Flower." *Maya Society Quarterly* 1(3):120–122.

Thompson, J. Eric S. 1939. *The Moon Goddess in Middle America, with Notes on Related Deities*. Carnegie Institution of Washington, pub. 509, contribution 29, 121–173. Washington, DC: Carnegie Institution.

Thompson, J. Eric S. 1950. *Maya Hieroglyphic Writing; An Introduction*. Norman: University of Oklahoma Press.

Thompson, J. Eric S. 1962. *A Catalog of Maya Hieroglyphs*. Norman: University of Oklahoma Press.

Thompson, J. Eric S. 1972. *A Commentary on the Dresden Codex: A Maya Hieroglyphic Book*. Philadelphia, PA: American Philosophical Society.

Tiesler, Vera, and Andrea Cucina. 2006. *Janaab' Pakal of Palenque: Reconstructing the Life and Death of a Maya Ruler*. Tucson: University of Arizona Press.

Tokovinine, Alexandre. 2008. "The Power of Place: Political Landscape and Identity in Classic Maya Inscriptions, Imagery, and Architecture." Ph.D. diss., Harvard University, Cambridge, MA.

Tozzer, Alfred. 1941. *Landa's Relación de las cosas de Yucatán: A Translation*. Papers of the Peabody Museum of American Archaeology and Ethnology, Harvard University, vol. 18. Cambridge, MA: Peabody Museum.

Vázquez Álvarez, Juan Jesús. 2001. *Palabras floridas; pejkaj ch'utyaty; actividad oral de los choles dedicada a las deidades.* Tuxtla Gutiérrez, Mexico: Gobierno del Estado de Chiapas.

Vogt, Evon. 1976. *Tortillas for the Gods: A Symbolic Analysis of Zinacanteco Rituals.* Cambridge, MA: Harvard University Press.

Wald, Robert. 1997. *Politics of Art and History at Palenque: Interplay of Text and Iconography on the Tablet of the Slaves.* Texas Notes on Precolumbian Art, Writing, and Culture, 80. Austin: University of Texas at Austin.

Wald, Robert, and Michael Carrasco. 2004. "Rabbits, Gods, and Kings: The Interplay of Myth and History on the Regal Rabbit Vase." Paper presented to the Maya Meetings, University of Texas at Austin.

Wanyerka, Phil. 1991. "The Proceedings of the Maya Hieroglyphic Weekend, October 27–28, 1990, Cleveland State University." Presented by Dr. Peter Matthews, Department of Archaeology, University of Calgary. Transcribed by Phil Wanyerka. Manuscript in possession of the authors.

Webster, David, Barbara Fash, Randolph Widmer, and Scott Zeleznik. 1998. "Skyband Group: Investigation of a Classic Maya Elite Residential Complex at Copan, Honduras." *Journal of Field Archaeology* 25(3):319–343.

Whitmore, Sylvia. 2012. "Divination in Mesoamerica." PhD diss., La Trobe University, Melbourne, Australia.

Wichmann, Søren, ed. 2004a. *The Linguistics of Maya Writing.* Salt Lake City: University of Utah Press.

Wichmann, Søren. 2004b. "The Names of Some Major Classic Maya Gods." In *Continuity and Change: Maya Religious Practices in Temporal Perspective,* ed. Daniel Graña Behrens, Nikolai Grube, Christian M. Prager, Frauke Sachse, Stefanie Teufel, and Elizabeth Wagner, 77–86. Markt Schwaben, Germany: Anton Saurwein.

Wilson, Richard. 1995. *Maya Resurgence in Guatemala.* Norman: University of Oklahoma Press.

Zender, Marc. 2004a. "The Glyphs for 'Handspan' and 'Strike' in Classic Maya Ballgame Texts." *PARI Journal* 4(4):1–9.

Zender, Marc. 2004b. "A Study of Classic Maya Priesthood." PhD diss., University of Calgary, Canada.

Zender, Marc. 2005. "The Raccoon Glyph in Classic Maya Writing." *PARI Journal* 5(4):6–16.

Zender, Marc. 2014. "On the Reading of Three Classic Maya Portrait Glyphs." *PARI Journal* 15(2):1–14.

Index

18 Ub'aah Chan, 38, 169, 175, 188–89, 257
819 day count, 89, 105, 106, 108, 131, 134, 235, 240

accession events, 19, 21, 57, 74–75, 86, 92, 100, 110, 125, 127–28, 130–38, 140, 152, 153, 156, 162, 177, 180, 181–82, 192, 194, 197–98, 202–03, 206–207, 219–20, 226, 227, 231, 238, 240, 243–45, 247–62, 264–65, 268, 269–71
Aguateca, 35, 146, 257
Ahkal Mo' Nahb I of Palenque, 121, 123, 206, 214–15, 217–18, 247
Ahkal Mo' Nahb II of Palenque, 121, 123, 206, 214–15, 217–18, 243, 247
Ahkal Mo' Nahb III of Palenque, 42, 57, 126, 128, 138, 162, 176–77, 179–82, 192, 193–95, 197–99, 202, 203, 227, 232, 253–55, 257, 261, 263–65, 268, 269
Ahkmo' of Site R, 185
Aj Chak Maax of Laxtunich, 185
Ajen Yohl Mat of Palenque, 121, 123, 207, 214–15, 219–20
Ajk'uhuun, 76, 220
ak'ab "night, darkness," 13, 52, 63, 77–78, 83, 85, 144–45, 147–48, 212, 238, 241–42, 267, 268
Altar de Sacrificios, 167–68
artisans, 57–58, 71, 75
Aztec, 37, 60, 65, 82, 94

Baakal Waywal title, 232, 234–35
bah ch'ok, 74, 130, 132, 133, 134, 159, 180, 182–83, 231, 248, 263
banded-bird title, 176, 179, 183, 227, 232, 245, 247, 254, 257–58, 261, 263
Basket Grass, 69–70
Bird Jaguar of Yaxchilán, 14, 19, 21, 22, 46, 100–105, 140, 147, 153, 156, 158, 159–61, 173, 176, 185, 256, 259, 268
bloodletting, 33, 130–34, 136, 144, 145, 174, 178, 180, 187, 238, 252–53, 266, 267, 268, 271
Bolon Yokte' K'uh, 60
Butz'aj Sak Chiik of Palenque, 247

Calakmul, 86, 139, 207, 208, 225–26, 262
calendar, 89–107
caption text, 19, 22
Casper of Palenque, 192, 243, 247
Casper-U Kokan Chan of Palenque, 180–82, 192
cattail, 230
cave, 16, 49–50, 54, 59, 64, 70–71, 73, 99, 143, 209, 228, 250
centipede, 60, 170
Centipede-snake, 49, 59, 209, 213, 256
Cerro El Mirador, 228–29
ch'ab-ak'ab couplet, 145, 238, 241–42
ch'ajom title, 14, 104, 183, 189, 261

ch'ok "youth" title, 36, 74, 132, 137, 179, 181, 182, 235, 264
Chacamax River, 228
Chahk deities, 16, 29, 30–37, 46, 49, 51, 57, 73, 85, 143, 144, 147, 150, 153–55, 180, 252, 257, 262, 266, 267
Chak Chan of Palenque, 220–21, 227
Chamá, 164–65
Chan Te Chuwen deities, 57–58, 88
chiasmus structure, 11–12, 169–72, 173, 183–189, 190, 191, 195, 234, 241, 269, 271
Chichén Itza, 60, 265, 271
co-essence, 29, 36, 37, 42, 166–68, 211
color, 17, 18, 29, 30, 47, 52, 76, 81, 143, 146, 165, 260
complementary opposition, 13, 19, 27, 35, 39–40, 48, 52, 59, 68–88, 98, 156, 212
conch shell, 41, 43, 44, 45, 52, 144
Copán Bench: 10K-2, 53, 60; Bench 8N-11, 35, 84–86, 170, 269, 271; Margarita panel, 62, 150–51, 163, 184; Motmot Marker, 62, 184; Stela A, 139; Stela D, 20, 151, 184; Stela H, 34, 139; Structure 10L-26-1, 169; Temple 11, 184
corn, 13, 32, 36, 39, 48, 52–55, 69–75, 78–82, 87, 88, 94, 211, 224, 259–61
creator grandparents, 11, 16, 27, 38–40, 45, 47, 48, 53, 56, 58, 67, 68, 75, 77, 87, 98, 272

dawn, 34, 53, 60, 70, 72, 73, 74, 77, 117, 136, 138, 170, 224, 230
Descending Quetzal Mountain. *See* Yemal K'uk' Lakam Witz
Dieseldorff vase, 164
directions, 17, 18, 52, 59, 81, 267
Distance Numbers, 100
Don Juan Mountain, 228, 232
Dos Pilas, 37, 86, 146, 211–12, 252
Dresden Codex, 17, 34, 61, 65, 72, 82–83, 95, 96, 149, 172, 192, 230, 267
dwarf, 36, 258, 262

eagle, 60

fire, 29, 30, 34, 35, 37, 38, 46, 54–56, 61, 70, 98–99, 224, 230, 231
flatsedge, 230, 260
flint shield, 13, 126–27, 138, 143, 176–77, 189, 192, 258, 264, 268

flint, 57, 58, 59, 73, 143, 189, 237, 252, 256, 257, 259, 262, 267, 268
flowers, 11, 58, 59, 63–66, 82, 144, 146, 153, 194, 250, 252, 260
Four Crocodile place, 62–63, 148–49
framing convention, 105, 116, 127, 151–59, 189, 211, 252, 270
fronting, 121, 122, 123, 124, 201, 248

Gathered Blood, 16, 69, 71, 77, 82
GI (deity), 30, 32–34, 57, 65, 129, 131, 134, 155, 169, 176, 181, 194, 226, 232, 238–40, 247–49, 250–52, 264–65, 267
GII (deity), 30–31, 35–37, 54, 62, 100, 106, 131, 134, 153, 154, 181, 208–209, 211, 226, 234–35, 240–41, 247–49, 259, 260, 263–64
GIII (deity), 30–32, 34–35, 38, 54, 84, 89, 105–106, 129, 131, 134, 181, 208–209, 226, 228, 233, 240, 247–49, 255–59, 264
Glyph C of Supplementary Series, 84
Glyph G of Supplementary Series, 93, 94, 101
God D, 29, 56, 57
God K, 36
God L, 16, 77, 83, 99, 236, 253–54, 257–58, 262
God N, 29, 32, 35, 37, 43, 45, 53–54, 56, 67
goddesses, 48, 63–64, 69, 70, 71, 72–73, 80–84, 87, 95, 223

haab, 73, 89–93, 105, 106, 162, 191, 265
head variant, 20, 51, 62, 84, 85, 102, 103, 104, 106, 144, 193–97, 202, 203, 204, 218, 267
headdresses, 29, 32, 34, 35, 43, 45, 54, 56, 60, 62, 63–64, 74, 76–77, 94, 97, 129, 140, 144, 146–47, 159, 161, 169, 173, 174, 176, 180, 183, 188, 189, 207, 208, 209, 216, 224, 236, 237, 253, 254–55, 256–57, 261, 270
Heart of Earth, 39, 40, 45, 47, 98
Heart of Sky, 39, 40, 54, 98, 267
heart, 97, 146, 246, 267
hearthstones, 30, 54–56, 98–99, 191, 231, 238
heat, 29, 54, 55–56, 59, 61, 74, 75, 111–12, 156
Hero Twins, 43, 48, 69, 71, 73, 75, 77, 78–80, 83, 85, 94, 132, 224, 260
Hix Witz, 171
house metaphors, 53–54
Houston Museum of Fine Arts, 254
hummingbird, 63–65, 146
Hunahpu, 16, 27, 43, 69, 71–79, 82, 224–25

hunchback, 258
Huracan, 30, 39, 267

Initial Series, 93, 191, 233
Itzamnaaj K'awiil deity, 37
Itzamnaaj K'awiil of Dos Pilas, 211
Itzamnaaj, 16, 25, 29, 37, 38, 40, 43, 45, 52–54, 56–58, 60–61, 63, 65–66, 76, 77, 78, 82, 88, 96–99, 147, 165–66, 176–77, 194, 197, 253–54, 260, 266, 267–68
Ix Chel, 16, 29, 40, 51, 82

Jaguar Paddler God, 257–58
jaguar, 13, 34, 38, 42–43, 60, 61, 77, 78, 88, 114–15, 117–18, 146–47, 171, 178, 197, 199, 202, 216, 254, 257
Janaab Ajaw of Palenque, 176, 258
Janaab Pakal of Palenque, 122–23
Jasaw Chan K'awiil I of Tikal, 242
Jester God, 75–76, 88, 127, 191, 209, 253, 262, 263–64
Jewel Bird, 220–21, 227

K'ahk' O' Chahk, 174, 189, 190–91
K'ahk' Tiliw Chan Chaak of Naranjo, 87
K'ak' Tiliw of Quiriguá, 170
K'an Joy Chitam I of Palenque, 121, 123, 214, 217, 219, 220, 245–48, 250
K'an Juub Matwiil, 260
K'an Mo' Hix of Palenque, 122–24, 146, 215–16, 219–20
k'atun period, 66, 75, 76, 83, 89, 90, 93–98, 107
K'awiil, 37
K'inich Ahkal Mo' Nahb III of Palenque, 126, 128, 138, 162, 176–83, 192, 193, 194–95, 197–98, 202–203, 264, 268
K'inich Ajaw Itzamnaaj, 61
k'inich ajaw title, 34, 35, 61
K'inich Janaab Pakal I, 65, 74, 86, 118, 120–27, 130–37, 146, 153–54, 156–59, 170, 176, 179, 180, 182, 191, 193–95, 198–200, 202–204, 206–209, 211–17, 219–32, 237–38, 248, 250, 252–54, 259, 261–63, 268, 271
K'inich Janaab Pakal II, 193
K'inich Kan Bahlam II of Palenque, 130–38, 156–59, 181, 183, 191–93, 194, 206–207, 222, 224–226, 230–69, 271
K'inich K'an Joy Chitam II of Palenque, 30, 45, 74, 86, 125, 127, 131–38, 154–55, 162, 176–77,

181, 192–95, 197, 198, 201–206, 254, 258, 264, 266, 268, 269
K'inich K'uk' Bahlam II of Palenque, 162, 182, 193–204
K'inich K'uk' house, 231, 248
k'inich title, 34, 35, 61–62, 156, 218, 225
K'inich Yax K'uk' Mo' of Copán, 61–62, 150–51, 184
K'uk' Bahlam I of Palenque, 247
Kaloomte', 38, 102, 104, 105, 131, 132, 135, 237, 254–55
Kan Bahlam I of Palenque, 121–23, 206, 214–18
kin bowl, 213, 224, 267
kinship, 15–17, 27, 87
ko'haw headdress, 127, 129

La Corona altar, 54
La Pasadita Lintel 2, 147, 172
Lady Blood of the Popol Vuh, 69, 71, 79, 81–83, 86, 94–95
Lady Bone Water of the Popol Vuh, 68–71, 80–82
Lady Great Skull of Yaxchilán, 21, 22
Lady K'abal Xook of Yaxchilán, 187–89
Lady Kinuw of Palenque, 237
Lady Ohl of Yaxchilán, 174, 187–89
Lady Sak K'uk' of Palenque, 122, 124, 146, 214–16, 219–21, 226
Lady Six Jalam Chan Ajaw of Yaxchilán, 160–61
Lady Six Sky of Naranjo, 86–87
Lady Tz'akbu Ajaw of Palenque, 86, 125–27, 131, 153, 156, 176, 207, 232, 237–38, 248, 253, 264
Lady Yohl Ik'nal of Palenque, 92–93, 121, 123, 207, 209, 214–15, 218–20, 226
Lakamha' place, 232, 234, 236, 250
laughing falcon, 56, 77
Laxtunich, 185–86
Leiden plaque, 14, 92, 161–62
lunar cycle, 71, 82–84, 86–87, 88, 89, 94–95, 107, 170, 191

macaw, 62, 146, 149–50, 163, 216
Madrid Codex, 230
Matwiil, 132, 170, 182, 232–35, 238, 240–42, 248, 260
meteors, 29, 34, 37–38, 144, 169, 173, 189, 211, 257
metonyms, 10–13, 44–45, 66, 145, 169, 250, 263, 268

Milky Way Crocodile, 34, 62, 70, 97, 148–52, 223, 251
Milky Way, 34, 51, 52, 96, 149, 211, 223, 251, 255
Mixtec, 60
Motul de San José, 171, 245
Muwan Mat of Palenque, 207, 219, 225
Muwan Mat, mythological figure, 105–106, 238–245

Nah K'an Jal, 230, 241, 260, 267
name tag, 161, 190, 270–71
Naranjo, 37, 86–87
New Year, 37, 61, 91–92, 107, 266
Nine Fire-Vase Mountain, 259, 266, 267
Nine Place, 151, 184, 192, 251, 255–256
Nuk Yajaw Chan, 231, 245, 247, 248, 254, 262
Nuun Ujol Chahk, 207, 225, 226

obsidian, 37, 38, 73, 77, 144–46, 173, 237, 252, 256–57, 261, 267, 268, 270
ochb'ih "death," 119, 222–23
okte' ritual, 252–53, 255
One Batz and One Chouen, 16, 27, 69, 71, 75, 81
One Hunahpu, 16, 27, 68–69, 71–73, 75–77, 79–82, 85, 95, 224
One Ixim, 38, 48–49, 63, 68–69, 72–73, 79–87, 95, 106, 164–66, 170, 173–74, 191, 211–13, 223–251, 258, 261, 263
Otolum River, 229, 233
otot "house," 129–30, 148, 154, 163
owl, 38, 51, 77, 147, 257

Pa' Chan, 148
Paddler Gods, 66, 77–78, 83, 98, 251, 257–58, 262
Palenque: Cross Group sanctuary jambs, 235–36; Cross Group sanctuary piers, 236–37, 263; Dumbarton Oaks Tablet, 30–31, 46, 138, 153, 155, 158, 266; Group D, 229, 248, 249; Oval Palace Tablet, 86, 194; Palace Bench 1, 249, 251; Palace House A-D, 125–26, 130, 133, 268; Palace House C, 34, 226; Palace House D, 33, 267; Palace House E, 64, 65, 148, 162, 170, 194–96, 198, 199, 204; Palace Tablet, 86, 117, 125–40, 176, 177, 179, 221, 222, 258, 264, 266; Tablet of the 96 Glyphs, 24, 85, 162, 182, 193–204, 205;
Tablet of the Orator, 170, 195; Tablet of the Scribe, 170, 195; Tablet of the Slaves, 128, 138, 177–178, 179, 195, 255, 268; Temple of the Cross, 19, 21, 30, 32–33, 36, 54, 105–106, 155–59, 162, 176, 180–82, 190, 210, 218, 226, 229–234, 236–56, 259, 261–65, 267, 268, 271; Temple of the Foliated Cross, 30, 32, 74, 78, 79, 105, 106, 157, 159, 229–30, 234–38, 240, 242, 244–50, 259–63, 267; Temple of the Inscriptions, 32, 34, 91, 118, 120–24, 129, 131, 141, 144, 146, 169, 204, 206–26, 232, 249, 250, 251, 253, 261, 262, 263, 267, 272; Temple of the Sun, 30, 32, 35, 105–106, 229, 230, 233–34, 236, 237–38, 240–41, 244–245, 247–50, 255–59, 262–64, 266; Temple XIV, 49–50, 86, 158, 264; Temple XIX platform, 57, 65, 126, 128, 138, 176–77, 179, 180, 181, 192, 204, 227, 229, 232, 253, 254, 255, 258, 261, 263–65, 267, 268; Temple XVII Panel, 74, 181, 229, 237, 256, 268; Temple XXI bench, 178–83, 192, 229, 261, 265, 269; Tower Court, 194–95
Paris Codex, 76, 96
Paxil Mountain, 54, 70, 71, 259
peak event, 20, 113, 115–17, 121–23, 125, 135–40, 162, 185, 197, 198–200, 215–16, 243, 244
pib nah, 230–32
Piedras Negras, 8, 9, 20, 65, 96–97, 128, 144, 146, 152–53, 195, 252, 269, 270
Place of Duality, 39–41, 44–48, 53–54, 56, 58–59, 63
Popol Vuh, 66, 68–75, 77–79, 81–83, 94, 98, 161, 224, 235, 255, 260, 267
pre-accession events, 86, 125, 138, 156, 158, 179, 180–83, 191, 231, 238, 247–62, 264, 268, 269
Primary Standard Sequence, 58, 162, 190, 212, 213, 214, 266, 271
Principal Bird Deity, 38

quadrilateral world, 51–53, 59, 98, 190, 212, 217, 263
Quadripartite Badge, 32–34, 129, 207, 209, 211, 213, 223, 224, 236, 250–54, 265, 267
quetzal, 39, 46–47, 62, 82, 146, 150, 163, 191, 219, 224–225, 229, 236, 249, 250, 268
Quiriguá, 8, 19, 98–99, 139, 140, 153, 170–71

Río Azul, 67, 76, 259, 266
Ritual of the Bacabs, 168

Sacul Stela 1, 257
sak huun "white paper" headdress, 74, 77, 128, 131, 132, 138, 176, 177, 202, 231, 232, 240, 253–55, 258, 263, 268, 270
Santa Elena, 207, 225–26
semantic markers, 142–46
Seven Hunahpu, 16, 27, 68, 71, 75, 82
Seven Place, 184, 192, 255
shell, 30, 32, 33, 41, 43–45, 47, 49, 52, 59, 104, 129, 144, 147, 251–52, 260
Shield Jaguar III, 14, 19, 62, 140, 189, 258, 268
Shield Jaguar IV, 22–23, 100, 153, 158, 159, 185
Site R, Panel 3, 185, 187
sky band, 52–53, 56–59, 62, 84, 96–97, 118, 170, 211–12, 220, 251
solstice, 51–53, 59, 192, 227
stingray spine, 32–33, 77, 180, 251–52
sun god, 32, 34–35, 53, 57, 59–62, 66, 67, 74, 85, 86, 89, 98, 148–50, 170, 255

T24/T1017 "luminous/lightning flash," 85, 144, 170, 251, 255, 260, 261
T504 *ak'ab* "night, darkness" sign, 144–45, 238, 242
T712 *ch'ab* sign, 144–45, 238, 241–42
Teotihuacán, 37–38, 128, 129, 146, 149–50, 157, 169
Thorn Broom, 69–72
Tikal, 64, 65, 66, 86, 99, 128, 139, 144, 157, 164, 221, 222, 231, 242, 250, 251, 254, 271
Tilom of La Pasadita, 147
Tiwol Chan Mat of Palenque, 74, 193, 195, 237, 268
Tlaloc, 16, 35, 37–38, 64, 73, 86, 129, 131, 147, 169, 173–75, 188–89, 237, 254–57
tok'-pakal, 13, 126, 127, 138, 176, 177, 189, 192, 258, 264, 268
Toniná, 194, 237
Tortuguero Monument 6, 230
Tres Islas, 149–50
turtle, 29, 43–45, 47, 52, 69, 78, 260
tz'ak "whole, complete," 13, 52, 59, 66, 77, 83, 85, 86, 135, 154, 169, 197–98, 202, 203, 240, 242
tz'ikin "bird," 60, 204

U Kokan Chan of Palenque, 180–82, 236, 240, 243, 244
U Pakal K'inich. *See* K'inich Janaab Pakal II
Uhuk Chapat Tz'ikin "Seventh Centipede Bird," 60

Underworld, 16, 17, 34, 38, 40, 47, 68, 69–71, 73, 77, 79, 82, 87, 94–95, 99, 107, 120, 149, 209, 239, 223, 224, 249, 250, 260
Ux [Ch'akan] Mat of Palenque, 125, 127, 130–34, 236–37
Ux Bolon Chahk, 154–55
Ux Yop Huun headdress, 126–28, 130–32, 134–38, 176–77, 194, 268
Ux Yop Huun, 126–28, 130–38, 176–77, 194, 268
Uxte'k'uh, 237, 263

Venus, morning star, 16, 72, 83, 85–86, 89, 93, 95, 107, 170

Water, 13, 40–50, 51, 52, 65, 67
Waterlily Bird-Serpent, 45–49, 69, 176
Waxaklajuun Ub'aah K'awiil of Copán, 184
Wok, 267

Xbalanque, 16, 27, 43, 69, 71–73, 75, 78–79, 82, 94
Xpiyacoc and Xmucane, 11–12, 16, 27, 39–40, 43, 58, 68, 73
Xulu and Paqam, 78

Yahawte' K'inich, 171
Yajawk'ahk' "vassal of fire," 34, 35, 76, 195, 221, 227, 257
Yax Bolon, 43, 78, 88, 132, 191, 212
Yaxchilán, 8, 51, 103–104, 105, 147, 148, 149; Lintel 1, 22, 101–102, 104, 161, 259; Lintel 2, 22, 100, 102, 104, 153, 156, 158, 159, 161, 172, 268; Lintel 23, 139, 273; Lintel 24, 186, 189; Lintel 25, 147, 174, 186, 188; Lintel 26, 186; Lintel 3, 22, 100–101, 103, 104, 161; Lintel 5, 22, 160–61; Lintel 8, 173–74, 256; Stela 1, 58, 172; Stela 11, 19, 46, 140; Stela 12, 14–15; Stela 3, 65; Stela 35, 174–76, 188–89; Structure 12, 21, 140, 216; Structure 22, 21, 140; Structure 33, 22, 100–104; Structure 44, 62, 63, 148; Structure 54, 22
Yaxhal Witznal, 241, 259–60
Yemal K'uk' Lakam Witz "descending quetzal big mountain," 229, 236, 249, 250
Yopaat Chahk, 236, 238
Yuhk Mak'abajte' of Palenque, 220, 221, 227

zenith passage, 51–52, 55, 58, 59, 72, 120

www.ingramcontent.com/pod-product-compliance
Lightning Source LLC
Chambersburg PA
CBHW070909030426
42336CB00014BA/2343